WE
OFFER
THEE
O LORD
THE
CHALICE
OF
SALVATION

Joe Kotcka

SEVEN BRITONS IN IMPERIAL RUSSIA

(1698-1812)

PRINCETON STUDIES IN HISTORY

VOLUME 7

Seven Britons
in Imperial Russia
1698-1812

EDITED BY PETER PUTNAM

✧

PRINCETON, NEW JERSEY

PRINCETON UNIVERSITY PRESS

1952

Printed in the United States of America
By Princeton University Press at Princeton, New Jersey

TO MY WIFE DURINDA
IN THE HOPE THAT THE DEDICATION
OF THIS BOOK TO HER
MAY IN SOME SENSE
COMPENSATE FOR THE DEDICATION
OF HERSELF TO IT

ACKNOWLEDGMENTS

MOST GRATEFUL acknowledgments are owing to the librarians of Princeton and Yale Universities and of the Library of Congress, especially Malcolm Young, Reference Librarian of the Harvey S. Firestone Memorial Library, whose unfailingly courteous cooperation so greatly facilitated my access to the materials of research; to my auxiliary readers, Mrs. Valerie Koerber, Mrs. Ernest Condell, and my mother, who, together with my wife, spent many long hours reading aloud to me from these materials; to Mrs. Kate Tredennick for her painstaking devotion to the task of proofreading my manuscript; to Otto Bettmann, whose assistance in providing illustrations was invaluable; to H. Lester Cooke, Jr. for preparing the maps; to Harriet Anderson, P. J. Conkwright, and Datus Smith, whose interest and constructive criticism have made the preparation for publication a genuine pleasure; to the late Allison Bunkley, for the many enjoyable conversations which helped to sharpen my total perspective; to Dietrich Gerhard, for the book which first opened many areas of my investigation and for the kindly encouragement which confirmed me, at a moment of doubt, in my determination to pursue it; to Cyril E. Black, whose bibliographical suggestions, technical assistance, and broad general knowledge of Russia have generously facilitated the composition of these pages; and, finally, to Robert R. Palmer, who, from first to last, by a seemingly inexhaustible patience, conscientious interest, and extraordinary critical ability has encouraged, guided, and inspired my total endeavor.

INTRODUCTION

BRITISH TRAVELERS to Russia between 1698 and 1812 moved across an historical stage whose scenery was constantly shifting. Throughout the period, the changes were remarkable in both countries, but the specific terminal dates have peculiar significance for Russia in particular. In 1698, young Tsar Peter, first Russian ruler in over six centuries to leave his dominions, having assumed an incognito among a small and motley band, and quietly departed the political, economic, and cultural backwater which was ancient Muscovy, was engaged in investigating the techniques of a superior European culture. In 1812, Alexander I with the eyes of the western world upon him, crossed the frontiers of his mighty empire at the head of a victorious army in the growing resolve to give order and stability to a civilization which, after twenty years of war and revolution, seemed on the verge of self-destruction. In the intervening span of years, all aspects of the national lives of both Russia and England had undergone more or less striking metamorphoses, and a survey of the corresponding intellectual, political, economic, and social developments of each nation illustrates many contrasts in the changing features of the two historical epochs, as well as in the evolving characteristics of the two nations whose growth they witnessed.

In her intellectual and artistic contributions, Russia, upon the threshold of her emergence from centuries of isolation, could not be expected to compete with an England which was assuming a major role in the cultural life of Europe. At the close of the seventeenth century, two Britons, Newton and Locke, had pioneered scientific and philosophical frontiers for generations yet unborn, and a mere catalogue of the great names will suffice to show the importance of British achievement in the century which followed. Berkeley, Hume, and Bentham distinguished themselves in the field of philosophical speculation; Gibbon composed his monumental history; and Adam Smith revolutionized economic thought. Poetry passed from Augustan neo-classicism to the spirit of romanticism in the hands of Pope, Young, Gray, Ossian, Blake, Wordsworth, Coleridge, and Byron. A new literary form, the novel, came of age in England with Defoe, Richardson, Fielding, Sterne, Smollett, Jane Austen, and Walter Scott. The century brought the journalism of Addison and Steele, the satire of Swift, the drama of Goldsmith and Sheridan, the biography of Boswell, and the literary criticism of Dr. Johnson. The stately Georgian style of architecture graced buildings whose spacious interiors were adorned with the furniture of Chippendale, Hepplewhite, and Sheraton, and, for the first time in her history, England produced painters of genius in Gainsborough, Romney, Reynolds, West, Constable, and Turner.

By contrast, Russia contributed little to the west. In the infancy of her cultural activity, she tended to be less creative than imitative and acquisitive. By aping the manners and customs of their European brethren, the Russian nobility gradually accumulated the mental, as well as the physical trappings of western civilization. Divesting themselves of their flowing Muscovite caftans, they donned coats, waistcoats, and breeches of Parisian cut and spoke French, rather than Russian, in the conversations of their elegant salons. Italian and Dutch paintings were hung beside the Russian ikons, volumes of Voltaire and Schiller appeared next to *The Lives of the Saints*, and the fashionable noble was more often seen at the play and the opera, than at the Greek Orthodox mass. Russian ladies emerged from the oriental seclusion of the terem and conducted their households no longer in the timbered Muscovite "beehives," but in magnificent palaces of brick, stucco, or stone, set tastefully in gardens landscaped according to the English fashion. The transformation thus effected was so complete, that a visitor from pre-Petrine Muscovy, set suddenly down in Alexandrian Russia, might logically have concluded that his country had been conquered by an invading European army, which had then imported all the impedimenta of western civilization and settled its officers in the capitals and upon the landed estates to rule their subject peoples. The occasionally absurd excesses of imitation, balanced, here and there, by more solid achievements of the native genius, were all a part of a painful apprenticeship, which, however, prepared the ground for a later flowering. The branches artificially grafted upon the Russian trunk were ultimately to bear magnificent fruit with the ballet, music, drama, poetry, and, above all, the novel of the nineteenth century.

Politically, as well as culturally, Britain was more creative and more influential than Russia. Locke's political principles stimulated thought underlying both the American and the French Revolution, and, a century later, Burke, in endorsing the one and rejecting the other, gave brilliant expression to the theory of the organic development of indigenous political institutions. In the interim, Blackstone's *Commentaries* synthesized the achievements of British jurisprudence for the posterity of the western world. Russian intellectuals in the same period read widely among French and British thinkers, but original political works were scarce. Catherine's famous *Instruction* to the legislative assembly, widely acclaimed as evidence of her enlightenment, was largely an interpretation and digest of her reading of Montesquieu, Blackstone, and Beccaria. This same enlightened Catherine, a score of years later, disgraced and exiled both Radishchev and Novikov, patriotic liberals whose writings had favored emancipation of the serfs. The reforming ideas of Speranski enjoyed better success in the early reign of Alexander I, whose well-known political liberalism encouraged Jeremy Bentham to hope for his patronage in drafting a Russian constitution. Like Catherine, however, Alexander later found it expedient to renounce his former opinions. In 1812, Speranski, too, was exiled and, in his conflict with the French Revolution, the Russian Emperor identified himself with the party of reaction. For this reason, the liberal movements under Catherine and Alexander have been likened to the Roman Saturnalia, brief holidays during which slaves were permitted to rule their masters, followed all too soon by a return to bondage. Yet memories of these holidays were not entirely eradicated, and in politics, as in art, a period of awakening and education was a necessary precursor to subsequent development.

The outstanding political achievements in the two countries during this period were not theoretical, but practical. In England, the great Whig aristocracy had wrested power from the crown, in order to maintain its privileges under the revolutionary settlement, but, as the shift in the sovereignty from throne to Parliament was gradually confirmed, that body became the amphitheater of a bitter political struggle. King's men and opposition members, divided upon no principle but that of self-interest, employed bribery, the patronage, and all the corrupt electioneering methods of the "rotten borough" system, to obtain seats in the unreformed House of Commons. Paradoxically, this destructive and selfish contest had its unforeseen constructive consequences by assisting in the formation of two of the most useful political institutions of modern government: the two-party system and the ministerial cabinet.

In Russia, the contest for power was as naked of principle as in England, but it resulted in the formation of no comparable institutions. At the outset, Peter the Great, availing himself of the tradition of centuries, had succeeded in forcing the turbulent Muscovite nobles into the lifelong service of his military bureaucracy, but, by 1762, less than forty years after his death, they had liberated themselves from all obligations to serve the state. Peter's disruption of the legitimate succession, an era of largely unprecedented feminine rule, the influence of foreigners and favorites, and two unstable regencies so weakened the throne that it was unable to keep the nobility in check. This nobility, now fused into a unified class with a strong corporate sense, capitalized upon the disorder and used the Guard of the capital to arbitrate the rapidly changing succession, but was never equal to the task of challenging the principle of autocracy. The very privilege which was its chief concern, created an unbridgeable gap between the nobility and the vast majority of the third estate. Unable, therefore, to pretend to the role of champion of the public welfare, the nobility was forced, however little it revered the throne in practice, to appeal to its unlimited theoretical authority as the only legal sanction of its "vested interests." Hence, there arose a new incentive for union between crown and noble, and Catherine, acutely aware of this fact and, in her turn, fearing the wrath of the aristocracy, strengthened and stabilized this union by extending serfright into many new areas and offering a large measure of political autonomy to the nobles of district and province. The joint administration of crown and noble in the military bureaucracy grew ever stronger, collecting an increasing revenue, constructing public works, supervising the movements of persons and property, and, in general, imparting to Russian political life, a regulative character which it has never discarded.

In both countries, the internal redistribution of political power was accompanied by the geographical expansion of national sovereignty. While Russia was extending her borders to include the greatest territorial expanse of modern times, England was acquiring colonial possessions all over the globe. The incorporation of Scotland into the Kingdom of Great Britain in 1707, and the addition of Ireland in 1801 as a member of the United Kingdom were mere consolidations of ancient political connections, but the larger objectives of British policy ranged far across the seas. Despite a temporary setback in the War of American Independence, the British colonial empire grew rapidly, and, by the close of the Napoleonic Era, Britannia could number among her treasures Canada, Honduras, British Guiana, and a host of Caribbean islands in the New World, the strategic control points of Gibraltar and Malta in the Mediterranean, the Cape of Good Hope and the valuable slaving ports of the Gold Coast in Africa, an entire new continent in

Australia, and, in the Orient, Ceylon, the Straits of Malaya, and, above all, the fabled wealth of India.

Russia, meanwhile, was appeasing a huge territorial appetite upon the continent. Under Peter, the conquest of the Baltic provinces brought ancient Muscovy a new geographical and maritime proximity to western Europe. Under Catherine, successive partitions of Poland added many thousands of square miles of rich land and millions of inhabitants. In the same reign, vast cessions from Turkey along the coast of the Black Sea and the privilege of free navigation of the Straits gave promise that Russia might one day become a Mediterranean as well as a Baltic power. Throughout, the reduction of border tribes and the tightening of controls upon nominally subject peoples consolidated southern and eastern frontiers, and, indeed, every extension of the Russian boundaries lessened the danger of invasion. With each new advance and its concomitant advantages of increased population, new commercial opportunities, and additional agricultural land, the power and weight of Russia in the European scales grew.

Such prizes as these were won only by an energetic foreign policy, and the statesmen of the Age of Reason did not hesitate to call upon armed conflict to arbitrate their differences. In the span of years, both England and Russia were actually at war with one or another of their neighbors for more than half a century all together and never, with a single exception, at peace for more than two decades at a time. The British colonial empire was founded and maintained at the expense of three great maritime rivals: Holland, France, and Spain. By 1815, all three had been virtually destroyed as effective colonial powers, and the British fleet, under the leadership of such great captains as Anson, Hawke, Rodney, Hood, and Nelson, had risen to an indisputable superiority over the combined navies of all Europe.

Russia also pursued her territorial ambitions in competition with three main rivals, and, by the close of the period, she had far outstripped her three European neighbors, Sweden, Poland, and Turkey, in the race for empire. Against Sweden and Turkey, she had her maritime adventures, but she was primarily concerned with the creation of a military force to extend and guarantee the borders of the great land ocean which was the Russian Empire. It was Peter the Great, the father of Russian sea power, who first transformed the loosely organized, ill-equipped horde of feudal conscripts into a disciplined standing army capable of conquering one of the first military powers of Europe. From his time, the Russian army won nearly every campaign in which it was engaged and was repeatedly victorious in the final issue. As Narva was avenged by Poltava in 1709, so too, were Austerlitz and Friedland redeemed by the rout of the Grand Army of France in 1812, when Russia stood forth, at last, as the military arbiter of the entire continent.

Under the competitive states' system of eighteenth century Europe, armed conflict was closely integrated with economic activity, and the military and naval successes of Russia and Britain were accompanied by their commercial, financial, industrial, and agricultural advancement. While her fleets swept over the seas, the value of Britain's maritime commerce increased tenfold. The growing merchant class improved techniques of company organization, credit, and finance, and the Bank of England, founded in 1694, grew so rapidly, that, within a few short decades, London had replaced Amsterdam as the financial capital of Europe. Commerce and the accumulation of capital served to stimulate industry, and the technical progress of these years was an important influence in the transformation of England into "the workshop of the world." Wedgwood's huge pottery works demonstrated the efficiency of specialized division of labor. Textile manufacture was facilitated by a whole series of new inventions from "the flying shuttle" to the power loom. Coke replaced charcoal in the blast furnaces, and the metallurgical industry boomed with the introduction of rolling mills, blowers, and the "puddling" process. Nearly dwarfing these in significance was Watt's patent of a practical steam engine in 1769, enabling man, for the first time in his history, to generate and control power without dependence upon the natural forces of wind, water, or animal draft. Agriculture, too, made rapid advances. The application of manure and new fertilizers enriched the soil, the addition and rotation of root crops increased productivity, and the use of the new cultivator stimulated growth. Improved feeding and the selective breeding of livestock were found to double the weight of cattle brought to market. Enthusiasts for the new farming like Arthur Young inspired the landed classes to improve their holdings, and a wave of enclosures both increased the agricultural yield and forced tenant farmers off the land and into the growing mills and workshops.

During the same period, the Russian economy compensated for its lesser technical improvement by its greater quantitative expansion. Thus, although Muscovite financial methods were notably backward, the century witnessed a very marked increase in the amount and circulation of specie throughout the empire. Commercial and shipping operations were so clumsy that western merchants and vessels usurped the great bulk of the foreign trade; yet the value of this trade multiplied at double the rate of the British, or more than twenty times in little over a century. Whereas, during the greater part of the period, British technical improvements were accorded only a restricted application, the wider exploitation of Russian serf labor, mobilized into mills and mines, enabled it to compete successfully in the manufacture of cordage, sailcloth, and linens, as well as in the productions of heavy industry. It was not until the last decade of the eighteenth century that England equaled and surpassed Russian iron production. Agriculture, bound to the conservatism of the peasant community, made little technical progress, but its extension to the vast black-earth regions of southern Russia and the Ukraine greatly increased the total yield and enabled many landlords to export large surpluses of hemp, flax, and other farm staples. Finally, that significant, if mysterious index of economic activity, population growth, showed a far greater advance in Russia than in England. The inhabitants of the British Isles increased from about 7,500,000 in 1700 to about 16,000,000 a hundred years later, but the much greater number of Russian subjects within the boundaries as drawn in 1725 had shown a corresponding growth in only seventy-five years, exclusive of the millions living in the newly conquered provinces. If the inhabitants of the territories annexed to Russia by the end of the Napoleonic Era be also included, the total population is found to have reached the extraordinary figure of 45,000,000, or nearly four times the number of the subjects of Peter I in 1698.

It was the glory of the British colonial and commercial expansion that it was accompanied by an era of unprecedented prosperity for the nation as a whole. It was the tragedy of Russia's territorial and military advance that it retarded the living standard and crushed the liberties of the great bulk of the populace. For all its mercantilist restrictions, the British economic system tended to instill in its people a spirit of initiative and free enterprise, which played an important part in England's rise to commercial and industrial hegemony in the nineteenth century. The Russian people, on the other hand, were bound to a wheel which spun in a slow and vicious circle. The policies of the tsarist regime, ambitious beyond its financial means, weighed heavily upon the masses at the base of the servile system. The territorial conquests of repeated military campaigns were no compensation for the financial exactions which they laid upon the peasantry, nor did the international prestige of the Court of St. Petersburg justify the domestic humiliation of the Russian people. With security of neither person nor property, the lower classes entertained few prospects of retaining increased earnings and had little incentive to improve their productive techniques. Nevertheless, the increase of territory and inhabitants in a country magnificently endowed by nature with vast forests, rich mines, numerous river highways, and, above all, fertile plains enabled the primitive economic organization of the Russian people however precariously, to underwrite the ever growing ambitions of its military despotism. While Britain's thalassocracy rode before the wind, Russia's ponderous juggernaut lurched steadily forward.

Paradoxically, the contacts between the maritime, and commercial island kingdom under a constitutional monarchy and the vast military and agrarian autocracy of the continent were often of the greatest importance to their respective development, and the British travelers who witnessed the cultural, political, economic, and social changes of the eighteenth century played their part in the eventful history of Anglo-Russian relations. These relations had taken their rise only by sheerest accident; yet it was not the hand of fate, but the hardihood of the British mercantile spirit which placed them upon lasting foundations. In 1553, one of three ships, fitted up by a group of English merchants for the purpose of exploring for a northeast passage to the Orient, became separated from her companions in a northern gale and subsequently found her way into the little port of Archangel. There, the adventurous Captain Chancellor and his men disembarked to make the long overland journey to Moscow. They were kindly received by Ivan IV and returned the following year to England, bearing a cordial invitation from the Tsar to open a commerce with his subjects. The charter of privileges subsequently granted to a circle of British merchants, who incorporated as the Muscovy Company, promised them an exclusive monopoly of the trade of Archangel, and the Anglo-Russian commerce was launched. Among the many British travelers to Muscovy who followed, there were a number who left written records. Chancellor, Jenkinson, Turberville, Horsey, and Fletcher had all published accounts by 1591, and the extent of British commercial interest is even more clearly demonstrated by the fact that, in addition to various diplomatic missions of a commercial nature and the regular trading voyages to Muscovy, no less than six expeditions had traversed the entire breadth of the country into Persia before the close of the sixteenth century.

About the turn of the century, however, the British trade was impeded by that era of disputed successions, foreign invasions, and civil disorders, known to Russian history as "the Time of Troubles." Even after the restoration of order under the Romanov dynasty in 1613, the trade declined. The restrictive regulations of the Muscovy Company, the invasion of the British monopoly by Dutch competition, and the royal displeasure of Tsar Alexis at the execution of Charles I reduced the British trade and the number of British merchant travelers to an intermittent trickle until the end of the seventeenth century. Nevertheless, the contacts established with Europe in 1553 were never broken thereafter, and for this reason Chancellor's voyage and discovery of Russia to Europe was no less momentous an event for the subsequent development of Muscovy than Peter's famous tour and discovery of Europe to Russia a century and a half later.

If the relative importance of her merchants declined throughout the seventeenth century, British influence in Russia was represented by a new class of travelers. These were not mere visitors but expatriates, men who adopted the Muscovite service as a profession, and who, therefore, entered into a more permanent and more intimate relationship with the fabric of Muscovite society than their mercantile predecessors. During this period, they were predominantly soldiers of fortune. In the wars with Poland, the superiority of western military organization and equipment had recommended to the early Romanovs a policy of enlisting foreign assistants, both to train their troops and to establish native manufactures of military supplies. Among the European adventurers who flocked to the Muscovite standard the British and, more particularly, the Scottish nation was well represented. Members of old Scottish families, driven from their native country either by loyalty to the Stuart cause, by religious intolerance, by lack of economic opportunity, or by the mere love of adventure, underwent voluntary exile to serve as mercenaries upon the continent, and a number of these ultimately found their way to Muscovy. Various Gordons, Hamiltons, Keiths, Leslies, and Bruces, as well as the Generals Dalyell, Drummond, and Menezius won military recognition under the Romanovs. Some of these lived to exert an important westernizing influence upon Muscovite society. The sisters Hamilton, for example, one of whom married the uncle, and the other, the guardian of Princess Natalia Naryshkin, the later Tsaritsa and mother of Peter the Great, introduced a European element into the highest circle of the court. Bringing western influences to bear upon an even more important quarter, General Patrick Gordon, besides the distinguished performance of his military duties and his valuable support of Peter in two Muscovite insurrections, further served the reforming Tsar informally as a teacher and helped to inspire in him an admiration for European methods even more pronounced than that of his predecessors.

Peter's rapidly accelerated program of Europeanization both increased the numbers and widened the variety of the professional expatriates in the Russian service. On his return from the famous tour of the Germanies, Holland, and England, he brought with him a whole army of technical experts, including not only military, but naval officers, shipwrights, engineers, doctors, astronomers, gunfounders, smiths, textile workers, and mining experts. Among the Germans, Dutchmen, Frenchmen, Italians, and Poles were many important Britons. Worthy of particular notice in this era are Field Marshal Ogilvy, who supervised the discipline and training of the army, Count James Bruce, astronomer, general, and director of the schools of navigation, artillery, and military engineering, Dr. Robert Erskine, chief and founder of the Medical Chancery, one of a long line of Scottish physicians in the Russian service, and Mr. Farquharson, mathematician and surveyor of the great St. Petersburg-Moscow road. The master-builders, Brown, Ney, Cosens, and Dean, helped to construct a navy largely officered by foreigners, whose sizeable British contingent was led by Admirals Thomas Gordon and Thomas Saunders. All these, together with their fellow countrymen, played an important part among those foreign volunteers who assisted Peter to his ultimate triumph over Sweden in the long Northern War. In so doing, they helped to alter the balance of Europe and, thereby, to inject an entirely new element into the history of Anglo-Russian relations.

When Peter possessed himself of the Baltic provinces, he obtained both the sources and the outlets of a trade which was of the most pressing importance to the maritime powers of Europe. Without the timber, flax, iron, hemp, and other stores which flowed in ever-increasing quantities through the ports now under Russian control, the dockyards of Britain would have lacked many materials necessary for the construction and refitting of the great war and merchant fleet upon which her colonial and commercial empire absolutely depended. The recognition of this appalling fact spurred British diplomatic energies to the attainment of a commercial agreement with the Russian government to insure the export of an ample supply of these vital naval stores. The negotiations which followed were brought to nothing by the mutual political hostility of George I and Peter the Great, but here, as elsewhere, the individual initiative and technical skill of her merchant class came to Britain's rescue. The old Muscovy Company, reorganized as the Russia Company, was freed of the restrictions which had previously strangled the trade. Merchants of this company poured into Riga and the new port of St. Petersburg, and backed by the large capital and wide trading affiliations of the commercial houses they represented, secured a major portion of the Russian export in the face of fierce competition. As a result, it was these merchant travelers, rather than the diplomatic representatives of the Foreign Office, who paved the way for those concessions granted to Britain by the terms of the Anglo-Russian commercial treaty of 1734.

This remarkable treaty embodied and perpetuated a state of economic interdependence between the two nations. Whereas it guaranteed for Britain the delivery of those materials vital to the construction of her ever-expanding navy, it was justified, on the Russian side, by the huge payments of specie for goods received by the English merchants. British gold helped the perpetually impoverished Russian government to finance its extraordinarily ambitious program and the landowning nobility to support a newly luxurious scale of existence. Hence, although their commercial privileges enabled the British merchants to maintain Russian exports in a captivity nearly as confining as that of an English colonial dependency, they enjoyed a prestige with the government and the aristocracy accorded to the merchants of no other nation. Moreover, even though it was seriously threatened in 1780, 1800, and 1807, this British domination of the Russian trade remained a cardinal fact of international relations throughout the period.

In the meantime, a series of Russian military successes had been making a deep impression upon the minds of European diplomats, and the Court of St. Petersburg came to be wooed for political, as well as for commercial reasons. In the War of the Polish Succession (1733-1735), the Russians were not only completely victorious over the Poles, but actually defeated a French force sent to support a rival claimant to the throne, and, in 1736, Austrian diplomats negotiated the aid of 20,000 Russian troops against a French army on the Rhine. In 1748, a Russian expedition, dispatched under the terms of an alliance with England, materially hastened the conclusion of the War of the Austrian Succession, and, in the Seven Years' War, but for the sudden accession of the Prusso-phile Peter III, the Russian armies of the Austrian coalition might well have eliminated Prussia forever from the ranks of the great powers. In the reign of Catherine, the increase of Russian political weight amounted to a preponderance in the balance of Europe, and diplomats from every capital thronged to her court as competitors in a game whose stakes the British alone failed to grasp. The Foreign Office, preoccupied with commercial affairs and dazzled by the brilliance of the English victory in 1763, made only apathetic efforts toward a military alliance eagerly sought after by Britain's deadliest enemies. With no promise of reciprocal gain, it first encouraged Catherine's Mediterranean ambitions by granting her the naval assistance which helped destroy the Turkish fleet in 1770; then, in 1773, with utter indifference, permitted her to partition Poland with Frederick II and Maria Theresa; and, finally, with righteous indignation, found itself "betrayed" in the Armed Neutrality of 1780, which both challenged Britannia's supremacy on the seas and made a material contribution to the cause of France and the American Revolution. Paul I attempted a second declaration of maritime independence from Britain in the Armed Neutrality of 1800, but this time the dissatisfaction of the nobility at the prohibition of the lucrative English trade aggravated the general dissension culminating in his assassination. The same dissatisfaction was operative in Alexander's revocation of the Continental Blockade, extended to Russia under the terms of the Treaty of Tilsit in 1807, and the history of Anglo-Russian relations in this period was climaxed in 1812 by the union which sealed the doom of Napoleon and decided the fate of Europe.

The activities of the professional expatriates, the merchants, and the diplomats had all been calculated in some way to affect the course of Russian history, but, from the time of the accession of Catherine the Great, there appeared a group of passive spectators who constituted the last of the four main types of British travelers in the eighteenth century. These were the pleasure seekers and wealthy tourists who had previously visited only the older European capitals, but who were now attracted to St. Petersburg by the brilliance of Catherine's reign and her reputation for enlightenment. There were men of leisure, who traveled merely to escape ennui or to satisfy an idle curiosity about foreign lands. There were sons of the nobility and rich bourgeoisie with their tutors, who toured the continent with the ostensible purpose, at least, of completing their educations. There were also a few "professional" travelers, who used their experiences abroad as material for books pretending to literary or scholarly distinction. Whatever their aims, it may be said of them in common that they contributed little to Russia aside from their personal presence in the already cosmopolitan society of the capital. Their significance was rather as an index, than as an aid to Russian progress.

Their books revealed the extent to which the Russian aristocracy had become Europeanized and illustrated the increasing interest of the British reading public in the character of Russian society. Therefore, although they participated in Russian life in no immediately effective sense, as the bearers of ideas and information between the two countries, they, too, must be assigned a place among those British travelers who played a role in Anglo-Russian relations of the period.

Exclusive of the voluminous official correspondence of the various diplomats, there are some twenty-six British travelers between 1698 and 1812 who recorded their impressions of Russia in published volumes. They vary widely in almost every respect. They range in size from brief memoranda to ponderous tomes; in form, from edited epistles and journalistic narrative to encyclopedic tracts; in matter, from autobiographical anecdote and social gossip to comprehensive historical and social surveys; and in tone, from personal intimacy to scientific objectivity. Aside from an unwillingness to deal with works which have already been given critical treatment, the selection of seven from among the many volumes has been guided by three considerations: the character and background of the author, the contents of his work, and the significance of the historical period or phase which he described. In the first category, it seemed advisable to choose the works of only those men about whom sufficient biographical data were available to furnish a basis upon which to interpret their opinions. Moreover, it was desirable that, among those selected, there should be represented at least one of each of the four main types of travelers in Russia. In the second place, it seemed essential that these writings should contain observations on matters of sufficient importance, viewed with sufficient understanding, and expressed with sufficient facility to offer interest, enlightenment, and readability to the modern student. Finally, it seemed important that their visits should have been timed and their itineraries arranged so as to coincide with the historical events or trends prominent among the major developments in the history of Russia, in general, and of Anglo-Russian relations, in particular. A brief chronological survey of the available works will illustrate how these principles have operated in the selection of seven specific authors and serve as a preliminary introduction of them and their fellow travelers to the reader.

Of six accounts published by visitors to the Russia of Peter the Great, five have proved themselves more or less inadequate to the requirements of this anthology. *Passages from the Diary of General Patrick Gordon*, who arrived in Muscovy in 1661 to begin a career of nearly forty years in the Russian Army, gives much valuable and interesting information of Peter's early reign and the author's many services, but, since it concludes with his death in 1699, it fails to describe Peter's program of Europeanization at the accelerated pace it assumed upon his return from the western tour in 1698. *An Account of Russia as it was in the Year 1710* is a brief, concise, and straightforward survey by Charles Whitworth, envoy extraordinary to Russia from 1705, but, even aside from the fact that the book has been only recently reviewed, it would have been inappropriate to select a diplomat as a representative of British travelers at a time when the influence of the professional expatriates was at its peak. John Bell, who typified this latter class, entered the Russian service in 1715 as the protégé of Dr. Erskine and accompanied several important embassies to Persia and China. He wrote fine narrative descriptions of the regions through which he passed, interesting from the standpoint of Russian expansion to the south and east, but irrelevant to those western ambitions which comprised the most striking feature of Peter's reign. Peter Henry Bruce, a nephew of the influential Count James Bruce, published an entertaining and readable recital of his thirteen years' service in the army, but, although his paternal ancestry and last residence were Scottish, his maternal kin, birthplace, and early training were so entirely Germanic that his observations cannot be regarded as reflecting British opinion. *The History of the Russian Fleet during the reign of Peter the Great by a contemporary Englishman*, written in 1724, concerns the most striking and original aspect of Peter's entire program, but, in addition to being rather tedious, fragmentary, and overspecialized for an anthology of this sort, the anonymity of its author precludes any analysis of either his character or the specific circumstances of his visit. John Perry's *The State of Russia under the Present Czar* answers nearly every objection which can be raised against other contemporary accounts. A former British naval officer, Captain Perry was introduced to Peter in England during the famous tour and enrolled in that army of technical advisers whom the Tsar enlisted in his service. His fourteen years as an hydraulic engineer on canal and dockyard construction not only offered him an insight into Peter's naval ambitions, but took him far into the interior of the country, and his book, in addition to a specific account of his personal experiences, included many general observations upon the Russian Empire as a whole.

The thirty-eight years separating the great reigns of Peter I and Catherine II were less productive of travel literature than the preceding period. Three of the four authors have left but scant record of their lives and backgrounds. Two of these are relatively unimportant. Mrs. Vigor who came to Russia in 1729, apparently as the wife of a member of the Russia Company, remained after his death to re-marry Claudius Rondeau, one of the British plenipotentiaries in the important commercial treaty of 1734. Despite these affiliations, however, she appeared entirely unconcerned with either diplomatic or commercial affairs, and her sentimental epistles, when not devoted to the narrative of her personal vicissitudes in the affairs of the heart, confine themselves to inconsequential anecdotes and court gossip. A contemporary, Mrs. Elizabeth Justice, finding herself in straitened circumstances upon the desertion of a ne'er-do-well husband, was employed for three years, beginning in 1734, as the governess to the three daughters of Mr. Evans, a British merchant in St. Petersburg. Her more general account of the food, costumes, houses, and manners of the natives makes very pleasing reading, but its extreme brevity permits only the most cursory treatment. An obscure Scottish physician, John Cook, whose failing health suggested the unusual expedient of a change to a Russian climate, in 1736, recorded his many adventures at much greater length. As a medical officer in the Russian service until 1750, he traveled far and wide, from St. Petersburg to Moscow, from Astrakhan to the Ukraine, and even accompanied a Russian embassy to Persia. The narrative of his personal experiences is enhanced by a wry humor and fine sense of detail, but it may be said of his general observations that, where they are not so entangled in the web of anecdote as to make them unwieldy of quotation, they are often more felicitously stated in the work of another author. Moreover, his adventures were unrelated to the main developments of Anglo-Russian relations, while those of his contemporary, Jonas Hanway, a merchant of the Russia Company, as narrated in *An Historical Account of the British Trade over the Caspian Sea* serve as an introduction to the vital question of the Anglo-Russian commerce. As Hanway's was the only book of the entire period to award a full treatment to this primary consideration any anthology of British travel in Russia without it is unthinkable.

Even in its earliest years, the reign of Catherine II witnessed the composition of a number of travel books which subsequently appeared in print. One of the most lucid and best written of these was the work of the distinguished Sir George Macartney, whose diplomatic mission was signalized in 1766 by the renewal of the earlier commercial treaty of 1734. However, both the mission and the book which was its consequence have already been given full and brilliant treatment by W. F. Reddaway, and the commercial relations which underlay Macartney's most important and successful negotiation had not sufficiently altered since Hanway's day to warrant a re-examination of the ground. Two unknown authors, John Williams and Joseph Marshall, visited Russia at nearly the same time. Williams was too taken up with simple historical chronicle to allot much space to either original observation or the description of his firsthand experiences. Marshall, a traveler for pleasure, employing a journalistic and narrative style, attempted a serious and objective survey of the contemporary scene on a circuit which led him from St. Petersburg southwest through the Ukraine and the Polish borderlands, and back across the Baltic provinces to St. Petersburg. In addition to the usual data on government revenues, trade, and the military establishment, he included conscientious descriptions of the peasant life and agricultural techniques of the regions through which he passed, but the value of this rather monotonous catalogue is lessened by his confessed ignorance of the subject of farming as a whole. The letters of William Richardson, published under the deceptively chatty title of *Anecdotes of the Russian Empire*, have been chosen in preference to the writings of his contemporaries for two reasons. His position as secretary to the British Ambassador, Lord Cathcart, in St. Petersburg from 1768 to 1772 leads naturally to a discussion of the Anglo-Russian diplomacy of the period, particularly as it was involved in the extraordinary Mediterranean expedition of the Russian fleet. Moreover, his letters represent a brilliant integration and refinement of various elements of contemporary British opinion in its attempt to interpret and evaluate the nature of Russian society.

The publication of the official correspondence of British representatives at the Russian Court has offered the widest possible range of choice in the selection of one of that class of diplomats who comprise the third of the four types of British travelers to eighteenth century Russia. In the earlier phases of Anglo-Russian diplomacy, the commercial agreements of 1734 and 1766 and the military subsidy treaties of 1748 and 1755, negotiations already fully dealt with by diplomatic historians, Russia had not yet assumed that political importance in Europe which she acquired under Catherine II. Moreover, since the death of Peter the Great, the growth of British ascendancy in Russia had appeared nearly unchecked. With Catherine's conquest of Turkey and the opening of the Black Sea in 1774, however, Russian foreign policy entered a new phase, and, during the War of American Independence, St. Petersburg became a hotbed of diplomatic activity in which rival British and French factions sued for support, while Catherine herself matured plans for the subsequent seizure of the Crimean Peninsula. The Armed Neutrality of 1780 was the first act of overt hostility to the British interest at St. Petersburg, and, therefore, the mission of Sir James Harris, British plenipotentiary from 1777 to 1783, embraces one of the most critical periods of Anglo-Russian diplomacy in the entire century. Moreover, Harris's lengthy public and private correspondence claims the attention of the historian not only for the significance of the events it describes but because it illustrates a wide variety of the problems faced by English representatives to the Russian Court as they appeared to one of the most astute diplomats of his time.

Tourist travelers abounded in the last quarter of the century. In 1774, Nathaniel Wraxall, then but twenty-three years of age, made a summer tour around the Baltic coast, which included six weeks in the Russian dominions. His letters, published as *Cursory Remarks Made on a Tour Through Some of the Northern Parts of Europe* were the first step of a rather undistinguished career as an author of travel books and historical memoirs. The brief narrative descriptions, interspersed with aesthetic and historical reflections, are light and readable, if only by virtue of their superficiality. John Richards' *A Tour from London to Petersburgh and thence to Moscow*, published in 1781, is a brief epistolary narrative of a journey made a few years later. It is equally superficial and abounds in errors, even by tourist standards, as when the author remarks the absence in Moscow of those social festivities and charitable institutions which were such a delight to other British visitors. Lady Elizabeth Craven enjoyed a far more interesting itinerary in *A Journey through the Crimea to Constantinople*, made in 1786, shortly after the Russian annexation. Her letters to her lover are both interesting and amusing, but her absorption in social diversions, romantic landscapes, and historical sites left her little opportunity to comment upon the present economic and political importance of the regions she visited. It was a different sort of tourist, the famous Archdeacon Coxe, a traveler to Russia in 1778 and again, in 1784, as the tutor to young Englishmen taking the Grand Tour, who compiled the most valuable literary record of his experiences in Russia. It might be objected that the solid scholarship and serious objectivity of Coxe's voluminous work have rendered it untypical of the tourist literature of the age. In any event, it is a happy flaw, and the fame as well as the merit of his Russian volumes have prompted their selection for detailed treatment.

Two distinguished visitors to Russia about this time deserve special notice. The first of these is William Tooke, who, in 1771, accepted a post as chaplain of the English Church at Kronshtadt. There and in a similar capacity at St. Petersburg, he passed the next twenty-one years, until the inheritance of a sizeable fortune freed him of his clerical duties and enabled him to devote his full energies to the historical scholarship which had long been his enthusiastic avocation. As a member of the Imperial Academy of Sciences and of the Free Economical Society at St. Petersburg, he had access to much valuable information, which he employed to advantage in the composition of no less than four sizeable histories of the country. Only one of these, however, *A View of the Russian Empire during the Reign of Catherine the Second and to the Close of the Present Century*, dealt with contemporary Russia. Despite its general dullness of tone, it was admirably informative, but like the previous history of John Williams, the absence of original observations or eyewitness accounts render it unsuitable for special treatment. Far more provocative reflections upon the character of Russian life might have been expected from the pen of Tooke's famous contemporary, Jeremy Bentham, who, in February 1786, joined his brother Samuel in the government of Mogilev in White Russia, where the latter was employed by Prince Potemkin in various projects for the economic improvement of the region. Unfortunately, the very fragmentary nature of the publication of his correspondence and memoirs and the editor's frequent substitution of his own paraphrase for the original text have rendered them virtually useless for the purposes of this anthology, nor does the catalogue of Bentham's manuscripts in the Library of the University College in London suggest the existence of any body of material devoted to Russia. Bentham's strange silence upon this point may possibly be explained by his preoccupation with speculations of an entirely independent nature. At one point, he remarked that it was only the solitude of his life in Russia which made his residence there attractive to him, and, although he had originally entertained the hope that Catherine might employ him in work upon the new legal code, he became so entirely engrossed in his other projects that he seems quite to have forgotten the notion and did not even, upon the occasion of her passage through Mogilev on the way to inspect the Crimea, deign to seek an audience which his brother's connections and his own reputation might easily have opened for him.

From this time, although Anglo-Russian relations were far from static, and although their changing facets profoundly influenced the reactions of individual Britons, they underwent no alterations calculated to introduce any new genus of British traveler to the Russian scene. An unknown author, Andrew Swinton, seems to have been a member of the tourist class, and the letters of his *Travels into Norway, Denmark, and Russia in 1788, 1789, 1790, 1791* are lively and entertaining and give particularly informative details of peasant life and land cultivation. As a kinsman of the Scottish Admiral Greig, whose death had recently concluded a career of nearly twenty years in the Russian service, he devoted considerable space to the naval operations of the current Russo-Swedish War, and he reflected the overwhelming majority of British public opinion in condemning the anti-Russian policies of Pitt, who, almost alone in his recognition of the potential Russian threat to England in the Near East, was attempting to curb Catherine's territorial claims in the peace negotiations then pending with Turkey. Mrs. Maria Guthrie, wife of Dr. Matthew Guthrie, a Scottish physician to the Court of St. Petersburg, and herself an acting directress of the Imperial Convent for the Education of the Female Nobility of Russia, was a studious tourist throughout her Crimean travels in 1795 and 1796, but her observations in the letters to her husband are so taken up with scenic beauties, archeological antiquities, and the ancient history of the various nations, tribes, and nomadic peoples, as to virtually obscure her meager references to the importance of the region for Russia's Mediterranean ambitions. Dr. Edward Daniel Clarke, a celebrated geologist, archeologist, and antiquarian, like Coxe, played the role of traveling tutor in his early career and, in 1798, embarked with a pupil upon an extraordinary tour which, in the course of three years, took them through Russia, the Baltic countries, the Middle East, Egypt, the Balkans, the Germanies, and France. Only a small, but still sizeable portion of his six volumes of travel dealt with Russia and the narrative of his journey from St. Petersburg to Moscow and, thence, southward to the Crimea, contains some of the most amusing passages of the entire literature. Envenomed by the anti-British policy of the Emperor Paul in the Armed Neutrality of 1800, Clarke displayed a gift for satiric virtuosity and splenetic hyperbole in picturing in turn the degeneracy, incompetence, drunkenness, indolence, superstition, dishonesty, and abysmal ignorance of tsar, noble, and peasant alike. However readable, his caustic tirades are too far removed from the norm of British opinion to justify their inclusion in the following pages.

With the accession of Alexander I in 1801, Anglo-Russian relations were restored, and the British travel literature of his early reign followed the diplomatic trend. A literary raconteur, John Carr, revealed largely favorable impressions on his Russian tour in 1804, but his *Northern Summer* betrayed much of the superficiality of the typical tourist. *The Russian Journals of Martha and Catherine Wilmot, 1803-1808* are of greater interest. As guests and intimates of the famous Princess Dashkov, whose memoirs Martha subsequently edited, the Wilmot sisters were close to the life of the Moscow and provincial nobility and of the peasantry upon the landed estates, and their many portraits and impressions of aristocratic society far from the glitter of the imperial court are tempered with many homely details of daily routine not to be glimpsed in the works of more transient visitors. A refreshing contribution to the latter is the inclusion of two letters by their uncultivated maidservant, Eleanor Cavanagh. *The Russian Journals* have been omitted from this anthology not merely because publication in 1936 has already made them easily available to the modern reader but because, despite the occasionally penetrating insights of their Irish wit, many of the sisters' most interesting impressions have been closely paralleled and more fully and felicitously expressed by a contemporary acquaintance. This was the painter, Robert Ker Porter, who divided his time between St. Petersburg and Moscow from 1805 to 1807. Ker Porter was employed by the Russian government to paint a number of canvases for the new Admiralty in St. Petersburg, but his letters to his sisters reveal the attitude not of the professional expatriate but of the traveling pleasure seeker, and, taken together with the more serious studies of Coxe, they help to fill out the portrait of the tourist type, besides furnishing magnificent and readable word pictures of peasant scenes, noble life, and the Russian landscape. With the rupture of Anglo-Russian relations after Tilsit in 1807, Ker Porter was forced to return to England, but another sudden diplomatic revolution in 1812 brought as his successor, Brigadier General Sir Robert Thomas Wilson, the final representative of British travel in that epoch and an exciting figure in the last dramatic act of the Russian emergence into the European family of nations. A soldier who had fought in the British cause ever since 1794, Wilson accompanied the main Russian army throughout a major portion of the Napoleonic invasion of 1812, and his diaries and the correspondence in which he recorded his experiences are still valuable sources for the diplomatic and military history of that memorable year.

With Ker Porter and Wilson, the roll call of the seven Britons selected from among the number who left published records has been completed. These seven are representative, not only of the four traveling types, the expatriate, the merchant, the diplomat, and the tourist, but also of seven different professions tending to inculcate distinctive mental attitudes in their adherents. In order of their appearance in Russia, they were an engineer, a merchant, a humanist scholar, a diplomat, a traveling tutor, a painter, and a soldier, and each was distinguished in his field. Moreover, the circumstances of each of their visits illustrates some distinctive phase in the development of Russian relations with the west, whether political, economic, or cultural. They are divided into four generations. Perry, the expatriate engineer, departed the dominions of Peter in 1712, the date of Hanway's birth. Hanway, the merchant, whose Russian adventures exemplified the growing commercial traffic between the two nations, arrived in St. Petersburg in 1743, the same year in which Richardson was born. Richardson, Harris, and Coxe, within four years of the same age, were all visitors to Catherine's Russia during the first flowering of European culture among the Russian nobility and the new maturity of Russian diplomatic influence in the European balance. Ker Porter and Wilson began life during Harris's critical embassy to the Court of Catherine and, in their sojourns to Russia, witnessed Alexander's manipulation of Russian military might in deciding the fate of Europe.

In the following pages, the works of these seven authors have been treated in seven separate chapters, each of which is divided into two parts. The first of these two parts includes a brief biographical sketch of the author, an outline of the historical background affecting the circumstances of his visit, and, finally, a critical analysis of his writings in terms of both character and background. The second is composed of selections from his publications, journals, or correspondence. The preservation of the flavor of the original and the interest of the observations will, it is hoped, compensate for the length of these extracts. The editor has taken the liberty of dividing them into sections and sub-sections under captions of his own invention both to facilitate reference and to emphasize the predominant slant of their author's ideas. Throughout, quotations from the writings of other authors have been interpolated, either in footnotes or in the text of the introductory essays, to elaborate particular points or to round out the picture of contemporary opinion.

In the end, the reader may yet be inclined to question the objects of such an organization. Although it is not a series of biographical sketches, it is hoped that the handling of the biographical material may help to bring into focus against the background of an historical era the personalities of seven distinct individuals who lived and breathed the atmosphere of eighteenth century Britain. Although it is not a study of Anglo-Russian relations as such, it is believed that the interpolated history of the economic, political, and cultural intercourse between these two nations can illuminate the development of an international relationship integral to the history of modern Europe. Although it is not an analysis of the political, economic, intellectual, and social trends of Russia in the eighteenth century, yet it is felt that the critical examination of the observations and experiences of these travelers will serve to reincarnate the character of all these changes in the emergence of a great national people upon a new stage. The sum of all these objects, for better or for worse, is merely to clothe in flesh the skeletal structure of previous historical research. As an original contribution to historiography, it must be judged as a sort of historical adaptation of a public opinion poll applied to the field of international relations. As such, it seeks to demonstrate how the mental constitutions of seven individual personalities which had grown to maturity in the intellectual soil of Britain reacted to the atmospheric pressures of a totally foreign social climate.

CONTENTS

CHAPTER SEVEN

ILLUSTRATIONS

Title-page decoration from a drawing by Damame-Demartrait and Ker Porter in *Russland: Sitten, Gebrauche und Trachten*, Budapest, 1816. *Bettmann Archive.*

MAPS

CHAPTER ONE

John Perry

John Perry:

ENGINEER TO THE GREAT TSAR
(1698-1712)

IN THE LIFE OF JOHN PERRY is presented a striking instance of one of those unfortunate men who, despite an apparent abundance of talent, perseverance, and even opportunity, never attain the success which fate seems to have intended for them. His professional life was a tragedy in three acts. In the first, his aspirations as a British naval officer, possessed of a ship's command when but twenty-three years of age, were suddenly crushed in the humiliation of public dishonor and imprisonment. In the last, as an hydraulic engineer over a quarter of a century later, he seemed about to redeem the promise of his youth by successfully damming a breach in the Thames embankment which for fourteen years had been imperiling the navigation of one of the world's greatest marine highways. This feat, which had bid fair to baffle the engineering talent of England, won him the official gratitude of Parliament and a permanent, if minor, place in the annals of engineering,[1] but his overly optimistic estimate of the probable cost deprived him of so much as a farthing's profit for five years' wearied efforts, and he dragged out the remainder of his professional life in desultory and incomplete projects for harbor improvement and fen drainage. An intervening period of fourteen years' service on the rivers, canals, and dockyards of Peter the Great brought him neither professional satisfaction nor financial reward and were terminated in ignominious flight in fear of his very life. Nevertheless, the book which was their consequence was widely read and outstandingly influential on both British and French opinion of Russia throughout the century.[2] It was long considered "an accurate account of this vast empire, the first, indeed, that may be said to have introduced a knowledge of it into Eng-

---

[1] An entire chapter, most complimentary to Perry, is devoted to the stopping of the Dagenham Breach in Samuel Smiles, *Lives of the Engineers*, London, 1861, 1, 107ff.

[2] D. S. von Mohrenschildt, *Russia in the Intellectual Life of 18th Century France*, New York, 1936, pp. 184ff.

land,"[3] and, if subsequent scholarship has disclosed a variety of errors of both fact and judgment, Perry's book is still of great interest to the modern reader as an expression of contemporary opinion by one engaged at first hand in one of the most remarkable aspects of a great epoch in Russian history.

Little is known of the ill-starred engineer's early life. He was born in 1670, the second son of respectable, but undistinguished parents, in Rodborough, Gloucestershire. In all probability, his formal education was much abridged by his entrance into the British Navy at the usual early age, but he advanced rapidly in the school of the sea. In his twentieth year, shortly after an action with a French privateer in which he received a severe wound in his right arm, he was granted a lieutenant's commission on board the *Montague*. In 1693, he demonstrated his mechanical aptitude by improvising an engine for pumping water from the drydocks at Plymouth and later in the same year was awarded the sole command of the fireship *Cygnet*. He was not left long in the enjoyment of this post, however, for in September of the same year both the *Cygnet* and the *Diamond*, a larger vessel to which it was attached, were captured by French privateers, and, worse still, the mutual recriminations between the two British commanders ultimately resulted in Perry's court-martial. Found guilty of dereliction of duty, he was not only fined £1,000 but sentenced to ten years' imprisonment in the Marshalsea.

All further hope of an honorable career in the service of his country now seemed blighted, but with a stubborn determination characteristic of his later life, Perry refused to accept his fate. From his captivity, he wrote a spirited defense of his position, dated December 18, 1695, and published it as an appendix to a pamphlet entitled *Regulations for Seamen*. Perhaps as a consequence of this pamphlet, he obtained his release before the expiration of his sentence, and, in April of 1698, his career took a new direction. It was at this time that Perry was introduced to Peter the Great, then visiting in England, and, without any prospects in his native land, he seized the opportunity to seek his fortune abroad. Having been recommended to the Tsar as an hydraulic engineer, he negotiated a contract to serve in that capacity with a captain's commission, an annual salary of £300 above and beyond a subsistence allowance, and the promise of further liberal rewards at the conclusion of tasks of particular value. Still but twenty-eight years of age, Captain Perry departed England without delay, buoyant in the

[3] S. A. Allibone, *A Critical Dictionary of English Literature*, Philadelphia, 1902, ii, 1566.

anticipation of an adventurous and profitable role upon the vast new stage of the Muscovite dominions.

Optimistically as it began, Perry's account of his years in Russia soon became a wearisome recital of nearly unrelieved frustration. In addition to the ordinary inconveniences of exile, his professional life was subject to a thousand harassments. Supplies of money, material, and above all, of skilled labor were continually inadequate for the performance of engineering projects which might have taxed the genius of a De Lesseps. The asperities of the Russian winter enforced long months of idleness annually, the violence of the spring floods often destroyed or damaged the accomplishments of the preceding summer; and the exigencies and vicissitudes of Peter's military campaigns caused delays, postponements, and even the entire abandonment of his most cherished projects. The greatest of all the obstacles in Perry's eyes, however, was the ignorance, corruption, and hostility to innovation of the old Muscovite nobility who impeded the progress of the Tsar's "grand designs" in a thousand ways.

Every one of these difficulties was manifested on Perry's very first assignment. Typically ambitious in conception, this was a project for the construction of an all-water route to link the Don and Volga rivers, separated by nearly a hundred miles (or about twice the length of the Panama Canal). In addition to the construction of many locks and sluices necessary to improve the navigation of the tributary streams, the project demanded the digging of a canal some three miles in length. Perry accepted this monumental commission eagerly, but he soon encountered many difficulties. Arriving upon the site in the province of Astrakhan, he was greeted by its governor and his commander, Prince B. A. Golitsyn,[4] unceremoniously shown a gallows, and threatened with hanging, unless he undertook to begin work just where it had been abandoned in a previous and thoroughly impracticable attempt. Perry succeeded in overruling the Prince on this point, but found in him an implacable foe, and in addition to the natural obstacles of climate and geography, he was confronted by many man-made difficulties. Without adequate supplies of materials, and granted less than half of the entirely unskilled labor force originally promised him, he struggled along for three summers until 1701, when the loss of the

[4] Prince Boris Alekseevich Golitsyn (1654-1738), descended from one of the great noble families of Russia, had recommended himself as a favorite to Peter through his support of his cause against the attempted usurpation of his half-sister in 1689.

Battle of Narva so impoverished the Russian government that the
entire project had to be abandoned in a state of half completion.

Under such circumstances as these, it is not surprising that the ambitious young engineer soon began to regret his enlistment, and the tale
of his subsequent discouragements in the Russian service often assumes
the character of a ponderous legal indictment. Perhaps the ultimate in
professional frustration occurred at Voronezh, where he was appointed
Comptroller of Russian Maritime Works in 1701. There, he was ordered
to supervise the refitting of a river fleet which had been so haphazardly
constructed that its rotten and sinking hulks could not be careened for
repairs. Undismayed by the challenge to his skill, Perry devised an
ingenious solution. By damming the river, he was able to float fifteen
ships at once over cradles built for their reception upon the bank and,
by letting off the water through sluices, to lower them gently into position. Triumphantly, he pointed out the superiority of this method to
that of even the English drydocks, which received only one or two
ships at a time and depended upon the incidence of the tide, rather
than upon artificial control, for raising and lowering the water. However, the stupidity of his Muscovite subordinates soon destroyed the fruits
of his labor, for "proper care not being taken to keep the sluices open
in the spring, when the floods come down and brought vast quantities
of sand washed off the neighboring mountains, the channel began to
choke up, scarce six feet of water remaining where seventeen were
formerly."[5]

Granted adequate financial compensation, Captain Perry might have
been persuaded to overlook these many professional annoyances, but he
found the payment of his annual salary repeatedly postponed through
a succession of ruses. At the outset, Golitsyn had insisted that he procure some bond for his intention to remain in the service until the
Don-Volga canal was completed, arguing that his predecessor on that
project had fled the country directly upon the receipt of his first year's
salary. Unable as a stranger to secure any satisfactory pledge, Perry
had reluctantly consented to permit the arrears due him to accumulate.
At Voronezh, Admiral Apraxin,[6] his new commander, showed himself equally adept in the art of evasion, and the situation was further
complicated by Perry's refusal to accept any payment in the recently
devaluated currency of the Muscovite treasury. As the years dragged

[5] Charles Whitworth, *An Account of Russia as it was in the Year 1710*, Strawberry-hill, 1758,
p. 120.
[6] Fëdor Matveevich Apraxin (1671-1728), a Russian admiral and a favorite of Peter,
became one of the most influential members of the court after 1700.

by, Perry's petitions and remonstrances both to Apraxin and to the Tsar himself became increasingly vehement, and, while they did nothing to allay his financial grievances, provided a continuous source of altercation between himself and his commander.

An instance of the growing mutual hostility between the British Captain and the Russian Admiral occurred in connection with the construction of some new drydocks on the river. Having surveyed and selected a suitable site for these docks, Perry found himself overruled in favor of a Russian engineer whose recommendation of a much inferior sandy strip of bank was based upon a conspiracy with its owner who would be compensated for its loss to the government by a grant of much more valuable property elsewhere. Over Perry's bitter protests, the foundations were laid in the shifting sands of the river bank, and the work proceeded in the face of the difficulties which he had predicted. Events ultimately vindicated his prophecy of disaster, and, as Whitworth reported, in 1709, in defiance of their orders to lay the keels of several new ships on this site, "the carpenters resolved to open the gates in the floods, and let in the water, rather than have the foundation of the docks torn up and the carcases of the ships spoiled at the same time, as happened to one the year before."[7] In view of the British engineer's bitter denunciation of the entire procedure, it is more than likely that Apraxin suspected him of complicity in this piece of insubordination, and the whole incident is but one of many examples of their growing animosity.

Convincing as was Perry's narration of his maltreatment in the Russian service, the objectivity of his motives is more than a little suspect. By his own admission, the account of his professional experiences had been written, not for publication, but "only with intention of presenting it in manuscript to some persons of honour, in order of my being employed at home . . . , and not without some hopes also that . . . , touching the hardships done me . . . , I may obtain the King's most gracious orders to his Ministers for my being relieved as to the wages due me. . . ."[8] In short, the manuscript had been intended both as a sort of professional advertisement, and as a petition of grievances to secure redress from the Russian government through British diplomatic channels. It was not to be expected, therefore, that either his engineering talents, or the injustices done them should suffer in the telling.

A comparison with contemporary sources tends to show that Perry

[7] Whitworth, *op. cit.*, pp. 116-117.
[8] John Perry, *The State of Russia*, London, 1716, pp. 58-59.

was unfair in both his characterization and his official treatment of
Admiral Apraxin. In sharp contract with his black portrait of the
Admiral is the description by another Englishman in the Russian
service as a sincere, austere, and dignified gentleman with emphasis
upon the trust which might be placed in his word. In a passage which
can only be interpreted as a reference to Perry's account, he went on
to say: "This is his just character and the result of my personal observations, though I am sensible a different account has been given . . . ,
and, peradventure, in some few instances, when his spirit has been
exhausted by intense application to a multiplicity of weighty affairs,
and his temper ruffled by an importunate address, he may have received
some persons with incomplacence."[9]

In addition to the impatience, sense of superiority, and "importunate
address," which characterized all Perry's dealings with the Admiral,
he was guilty of at least one instance of real subterfuge. His success in
floating the rotting river fleet upon stocks for repairs having suggested
to his fertile imagination a means of storing all war vessels not actively
in use upon dry land under protective sheds, he proposed the construction of a number of "dry havens" as a means of preserving the Russian
fleet from premature decay in peacetime. Peter had given a preliminary
endorsement to the plan, but when his prolonged absence upon a
Polish campaign had brought the work to a standstill, Perry applied
to Apraxin for a short leave to England until some further use for his
services could be found. The Admiral refused with the accusation that
"this innocent request," as Perry termed it, was only a trick by which
to escape the Russian service, and he brought the more serious charge
that Perry disloyally intended to use a plan conceived and brought to
maturity during his Russian service in the interests of the politically
hostile British government. Despite Perry's repeated protestations, it is
clear from the correspondence of Charles Whitworth that Perry had
actually attempted to contract for the construction of "dry havens" for
the British Navy.[10] Apraxin was not only justified, according to contemporary standards, in refusing Perry's leave, but was furnished with
still further grounds for scrutinizing his hostile subordinate's motives
with the utmost suspicion.

On the other hand, the widely attested unscrupulousness of the
Russian government in dealing with its foreign servants proves that

[9] C. A. P. Bridge, ed., *History of the Russian Fleet*, London, 1899, p. 80.
[10] Whitworth to Harley, July 18/29, 1705, *Sbornik*, xxxix, 135-136; Whitworth to Harley,
March 10/21, 1707, *Sbornik*, xxxix, 473.

Perry's grievances were far from imaginary. The same anonymous naval officer who had contradicted Perry's appraisal of Admiral Apraxin complained bitterly of salary losses through inflation of the coinage, reduction of subsistence allowances, assessments in return for promotion, and long delays in the payment of arrears due to the members of Peter's foreign contingent. "These reductions and defaultations have reduced them to very mean circumstances. . . . Very few foreigners in his service, either by land or sea, have been able to make any considerable advantage, and, of those few, rarely one permitted to depart the country. Besides long attendance and great expense to procure dismission, various stratagems have been used to impoverish 'em in their fortunes. No one maxim obtains more generally than this. . . ."[11]

The Muscovite government could not afford to pay a price equivalent to the value it placed upon its foreign experts, but it esteemed them too much to permit them to leave the service at will. Even so worthy a servant as General Patrick Gordon met with obstinate refusal on this point. In nearly forty years with the Russian Army, he petitioned for his leave unsuccessfully no less than four times and, in one instance, with the backing of a letter from Charles II himself, but these requests were answered with threats of degradation and banishment to Siberia. Upon the one occasion on which he was granted a furlough to England, his wife and children were held as hostages for his prompt return.[12] Captain Peter Henry Bruce, who entered the Russian service in 1711, also remarked "the difficulties strangers have to encounter in endeavouring to get out of this country," observing that "the Russian policy is that money saved by the government servants should remain in the country. . . ." He, like Gordon, failed in four petitions for his release, but succeeded in a fifth attempt through the ruse of a temporary furlough, being unencumbered by a wife or children to constitute effective hostages. However, he was unable to secure the arrears of two years' salary, "and, at the expiration of my furlough, every thing I had left here was seized, so that I had no reason to boast of any advantage I reaped in Russia after thirteen years' service."[13] Under these circumstances, stratagem appeared to be the sole means by which Perry might hope to escape his unprofitable service.

The prolonged stalemate of his dealings with Apraxin was suddenly broken by the unexpected turn of military affairs in 1711. In that year,

[11] Bridge, *op. cit.*, pp. 99, 101.
[12] Patrick Gordon, *Passages from the Diary of General Patrick Gordon*, Aberdeen, 1859, pp. 47-48, 57-58, 105, 109, 158-160.
[13] Peter Henry Bruce, *Memoirs*, London, 1782, pp. 114-115, 172, 210, 223, 350, 364.

a crushing defeat by a Turkish army on the Pruth lost Russia Azov, her sole foothold on the Black Sea, and completely nullified the value of those maritime projects upon which Perry had been employed on the Don and Voronezh rivers. He was therefore recalled to St. Petersburg, from which the energetic Peter now contemplated the construction of an all-water route to the Volga as a means of supplying his new capital from the interior. The preliminary survey for the site of this waterway was entrusted to Perry, and the British Captain, rejoicing in his transfer from the command of the hostile Admiral to that of the great favorite, Prince Menshikov,[14] set enthusiastically to work upon a task of greater magnitude than any he had previously attempted. When, in the spring of 1712, he reported his recommendations in St. Petersburg, it was determined to commit the entire project to his supervision, but Perry, although Menshikov had duly paid him his first annual salary, now refused to accept any further commissions unless first satisfied as to the full amount of his long arrears from Apraxin. The altercation became so bitter and Perry's refusal to compromise so antagonized the Russian Admiral that he threatened to employ force. Perry stood his ground as long as he dared, but upon hearing of the Tsar's extreme displeasure, he became so alarmed for his personal safety that he put himself under the protection of the British envoy. When shortly afterwards Whitworth departed the country for England, the embittered engineer accompanied him under the shelter of diplomatic immunity, but "without any money, pass, or discharge."[15] In short, with the exception of the £300 paid for his last survey, his fourteen years' service in the Russian Empire had gone entirely unrewarded.

Not until 1716, four years after his return to England, was Perry's book published. It included, in addition to the original manuscript which had been intended for private circulation only, a further general account of an even greater scope than that suggested by its imposing title. Although the two parts taken together cover only 281 pages, the author's observations range widely, from a description of Peter's personal history to reflections upon meteorological principles, from comments upon the habits of the nomad tribes to a critique of the fiscal administration of Russia. A rough scheme of organization is discernible, if only as a sequence of ideas, but even this is much blurred by the

---

[14] Prince Aleksandr Danilovich Menshikov (1672-1729) rose from obscure and humble origins to become the chief favorite of Peter, holding high office in both the military and civil administration. In 1727, after Peter's death, he was disgraced and banished to Siberia.

[15] Perry, *op. cit.*, p. 54.

inclusion of "curious anecdotes" and generalizations not relevant to the immediate subject matter. In the selected quotations below, this sequence has been preserved in the main, but mere historical narrative has been largely omitted unless expressive of some original interpretation by the author. In general, three outstanding impressions emerge: the author's enthusiasm for the immense potential strength of Russia, his admiration for the person and policies of Peter, and his disgust with the reactionary and primitive character of the Muscovite people. These sentiments underlie the whole fabric of the book, and in their continual interplay are revealed both the character of the author and the influences which conditioned his attitude towards the historic epoch he witnessed.

As an engineer, it was Perry's function, by the application of scientific principles to nature, to make available to man the wealth of the world's resources. Accordingly, physical Russia appeared to Perry as a vast storehouse of hidden treasure crying out for exploitation by ambitious and intelligent men. With an enthusiasm which sometimes became positively lyric, he described the forests and rivers, the fish and game, the agricultural and mineral wealth. Occasionally, it seems as though a romantic echo of his adventurous youth on the sea responded to the call of this great land ocean, but more often the reader is reminded of the enthusiasm of American technical advisers called to the Soviet Union in the 1920's. With them, as with Perry, Russian natural wealth stirred not mere poetic admiration, but the desire for active exploitation. Such an attitude was diametrically opposed to that of the Russian boyar, Prince Golitsyn, who had said of the Don-Volga canal that "God had made the rivers to flow one way, and it was presumption in man to think to turn them another."[16] The irreconcilability of these positions largely accounted for Perry's antipathy for the character of the typical Russian.

In the geographical survey of the Russian Empire with which his book began Perry invariably oriented his evaluation of its resources towards two activities: "war and trade." They were his insistent preoccupations. Although Russia was engaged in a life and death struggle with Sweden at the time, and although there were less than two years of peace in Peter's entire reign, in his description of the eastern and southern borders Perry suggested, almost recommended, a military conquest on every frontier. Siberia, Great Tartary, the Caspian basin, the Kuban, Georgia, and the Crimea were all to be theaters of

[16] *ibid.*, p. 6.

future military operations. Similarly, every border was a potential trade route. The Tsar intended one day to carry on commerce over the Baltic, the White, the Black, and the Caspian seas and also to explore for a northeast passage to the Indies by way of the Tartarian Sea. In short, war and trade were to be the dual occupations of the Russian people, and it was in the opportunity to prosecute these pursuits that the potential strength of the Russian state consisted.

The basic innovation of Peter's reign was the consciousness of this connection between commercial and military operations. To Perry, as was natural to a foreign contemporary, Peter's entire program of Europeanization was new. He did not recognize the very extraordinary extent to which the points of this program could claim precedent in the Russian past.[17] Nevertheless, Perry recognized the traditional character of Russian commercial and military policy. He knew that Russia had enjoyed a maritime traffic with Europe for over a century and a half. He knew also that most of the military designs which he imputed to Peter were merely extensions of the intermittent warfare of the Russian frontier. Yet this knowledge never seemed to modify his sense of a new force at work. Intuitively, he felt the fact that Peter's wars possessed a new logic. They were fought not to increase the dynastic patrimony but to open commercial connections, not to levy tribute and confiscate wealth but to construct a commercial empire. Every military conflict of Peter's reign was oriented towards commercial ends.[18]

This correlation of war and trade, a cornerstone of European mercantilism, whether the distinctive contribution of Peter or no, under his application involved Russia in the European orbit and precipitated problems similar to those faced by the western nations. During the major portion of John Perry's life, Europe was engaged in an epoch which may with some cogency be called the first world war. In two separate but connected struggles, Louis XIV, on one side of Europe, and Peter the Great, on the other, engaged their neighbors in a conflict which was, for duration, scope, and intensity, unprecedented in the history of modern Europe. From its settlement at Utrecht (1713) in the west and Nystadt (1721) in the north, nothing like it was seen again until the Napoleonic Wars. Each witnessed an advance in military techniques and in each Russia played a new and influential role;

---

[17] Nearly all later historians have emphasized that Peter was less an innovator, than an accelerator of an already marked growth of European influence. Admiral Bridge, in his introduction, includes a particularly neat summary of Russian precedents for Peter's policies, from the adoption of European dress to the hire of foreign shipwrights. Bridge, *op. cit.*, pp. xi-xiv.

[18] E. Pernet, *La Politique Economique de Pierre le Grand*, pp. 33-40.

but the most important fact to note is that each necessitated an intensive reorganization of the resources of the national states involved.
It was this epoch of the first world war which witnessed a major stride
towards the organization of the power state and in this sense, the reforms of Petrine Russia represented only one facet of a European wide
development. For this reason, Perry was fitted by the political climate
of Europe to understand and sympathize with the efforts of Peter to
mobilize and regulate the resources of the Russian Empire.

Peter was the ideal monarch because he sought to exploit and improve
the latent natural wealth of his country. Perry's admiration for Peter
increased in proportion as his esteem for the national character of the
Russians diminished. He found a country, endowed with every natural
blessing, inhabited by a people totally unworthy of it, ignorant, superstitious, dishonest, and reactionary, clinging to primitive techniques
and primitive institutions. The single hope for reform lay in the enlightened Tsar, the only dynamic element of Russian society.[19] This fact
was repeatedly emphasized in Perry's treatment. Long passages resemble a catalogue of Russian deficiencies, to each of which is appended
a description of the measures Peter has taken to repair them. Perry
exempted Peter at every point from the censure which devolved upon
his people. Such blame as attached to governmental policy was always
attributed to some parasitical and corrupt adviser, who had misrepresented the true state of things to his faultless monarch. In Peter, Perry
presented the ideal of an enlightened despot, fifty years before the
heyday of enlightened despotism.

The impulse which initiated the entire process of reform was generated in the mind of Peter, and, in his analysis of this mind, Perry again
revealed his feeling that the aim of a commercial expansion was the
central concern of his regime. Commerce, to Perry, meant shipping,
and it was Peter's interest in shipping which led him step by step to his
later reforms. The chance coincidence of Peter's hereditary genius and
his fortuitous exposure to foreign influence at an early age were interpreted as the circumstances which conditioned an entire historical
epoch. From the naval games of his childhood to the success of his new
fleet in the taking of Azov, Peter's interest grew until, following the
famous European tour, he embarked upon the remarkable resolve to

---

[19] Whitworth reflected a similar adulation of the great Tsar: "He is extremely curious and
diligent and has further improved his empire in ten years than any other ever was in ten times
that space and which is more surprising, without any education, without any foreign help, contrary to the intentions of his people, clergy, and chief ministers, but merely by the strength of
his own genius, observation, and example." Whitworth, *op. cit.*, pp. 57-58.

transform the world's largest land empire into a naval power. As an engineer and a practical working man, Perry was naturally attracted to the Tsar's pleasure and skill in mechanical pursuits. As a European, he was gratified by a Russian's recognition of the superiority of western techniques. As a former English naval officer, he approved Peter's interest in shipping and was flattered by his preference for English to Dutch marine construction. Understandably, all these causes contributed to Perry's admiration for the Tsar and his sympathy for the program which he imputed to him. Whether or not he exaggerated the importance of Peter's commercial designs, it cannot be denied that it was Peter's naval projects which represented his most striking break with the past. It would have been a cause for wonder had they not occupied an important place in the observations of any contemporary.

Between the energetic and enlightened Peter and the vast natural wealth of the Russia he ruled loomed the monolithic bulk of Muscovite society. To articulate and mobilize this static mass into an active mercantile state represented a far more difficult task than did a similar process in the more dynamic western societies. To Perry, Peter, endowed with a European education, hereditary genius, and a despotic political power, represented an irresistible force, but in the great Muscovite community he strove to reform he encountered a nearly immovable object. The problems were immense. In technical ability Russia was far behind her European rivals. Politically, the exigencies of war and the confusion of an archaic administrative system either obstructed or perverted many of Peter's schemes. Economically, the lack of capital, difficulties of transportation, and ignorance of modern commercial methods hampered progress. Socially, a deeply rooted tradition froze the various elements of the population in a rigid structure, stubbornly unreceptive to all new patterns of activity. Perry discussed, rather lightly in some cases, a majority of these problems, but his attention focused largely on the human, rather than on the institutional deficiencies of the Russian people. To Perry, Peter's fundamental problem was the national character of his people.

A primary cause for the irritating inertia of Muscovite society was the reactionary influence of Greek Orthodoxy. The secular power of the church concerned Perry little, because Peter so easily incorporated it under his own political authority, an act which the Englishman, himself a member of an established church, heartily approved. It was as a cause of the intellectual and moral turpitude of the people that Perry

really despised the Russian faith. In an extended passage he condemned
it as the sponsor of illiteracy, irrationality, dishonesty, idolatry, drunkenness, and criminal degeneracy. That Perry, in this crushing indictment of the Russian national character, should seek to make the church
the scapegoat is partially explained by his own religious prejudices
which led him into both exaggeration and error. As a member of the
Church of England, he shared the Anglican bias against Papistry to
which he likened Orthodoxy, and, as a devotee of scientific reason, he
decried the superstition and obscurantism of the church with the ardor,
if not the wit, of a Voltaire.[20] Seeing it as a specific evil, he generalized
and exaggerated its scope and, with minor exceptions, tended to exempt
economic and political influences from their share of the responsibility
in the formation of the national character. Rather, in consideration of
these latter, he reversed the position of cause and effect as understood,
for example, by a doctrinaire Marxist. It was less economic impoverish-
ment which had debased the character of the Russian peasant and perverted his religious concepts than it was the debasement of his character
by a religious virus, which obstructed the development of commercial
prosperity. Like those sixteenth-century reformers of western Europe
who found the ethical standards of the Catholic Church unsuitable for
the new bourgeois society, Perry indicted the Greek Orthodox Church
for the obscurantism and dishonesty which undermined the development of a better way of life.

In addition to religious and secular education, begun by the Tsar,
these evils might be attacked on other fronts. In religious conservatism
Perry saw the cement of the whole inert social edifice, pervading its
every compartment, retarding every attempt at progress. The literal
mentality of Greek Orthodoxy had produced a crystallization not only
of ecclesiastical, but of all social forms. It furnished a moral sanction
for "the cult of immobility" which paralyzed Muscovite society.[21] In
opposition to it, there was justified an assault of such scope and violence
as to approach iconoclasm. In this light, Peter's insistence on the adoption of the merely external trappings of European civilization seemed
less naive to Perry than to many later observers. Every break with the
past was another breach in the bastion of reaction.[22] Peter must regulate

---

[20] It is noteworthy that the great Frenchman, in using Perry's book as a source for his
history of Peter the Great propagated and gave wide currency to many of his false notions about
Greek Orthodoxy. For example, he stated that one of its converts was first required to spit
three times upon his former faith. Mohrenschildt, *op. cit.*, p. 135.

[21] Pernet, *op. cit.*, pp. 1-15.

[22] Eugene Schuyler, *Peter the Great*, New York, 1884, 1, 342.

not only commercial, but social relations; he must establish not only European military discipline, but European dress; he must destroy not only the power of the religious reactionaries, but the beards which symbolized their reaction. As in every other instance, Perry here endorsed Peter's program, believing that the end would justify the means. With the removal of the debris which cluttered the literal Muscovite mind, the European enlightenment would begin; with the destruction of the archaic forms which paralyzed the machinery of Muscovite society, the manifestly superior European mores would take their place.

Politically, beyond the various revolts and attempts to dethrone Peter, the task of government was rendered extraordinarily difficult by the unwieldiness of the administrative instrument. In consideration of the fact that Peter's reforms were directed at so many phases of Russian life, the inefficacy of his administrative control was a real tragedy. The incompetence of "the omnicompetent state" resulted both from its organizational weakness and from the stupidity and corruption of its officials. Perry painted a black picture of these combined evils. There was no separation of powers. Officials possessed judicial, executive, and, in determining the assessments of the taxes, legislative functions to such a degree "that they might be said to have the sole power of men's lives and fortunes in their hands." Moreover, these powers were so loosely disseminated through the official hierarchy that they tended to become entirely personal. Even subordinate officials, unchecked by a regular discipline, became practicing despots, disposing all affairs in accordance with their private caprices. Such a system gave full scope to the Muscovite propensities for corruption, and the cost to the state in terms of the collection of taxes was enormous. Actually, it is now estimated that of every hundred rubles collected from the people, only thirty ever reached the imperial treasury.[23] Peter, driven by the exigencies of his military campaigns, was unable to carry on any extensive reforms of his administration during the time that Perry was in Russia, but he did attempt to improve his taxgathering machinery by setting up the new office of the ratusha. Using a Dutch model he broadened the base of his government to include the infant bourgeois element of the population. Perry, a member of the middle class, heartily approved this step, but his enthusiasm led him to exaggerate the actual benefits accruing to the state, for, in truth, the Russian merchants proved to be quite as corrupt as their noble brethren.[24] In general,

[23] James Mavor, *An Economic History of Russia*, London, 1914, I, 141.
[24] V. O. Kliuchevsky, *A History of Russia*, New York, 1931, IV, 155; Schuyler, *op. cit.*, I, 344.

Perry's analysis of the administrative organization of Russia was not searching. With the exception of the ratusha, there were no general administrative reforms to focus his attention on the problem. Moreover, then as later, English political practice left a large share of the functions of government in the hands of an amateur gentry, whose greatest check was their own political morality, and, with this background, he tended to condemn as the basic weakness not the administrative system as such but the ethical character of the officials who manned it.

Perry's description of the military reforms showed more insight into the nature of the administrative problem. It has been pointed out that the military establishments of the eighteenth century exercised an important influence by providing models for the reorganization of the civil administration.[25] These new armies organized a body of salaried experts for the performance of specialized functions and held them strictly accountable for their actions. As such, they represented a sharp contrast to the semi-feudal administrations of irresponsible, nonsalaried, amateur nobles, holding office as property through privilege. Perry's description of Peter's military reforms presented a striking instance of this contrast between the civil and military organizations. In his army, Peter attempted to correct those deficiencies which made his civil administration so imperfect a control instrument. Systematic division of labor, employment of foreign experts and the specialized education of Russians, the payment of salaries, promotion, not through privilege, but as a reward for meritorious service, and punishment for offenses were all part of a program, carried on "that the Tsar might have men fit to serve him in his army and navy and in all manners of business." In essence, this aimed at a total mobilization of the aristocracy to the uses of the state. It foreshadowed the publication of the famous Table of Ranks (1718), equating military and civil commissions, and making all rank dependent, not upon hereditary privilege, but upon service to the state. Perry did not witness this last extension of the obligation to state service, nor did he recognize that in these earlier phases Peter was only furthering a traditional policy of his predecessors,[26] but in his consciousness of the implications of the present, there was a foretaste of things to come.

Whatever the success of Peter's military reforms, the corruption, stupidity, and oppression of the civil administration still undermined

[25] W. L. Dorn, *Competition for Empire*, New York, 1940, p. 14.
[26] G. T. Robinson, *Rural Russia under the Old Regime*, New York, 1932, pp. 1-33.

the all-important commercial prosperity of the nation. Perry emphasized this point by his insistence upon the extraordinary natural wealth
of Russia, while depreciating the extent of both those successes already
attained and of the enormous problems still confronting the government. For example, Perry simply listed the iron mines and foundries,
the powder mills and naval stores as items of the produce of Russia
without any mention of the remarkable program of development
which Peter had conducted to make the raw materials available to
human uses.[27] Again, he extolled the magnificent system of waterways
without regard for the immense effort necessary for their artificial
improvement. From an impoverished government, locked in a deadly
armed conflict with one of the foremost military powers of Europe, he
had cavalierly requested the extraordinary number of 30,000 workmen
for his Don-Volga canal and had expressed chagrin at receiving only
half that number, yet, in terms of relative population, Perry's demand
would have been equivalent to a force of over 300,000 men in the
contemporary United States. Perry's vision of the potentialities of a new
mercantile Russia made him impatient of all obstacles to its realization.

In his analysis of the state of the Russian economy, he launched a
vehement attack upon the policies of the corrupt and ignorant Muscovite officials. The inflation of the coinage, arbitrary price-fixing, and
sudden impositions of new duties had seriously undermined the confidence of foreign merchants in the trade, to say nothing of the government's frequent violations of its own "most solemn contracts and
agreements." Yet even when the irresponsible practices of the Tsar's
lords and favorites were not aimed at self-enrichment, their inopportune
attempts to encourage Russian competition with foreign manufactures
or failure to stimulate indigenous productions tended to injure international commerce.

Still more deadly than these impediments to existing traffic was the
paralyzing effect of official practice upon the very mainsprings of all
economic activity. Taxation was so burdensome and was so oppres-
sively collected, that it had deprived the people of all security of property. In dread of confiscation and torture, the peasantry were driven to
alternative economic sins. Either they buried their money in the ground,
removing it from circulation, or they slowed their production to a
subsistence level, working only during the summer months in their

[27] In 1718, Russian foundries smelted over 104,000 tons of iron, while, more than twenty
years later, England produced only 17,000 tons, or less than one-sixth of that amount, and only
in 1796 did British production reach 125,000 tons. Mavor, *op. cit.*, I, 129.

fields, and spending the long winter in idleness.[28] Idle money and idle hands were unthinkable evils in an impoverished and undeveloped country. In England "and the other free countries," the possessions of wealth and technical skill were prized and furnished stimuli to activity; in Russia, wealth and ingenuity were only the occasions for tyrannical oppression, curses to be avoided or concealed from the cruel officialdom.

Here, for the first time, toward the very end of his book, Perry came face to face with the great underlying contradiction of Peter's regime. Peter, the great reformer and revolutionary, never opposed the most important continuous development of the past two centuries of Muscovite history: the progressive enslavement of the peasantry. Such modifications as Peter did make in the institution of serfdom were rather legal confirmations and extensions of existing practice.[29] Peter's Europeanization program actually touched only the upper class, and its ultimate historical consequence for the old Muscovite community was to split it into two parts as distinct as two nations, of which the first a wealthy, educated, and privileged nobility, endowed with the mental equipment of the enlightenment, weighed heavily upon an impoverished, ignorant, and reactionary slave class. Never foreseeing this outcome, Perry did not really condemn serfdom as an institution. His concern was less humanitarian than economic, and less theoretical than practical. The great evil was the "check and discouragement to ingenuity" and hence to national prosperity, and its implied remedy was not a constitutional reform but the enlightenment of the existing ruling class. The emphasis upon the personal, rather than the institutional, was revealed in Perry's most pessimistic statement about the future of Russia: "this is certain, that if the present Czar should happen to die, without the greatest part of his present old boyars go off before him, the generality of things wherein he has taken so much pains to reform his country, will for the most part revolve into their old forms. For it is believed that his son, the present Prince of Russia ... will easily be prevailed on to come into the old methods of Russia. . . ."[30] The conditioning elements here were entirely personal, and on the reverse side of the medal Perry implied that should the old boyars go off first,

---

[28] In the absence of security of property, Whitworth saw the same pernicious influence on the peasantry. "This country is a perfect model of Bayes Grand Dance, where everyone has his share of slavery and worship, except the peasants, who are perfect slaves subject to the arbitrary power of their lords and transferred with goods and chattels. They can call nothing their own, which makes them very lazy, and when their master's task is done, and a little bread and firing provided for the year, the great business of their life is over, the rest of the time being idle or slept away; and yet they live content." Whitworth, *op. cit.*, p. 39.

[29] Robinson, *op. cit.*, pp. 25-26.   [30] Perry, *op. cit.*, p. 261.

all might yet be well. An enlightened and Europeanized aristocracy would know how, as Peter did, to "give encouragement" to the people regardless of their institutional status.

The great concrete manifestation of Peter's policies and the lasting monument of his reign was the capital he fixed on the shores of the Baltic, and in his description of St. Petersburg, Perry again showed confidence in the aims and methods of Peter. St. Petersburg was the very symbol of absolutism. Its site had been captured by military force; its buildings had been raised by slave labor; its population had been settled by despotic decree. It still struggled for survival against the natural disadvantages of its terrain and the psychological opposition of the "old boyars," and the realization of its true worth involved still other gigantic undertakings but Perry, like Peter, was so dazzled by the bright vision of the future that he often seemed blind to present difficulties. Thus, he described the St. Petersburg-Volga canal only in terms of its advantages.[31] To the very last Perry failed to resolve the discrepancy between future hopes and present problems. His book ended abruptly with a description of yet another of Peter's schemes for the improvement of the new capital. Appropriately, it was impetuous in conception, autocratic in design, and incomplete in execution. Disregarding all natural difficulties, Peter had arbitrarily decreed the construction of a road between St. Petersburg and Moscow in a straight line, but its construction had been postponed. Perhaps Perry's closing words expressed a subconscious intuition of the great pathos of the dynamic Peter, forever driven by the exigencies of war and finance, forever striving to perform the impossible. His last words have an almost wistful ring: "and the Czar does design to have a road accordingly made when he has peace and can better spare men and money for it."[32]

---

[31] Whitworth was not so sanguine of the gains to be realized through this canal. He conjectured: "This communication seems to be more for curiosity than for use, for the frigates now bringing from Kazan have been three years in their passage. They are frozen up for the six winter months. During the spring floods for five or six weeks it is scarce possible for them to mount the Volga against the current. During the autumn the waters are very low, and they are often forced to warp around the points of land and sandbanks." Whitworth, *op. cit.*, p. 156.

[32] Perry, *op. cit.*, p. 281.

EXTRACTS FROM: *The State of Russia under the Present Czar, in relation to the several great and remarkable things he has done, as to his naval preparations, the regulating his army, the reforming his people, and improving his countrey. Particularly those works on which the author was employ'd, with the reasons of his quitting the Czar's service after being fourteen years in that countrey; also an account of those Tartars and other peoples who border on the eastern and extreme northern parts of the Czar's dominions, their religion and manner of life: with many other observations. To which is annex'd a more accurate map of the Czar's dominions than has hitherto been Extant.*

by John Perry

CONTENTS

....

EDITOR'S NOTE

THROUGHOUT the selected extracts, the original spelling and punctuation have
been preserved with relatively few exceptions. After the first appearance of a
Russian word, the modern spelling has been added in brackets; and where
an old geographical name has been superseded, the modern name also has
been added. Brackets have been used for page references at the end of each
extract, and dates inserted to clarify the text have been placed in italics. The
only interpolated material not in brackets are the titles, supplied by the editor
to describe and divide the extracts.

    In arranging the material, the original sequence has been maintained in the
great majority of cases; but where chronology is of little or no importance, it
has occasionally been altered in the interests of organization.

I · NEW PROSPECTS ON OLD FRONTIERS

1. TOWARD THE TARTARIAN SEA: SIBERIA

THE KINGDOM OF SIBERIA, and provinces thereto belonging, is accounted
the eighth part of the Czar's dominions (as divided into provinces
about six years since), and brings a considerable revenue into the
Czar's treasure, besides maintaining the garrisons in the countrey and
sending constant recruits to the Czar's army, particularly, the Sibersky
[Sibirsky], Tubollsky [Tobolsky] regiments, both of foot and dragoon,

are reckoned as good as any the Czar has, excepting the Guards, which are men chosen out of all the regiments.

Besides these advantages, and the farther prospect of extending the Czar's conquests quite on to the Tartarian Sea, when there shall be a time for it, where the richest furs are always found: By way of this countrey the Russes now carry on a beneficial trade quite to China, there going every year a considerable carravan of merchants, that carry thither chiefly the rich furs of Siberia, such as black foxes, sables, tigers, ermine, etc. and some small goods also imported at Archangel, and return from China tea in great jars, damask silk, with a sort also of linen which is mixed with cotton . . . dyed some red, some blue and other colors, very much worn by the Russ women. They make some return also of pearl and of gold in ingots from China. Besides the Russes themselves fish up pearls in some of the eastern rivers bordering on the dominions of China; between which and the Tobolsks [Tobolsk] in the way towards China, they have built several towns and places where the Russes keep garrison. And . . . since I came from Russia . . . the Russes have found upon a river that flows from the southeast part of that province, and falls into the Caspian Sea, a considerable quantity of gold dust, which they hope will turn to good account. There are also several iron works in Siberia, and the iron that is brought from thence, is so much esteemed for its goodness, that it is sold for a third part better price than any other iron in Russia: Also, there is a sort of ivory brought from thence, being the tooth of an amphibious creature call'd a behemot [behemoth]. . . .[33]

All informations agree that the whole way between the River Wolga [Volga] and the walls of China, the countrey is interlined with plains and woods, with lakes and rivers, some falling toward the Caspian and others toward the Tartarian Sea, and is for the most part pleasant and fruitful. [79-83]

2. TOWARD THE CASPIAN SEA: THE LOWER VOLGA

The next people that I shall take notice of are the Caban [Kuban] tartars, who are a very strong bodied, well proportioned people. . . . They inhabit to the westward of the River Wolga along the northeast coast of the Black Sea and between that and the Caspian Sea, from whence they make frequent incursions into the outparts of Russia, plunder and fire villages, and often carry off cattle and horses and

---

[33] Doubtless, the walrus of the northern waters. It was easily killed on land and was long valued for its ivory tusks, as well as for its hide, oil, and meat.

people, by reason of which there is a great tract of land on the west side of the Wolga all the way between the town of Saratoff [Saratov] and the Caspian Sea lies wholly uninhabited, save only the islands about Astracan [Astrakhan] and the people that live within the town of Camishinka [Kamyshin] Czaritza [Tsaritsyn] . . . and Terki [Terek], the nearest of which are from 150 or 160 to above 200 miles distance from each other, (as the road lies) where garrisons are kept at each particular place, and are always ready for an alarm. And by reason of the incursions of the said tartars, the Russes do not plow and sow in these parts (though the land is extremely rich) but have every year corn brought down to them by the River Wolga, and the same vessels go back laden with fish and rock-salt, etc. of which the greatest part of Russia is supplied from a place thirty miles below Camishinka, as also from Astracan there is returned every year some small matter of rich goods from Persia and Armenia, as wrought silk, calicoes, etc.

The said tartars when they make their incursions, it is usually in the summer time, when there is grass enough on the ground; and each man for expedition sake, takes two horses, which they change as they ride, sometimes sitting upon one, and sometimes upon another. They always travel with sentinels at a convenient distance from all sides of their main body, to prevent being discover'd. . . . They come on with that swiftness and caution, that there seldom is any advice of them; and immediately fall upon what booty they can find, and do what mischief they can, and then return again with the same expedition as they came on, before the Russes can . . . cut off their retreat: And those that happen to be taken, on either side, are used very barbarously, which seldom or never have any redemption from their slavery. One of the advantages, therefore, which was proposed for making a communication between the Wolga and the Don, was to have a barrier to prevent these tartars from advancing farther into Russia.

Whilst I was employ'd at Camishinka, there was an army every year of two thousand gentlemen on horseback . . . with four thousand foot and twelve field-pieces,[34] who were sent to cover the workmen from the incursions of the said Cabans; and guards and out sentinels were placed at several miles distance, on the tops of hills and proper places, to prevent our being surprized: But notwithstanding all our guards and watches that had been placed, a party of between three and four

---

[34] As, according to Perry's own account, he had never had as many as 15,000 workmen, the proportion of soldiers to laborers must be computed at 2 to 5, a remarkable instance of the drain of military manpower occasioned by Russia's unsettled frontier.

thousand of these tartars once came just as it was day in the morning, without our having the least advice of them, up to our very camp; and when they found that the alarm was taken, and our cannon began to play upon them from our lines, they immediately retired with the same speed they came on, before our men could mount or get in any order to attack them. . . . They carried off in all about 1400 horses, some of which belonged to the army and others to the workmen; with several people that were looking after the horses where they were feeding in the meadows, at some distance from the camp; there being no inclosures in that countrey.

The countrey, all the way from Camishinka to Terki, as it is in the best climate in the world, so it is for the most part extremely fertile and pleasant to inhabit. In the spring of the year, as soon as ever the snow is off the ground, which usually does not lye above two or three months in these parts, the warm weather immediately after takes place; and the tulips, roses, lilies of the valley, pinks, sweet williams, and several other flowers and herbs spring up like a garden, in a very great variety. Asparagus, the best I ever eat, grows so thick, that you may in some places mow it down, and the common grass in the meadows is up to the horse's belly. Liquorish, almonds, and cherries, the fields are cover'd with; but the trees are low, and the fruit small. As also in autumn appear ripe several sorts of grain, and the fruits of the earth which by cultivation might be much improved. There is a great variety of birds, and wild-fowl in abundance of all sorts, both of land and water: As also small fallow-deer, rayn-deer, elks, wild-boars, wild-horses, wild-sheep, of which I once eat part of one, that being chased by a wolf, was taken by a fisherman into his boat on the River Wolga; it eat tenderer, and was much preferable to common mutton. . . .

It is a thousand times to be lamented, that so rich and noble a countrey, situated on the side of the great River Wolga, which is perhaps the best stored with fish of any river in the whole world, and where many small rivers (not described in the map) fall into it, should now lye in a manner waste without inhabitants, whilst . . . many of the northern Russes I have seen for want of sun enough to ripen their harvest, mingle roots of grass and straw with their corn to make bread.

Therefore it will be worth the Czar's thoughts to settle and cultivate a good understanding with the said tartars, and by giving them his protection, improve and better people his country to the southward; as also by way of the Wolga, since he has fallen on thoughts of shipping and improving sailing vessels for the use of the Caspian Sea, which his subjects before knew little of: He has an opportunity to invite and settle, not only trade and commerce with the Persians and Armenians, who are naturally a trading people, and with whom the Russes at present have some correspondence, but also to settle a trade with Great Tartary by means of the rivers that extend that way, and the several other countries bordering on the Caspian Sea; which it is believed by our English merchants, whom I have talk'd with in Mosco [Moscow] on this subject, might in time prove a means to vend considerable quantities of English cloth this way, as well as linen, corn, and other things, the product of the Czar's countrey, which they might, no doubt, in the course of time, be brought to the desire and use of. . . . [87-94]

3. TOWARD THE BLACK SEA: THE CRIMEA

The next people that I shall give an account of are the Crim-Tartars [Crimean Tartars], who border on the Black Sea, and on whom the Czar has the most thoughts of extending his southern conquests. They are in possession of a very fruitful and pleasant countrey, which is almost as an island surrounded partly with the waters of the Black Sea, and partly with those of the Palus Maeotis [The Sea of Azov] . . . and they have also a good tract of countrey farther to the northward, and to the westward as far as the mouth of the Nieper [Dnieper].

The said Tartars were formerly victorious against the Russes. They have often penetrated into the heart of Russia, and in anno 1671,[35] they burnt the city of Mosco, and by the articles of peace concluded in the time of the Czar's predecessors, the Russes were obliged to submit to very scandalous terms; not only to be tributary to the said Tartars, but even to have it inserted in their articles, that the Czars of Russia should hold the stirrup to the Great Cham, in case of their happening to meet together. But if the princes of Christendom should again be jointly engaged in a war with the Turks, and the Czar be disengaged but a little time from his present war with the Swedes, the Crim will then certainly be a bloody seat of war, and the Czar will revenge these indignities, with exerting his utmost for the conquest of it, thereby to make his way into the Black Sea.

I have often heard the Czar say, when he was building of his ships, and preparing magazines on that side . . . that he hoped, in case he

---

[35] This is an error, perhaps typographical, for in reality, the Crimean Tartars had burned Moscow a hundred years before, in 1571, and never seriously threatened it during the seventeenth century. Nevertheless, large raiding parties penetrated deep into Russia for many years. B. H. Sumner, *A Short History of Russia*, New York, 1943, p. 33.

lived, that it would not be many years before he could make himself master of Kertzi [Kertch] and have that place for laying up and rendezvous for his navy: There being on the bar of Azoph [Azov] commonly not above seven foot draught of water . . . whereas at Kertzi, there is water enough for the biggest ships the Czar can propose to build, and where may easily be made good security for the greatest navy in the world.

The views which the Czar has, and the success that he promises himself one time or other to obtain on this side, is, that he will either by force or consent, oblige the Turks upon paying them tribute, (as is used in the Sound) to let him trade with his ships into the Mediterranean. [136-140]

II · THE TRAIL TO EUROPE

I. FIRST THOUGHTS OF SHIPPING

THE occasion of his [the Tsar] first falling upon thoughts of shipping, and his traveling to inspect the improvements of other countries, was owing chiefly to his early genius and curiosity to enquire into the reason and causes of things; which method in his common conversations, he still uses with indefatigable application in minutest things. And next was also owing to an accident that happened, which led him to a liking and pleasure in conversation with foreigners. . . .

It happened that one LeFort,[36] a Frenchman, who had been apprentice to a merchant in Amsterdam, and was then a captain in the Russ army, was appointed one of the officers that commanded the Guards that were chosen to secure the Czar's person . . . : and he being of an active and ingenious temper, happened to be very much taken notice of by the Czar, who was then but 12 years of age . . . and he from that time kept him always near his person, and took a particular affection to him, and was pleased with the discourse that he often entertained him with; of the countries he had been in, of the regular discipline of the armies, and of the naval powers; the riches and trade that was extended through Europe, by other nations, over all the parts of the world, by the means of shipping. Whereupon the Czar at first ordered ships to be built for his pleasure, with masts and sails, and guns, upon

---

[36] François LeFort (1656-1699) was born in Switzerland of Scottish descent and raised in Amsterdam. This cosmopolitan adventurer, who met Peter by chance in the foreign quarter of Moscow, became a prime favorite and exercised a profound influence over him during his early development.

the Perrislausky [Pereiaslavskoe] Lake, not far from Moscow, where he often diverted himself with sailing upon the said lake, and had several sham-fights perform'd, in which he acted and commanded as a sea-captain, from which time he took that title upon him. [141-146]

2. THE TRIAL FLEET AT AZOV

And in the year 1694, when the Emperor, the Poles, and the Venetians were jointly engaged in a war with the Turks, the Czar also declared war against them, and commanded several small galleys and vessels to be built and equipp'd on the River Veronize [Voronezh], which he employed in the taking of Azoph. . . .

The first summer, the Czar march'd against the place with an army of 80 or 90 thousand men, (which was in the year 1695) but the Turks got succours into the town by water, made frequent sallies, and held out a resolute defence. . . . But the second year, the Czar having ordered a strong recruit of his army, and prepared a fleet of small vessels and galleys, to prevent the relief of the town, when the Turks came with their fleet, by way of the Black Sea, before the Barr, with a new supply of men, provisions, and money, and attempted with a great number of half galleys, boats, and vessels to have thrown fresh succours into the town, as they had done the year before: The Czar with his aforesaid vessels and boats, (on board of which he acted in person) laid an ambuscade behind a small island, and after having first made a shew to retire before the face of the enemy, when they were got a little way within the river, he fell upon them, sunk and took several of their vessels, with soldiers, provisions, and money on board; and at another time, beat them back over the bar. . . . The enemy finding themselves thus every way distress'd by the most surprising and vigorous behaviour of the Czar and his army, and no prospect of the relief which they had expected by their fleet, they were obliged to surrender themselves, upon conditions, that they should have liberty to march out of the place without their arms. [146-149]

3. MARITIME PLANS FOR MUSCOVY

The Czar pleased with the success of his new built fleet, and the reduction of so important a place, which open'd a way into the Black Sea; upon his returning to Mosco in triumph, he was complimented upon this victory by his boyars, as being principally owing to his fleet, and his Majesty's personal vigour and conduct on board the same, by which he prevented the relief of the town. His Majesty on this occasion finding the great advantage of a maritime force, declared to his Lords that he was resolved to establish a navy on that side, that he might maintain this important place, and be able to meet the Turks and oppose them in the Black Sea; and commanded them immediately to send for builders and artificers from Holland to build his ships, and from Italy and Venice to build his galleys, and resolved to have a fleet ... to be built, and equipp'd with all things ready to put to sea, within the time of three years that was given for the doing it. A list accordingly was prepared and agreed on in council, which the Czar called for this purpose, by which several of the great lords (who had great estates, and a great many slaves at their command, in which their estates was accounted to consist) were obliged to build each of them a man of war at their own charge, and were at liberty to call them after their own names when built. The monasteries also, and the cities and towns, the merchants and the gentlemen through all the districts of his dominions, were to pay their proportion to the charge of this new undertaking, besides the ordinary course of the taxes for maintaining the army, and carrying on the war that was then in hand. . . . His Majesty declared also at the same time his intentions to travel whilst this fleet was preparing, and appointed several of the young nobility and gentry of his countrey to go with him, to see and learn the improvements of other nations, commanding some of them to travel to one place, and some to another, to make all the observations where possible through all the parts of Europe. [150-151]

4. THE WORKMAN TSAR IN HOLLAND

The Czar, having thus dispos'd the condition of things in his absence, in May 1697, he set forward upon his journey. . . . [157] His humour did not lead him to the courts of princes to observe the politeness of government, or the pleasures and splendor there, but he employ'd his time in conversing with common artificers, that were masters of such arts as were wanting in his countrey, (his people not being then masters of the grounds and rules of any art or science whatsoever) but was most strictly curious in making his inspections in the improvements of shipping and trade, and the arts and discipline of war. . . . Most commonly when he came to any seaport he went about in a Dutch skipper's habit, that he might go among the shipping, and be the less taken notice of. He did not stay long at any of the seaports in the Baltick,

[Baltic] . . . but . . . was desirous, above any other place, to be at Holland.

The magistrates . . . had prepared for him a very magnificent house for his residence. But the Czar having taken a particular fancy and resolution on his own part to learn the art of ship-building, . . . refused all importunities made to him to accept of any lodging in the city, and chose to take a small house on the East-India wharf, (or ship-yard) just by the water side, where there were strict orders given, that neither any mob from abroad, nor the people in the yard, should gaze and disturb him; a thing he was the most averse to imaginable. Here he lived for some months, with two or three of his favourites, whom he took to be partners with him in learning the art of ship-building. He wrought one part of the day with the carpenter's broad ax among the Dutchmen; and for the better disguise, wore the same sort of habit which they did: And at other times diverted himself with sailing, and rowing upon the water.

He admitted nevertheless of the private visits of some of the most considerable men of the city, who brought to him all the collections of art and nature that Holland could afford. He went often, during his stay at Amsterdam, sometimes in one habit, and sometimes in another, to burgomaster Whitson, and some others, to private entertainments that were made for him; where he would be very free and merry with a few persons, which to this day is his way, and is most agreeable to him. [159-163]

5. THE QUEST PURSUED TO ENGLAND

He had in this time seen several of our English built ships, and being pleased with the proportion and beauty of them, after he had been some time at the Hague, (where his ambassadors made their publick entry) and had had a private interview with King William, he went to England, where a house was first provided for him in York-Buildings by the water side. He spent some few days in the city of London, and had several interviews with the King . . . and many of the English nobility; but was more particularly, and above all, taken with the conversation of the then Marquis of Carmarthen,[37] who complied with him in his humour, and assisted him in his pursuit after the knowledge

---

[37] Thomas Osborn, first Earl of Danby, Marquis of Carmarthen, and Duke of Leeds (1631-1712). This "famous wag and heroic drinker" was delegated guide and entertainer of the Russian Tsar during his residence in England. E. J. Simmons, *English Literature and Culture in Russia (1553-1840)*, Cambridge, Mass., 1935, p. 56.

of shipping, and would row and sail with him upon the water, which was his delight; of which obligations and kindness of my Lord Marquis to him, I have many times since heard him speak with great affection; as indeed he often does of England in general, and what he observed here. And I have often heard him say, that he designs to take a turn hither again when he has peace settled in his own countrey: And has often declared to his lords, when he has been a little merry, that he thinks it a much happier life to be an Admiral in England, than Czar in Russia.

A house in London not suiting his humour and the intentions of his travels, some few days after his arrival, Mr. Evelyn's[38] house, an agreeable seat at Deptford, was prepared for him, where there was a backdoor open'd into the King's yard, very convenient for his intended business of conversing with our English builders . . . and artificers for his navy that he intended to establish.

The Czar was mightily pleas'd with our Armory in the tower, and with our way of coining of money, which is the most perfect in the world. He was about three months in England, in which time the King was pleased to send Admiral Mitchel down with him to Portsmouth, to put the fleet that lay at Spithead to sea, on purpose to shew him a sham engagement; and which had before been shewn him in Holland, but not so satisfactory to him as that in England. He took also a tour to Oxford to see the University. He was once to see the Archbishop of Canterbury at his palace, and went often to our churches and cathedrals to see the order of our establish'd religion; and also had the curiosity to see the Quakers and other meeting-houses, in the time of their service.

He was likewise shewn both Houses of Parliament when they were sitting, and was prevail'd upon to go once or twice to the play, but that was what he did not like. He spent most of his time in what related to war and shipping, and upon the water. He often took the carpenter's tools in his hands, and often work'd himself in Deptford Yard, as he had done before in Holland. He would sometimes be at the smith's, and sometimes at the gun-founder's, and there was scarce any art or mechanick trade whatsoever, from the watch-maker to the

[38] John Evelyn (1620-1706). Noted diarist, minor public official, a prominent member of the Royal Society and a gentleman of extraordinarily diversified interests. A famous and enthusiastic gardener, he was dismayed to find, among other evidences of abuse to his house and property, severe damage to his prized holly hedge "caused by the Czar amusing himself by being driven in a wheel-barrow through the hedge as a morning exercise." Arthur Ponsonby, *John Evelyn*, London, 1933, p. 59.

coffin-maker, but he more or less inspected it, and even caused a model of an English coffin to be sent into Russia, as he did also of many other things.

His Majesty, whilst he was here, order'd his said ambassador to contract with some merchants for exporting yearly into Russia, a considerable quantity of tobacco, upon condition of being first licens'd by the Lord Marquis of Carmarthen; which he granted him, in return of the obliging conversation he had receiv'd from him: The benefit my Lord made of this licence, was 5s. per hogshead,[39] tobacco having been before prohibited in Russia, by order of the Patriarch, as an unclean and irreligious thing; and to this day a priest will not come into any room where tobacco is smoak'd.

The King gave him free leave to take such of his subjects into his service as he should have occasion for; and at his departure made him a present of the Royal Transport, which was much the finest and best yatcht then in England, built frigate fashion, carrying 24 guns. . . . The . . . mathematicians, ship-builders and artificers, together with several other officers, bombardeers, and other persons, who were entertain'd, were sent over in the Royal Transport, and by other passages to Archangel; and within four days after, an agreement was made with me, his Majesty going over to Holland. . . . I was order'd to attend him . . . to Amsterdam. . . . I had but seven or eight days time given me in Amsterdam; and leaving the Czar, who design'd his journey from thence to Vienna and other parts, I was sent directly by the way of Narva to Mosco. . . . [163-169]

III · THE EVILS OF ORTHODOXY

I. THE PROBLEM OF POWER: THE PATRIARCH

The Russes relate that the Patriarch deriv'd his authority and jurisdiction from the Patriarch of the Greek Church. . . . However true this is, I know not, but this may be said of the Patriarch of Mosco, that he was in very high esteem with the people, and indeed might be said to bear a kind of share in the sovereignty of the empire, having not only been supreme judge of ecclesiastical causes, but had a power also

---

[39] The extent of the favor thus returned for Carmarthen's "obliging conversation" can be understood only when it is realized that this monopoly, providing a very considerable stimulus to the Anglo-Russian trade, is estimated to have netted the British merchants £120,000, annually. D. K. Reading, *The Anglo-Russian Commercial Treaty of 1734*, New Haven, 1938, p. 36.

to reform whatever he thought prejudicial to good manners, by his own authority, and to pass sentence on those he adjudg'd to death, without acquainting the court of it, and which had been the orders of the former Czars of Muscovy, to be put in execution without the least contest or hesitation.

But upon the death of the late Patriarch, ... the Czar refus'd to have any other patriarch elected, and took upon himself to be the sole head and governor of his church; only after the death of the said patriarch he appointed the present metropolitan of Razan [Ryazan], whom he found to be the most learned and ablest among his clergy ... to take upon him the administration of ecclesiastical affairs, but so as that he should from time to time, in all matters of moment make a representation of them to His Czarish Majesty and receive his particular directions and orders therein. ... Upon this notable resolution of the Czar, very bold writings were dropp'd in the streets of Mosco, which is the way of Russia, (for no man ever dares to print or disperse any libels there). ... [206-208]

2. THE PROBLEM OF POWER: THE MONASTERIES

The Czar ... soon after his return from his travels, gave orders to the precause [prikaz], or office belonging to the monasteries, that for the increase of his revenue, to ease in some measure the trading part of his people, a tax should be levied upon the monasteries through all Russia, they having a great part of the best lands and villages belonging to them. As also soon after, His Majesty made an order, that no person but what exceeded the age of fifty, should be admitted into the monasteries; for the Czar observ'd, that the shutting up of so many young people ... prevented by so much the increase of his people, which were wanting in his wars. And besides this, the Czar had another political end in it, for he found that, by reducing their numbers, he might take part of their revenue to himself, for a less number of villages would then serve to maintain them. [194-195]

3. THE LEGACY OF IGNORANCE

It was a very rare thing in Russia before this present Czar's time to have found any man, even among the highest and most learned of the clergy, to have understood any language but their own; and as they were themselves void of learning, so they were wary and cautious to keep out all means that might bring it in, lest their ignorance should be discovered . . . for which reason the learning of foreign languages and books were always formerly discouraged; even as they are to this day in the Turkish Empire. . . .

There came once a press and letters out of Poland to Mosco, where a printing-house was set up with the approbation of one of the former Czars; but not long after the house was fir'd in the night-time, and the press and letters were burnt, as was thought by the procurement of the priests, they looking upon all other books except the history of their own countrey, and the exploits and victories of their Czars, and the lives and miracles of their saints, to be as dangerous as witchcraft.

This ignorance was not so much to be wonder'd at when it is consider'd that they neither suffer'd their sons to travel, nor was there ever any university in the countrey, or considerable school of any learning, till this Czar's time. . . . Soon after the Czar came over, he caused a large school to be erected . . . in which a great number of boys have been taught arithmetick* at the Czar's proper charge . . . to such of them as will voluntarily come and learn: And out of them have been chose some of the most ingenious to learn the mathematicks; and near one hundred of these, who have been taught navigation, have been sent abroad to England, to Holland, and to Italy, to qualify themselves to make officers for the service of His Majesty's fleet. . . . His Majesty has order'd very good telescopes to be brought into his countrey as well as all other useful instruments and books. . . . His Majesty has always his lords about him, and is himself very curious in observing the eclipses that happen, and in describing and discoursing of the natural cause of them to his lords and people about him, and of the motions of those other heavenly bodies within the system of the sun, according as the great Sir Isaac Newton has indisputably demonstrated to the modern world. . . . [209-212]

4. THE POISONING OF MORALS

The ministers of their churches . . . never preach to the people, for that is a thing they have no skill in, only there are now some few of the chief men, who sometimes preach before the Czar, and on great holidays in the cathedral churches; but the height of the learning which the

---

* There never has been any school before to teach arithmetick, nor did they know the use of figures, I believe, not twenty men in the whole countrey, but they made use of a kind of bead . . . which they set upon wires in a frame, like that which our women in England use to set their smoothing irons on, . . . by crossing of which beads together and again, they could multiply and divide any sum after a very tedious way and liable to gross mistakes, which method they yet use. . . .

common clergy can be said to be masters of . . . is this: That they can sing and read over distinctly the service of the church; that they stand in no evil reputation with their neighbors; have a good clear voice, and can say over "Hospidi pomilio," (that is, "Lord have mercy upon us") as fast as ever they can utter it, twelve or fifteen times in a breath, which is their manner in their churches, or elsewhere, when they are at prayers. . . . Nor are their priests able to defend, or hold any tolerable argument for, their religion. And whenever you enter into any points of divinity or morality with them, the chief things which they or the laiety reason for, is the addressing to saints, the keeping of fasts, that is, the abstaining from flesh, which they must strictly do, at least half the days in the year: The doing some short penance for sins past, when enjoin'd, and the asking forgiveness of the priest, which when he has cross'd them and pronounc'd their pardon, they go away as well satisfied as if they had never done any harm, though they have committed the most detestable crimes in the world: Which . . . occasions that perfidiousness and ungenerousness of spirit, that the Russes are generally known to practice towards all that have to deal with them, in prevaricating and falsifying their word; which occasions a saying among the foreigners in that countrey, "that if you would know if a Russ be an honest man, you must look if he has hair grows on the palm of his hand; but if you find none there, don't expect it." When they flatter and soothe, and profess with the highest oaths and asseverations, the respect they have for you, which is their common way to lead you to a dependence on them . . . you must be sure to be upon your guard, for then they have the greatest intention to betray you. And so far are the generality of the people from having any sense of shame for doing a base thing, that to be a sharper is a commendable quality: And they say "that such a man understands the world, and no doubt, will thrive": But of an honest man they say, ". . . He is a blockhead and does not know how to live." And so little regard have they for their word, and so void of any notion of honour in the true and genuine sense of it, that they have not so much as any word in their language that expresses it. . . .

The Czar, to instil principles of virtue into the minds of his people, and to give them better notions of humanity and conscience, has for eight or nine years past employ'd several persons to translate out of foreign languages, many excellent books in divinity and morality, as well as relating to war and useful arts and sciences, and has set up printing houses, and caus'd them to be printed in Mosco, and dispers'd throughout his dominions, *maugre* all the opposition made thereto by the clergy; and further, has commanded several schools of learning to be set up, and made an order, that whoever in his countrey that is master of an estate to the value of five hundred rubles per annum, and doth not teach his son to read and write, and learn Latin, or some other foreign language, such son shall not inherit his father's estate, but the same shall be forfeited to the next heir of the same family. As also His Majesty has commanded, that the clergy of his countrey for the future, shall be obliged to learn Latin, or not to officiate in the priestly office. Whereby it is to be hoped, that in time his people will be brought to a better understanding in the grounds of religion and moral virtues, as well as in the arts of war and trade, and other useful sciences.

His Majesty has not only done this, but takes occasion in all his private conversation to argue moderately with the chief men of the church, as well as the nobility, desiring them to be very free in satisfying him in the reasons they are able to produce for their biggottry and superstition, in adhering to their old customs. [216-221]

5. IDOLATRY AND SUBSERVIENCE

It was the manner of the Russes . . . to have their rooms . . . cover'd with the images or pictures of their saints; and it is still the custom, that when any person comes into a room to pay a visit or otherwise, the first thing they do as soon as they set their feet within the door, is to cross themselves, saying, "Hospodi Pomilio," that is, "Lord have mercy upon me"; at the same time with great reverence bowing to the pictures, and then to turn and make their complements to the master of the house, and so round to the rest of the company. But if it be in a poor man's house, that has perhaps but one of these images or pictures, and it happens to be a little dark in the room, and the print of the picture perhaps half worn off, and become almost of the same colour with the wall, occasioned by the smoak that is in the Russes' houses, and there be no wax-candle set up before the picture, (which is a thing done only on holidays); when I say it happens that a man that is a stranger comes into the room, and does not at his first entrance see the picture or image set up, he presently enquires, "Where is God?" upon which some body or other presently points at, and shews him the picture that hangs on the wall, and then they pay their devotion, . . . and sometimes as the humour takes them, bow down to the very ground, and knock their heads on the floor.

This way of knocking their heads on the floor, is often done also to great men. When you reason with them against this idolatrous way of bowing down to mere pictures, they tell you, that it is absolutely necessary to have something to cross themselves to, and that it is a thing both very reasonable and decent, that you should first make your complement to God, and then to the rest of the company, at the entrance into a room or a house, for which they allege the direction of their holy saints, and the customs of their fathers. . . . But the Czar who has a more rational sense of God and religion, seeing the stupid folly, as well as bigottry of his subjects in these matters, and being willing to reform them from the error of their ways, has reduced the number of his saints in his own houses of residence . . . to the Cross, or the picture of Our Blessed Saviour only. And the lords and other persons who are his favorites, have been brought in a great measure to follow his example in it, excepting some few of the old lords, who, notwithstanding they are his favorites, will not be brought out of their old way in this thing. [221-224]

6. THE MODELS OF DISSIPATION

I shall conclude this part of my discourse with this observation of the Russ way of life; that notwithstanding their pretended purity in keeping their fasts, and abstaining from flesh, there is nothing more common than to have both the people and the priest, too, go to church on a holiday in the morning, and get drunk in the afternoon long before night; especially the greater the holiday, the more it is excusable, and the custom, to be drunk. It is very ordinary at such times, if you ride through Mosco in the evening on a great holiday, to see the priests, as well as other men, lie drunk about the streets . . . and so far from it being accounted a scandal to be drunk, that the very women, not only the meaner sort, but even women of distinction and fashion, will make no scruple to own, that they have been very drunk; and in publick company will thank them for the civility and kindness, as they call it, of making them drunk, when they have been entertained any place, the next time they meet them. And, indeed, when I first went into the countrey, and for some years after, it was the common way, not only at all great entertainments where the court was invited and present, but even among private friends, to make their visitants drunk before they parted, or it was not accounted that they had been made welcome; and it was the way to press and force them to it, even to that degree that it was usual to lock up the gates and doors, and to set a guard, that no man should go away before he had his load . . . and which custom extended even amongst the foreigners, as well as the Russes. But in the year 1705, upon the coming of the Honorable Mr. Whitworth, the late Majesty's envoy extraordinary into the countrey, he made such effectual representations against his own not having his liberty . . . and gave himself such an example at all the noble and agreeable entertainments which he frequently made, that it thereupon gave occasion of breaking the neck of this most destructive custom, and for some years past there has been no force us'd at any publick entertainments any more . . . But it is still the prevailing custom among the generality of the common people, who hold it as it were religious, that they shew a respect for their saints to be drunk upon their holy-days, of which they have a great many in the year. What obscenities, murthers and wickedness attend this custom for want of being better taught by the priests, who even join with them in the example . . . I will leave the reader to judge; even the horrible sin of sodomy being scarce look'd on as a crime in this countrey, which they are very much addicted to in their drink; and there is nothing more common in the time of the Russ carnivals, and the next morning after great holy-days, than to hear of murders that have been committed, and to see people lie stript and dead in the streets of Mosco, it being very rare but that the Russes kill those who they rob, barbarously saying that the dead tell no tales. [227-229]

IV · THE ASSAULT UPON MANNERS

I. A RUTHLESS RAZORING

IT HAD BEEN the manner of the Russes, like the Patriarchs of old, to wear long beards hanging down upon their bosoms, which they comb'd out with pride, and kept smooth and fine, without one hair to be diminish'd. . . . The Czar, therefore, to reform this foolish custom, and to make them look like other Europeans, ordered a tax to be laid, on all gentlemen, merchants, and others of his subjects (excepting the priests and common peasants, or slaves) that they should each of them pay a hundred rubles per annum, for the wearing of their beards, and that even the common people should pay a copeck at the entrance of the gates of any of the towns or cities of Russia. . . . This was look'd upon to be little less than a sin in the Czar, a breach of their religion, and held to be a great grievance for sometime, as more particularly by being brought in by the strangers. But the women liking their husbands and sweethearts the better, they are now for the most part, pretty well reconciled to the practice.

It is most certain, that the Russes had a kind of religious respect and veneration for their beards; and so much the more, because they differed herein from strangers, which was back'd by the humours of the priests . . . and which nothing but the absolute authority of the Czar, and the terror of having them (in his merry humour) pull'd out by the roots, or sometimes taken so rough off, that some of the skin went with them, could ever have prevailed with the Russes to have parted with their beards. On this occasion there were letters drop'd about the streets, sealed and directed to His Czarish Majesty, which charged him with tyranny and heathenism. . . .

About this time the Czar came down to Veronize, where I was then on service, and a great many of my men that had worn their beards all their lives, were now obliged to part with them, amongst which, one of the first that I met with just coming from the hands of the barber, was an old Russ carpenter that had been with me at Camishinka, who was a very good workman with his hatchet, and whom I always had a friendship for. I jested a little with him on this occasion, telling him that he was become a young man, and asked him what he had done with his beard? Upon which he put his hand in his bosom and pull'd it out, and shew'd it to me: farther telling me, that when he came home, he would lay it up to have it put in his coffin and buried along with him, that he might be able to give an account of it to St. Nicholas, when he came to the other world; and that all his brothers (meaning his fellow-workmen, who had been shaved that day) had taken the same care. [196-197]

2. TYRANNICAL TAILORS

As to their cloathes, the general habit which the Russes used to wear, was a long vestment hanging down to the middle of the small of their legs, and was gathered and laid in pleats upon their hips, little differing from the habit of women's petticoats.

The Czar therefore resolving to have this habit changed . . . gave orders that all his boyars and people whatsoever, that came near his court, and that were in his pay should . . . equip themselves with handsome cloathes made after the English fashion. . . . And next he commanded, that a pattern of cloathes of the English fashion should be hung up at all the gates of the city of Mosco, and that publication should be made, that all persons (excepting the common peasants who brought goods and provisions into the city) should make their cloathes according to the said patterns; and that whosoever should disobey the said orders, and should be found passing any of the gates of the city in their long habits, should either pay two grevens (which is 20 pence) or be obliged to kneel down at the gates of the city, and to have their coats cut off just even with the ground, so much as it was longer than to touch the ground when they kneeled down, of which there were many hundreds of coats that were cut accordingly; and being done with a good humour, it occasioned mirth among the people, and soon broke the custom of their wearing long coats, especially in places near Mosco, and those other towns wherever the Czar came. [197-198]

3. FEMINISM BY FORCE

The women also, but more particularly the ladies about court, were ordered to reform the fashion of their cloathes too, according to the English manner, and that which so much the more and sooner reconciled them to it, was this: It had been always the custom of Russia, at all entertainments, for the women not to be admitted into the sight or conversation with men; the very houses of all men of any quality or fashion, were built with an entrance for the women apart, and they used to be kept up separate in an apartment by themselves; only it was sometimes the custom for the master of the house, upon the arrival of any guest whom he had a mind to honour, to bring out his wife the back-way from her apartment, attended with a company of her maids, to be saluted, and to present a dram of brandy round to the whole company; which being done, they used to retire back to their own apartment, and were to be seen no more. But the Czar, being not only willing to introduce the English habits, but to make them more particularly pleasing to the Russ ladies, made an order, that from thenceforward, at all weddings, and at other publick entertainments, the women as well as the men, should be invited, but in an English fashioned dress; and that they should be entertained in the same room with the men, like as he had seen in foreign countries; and that the evenings should be concluded with musick and dancing, at which he himself often used to be present with most of the nobility and ladies about court. . . . At these entertainments, the Russ ladies soon reconciled themselves to the English dress, which they found rendered them more agreeable. [199-200]

4. THE REMAKING OF MARRIAGE

It had been the custom of Russia, in case of marriages, that the match used always to be made up between the parents on each side, without any previous meeting, consent or liking of one another. . . . But the Czar taking into his consideration this unacceptable way of joining young people together without their own approbation, which might in a very great measure be reckon'd to be the occasion of that discord and little love which is shewn to one another afterwards, it being a thing common in Russia to beat their wives in a most barbarous manner, very often so unhumanly that they die with the blows; and yet they do not suffer for the murther, being a thing interpreted by the law to be done by way of correction, and therefore not culpable. The wives on the other hand being thus many times made desperate, murther their husbands in revenge for the ill usage they receive; on which occasion there is a law made, that when they murther their husbands, they are set alive in the ground, standing upright, with the earth fill'd about them, and only their heads left just above the earth, and a watch set over them, that they shall not be relieved till they are starved to death; which is a common sight in that countrey, and I have known them live sometimes seven or eight days in that posture. These sad prospects made the Czar in much pity to his people, take away the occasion of these cruelties as much as possible; and the forced marriages being supposed to be one cause thereof, made an order that no young couple should be marry'd together, without their own free liking and consent. . . . This new order is so well approved of, and so very pleasing to the young people, that they begin to think much better of foreigners, and to have a better liking of such other new customs as the Czar has introduced, than they ever did before. . . . [200-202]

5. THE REDUCTION OF RETINUES

It had been a very pompous custom among all of the great boyars, to retain in their service, as a piece of state and grandeur, a great number of useless servants or attendants, which when they went anywhere abroad in the streets of Mosco, some went before them bare-headed, and others follow'd after in a long train, in all sorts of dresses and colours; and when their boyars or lords went either on horseback, or in a coach or sled in Mosco, it was a piece of grandeur to ride softly, though in the coldest weather, that these people might keep pace with them on foot;[40] and the great boyars' ladies also used to have the like numerous attendance.

But the Czar, who always rides swift, had set them another pattern, for he went only with a few servants on horseback, cloath'd in a handsome uniform livery; his courtiers did the same; and commanded the example to be follow'd among all the boyars and persons of distinction; and that the same might be the more effectual, the Czar, soon after he came from his travels, order'd a list to be taken of all the loose attendants that hung about these boyars' houses, and order'd them to be sent into the army. This went very much against the grain, and great interest and intercession was made . . . but however, the Czar's orders were to be obey'd, and there was a draught made of several thousands of the unnecessary or supernumerary attendants, and sent to serve in the army. [202-203]

V · AUTOCRACY, OLIGARCHY, OR ANARCHY?

I. THE PROBLEM OF POWER: THE BOYARS

IN THE TIME of the former Czars of Muscovy, no common person or stranger, was to come near their persons: It was to detract from the lustre of their greatness. . . . The old boyars did this on purpose, or at least it is certain that it had this effect, that they kept thereby the government of things intirely in their own hands, and ruled the former Czars by whatsoever superstitious and biggotted schemes and notions they had a mind to; establishing this for a rule, That as it was not proper for sinful men to apply themselves directly to God, but to approach Him by the way of His saints: So also it was presumption on earth to think of coming any way to the Czar, but by addressing his boyars. Which maxim (notwithstanding all the steps the present Czar has taken) is still in some measure kept up . . . there being no juries in that countrey, nor counsel admitted to plead as in England, but the will of the judge, pretending to take some statute for his guide, decides the law as he pleases. [142-143]

---

[40] The Muscovite tendency toward ostentation in defiance of simple expediency, like many other aspects of the behavior of the nobility in this period, is reminiscent of the conduct of the nobility of the Northern Renaissance. One proud Parisian official of that era "was in the habit of never going his rounds without being preceded 'by three or four musicians playing brass instruments, which appeared a strange thing to the people, for they said that it seemed that he said to the malefactors: *Get away for I am coming.*'" J. Huizinga, *The Waning of the Middle Ages*, London, 1937, p. 34.

2. THE USES OF CASTIGATION

Discipline by the Batoags

The punishment by way of battoags is after this manner; the person to be punish'd is laid down flat on his face with his back all bare. . . . Two persons are appointed to whip him on his back with battocks, which are sticks or rods at least the thickness of a man's little finger; one of them places himself at the person's head that is to be punish'd, to hold him down with his head between his knees, whilst the other kneels upon the offender's legs . . . whilst the two plac'd at his head and feet continue striking his bare back with their battocks, keeping time as the smiths do at an anvil . . . and keep striking on, although their backs are all bruis'd and raw, until the person who stands by and directs the punishment says it is enough. . . . Both lords and peasants suffer this kind of punishment, and sometimes it is done with that severity that people dye of it; yet the power of this sort of punishment is lodg'd with all persons that have the superiority over others, as lords, gentlemen, officers or masters, who on any displeasure or pretended fault, without any form of tryal but will, may exercise this piece of cruelty: And there are two things always to be observ'd in this way of punishment; the first is, that the person so punish'd . . . must own himself faulty, or he must be battoag'd till he does: And the next is, that when his punishment is over he must come and fall down on his hands and his knees, and knock his forehead on the ground, at the feet of the person who directs the punishment, and thank him for the favour that he has been beat no more; and 'tis very common to have subdiack-shicks, [pod'iachii] and men in other like posts often to receive this sort of punishment with the botoags, and yet to be continu'd in their places; it being not the way of Russia to turn men out for the lesser crimes and knavish tricks they are guilty of, but only to inflict corporal punishment upon them, or to degrade them and put them in lower places. [217-218]

Trial by the Knout

The giving of the knout is of another nature, and not to be put in execution but by the form of tryal before some governor or judge, or by the command of some great man: . . . The knout is a thick hard thong of leather about three foot and a half long, fasten'd to the end of a handsome stick about two foot and a half long, with a ring or kind of swivle . . . to which the thong is fasten'd. . . . The hangmen, or knoutavoit master, strikes . . . so many strokes on the bare back as are appointed by the judge, first making a step back and giving a spring forward at every stroke, which is laid on with that force that the blood flies at every stroke. . . .

The second and most severe way of giving the knout, (which is otherwise call'd the pine) is when a man's hands are tied together behind his body, and then drawn up by a rope tied to his hands, whilst at the same time a great weight is fix'd to his legs; and being thus hoisted up, his shoulders turn out of joint, and his arms become right over his head, which when done with the weight still hanging to his feet, the executioner is order'd to lay on so many strokes as are appointed by the judge. . . .

This punishment is commonly executed very leisurely, and between whiles, a subdiackshik (or writer) examines the sufferer how far he is guilty of the crimes he stands accused of, or whether he has any confederates, or is guilty of such other crimes . . . such as treasonable things, or robbery, and murders, that the authors are not known. This being done they are taken down, and their arms put into joint again by the hangman, and perhap dismiss'd or sent back to prison. But, if the crime whereof any person is accus'd be accounted capital . . . there is a gentle fire made just by the gallows, and after the offender, (for it does not always prove that they are criminal) is taken down from the punishment, and denies the fact or any part whereof he is accus'd, then his hands and feet are ty'd, and he is fix'd on a long pole upon a spit, which being held at each end by two men, the person that stands charg'd with guilt has his raw back roasted over the fire, and is then examin'd and call'd upon by a writer aforesaid to confess. The writer takes down in writing all the answers he makes, and if any person charg'd with any capital crime, in case when the proof is not clear against him, cannot stand out this variety of punishments three several times, which is order'd perhaps three or four weeks, one after the other, without confessing guilt; or if his answers that he has made in the time of his punishment are not judg'd clear and satisfactory, he must after all this torture suffer death; but if he is so hardy as to stand it all out without owning himself or being otherwise proved guilty, he is acquitted. [218-219]

3. THE DECENTRALIZATION OF DESPOTISM: THE DIAKI

The assessment of the duties and taxes to be laid upon the people, the collecting of the Czar's revenue, and the sole decision of all causes, (excepting those within the ecclesiastical jurisdiction) had formerly been wholly committed to such of the chief lords who were favorites, and commonly were of the greatest families in Russia; who acted as sovereign princes under the Czar,[41] in the several provinces into which the Empire was divided; who had the liberty to make use of the Czar's name for their authority in the issuing forth their orders, and might be said to have the sole power of men's lives and fortunes in their hands. And for the examination of causes, and for the execution of their orders, each of these lords or princes held apart an office or court of justice in Mosco, where these great lords usually resided, and to whom there was an appeal from the district of all the lesser towns and cities in each respective province. A bench of diacks [diaki] (or chancellors) sate as judges in each of these principal offices or courts in Mosco, whose business it was to hear and determine matters; and to sign orders, as well relating to the treasury, and the military, as to the civil matters; and to make report from time to time of their proceeding to their respective lords, under whose commands they acted; and the said lords seldom coming themselves in person to hear any causes, the diacks represented matters to them in such forms and colors, as they thought proper: And beyond which, in case of any grievance, there was at that time no higher court of appeal. [187-189]

4. THE VENALITY OF JUSTICE: THE VOEVODI

Each of these lords had the sole power also lodged in them, to appoint and send governors to the several towns and cities, to which each province was again subdivided into lesser districts; and each of which governors in their respective stations had a diack or petty-chancellor, and an office or court of justice erected under them in each city, called a precause (or place for command as the word signifies) where they sate both as commissionaries, to transact business relating to the Czar's revenue; and as judges, with an absolute power to determine all causes, without any jury affix'd or council to plead for unfortunate men. Only in cases of life and death they were obliged to make representation by letter to the lord of the province in Mosco, before any man was executed; and which they never failed so to represent, as to make the punishment fall as they would have it.

These governors had their commissions granted them, and usually

---

[41] Pokrovsky here uses Perry extensively to prove the decentralized and independent character of the authority which the chief lords and their underlings arrogated to themselves under Peter. M. N. Pokrovsky, *History of Russia*, New York, 1931, pp. 293-296.

held their places at most but for three years, if they did not practice such open roguery and oppression as to be turn'd out sooner. They never had any salary appointed them; but on the contrary, it was the custom to give the lord of the province where they were appointed, the sum of 3 or 4000 rubles upon their being advanced to their governments, more or less, according to the ability of the place; besides what they privately gave in presents to the diacks or chancellors belonging to the head office, or precause, in Mosco, from which they were sent; and yet these weywods [voevodi] or governors were commonly known to make themselves rich within the term of three years above mention'd; by which (to say no more) it may easily be conjectured what equity they practiced towards the Czar, and towards the people committed to their power. I shall not dwell upon many particulars, but only observe to the reader, that throughout all the countrey of Russia, amongst the common people, in case of injuries received, or disputes arising between man and man, the bribery of the judge is the first step to go upon; money is known to be taken on both sides; and generally he who bids highest carries the cause, whilst the sufferer has no remedy, but to be content, which occasions a usual saying among the people, when they complain of a grievance done them, "that God is high, and the Czar is far off." [187-189]

5. THE RESISTANCE TO REFORMATION: THE RATUSHA

But the profits which these governors usually received by bribery, and which they are not yet deprived of, were not all the advantages they made by their commissions; there was another considerable article which they found equally beneficial to them. These governors, in their respective districts throughout all the Czar's dominions, had the power of the assessment of the taxes, and of appointing challavolnicks [tselov-alniki] (or collectors) under them to receive the Czar's revenues, and to return such sums as they collected . . . into the grand precause, or proper office of each boyar, residing in Mosco, where the account of the collections made in each province was made out, (such as was thought fit) with the account also of what was expended on the several pretended occasions, for the service of each respective province; and the rest sent into the office of the Great Treasury in Mosco. . . .

Now the Czar believing that a more faithful return might be made of his revenue, and to prevent the oppression of these governors in the unequal assessment of the taxes, His Majesty was pleased to call a Grand Council of his lords, and proposed to them, that there should be one general office erected in Mosco, for the better collection and improvement of his revenue; that the said office should be called the Ratehouse [Rathaus], (according to the Dutch name and model) and that a certain number of reputable men should be chosen out of the merchants who should be entitled Burgomasters, and that were to sit daily, five or more of them, to appoint clerks and officers in the first place to take an account, and to collect the revenue payable into their own office, within the district of the city of Mosco; and from whence they were to impower and commission such other persons as they should appoint, by the name of Burgomasters also, in all the lesser towns and cities of His Majesty's dominions, to collect and receive all customs, with relation to publick trade, as well as petty toll, in the market places, and the profit or excise accruing to His Majesty from the sale of beer, brandy and mead, which in Russia is not permitted to be brewed or made, but by particular license, and to be sold for the immediate profit of the Czar, at certain rates. . . . And only the levying of the land-tax, (or tax upon houses) and poll-tax, to be levied by the direction of the governors, as before.

But this useful proposition, when stated by the Czar to his lords . . . occasioned very great strugglings amongst the nobility, to have so considerable a branch of their power lopp'd off from them. They . . . implored . . . that His Majesty would not do them so much publick dishonour and affront, as to take away this trust from them, and to lodge it in the hands of boors and slaves that were not worthy to be named in competition with them. But . . . they were forced to comply; and the same was accordingly put into execution, and which continued for some years with good advantage to the Czar's revenue, till some wretched politicians, who were the Czar's favorites, proposed other methods to raise and force greater sums into the Czar's treasury; whereby, though they succeeded two or three years, they have at length so ruined trade, and brought so general an oppression upon the subjects thereby, that in several particular articles, which by the good management of the said Burgomasters, brought in before 100 or 200,000 rubles per annum, brings in now not above half the sum. . . . [189-194]

VI · THE TSAR AND THE ARMY

I. ENLISTMENT BY DECREE

I HAVE already mention'd how the Russ Army was cloath'd in their long habits, and when this Czar return'd from his travels, how he then cloath'd the several regiments in regular liveries, like the forces of other princes of Europe; as also observ'd his establishing a new discipline in their exercise, which he had taken from other nations, and his receiving foreign officers into his service; I think it may not be unacceptable to the reader, to shew what temper and method he took to make his own people soldiers, seamen, etc.

In doing of which, that he might have men fit to serve him in his army, navy, and in all manner of business, he order'd a list to be taken of all the lords and gentlemen of the countrey, how many sons they had, and what their estates were. Some he sent to travel, others he appointed to his army and navy, there to serve at their own charge, until they had fitly qualified and signalized themselves by their behaviour, so as to be recommended as deserving of some post, and to be enter'd into his Majesty's pay; and that the greatest lord's son, after some time serving volunteer, should only first be made an ensign, and so to rise gradually, according to his behaviour; and not to be taken notice of, or have any respect paid him, (at publick entertainments, or the like) but according to the post that they were in, and had merited in his service. [270-271]

2. ENLIGHTENMENT BY EXAMPLE

And that this order might the better take effect, and that all persons, whether those he sent into his army or navy, might be the better contented with it, he set an example, by taking upon himself both a post in his navy, and in his army, wherein he acted and took the gradual steps of preferment, like another man. Of which it will be necessary to be a little more particular.

The first title he took upon him was that of a sea captain, at the time when he first built ships upon the Pereslavski Lake; and afterwards, when he went against Azoph in the year 1695, he enter'd himself an ensign before his travels into Europe. Upon his return, when he changed the establishment and name of the Streletzes [Streltsy] to that of Soldiers, he took upon himself the command of a company in the first regiment of his Guards. And I have seen him march as a private captain at the head of his company through the city of Mosco, on occasion of going to bless the waters. . . .

Upon his Majesty's return from his travels, he drew a draught with his own hands, and set up a man of war of fifty guns upon the stocks at Veronize, and caused himself to be declared master builder, (by his mock Czar . . .) in presence of all his lords.[42] His jester harangu'd him on this occasion for his ingenuity, and the several degrees of knowledge that he had attain'd to in his travels, and the mock Czar assured him of his favour, and that he might expect farther preferment according to his merit.

These three titles he took upon him when I first came into the countrey; and no man was to accost him in any publick company, as at entertainments, or the like, but by the name of captain. He continued above eight years before he attained to the degree of colonel, which was upon his having some signal success in an action against the Swedes in Poland; and after he obtain'd the great victory at Poltava, and came to Mosco in triumph, he was made lieutenant-general. . . .

In all these several stations, as he was from time to time gradually preferr'd, he constantly received his pay, . . . which was always brought and deliver'd to him at some great entertainment, when all his lords were present; upon which the mock Czar usually complimented him as deserving well of the publick for his good service; and his health was thereupon drank as captain, or ship-builder, or colonel, or general, according as he took his money that day. . . .

These are the methods which the Czar has taken, with mirth and good-humour, to make his lords see that he expects they shall not think themselves nor their sons too good to serve their countrey, and take their steps gradually to preferment: And he has not only done this, but taken indefatigable pains to examine into the merit and behaviour of all who serve in his army, and to reward and punish those who deserve it, of which there are several remarkable instances. Whereby he has now very well furnish'd his army with good officers of his own nation, who are gentlemen of the first rank, and ought to be men of spirit and bravery. [271-274]

[42] The public ceremonials in which Peter acted as an officer in his own service before a mock tsar have often puzzled subsequent historians. One biographer has termed them "a mere farce," but it is obvious that Perry saw in them a conscious intent to implant the ideals of a responsible, specialized, and salaried bureaucracy into the minds of his hitherto irresponsible and selfish nobility, and the mere fact that this was the interpretation of a practical engineer without any special political training seems to lend weight to its acceptance. Schuyler, *op. cit.*, p. 132.

3. THE PERSONAL ATTENTION OF PETER

As the Czar has taken particular regard to have his own subjects qualify'd to serve him on all these occasions, and has spared no pains for it, but continually busies himself amongst these men, in ordering and giving his directions in every thing that relates to his army and his navy, and delights in it, so that it may be said of him, that he is from the drummer to the general, a compleat soldier; besides his being engineer, cannoneer, fire-worker, ship-builder, turner, boatswain, gun-founder, blacksmith, etc. All which he frequently works at with his own hands, and will himself see that every thing be carried on and perform'd to his own mind, as well in these minutest things, as in the greater disposition of affairs. [278-279]

After the loss of the said battel [Narva], the Czar spent the greatest part of his time in the effectually giving his order for the raising of his recruits, and in the placing his officers, the seeing his regiments exercised, and providing all things whatsoever that were necessary for his army, the care of which he would not trust to any of his lords, but saw it all done himself, even to the minutest particular. . . .

And though afterwards, during the course of the war, he spent most of his time with his army, yet all the while he neither neglected the preparation of his fleet at Veronize (whither during the first of the war he went every winter) nor the carrying on his resolution of reforming his people and government. [204-205]

One more thing I will mention. The places where his naval preparations are made and where his armies are disposed, being very far distant sometimes from another, which requires him very often to undertake long and tedious journeys from place to place. He has, I believe (for the proportion of time that I was in that countrey) travell'd twenty times more than ever any prince in the world did before him, and which in no countrey, but by sled way, could be perform'd; his usual method of travelling in the winter, being after the rate of more than a hundred English miles a day. . . . [279]

VII · COMMERCE: THE BLESSINGS OF NATURE

THE next thing I shall speak of is the trade of Russia, and the several discouragements and hindrances to industry which the Czar's subjects labour under, through the arbitrary constitution and ill administration of the government, which hath been, and is still like to be injurious to his countrey; and shall also name a few particulars, which have been directly contrary to the Czar's immediate interest. [241]

1. GOODNESS OF SOIL AND CLIMATE

Russia, to speak of it in general, is a very level and fertile country, abounding with whatsoever is necessary for human life; and as there are no burning hollow mountains, and being far from those deep places of the sea where there is no depth to be found till you come near the shore, so there is never any undermining or falling in of the land from the surface, nor any earthquakes ever felt in this countrey. The air is serene and good, with not the 20th part of the fogs, and I believe at least one fifth part less rain than we have in England or Ireland. The countrey is intermix'd with pasture and arable land, with woods, lakes and rivers, and everywhere through all the parts that I have travell'd (which has been almost on all the sides of the Czar's dominions), there are to be seen many pleasant and delightful situations. The Russes have a saying, that they are very rich in fish and in bread; and I may add that they have good store of horses and of cattle; and of wild game, they have of all sorts the greatest plenty in the world. [242]

2. EASE OF TRAVEL AND TRANSPORT

There are two remarkable times of the year when the Russes express their joy upon the alteration of the seasons; the one is when the snow first falls on the ground, and the winter is so strongly set in, that the rivers are so frozen up, that they can pass with their horses and sleds upon the ice; which change, when the wind shifts about and blows from the northward, happens so suddenly, that sometimes within 24 hours there is no ice to be seen, and the next day a horse and sled may drive over the rivers; and when the winter is thus strongly fix'd, they have on all sides across the land, the lakes, and the rivers, wherever the nearest way lies, an opportunity of land-carriage by sleds, which is certainly the most commodious and swiftest travelling in the world either for passengers or for goods; the sleds being light and conveniently made, and with little labour to the horses, slide smooth and easy over the snow and the ice; and the snow by often passing of the sleds upon it wherever there is a way made, becomes smooth and hard like ice. Against which season of the year, great quantities of goods are laid up in most places of Russia, for the easiness and cheapness of carriage in the winter, excepting where there is opportunity of water carriage by their floats, their boats and their vessels. The whole winter through when once the sled way is fix'd, there come several thousand sleds every day laden into Mosco, drawn usually but with one horse; and it is remarkable that in Russia the price of land-carriage in the winter upon sleds, is not above the fourth or fifth part so much as it is in the summer upon wheels. The Russes also usually use but one horse for their common carriage by waggons in the summer, their waggons being made light and the roads thereby preserv'd smooth, and are not cut deep.

The other time of their rejoycing is in the spring of the year, after the ice has been some days rotten and dangerous and then breaks away, the river becomes open and free for their boats and vessels to pass. On these two occasions the Russes hold a kind of festival, and are merry with their neighbours. [244-245]

3. PRODUCE FOR WAR AND TRADE

The product or manufactures of Russia with which commerce is principally maintain'd with foreign parts, is pot-ash, weed-ash, Russia leather, furs, linen, flax, hemp, seal-skins, train-oyl,[43] rosin, pitch, tar, caviar, tallow, honey, wax, isinglass of both sorts (the one of which is us'd in windows for ships, etc. and the other for making of glue;) as also masts, timber, plank, and firr; and if the Czar does ever live to perform the communication which is his intention to make for free water-carriage between the Wolga and Petersburgh, he will then be able to bring oak and timber with plenty of corn to that place at very easie rates, that the same may both pay a considerable duty to the Czar, and turn very much to the advantage of his countrey, by the being exported from thence to other parts of Europe; for corn may then be loaded much cheaper there than can be deliver'd, either at the ports of Riga, Dantzick [Danzig], or Konigsberg [Königsberg], from whence and other places in the Baltick [Baltic], the Hollanders alone load every year eight hundred or a thousand sail of ships with corn. . . .

There is also brimstone and salt petre made in the Czar's dominions, and there are powder mills built on several small rivers near Mosco, where a sufficient quantity of powder is by foreigners made, not only to supply the Czar's occasions, but may be spar'd to other nations: As also some copper mines are found in the province of Cazan [Kazan], and there are a great many iron mines and works in the Czar's coun-

---

[43] A lubricating oil, obtained from marine animals, especially the Right whale.

trey, particularly near Veronize, and near Mosco, and on the side of the Onega Lake; at each of which very great quantities of iron-work are made for all manner of occasions in Russia, with all sorts of arms for supplying the Czar's army, the making of which is now brought to pretty good perfection; and it is even pretended, that by reason of the price of provision being less, and labour cheaper than in other parts, they will supply other nations with arms and other iron manufacture, of which some patterns have been sent abroad, before I came from Russia.

These are the produce of the Czar's countrey for war and for trade; and if the advantage of the situation be considered by means of those grand rivers which every where spread their branches, flowing thro' the heart of Russia, and fall into four several seas, as I have already mention'd in another place, was but industry cultivated and incouraged as it is in England and other free countreys, the product of it might, it is certain, be much farther improv'd, trade be extended, the people made happy, and the Czars of Muscovy, as the extent of their countrey is very great, might in a short time become equal in power and strength to any monarch on earth; more particularly by reason of the great cheapness and plenty of timber and naval stores for equipping out a fleet, and by reason of its being easie to maintain an army on the side of Azoph, they would undoubtedly be more able to shake the empire of the Turks than any of those princes of Europe who usually have war with them. [245-247]

VIII · COMMERCE:
THE FOLLIES OF GOVERNMENT

But I must here observe two or three instances of the disadvantages to the Czar's revenue, thro' the vitiated temper and injudicious administration of his boyars, and of the general oppression which his people (notwithstanding all the reformations which the Czar has endeavour'd) do and are like still to groan under, and from whence it will always appear, that wherever trade is oppress'd the people must be poor, and by consequence the prince must be so too. [248]

I. THE INFLATION OF THE COINAGE

The first instance I shall name which has in my time prov'd very detrimental to the Czar's revenue, and injurious to his people, is this: When I first went into the countrey the biggest piece of silver of the coin of Russia was only copeeks or pence; and the least was some half-pence and farthings of the same metal; and this coin was of very good silver, and of full weight in proportion to the best money of other countreys, so that . . . the exchange was then at two or three per cent advance. But after the misfortune which the Czar sustain'd of losing almost all his army, with his whole artillery and baggage before Narva . . . being afterwards somewhat straightened to raise new forces to carry on the war . . . it was propos'd by one of his favourite boyars, and seconded by the rest, that all the Czar's old money should be call'd in and melted down, and that new copeeks and half copeeks should be coin'd in the place of the old, not three fifths of the weight, and yet to pass for the same value as before; and which is still worse, an alloy has been since order'd to be mix'd with the copeeks. . . .

The exchange on which trade more particularly depends, after this, soon fell to between 30 and 40 per cent. and the price of everything, more especially what there was occasion for from foreign parts, was soon advanced in proportion to the exchange. . . . Nor has it in any respect proved any other than false policy, at the foot of the account; for whatsoever the Czar's own immediate affairs require from abroad, whether for the cloathing of his army, or for all other foreign commodities which there is a demand for, and are sent to Russia, the price has been since raised according to the course of the exchange: But in a more particular manner this evil hath been felt in the late maintaining of the Czar's army in Pomerania, when 40 or 45 per cent. was given for the return of money thither; as also has been experienced in the purchase of those ships which the Czar has had occasion to buy in England and in Holland; so that the Czar's own immediate affairs have suffered their full share in this piece of ill conduct, as well as foreigners who have been wrong'd in their pay, and merchants and trade in general been injured thereby. [248-251]

2. MONOPOLIES, DUTIES, AND RESTRICTIONS

But this is not the only misfortune which the countrey labours under thro' the Czar's want of honest and able ministers to advise and assist him in things relating to trade, and the management of his revenue; which for the most part he leaves to his lords, who make such representations from time to time to him, as they think fit; whilst his Majesty busies himself principally in the disposition of affairs relating to his army, and in his naval preparations . . . and his boyars, who are content to have him diverted this way, in the mean time take care to keep to themselves the modelling of things more immediately belonging to trade, and the taxes laid upon the people. . . .

Several new officers were created, called prebulshicks [pribylshchiki] (or advancers of profit to be brought into the Czar's treasure) and these persons had a full power given them, in several schemes which were laid down (according to the old ways of Russia) to manage some one branch, and some another branch of the duties and customs to be paid to the Czar; whereby they proposed to bring more speedy and greater sums into the treasury: And the things wherein the trade has been directly injur'd and obstructed have been as follows.

First, By forestalling and monopolizing many of the principal commodities, the growth of the Czar's countrey, such as potash, tar, etc. by buying up large quantities of goods, and then setting an extraordinary value upon them, and forbidding any Russ merchant to sell the same sort of goods, until all goods thus bought for the Czar (as they call it) are first sold at the rate that is set upon them. Besides this monopolizing and raising the price of goods whereby trade is immediately deaden'd and oppress'd: it is also practised in Russia to lay on new duties on several species of goods, without giving timely notice of it; and often done after the factors in Mosco have written to their principals abroad, and the ships with their orders have been on their voyage too, and at other times even after they have been arrived at Archangel: In which cases the foreign merchants have been put under the greatest difficulties; for they have been obliged either to comply and take the goods at the price that has been advanced upon them by the new duties imposed, or the ships must go home again without freight, and their correspondents be disappointed of the goods that they have expected, and been perhaps under an engagement to deliver.

Secondly, When the Czar's occasions have been declared to require it, and goods from foreign markets have arrived at Archangel, it has been often order'd that no Russ merchant, or other person whatsoever, should dare buy any such goods as are come into port, until what the Czar has occasion for is first bought; whereby foreign merchants have often been constrained to deliver their goods at such prices as have been offer'd them by the persons who are commission'd to buy them for the Czar. So that in the first of these instances, the native, who is a merchant, does not know how to encourage goods to be prepared, nor what price he shall give for them at any time, lest he should be afterwards restrained from selling them to his own advantage. And secondly, foreign merchants have often, by these monopolizings, and by imposition of new duties, without timely notice given, been considerably injured and disappointed, which I will leave to the merchants themselves to relate; and how very scandalously, by cavilling pretences, they have been often dealt with, even in instances where the most firm contract and agreement[44] has been made with them in the name and publick offices of the Czar. For obtaining right in which several cases, publick complaints and remonstrances have been strongly made, before they have in any measure been relieved, and often never redress'd. For which reasons, and to prevent these evils for the future, pressing instances have been made for a treaty of commerce to be settled, at least the Czar might from time to time appoint such duties on goods either imported, or exported, as should be thought fit, yet that 10 or 12 months notice should be given of it, that merchants might regulate their affairs accordingly; But the lords and favourites of the Czar have oppos'd it; for they would thereby lose the opportunity which they now have of being sought to and enriching themselves by constant presents and bribes. [251-254]

3. THE DESTRUCTION OF CAPITAL

Thirdly, The aforesaid prebulshicks have been farther empower'd to go into all houses to search after goods, to assess and levy severe duties in all inland markets and trade, and to trouble and vex the people to the last degree through all the Czar's dominions, beside the general tax which every house and family is obliged to pay: So that through these things, the arbitrary practices, together with the oppression of the governors, of the diacks, and petty officers subordinate to them, the

---

[44] If English merchants were often "scandalously dealt with" by the Muscovites, British mercantile ethics in this period were hardly above reproach. When two English expatriates set up a shop for curing Circassian tobacco and, thereby, threatened the profits of the British import monopoly of that commodity, the government resorted to harsh measures. Charles Whitworth fully executed his orders to demolish the infant industry: "We spent the best part of the night in destroying the several instruments and materials, some whereof were so strong, that they obliged us to make a great noise in pulling them to pieces. I likewise broke the great spinningwheel, and above threescore reels for rowling: I then destroyed three engines ready set up for cutting tobacco, and took away the plates and cranes for two more, several large engines for pressing the tobacco into form have been pulled to pieces, their screws split, their wooden moles broke, copper carried away, and about 20 fine sieves cut to pieces, nor is the least thing left standing, except some great plain wooden presses and some ordinary wooden tables. The next day my servants returned and burnt all the remains of the wood, which we had broke and my smith is now working in my house on the rest of the iron and copper-machines; so that I have fully executed the honor of Her Majesty's commands in this particular, and I wish it may have the effect proposed of hindering the working of Circassian tobacco here." Whitworth to Harley, July 18/29, 1705, *Sbornik*, xxxix, 138.

common people have but very little heart or desire to any industry, farther than necessity drives them. For if at any time by their ingenuity and endeavours they do get money, it cannot rightly be said they can call it their own; but with submission they say, All that they have belongs to God and the Czar: Nor do they dare to appear as if they had any riches, in their apparel, or in their houses, it being counted the best way to seem poor, lest there should be any notice taken of them that they have money; and they are troubled and harrass'd till they must part with it, and always be making bribes and presents to be at rest; of which there are ten thousand instances. So that everywhere as you travel through the villages in Russia, for this reason you will see the general part of the common people idle in the streets, and in the houses, especially in the winter; the chiefest things which they take care for, being in the affairs of their husbandry, to sow and to reap in their seasons, and to make a coarse sort of cloaths to defend themselves from the cold. What money the common people get, it is their way often to hide it under the earth, so that 'tis certain great sums are thereby wholly lost when men come to dye. [254-255]

4. THE DEFIANCE OF NATURE

Through Interference

Another thing which I shall here take notice of, and which has been very injudiciously put in practice . . . is this; About 12 or 14 years since, an estimate was deliver'd in at the council table, of the great quantities of cloth that there was a demand for and brought into the countrey every year from England and Holland, and that it would be of great advantage to Russia to have cloth made in Mosco, to save this charge, particularly for cloathing the Czar's army. Upon which, though they were told by foreign merchants, that their wooll was abundantly too coarse, and not possible to answer the making of cloth with it: Yet a resolution was taken to try the experiment and orders were forthwith given to send for spinners, weavers, sheerers, dyers, etc. to come over from Holland, with all manner of instruments compleat for setting up a woollen manufactury in Russia. A large square for this purpose was projected and built with brick, on the side of the Mosco River, with workhouses for employing several hundred persons . . . the charge of doing which, amounted to several hundred thousand rubles, before the experiment of making one yard of cloth was produced; and when it came to be fully try'd, it was found that the Russ wooll, which is very short, and as coarse almost as dog's hair, would not make any thread for cloth; so that afterward they were obliged to send to Holland for wooll to mix with it; and at the foot of the whole account, it is found that even such coarse cloath, as has been made only fit for soldiers, can be deliver'd much easier to the Czar, than to have it made in Russia. [267-269]

Through Inattention

This is a thing that they would have forced against nature and against reason, when they have no wool for it; whereas on the other hand flax is the growth of Russia, wherewith other nations are supply'd from thence; and there is no doubt, had the Czar been but at the 40th part of the charge to have brought in a few foreigners to have instructed his people in the making and improving the linen manufacture, but with a very little teaching, and the use of the proper instruments to spin and to weave linen cloth, which hitherto they have not had, nor do not know the use of, his own subjects might long e'er this (with encouragement and protection) have brought it to tolerable perfection, and have been a means to have vended much greater quantities abroad into foreign countries, and at easier rates than from any other nation whatsoever. . . . The linen, which they make for ordinary shirting, being not made above twenty inches broad, so that four breadths must be used for that purpose, is what is generally complain'd of by all those who purchase Russ linen, or know anything of that trade. And yet this thing still remains unattempted: And notwithstanding all the persuasions of foreign merchants, the Russes still obstinately persist in their own way, and will make their cloth too narrow for any use. [269-270]

5. THE CHECK TO INCENTIVE

There are very many sinister ways which the governors and men in power take to oppress the people; among which the general and common way is to contrive some pretended fault to be charged upon a man, and to send for and examine him, with threats of the knout or battocks; or otherwise to encourage some petition or information against him; in which case, let justice be as it will, every man according to his substance must either suffer stripes, or buy off his punishment with money.

The common boors or peasants, who have been sent upon the works under my command, have complained to me with tears of wrongs and injuries that have been done them by the governors of towns, and the officers in the districts who have been under the governors, particularly when I was at Veronize: And when I have offer'd to represent the injustice done them to the present Admiral Apraxin, (who had then the command of that province) and have promised them that I would do my utmost, and engage to obtain right for them, they have thereupon earnestly begg'd of me by no means to mention the things which they have complained of; alledging this for their reason, That even tho' they should obtain right at this time, yet that they were sure afterwards to suffer, and to be ruin'd for their complaining of those in power over them, who would mark them out as informers.

There is this instance more that I cannot but mention, touching the misery of these people; namely, that if any poor man be naturally ingenious, or a better workman than his neighbours in a countrey town or place, or be sent upon any of the Czar's works, he usually endeavours to conceal it, and pretends to be ignorant, for these two following reasons.

First, If it be known in a countrey town or place where a man lives that he is ingenious, he gets no rest, but is constantly sent for and employ'd, either by the governor or petty officers under him, or by the gentlemen of the countrey, whose slaves they are, without being able to call their time their own, or having any suitable encouragement to themselves; but in the place thereof, if they do not please, or murmur, and are not content, they often get stripes for their labour.

Secondly, In case of any number of men being sent from the places where they live to go upon any of the Czar's works, if any artificers are more ingenious than their fellow-workmen, unless it be where the Czar himself is present, and takes cognizance of it, they have oftentimes more labour and care of work committed to their charge, but have no encouragement given them for their ingenuity more than another man. When I was at Veronize, I order'd a Dutch master carpenter who was under my command, upon occasion of an engine that was to be made, to chuse out two or three of the most ingenious persons that he could find among the Russ carpenters to be employ'd in it; upon which, among others, he named one to me, who, he told me, he believed was the best workman of them all: But I happening to differ with him in opinion, because he had never discover'd himself, he answer'd me, That he was assured the person whom he had named to me was a workman, by what he had observ'd of him in the handling of his tools, but that the man was in the right of it not to discover himself, for the reason abovemention'd; and when it came to be try'd, it proved to be as the Dutchman had represented it to me.

And notwithstanding all that I could do by the representations I have made on the works that I have been employ'd on, to have some small encouragement to be given to such as I found deserving out of the Czar's treasure, yet I could never obtain so much as one single copeek a day encouragement for any one person; it being not the manner of Russia, on any such works as I was employ'd on, to pay any money or wages at all to common artificers and labourers out of the Czar's treasure.

But that the reader may the better understand how such men, who are employ'd and sent on publick works are paid, it will be necessary to give the following account:

All the common people, or peasants of Russia, (who dress and till the land, etc.) are slaves, either directly to the Czar himself, to the boyars, to the monasteries, or to the gentlemen of the countrey; and when the Czar either gives any person a village, (which is often forfeited, and taken from one man and given to another,) or when any village or estate is bought and sold in Russia, the way of reckoning the value of the same, is not according to the extent of land that belongs to the same, but according to the number of inhabitants or slaves there are upon it; each house or family have their portion of land alotted to them, and are oblig'd to pay to their proper landlord such a proportion of money, of corn, and all manner of provision in specie. Besides the common taxes that are laid on them by the Czar's particular orders for carrying on his wars, it is the manner of Russia, upon occasion of all works and business belonging to the Czar, where any number of common labourers, carpenters, masons, or smiths, are required, to send an order into such provinces and districts for the respective governors of the towns, as is thought fit, to levy them from among such of the peasants or slaves, according as the order directs; which sometimes falls out, that every third, fifth, or tenth house, shall find a man, whether carpenter, smith, or labourer, sometimes with a horse, and sometimes without, for so many months or so much time as such order appoints, to be paid at the proper expence and charge of the towns and villages from whence they are appointed to be levied, till they are order'd to be relieved, and other numbers of fresh men, either from the same or some other districts are sent in their places. And I have known it sometimes, that even one half of the men belonging to all the villages in some particular district, have been sent alternately to relieve one another, without having any wages allowed them. And therefore this being the custom of Russia, when I have made my utmost application for the encouragement of some few persons who have been really ingenious, that they might have but a copeek a day reward allow'd them to animate the rest, I have received for answer, particularly by my lord Apraxin . . . that there was no such precedent for the giving of money out of the Czar's treasure for men to do their duty for which they were sent; but in the place of it they had batoags that grew in Russia, and if they did not do their work when requir'd, they must be beaten to it.

Upon these considerations, it is no great wonder that the Russes are the most dull and heavy people to attain to any art or science of any nation in the world, and upon every opportunity are the most apt to rebel, and to engage in any the most barbarous cruelties, in hopes of being reliev'd from that slavery that is hereditary to them.

The Czar, where he is present, does indeed give encouragement to some of those common artificers and workmen, who have the happiness to be under his eye, and whom he finds deserving, as particularly in the building and equipping of his ships, where he is daily among the artificers. . . . But his boyars are quite of another temper, and in all other places and occasions, through all the parts of the Czar's dominions, the generality of his subjects remain still under the same check and discouragement to ingenuity. [255-261]

IX · THE WINDOW TO THE WEST

I. THE PRIVATIONS OF PETERSBURG

WHICH leads me here to mention, that among some other causes, one of the chief which makes the generality of the nobility at present uneasy, is, that the Czar obliges them against their will, to come and live at Petersburgh, with their wives and their families, where they are oblig'd to build new houses for themselves, and where all manner of provisions are usually three or four times as dear, and forage for their horses, etc. at least six or eight times as dear as it is at Mosco; which happens from the small quantity which the countrey thereabouts produces, being more than two thirds woods and bogs; and not only the nobility, but merchants and tradesmen of all sorts, are oblig'd to go and live there, and to trade with such things as they are order'd, which crowd of people enhances the price of provisions, and makes a scarcity for those men who are absolutely necessary to live there, on account of the land and sea service, and in carrying on those buildings and works which the Czar has already, and farther designs to make there. Whereas in Mosco, all the lords and men of distinction, have not only very large buildings within the city, but also their countrey seats and villages, where they have their fishponds, their gardens, with plenty of several sorts of fruit and places of pleasure; but Petersburgh, which lies in the latitude of 60 degrees and 15 minutes north, is too cold to produce these things. Besides, Mosco is the native place which the Russes are fond of, and where they have their friends and acquaintance about them; their villages are near, and their provision comes easy and cheap to them, which is brought by their slaves.

As for the Czar, he is a great lover of the water, and entirely delights in ships and boats, and in sailing. . . . But his lords have no relish nor pleasure in those things, and though they seemingly complement the Czar whenever he talks to them of the beauties and delights of Petersburgh; yet when they get together by themselves, they complain and say that there are tears and water enough at Petersburgh, but they pray God to send them to live again at Mosco. [261-263]

2. THE MEANNESS OF MOSCOW

Mosco is situated near the centre of Russia, on a river of that name . . . and stands upon a large piece of ground, where every man of distinction hath (though in the midst of the city) both a garden and an outward court belonging to his house. Whenever any traveller comes within a fair view of the city, the numerous churches, the monasteries, and noblemen and gentlemen's houses, the steeples, cupolos and crosses at the tops of the churches, which are gilded and painted over, makes the city look to be one of the most rich and beautiful in the world, as indeed it appeared to me at first sight coming from the Novogorod [Novgorod] road, which is the best view of it; but upon a nearer view, you find your self deceived and disappointed in your expectation. When you come into the streets, the houses, excepting those of the boyars, and some few rich men, are every where built of wood, particularly those that front the streets, after a very mean fashion: The walls or fences between the streets and the houses are made of wood, and the very streets, instead of being pav'd with stone, are lin'd or laid with wood. . . . [263-264]

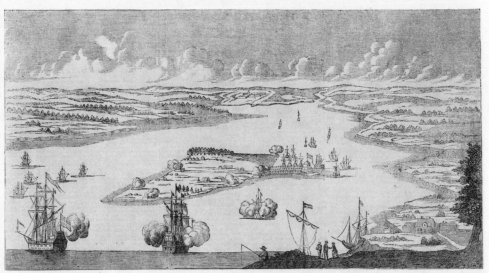

ST. PETERSBURG IN 1706

ICE HILLS ON THE RIVER NEVA

Engraved by T.Holloway.

JONAS HANWAY

3. THE UNFULFILLED FUTURE

His Majesty . . . for a long time had intentions to bring the trade from Archangel, and all the other parts of his countrey, to his said new favourite town, situate at the mouth of the Neva, which falls out of the Lodoga Lake into the Baltick Sea.

To which end, before I came from Russia, storehouses were building for merchants, and a great number of inhabitants already settled there; and though it be but a small part of what is designed in variety of undertakings, . . . with canals through the streets, like that of Amsterdam, and an artificial haven both for his navy and merchant shipping that are intended to trade thither; yet notwithstanding these his Majesty's new designs of increasing his strength and commerce there, it will be found very difficult and burthensome to his people, without a free communication be made to the more fertile parts of his countrey by water; for by reason of the tediousness of the way, the being oblig'd to wait for floods and rains at several shallow places, and the vessels and floats being often dash'd and staved to pieces against the rocks and falls that are by the way, and the goods often lost and spoiled; and by reason also of the very great scarcity and dearness of forage for horses where land carriage is required; corn and other provision of burthen is usually at least 3 or 4 times the price which the same is bought for between the towns of Rebna [Rybnoe] and Cassan, the first of which is from Petersburgh near 1000 Russ miles upon the said river Wolga: From which side of the countrey is brought also oak timber, and other naval stores for equipping out the Czar's fleets, the charge of which is equally augmented by the tediousness of the carriage: So that the Czar's ships, which are now built of oak at Petersburgh, though men's labour is abundantly cheaper, and that he has the iron work and cordage out of his own countrey, yet the building of his ships with oak are as dear as to have them bought in England. [40-41]

And particularly, to the end that Petersburgh may be render'd more agreeable, about seven years since he order'd . . . an exact survey of the road between Petersburgh and Mosco, to find the bearing of one place from another, in order to make a road the whole way, by a straight line through all the woods, and over all the lakes, morasses and rivers, by which it will happen about one fifth part nearer than it now is; and a tract has since been mark'd out through the woods for making the way on a direct line, which was finish'd in the year 1710. And the Czar does design to have a road accordingly made, when he has peace, and can better spare men and money for it. [281]

CHAPTER TWO
Jonas Hanway

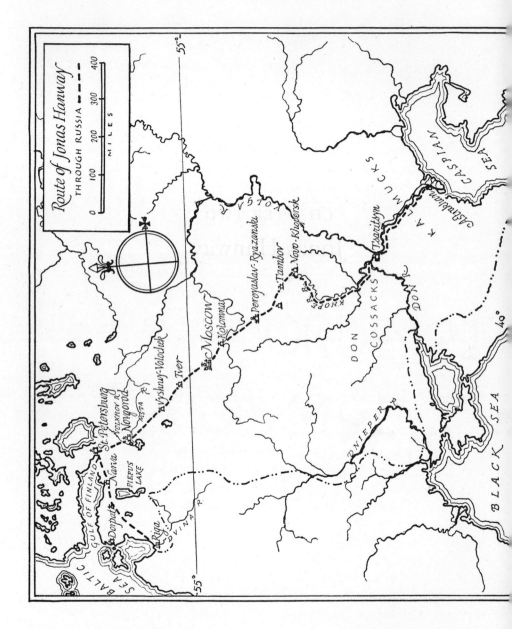

Route of Jonas Hanway
THROUGH RUSSIA

MILES
0   100   200   300   400

Jonas Hanway:

MERCHANT OF THE RUSSIA COMPANY

(1743-1750)

THERE was little in the early life of Jonas Hanway to distinguish him from the type of the ordinary English merchant. He was born of respectable parents on August 12, 1712,[1] in Portsmouth, where his father, Thomas, had been for some years agent victualler of the fleet. When the latter met with an accidental death, his widow moved with her four young children to London, where Jonas was first sent to school. The fact that his education included a course in accounting suggests that he was early intended for a business career, and, in 1729, when turning seventeen, the youth was apprenticed to a merchant in Lisbon. Instead of returning to England at the expiration of his term, young Hanway set up an independent commercial house which he conducted with moderate success for several years. When he did return to London, it was to depart again almost immediately upon a new venture, and, in the spring of 1743, as the partner of John Dingley, he embarked for St. Petersburg to launch upon those travels which were first to bring him into the public eye. Hanway shared with Perry a common middle class origin and an early experience of foreign travel but his position as a member of the favored Russia Company of British merchants placed him in a widely divergent relationship to Russian society. To Perry, with the precedent of only a few military adventurers and self-exiled Stuart sympathizers, the Muscovite service must have appeared a daring leap into the unknown realms of a barbarous and semi-oriental despotism. To Hanway, forty-five years later, the Anglo-Russian trade represented an almost prosaic enterprise, rooted in a long commercial tradition, and, if his subsequent adventures proved far from prosaic, his traditional privileges as a British merchant in Russia could not but influence both his impressions and the account which embodied them.

The publication date of Hanway's book, 1753, marked the bicentennial anniversary of that Anglo-Russian commerce of which it was a

[1] John Pugh, *Remarkable Occurrences in the Life of Jonas Hanway Esq.*, London, 1788, p. 1.

partial history, and although for the first century and a half the British traffic through Archangel had been rather restricted, events since the end of the seventeenth century had much accelerated the volume and altered the character of this trade. These events signalized the emergence of Russia into a European economy and, in their subsequent developments, led to the establishment of an Anglo-Russian interdependence which underlay their relations throughout the century. Their explanation does much to illuminate economic conditions in the two nations and to illustrate the character of contemporary mercantile thought and practice. For all these reasons, they are of interest to the modern student, but they are also particularly pertinent to an understanding of the travels of Jonas Hanway, for they not only explain the peculiar circumstances of his visit, but, by his consciousness of them, provided him with the mental furniture typical of his nation and class, and certain fundamental criteria upon which he based many of his opinions.

Trends about the turn of the century in combination with the same economic theories upon which Hanway was bred, inevitably inspired British merchants to conceive of Russia as a promising field of enterprise for the expanding national economy. A backward agrarian country, it offered both a market for finished goods and a convenient source of raw material, and could serve industrial and commercial England in the same capacity as one of her overseas colonies. The manufacture of British woolens, valued at £8,000,000 in 1699 and, year after year, estimated at half the annual export,[2] would profit immensely from uniform contracts for Peter's huge army. On the other hand, England, handicapped by dwindling forests and undeveloped coal resources, lacked fuel to smelt her native minerals, and therefore depended heavily upon imports of basic metals to supply her forges. Employing an estimated 200,-000 workers and second in importance only to the woolen mills, the British foundries drew some two-thirds of their bar iron from Baltic ports,[3] and Peter's new mines offered a valuable supplement to existing supplies. Hides, leather, furs, hogs' bristles, rhubarb, caviar, and train oil were among potential items of exchange for the tobacco, paper, pottery, pewter, woolens, and iron processed by English mills, and, of course, all such exchange would provide valuable freight for British bottoms. Above and beyond any of these considerations, however, a single driv-

[2] D. K. Reading, *The Anglo-Russian Commercial Treaty of 1734*, New Haven, 1938, pp. 4-5.
[3] T. S. Ashton, *Iron and Steel in the Industrial Revolution*, London, 1924, p. 104.

ing necessity spurred British energies to expand her commerce with Russia.

When Peter, in the long war with Sweden, occupied one after another of the territories skirting the Baltic coast, he upset more than the political balance of northern Europe. In these same regions he possessed himself of many valuable sources and even more valuable outlets for the naval stores which had long constituted the bulk of the Baltic trade. For more than a century, the great maritime powers in general and England in particular had been carrying an essential part of the materials necessary to build and re-fit their fleets from the shores of the Baltic. Timber for masts, spars, deals, and planks; pitch, tar, and turpentine as preservatives; tallow for ship's candles; flax for sailcloth; hemp for caulking and rigging; iron for cannon and fittings—all had been channeled in ever-increasing quantities through Baltic ports to British shipyards. Since 1658, made anxious by her dependence upon these vital commodities, England, like her rival, Holland, had striven to maintain a balance between Sweden and Denmark, so that neither should gain the sole power to check the vital flow.[4] To be sure, Peter's conquests did not grant him the complete monopoly of naval stores, but the hemp of the Ukraine and the great masts of Riga were essential to the British navy, and the political vacillations of the Northern War often made their procurement extremely precarious. The seriousness of one such crisis may be glimpsed in a passage from the correspondence of the Secretary of State, Charles Townshend: "It is our misfortune at this juncture, by the knavery of the Muscovites in imposing on our merchants last year, to have our magazines so ill provided with stores, particularly with hemp, that if the fleet of merchant ships now loading in the Baltick should by any accident miscarry, it will be impossible for His Majesty to fitt out any ships of war for the next year, by which means the whole navy will be rendered perfectly useless."[5]

With such a spur to action, the British Foreign Office was quick to realize the necessity of a commercial understanding with the Russian government, and from 1705 with the arrival of Charles Whitworth in Moscow until the rupture of diplomatic relations in 1719, it pursued a paradoxical policy only to be understood in the light of this problem of naval stores. Britain, while consistently importuning the Russian government for commercial privileges no less consistently opposed her

[4] R. G. Albion, *Forests and Sea Power*, Cambridge, Mass., 1926, pp, 139-199.
[5] William Coxe, *Memoirs of the Life and Administration of Sir Robert Walpole*, London, 1798, 1, 86.

politically at every turn in the hope of redressing the Baltic balance in favor of Sweden. Even beyond such hostile diplomatic gestures as the recognition of the Swedish as against the Russian candidate for the throne of Poland, she dispatched threatening naval expeditions to the Baltic on three occasions, and in 1720 Admiral Norris was in actual conflict with the Russian fleet.[6] Additional sources of friction with the Hanoverian George I were Peter's designs upon Mecklenburg and Holstein and his alleged support of the Jacobite conspiracy to return the Stuarts to the English throne.[7] Peter, for his part, pursued a policy in exact antithesis to that of the Foreign Office, for his newly discovered mercantilism was hostile to a commercial agreement which would weaken his own infant industries. He would have been willing to make commercial concessions only in return for the political alliance denied by the British government. Under the circumstances, it is hardly surprising that all negotiation came to nothing, and the recall of Captain James Jefferyes in 1719, marked a diplomatic rupture of eleven years' duration.[8]

The failure of English diplomacy is significant here chiefly as a contrast to the remarkable successes of that independent commercial enterprise of which Hanway and his fellow merchants were so justly proud. Without special privileges and in the face of fierce competition and political hostility, the Anglo-Russian commerce grew by leaps and bounds from 1700. From four or five ships a year, the number of British vessels stopping at Russian ports soon increased to sixty or seventy.[9] From 1701, at which time the trade had already gathered momentum, the value of English imports more than tripled, soaring from £90,000 in that year to £314,000 in 1733.[10] In a few short decades, the British merchants had built an insignificant commerce into a booming trade, equal in value to that of all the other nations of Europe combined. In the process, they not only maintained, however precariously, the vital flow of naval stores, but also established that economic community of interests which found its ultimate expression in the Anglo-Russian trade treaty of 1734.

That so thriving a commerce should spring into being so rapidly was, of course, largely a consequence of the compelling demand for

[6] Albion, *op. cit.*, p. 178.
[7] J. F. Chance, *George I and the Northern War*, London, 1909, pp. 105ff.; pp. 208ff.
[8] D. B. Horn, *British Diplomatic Representatives (1689-1789)*, London, 1932, p. 110.
[9] Reading, *op. cit.*, p. 35.
[10] Charles Whitworth, *State of Trade of Great Britain*, London, 1776, Part II, p. 29; compare J. J. Oddy, *European Commerce*, Philadelphia, 1807, I, 205.

naval stores, but the relative ease with which the British overtook and surpassed their foreign and particularly their Dutch competitors is a credit to the peculiar felicity of their commercial organization. The Russia Company, in whose hands the entire trade was lodged, was a regulated, rather than a joint stock organization. In the seventeenth century it had fallen under the control of a monopolistic oligarchy which had nearly strangled the trade, but in 1698, when such restrictions threatened to discourage the new tobacco exports,[11] Parliament had redefined its charter, offering membership to any Protestant, native-born Briton on the payment of but £5. The greatly increased membership resulting was composed of individual representatives of various British firms. In addition to the wide latitude of action permitted by the liberal terms of this new charter, the members enjoyed powerful financial backing from their connections at home. Moreover, since these firms had commercial affiliations with other parts of the world, their operations possessed greater elasticity than operations of individual traders. An analysis of the conditions governing the conduct of the Russian trade will show how the freedom, financial power, and wide scope of operations helped the members of the Russia Company both to shoulder aside their foreign competitors and to create a Russian dependence upon their transactions.

The prevalence of governmental monopolies in Russia soon favored the English interests. Prior to the accession of Peter I, two-thirds of the export trade of Muscovy had been engrossed in governmental monopolies, and the expense of the Tsar's many enterprises induced him to extend the list of crown goods. It was natural that the perpetually impoverished government should prefer large-scale cash purchases to piecemeal buying. It was here that the capital resources of British company organization helped their merchants to outbid the foreign competitors who traded largely as individuals. The iron, copper, rhubarb, and potash monopolies fell almost exclusively into English hands.[12] As the trade grew, the Russian government found itself increasingly dependent upon these cash purchases. Despite open political hostility in 1719, Peter, as Hanway proudly noted, twice issued proclamations to the British merchants assuring them of his protection in their trade. Similar announcements in the reign of Catherine I attested the continuance of this policy.[13] If the British dockyards were starving

[11] Dietrich Gerhard, *England und der Aufstieg Russlands*, Munich, 1932, p. 36.
[12] Reading, *op. cit.*, p. 45.
[13] P. B. Struve, "The Anglo-Russian Treaty of 1734," *Russian Review*, I, 1912, p. 24.

for Russian naval stores, the Muscovite treasury was athirst for English gold.

In still another way, British financial strength was complementary to the conditions of the Muscovite trade. The vastness of the Empire and the relatively short shipping season of its northern ports forced a peculiar rhythm upon Russian commerce. Goods were months and sometimes, as in the case of timber, years in their transit from the interior. Russian merchants usually came to St. Petersburg in the early winter in order to make contracts for the delivery of goods in the following spring and summer. Here, as with the government contracts, capital resources were of great use. The extension of long-term credit, although not initiated by the British, was most effectively used by them to dominate the market. Credit for terms from six months to as much as two years became customary, and the Russian merchants much preferred this method of doing business, regardless of the interest rates entailed. It is difficult to estimate to what extent British credit operations affected the economic structure of Russia,[14] but it can scarcely be doubted that they encouraged a considerable dependence upon the English trade.

Finally, the wide affiliations of British company organization enabled their representatives to redress the balance of trade so unfavorable to them and so gratifying to the Russian government. British merchants in Russia were and remained largely exporters of Russian goods. As the demands for Russian naval stores grew, so too did the surplus of British imports over exports, until by the 1720's the British merchants were shipping annually £200,000 of bullion into Russia. The mercantilists of Russia exulted, while those of Britain despaired. Actually, however, the balance was far more favorable to the English than theoretically supposed. The commodities which they took from Russia were largely staples, and the British commercial houses knew how to turn them to account in their world trade. Hemp, tallow, fir, isinglass, potash, rhubarb, and caviar were reexported to Italy, Turkey, the Indies, the British colonies, and even, by dint of extensive smuggling, into Spanish America, none of which enjoyed a direct commerce with Russia. If England lost £200,000 annually in the direct trade with Russia, the

---

[14] In a report to the Board of Trade, December 30, 1800, Stephen Shairp, Consul-General at St. Petersburg, remarked that in the hemp trade, at least, British advances of credit to Russian merchants extended by means of traveling middle men as far down in the economic scale as to the peasant, in order "to engage his stock and to enable him to pay his yearly rent to his landlord." Gerhard, *op. cit.*, p. 425.

goods thus purchased brought in more than twice that sum from her world market.[15] Even if this estimate be taken as exaggerated, its main thesis cannot be disputed. Moreover, the profits to the carrying trade were very considerable, particularly in such items as timber, in which the freight was several times the value of the actual cargo. The Muscovites, for their part, incapable of such extensive operations and seeing only the immediate fact, were more than ever disposed to favor the British commerce.

However profitable this trade was to the merchants of the Russia Company, their complaints of grievances continued to exert pressure for a commercial agreement. As Perry had pointed out, corrupt Muscovite officials, in the hope of being bought off, could interpose a thousand obstacles in the path of business. Freedom of movement was restricted and security of person and property, precarious. Neither government nor private contracts could be entirely trusted, and there was no adequate machinery for redress of grievances. Credit default and fraudulent packaging of goods, particularly hemp, were among the most frequent violations of mercantile ethics. These had been more or less constant sources of irritation from the outset, but during the period of the diplomatic rupture, further causes of complaint arose. In 1724, Prussia wrested from England the valuable army cloth contracts, and in the same year the Armenians obtained the monopoly of the trans-Caspian trade into Persia and stopped the exchange of British woolens for raw silk through Russian merchants. Hence, the balance of gold exported from England rose even higher; and when the deaths of Peter the Great (1724) and George I (1727) had removed a source of political contention, the clamor of the British merchants was finally heard at the Foreign Office, and diplomatic relations were at last resumed.

The details of the negotiations of the commercial treaty of 1734 are here relevant only in their illustration of three elements underlying the Anglo-Russian trade of the period as a whole: the effective influence of the Russia Company as a diplomatic pressure group in the formation of British policy, the prevalent concept of the character and value of the trade to both Russia and Britain, and the resulting advantages secured to each nation by the terms concluded. In regard to the first of these points, it is clear that the wishes of the Russia Company were consulted at every turn. Upon this basis were drawn up the instructions of both Rondeau and his successor, Lord Forbes, the English pleni-

[15] William Wood, *A Survey of Trade*, London, 1722, pp. 90-91.

potentiaries for the negotiation. Nominally, the Lords Commissioners of Trade and Plantations were responsible for the conduct of the affair, but in practice they acted very nearly as a rubber stamp for the merchants, who draughted projets, edited counter-projets, and, in the event of the delay of instructions from home, worked directly with the English plenipotentiaries. The influential political affiliations of the Russia Company[16] maintained its power nearly unchecked throughout Hanway's time, and, even in 1765, Sir George Macartney, negotiating a second commercial treaty, admitted to the influence of its members in accepting terms expressly denied by his superiors at the Foreign Office because "the terms granted were better than any of our merchants had flattered themselves with hopes of" and "those merchants are highly satisfied with the Treaty in its present form."[17]

Like the political influence of the Russia Company, the line of argument adopted by the British plenipotentiaries and, to a large extent, accepted by the Russian negotiators continued as an element in their commercial relations well beyond Hanway's time. In the first place, they pointed to the immensely favorable balance in gold enjoyed by the Russians as a reason for making concessions, and as an alternative they threatened that, in the event of a Russian refusal, England would be forced to turn to her American colonies to obtain the necessary naval supplies at the heart of the trade. In reality, England had long been attempting, by means of subsidies and certain restrictive regulations, to foster the procurement of necessary naval stores in the colonies. As early as 1705, the novelist, Daniel Defoe, had pamphleteered in behalf of this policy.[18] Actually, the expense of the Atlantic voyage, the high cost of American labor, and the general antipathy of the colonists to such regulations had rendered this program highly impracticable,[19] but the Russians appear to have credited the bluff, and the idea continued to hold some currency in the minds of British travelers until the Revolution. Hanway himself advocated a plan for stimulating American iron production, considering that "as there is no want in that country of ore or wood to work it up, it ought to be presumed that we

---

[16] One source of the domestic influence of the Russia Company was the prestige and importance of certain of its members. John Thornton, for example, one of its directors, was an extremely wealthy and well-known financier and director of the Bank of England, as were also his sons, Samuel and Henry, in addition to being members of Parliament with a widespread political acquaintance. Many other Company members enjoyed a similar, if lesser prominence. Gerhard, *op. cit.*, pp. 63ff.

[17] Macartney to the Duke of Grafton, August 8/19, 1765, *Sbornik*, XII, 210.

[18] Daniel Defoe, *A Plan of English Commerce*, London, 1705.

[19] Albion, *op. cit.*, pp. 240ff.

might make a considerable progress toward equaling our European neighbors,"[20] and a score of years later, Joseph Marshall's detailed discussion of the possibility of cultivating hemp in America proved that the idea still lingered in the British consciousness.[21] Far more important, however, was the belief that the value of British commerce to the Russian revenues guaranteed a favorable treatment to her merchants and provided a broad basis for Anglo-Russian friendship on other counts as well. Hanway expressed it repeatedly, and the frequency with which it was touched upon in some way or another by a series of his successors supports the classification of it as part of the contemporary dogma of the Anglo-Russian commerce. The most conclusive evidence of the prevalence of this feeling, however, was the extraordinary commercial privileges which its propagation wrung from the Russian plenipotentiaries.

The consequences for the Russia Company, the Anglo-Russian trade, and the relations of the two nations in general were immense. The terms of the treaty removed nearly every cause of complaint. All affairs relating to English merchants in Russia were placed under the jurisdiction of the College of Commerce only,[22] thereby remedying the multiplicity of courts and legal chaos which had so plagued them in the past. Concentrated under one head, against which diplomatic pressure might be brought to bear, justice for the members of the Russia Company now seemed secure. In addition, it was provided that there could be no seizure of British property, except in case of bankruptcy, even by an imperial decree. The books of the British merchants might be inspected only in cases of suit, and then, not by Russian officials, but by a board of four foreign merchants appointed by the College of Commerce for that purpose. Merchants of the Russia Company might build, buy, or rent houses, and yet be exempt from the quartering of soldiers in the cities of St. Petersburg, Archangel, Astrakhan, and Moscow. English ships were promised prompt clearance, and a Russian law threatening punishment to native officials who created delays attested the good faith of this provision. Representatives of Russian merchants must be furnished with credentials to insure that all contracts made by them should be binding, and the police machinery of the government was to be employed in punishing defaulters. Finally, a system of inspection of the packaging of goods was to guarantee against fraud and

---

[20] Jonas Hanway, *An Historical Account of the British Trade*, London, 1754, I, 368.

[21] Joseph Marshall, *Travels*, London, 1773, III, 180-183.

[22] The entire text of this treaty has been reproduced in Reading, *op. cit.*, pp. 302-312.

to standardize quality. In short, together with some others, these articles provided legal equity, security of property, freedom of movement for the goods and persons of the merchants, and guarantees of contract in regard both to payment and honest measure. It awarded to the British merchants privileges and immunities even beyond those allowed to the Russians themselves and, in this sense, made of the Russia Company a sort of state within a state.

All these privileges were theoretically reciprocal, but in practice, Russian merchants were virtually excluded from any share in the English trade beyond the borders of their own empire.[23] Even aside from the restrictive mercantilist legislation of Parliament, the superiority of British commercial techniques made Russian competition impossible. In addition to those terms already mentioned, however, three further concessions granted even greater advantages to the merchants of the Russia Company. The first of these was the permission to pay their tariff duties in Russian currency. In the absence of any direct monetary exchange, the bullion-starved Russian government had decreed the payment of all duties in Dutch reichsdollars, and beyond the mere inconvenience of obtaining these at Amsterdam, foreign merchants had long been plagued by the Muscovite policy of undervaluing them. At the accession of Peter the Great, a reichsdollar had an intrinsic worth equivalent to fifty copecks, but the deliberate inflation of the Russian coinage so violently condemned by Perry had, by 1734, raised the value to 121 copecks. Ignoring this fact, the customs officials continued to peg the price of the reichsdollar at 50 copecks, and thus foreign merchants found themselves paying a duty nearly two and a half times the ostensible charge.[24] In this light, the British privilege of paying the customs in Russian currency at the rate of 125 copecks to the reichsdollar offered a very considerable advantage over other foreigners.

Not content with this general tariff reduction, the British merchants obtained a provision lowering by one-third the duties on three kinds of woolen goods: "soldiers' cloth; . . . the coarse cloth of the county of York, . . ." and "heavy flannel," with the immediate consequence that they recaptured the valuable army cloth contracts from the Prussians. Finally, upon the payment of 3 per cent. of value, British goods and merchants were promised free passage from St. Petersburg across Russia and over the Caspian Sea into Persia, a land and water voyage of some 1500 miles within the Russian borders which was to provide the main subject matter of Hanway's Russian account. Taken all in all,

---

[23] Gerhard, *op. cit.*, p. 41.   [24] Reading, *op. cit.*, p. 260.

it is easy to concur with the verdict of the Board of Trade which, in reviewing the terms of the treaty of 1734 some thirty years later, characterized it as more favorable to British interests than almost all other commercial treaties concluded up to that time.[25]

While the Anglo-Russian trade in general continued to boom throughout the entire century,[26] that portion of it that was carried over to Persia terminated in ruin after a brief and curious episode. It was with this episode that Hanway's *An Historical Account of the British Trade over the Caspian Sea* was primarily concerned, and rambling as was its style, the book nevertheless presented a very complete picture of the ill-fated trade, from its earliest roots to its final demise. From 1553, the date of Chancellor's first voyage to Archangel, until 1581, no fewer than six British expeditions had traversed Russia and made their way into Persia. Since that time, sporadic interest had achieved nothing material until the inclusion of Article VIII in the commercial treaty, and even afterwards, the merchants of the Russia Company, apprehensive of the turbulence of faction and civil war in Persia, made no attempt to avail themselves of their new privilege "till the year 1738,

[25] Gerhard, *op. cit.*, p. 39.

[26] The analysis of primary sources of data on the amount of the Anglo-Russian trade has been complicated by a number of inaccuracies. The steady increase of prices must be kept in mind where the figures are in terms of the value of the goods. Moreover, the official assessments of the British customs were often erroneous. Merchants exporting to Russia tended to exaggerate the value of their goods, in order to make their trade appear more prosperous than it really was, and thereby to expand their credit at home. Imports from Russia were not infrequently appraised either too low or too high, according as the price of various articles had risen or fallen since the last official computation. Professor Gerhard, in checking Oddy's statistical tables, from which the list below has been drawn, has confirmed Oddy's scholarship in compensating for these inaccuracies. Moreover, Oddy's figures, in contrast to those of Chalmers and Whitworth, have the additional advantage of extending down to the very end of the century. Finally, whatever errors still exist, will not materially impair the value of these figures in showing the extraordinary over-all expansion which took place.

Years	Imports	Exports	Years	Imports	Exports
1701	£ 90,581	£ 69,201	1755	£ 661,740	£ 85,327
1705	142,234	74,247	1760	474,680	38,710
1710	115,725	212,318	1765	965,339	76,170
1715	241,876	105,153	1770	1,046,610	145,743
1720	169,932	92,229	1773	850,112	196,229
1725	250,315	24,847	1782	1,185,844	196,577
1730	258,802	46,275	1785	1,606,668	233,998
1745	294,704	62,702	1790	1,710,373	434,288
1750	584,091	111,846	1795	1,857,977	862,265
			1800	2,382,098	1,025,333

Oddy, *op. cit.*, I, 205; compare George Chalmers, *An Estimate of the Comparative Strength of Great Britain*, London, 1782, p. 72; and Whitworth, *op. cit.*, pp. 29-30. For discussion of statistical complexities, see Gerhard, *op. cit.*, p. 33.

when an unexpected incident happened which opened a new scene of commercial adventures."[27]

The incident referred to was the daring exploit of a British adventurer, Captain John Elton. He had first attracted attention in 1732 when, as a naval officer, he approached the Russian ambassador in London with a scheme for exploring a northeast passage to China. Shortly thereafter, he left England and, like Perry, enrolled in the Russian service with the rank of captain. There he spent several years with a military expedition on the eastern banks of the Volga, constructing forts and attempting unsuccessfully to establish an overland communication with Bukhara. Apparently disgusted with the Russian service, he quitted it in January 1738, but his experiences had suggested a new field of endeavor and in St. Petersburg he mustered sufficient backing from the merchants of the Russia Company to finance a small caravan of woolens with which he set out to prove the practicability of the trans-Caspian trade. After a hazardous journey across the forests and steppes down the pirate-infested Volga and over the treacherous Caspian, he and a single partner arrived in strife-torn Persia in 1739. His eloquence and bold address soon won him the confidence of the reigning usurper, Nadir Shah, and in the following year he returned to St. Petersburg with an extensive charter of privileges for British merchants and a valuable cargo of raw silk.

The developments which then followed showed British mercantilist machinery to good advantage and once more demonstrated the political vigor of the Russia Company. Elton immediately drew up a memorial depicting, in the most glowing terms, the advantages to be gained through the trans-Caspian trade and presented it to the Honorable Mr. Finch, His Majesty's representative at St. Petersburg. This memorial passed from Finch to the Duke of Newcastle, the Secretary of State, to the Lords Commissioners of Trade and Plantations, to the Russia Company, back to the Lords Commissioners, and finally to the King himself, with the recommendation that it receive the most serious consideration. The fact of the matter was that, although the Russia Company had forehandedly procured the concessions of Article VIII, a trans-Russian trade to Persia was outlawed by the terms of previous Parliamentary legislation. The charters of the East India and Turkey Companies granted them trade monopolies of Persian goods, and the Acts of Navigation forbade the importation of goods from any country other than that of their origin unless such importation had been legal-

[27] Hanway, *op. cit.*, 1, 8.

ized through long usage. However, French competition in the Levant had long denied the British silk industry a sufficient quantity of raw silk, and the Russia Company, scenting profit, set about securing the necessary legal exemptions. Despite the vigorous opposition of the Turkey Company, the desired legislation was passed in 1741. Moreover, on Elton's recommendation, the company obtained the permission of the Russian government to construct its own ship of 180 tons for the navigation of the Caspian. Characteristically, Elton built not one, but two ships, and the trade was launched. The whole process was a credit to British mercantile practice.

Promising as were these beginnings, the trans-Caspian venture was, as Hanway said, "devoted to ruin."[28] Initial British successes incited the jealousy of Russian and Armenian merchants who had previously shared a monopoly of the Persian trade. Fortunately for them, Elton's ungovernable energies soon offered an opportunity to intrigue against the English merchants as a body. The captain, given a new theatre of operations, apparently began to fancy himself in a more exotic role than that of a mere wool trader. In his intercourse with Nadir Shah, he so far excited the respect and confidence of that potentate that he was offered the command of a non-extant Persian navy, which it was to be his first duty to bring into being. Attracted by the parade of oriental life, the ebullient Elton accepted and immediately set to work upon the construction of a Persian warship in utter disregard of the hostility this was bound to create in the Russian government. Rumors of these activities in far-off St. Petersburg were at first discredited by the merchants of the Russia Company as the malicious slander of the envious Armenians, but, in 1743, alarmed by the repeated complaints of Muscovite officials, they decided to send one of their number into Persia to ascertain the real truth and, if necessary, to dissuade Elton from this reckless undertaking. It was Jonas Hanway, but recently arrived in St. Petersburg, who was recruited for this mission.

Great was the contrast between the newcomer and the veteran of the Persian trade. The one was a sober and devout merchant; the other, a swashbuckling adventurer. Each, in his way, was a pioneer, but whereas Elton launched the first Persian warship on the Caspian, Hanway, by braving public derision for many years, introduced the first umbrella into the streets of London, and, of the two, it cannot be denied that Hanway's was the more lasting gift to posterity. Elton traveled into foreign lands to appease the restless energy of his spirit,

---

[28] *ibid.*, I, xiii.

while Hanway suffered exile only in order to gain financial independence for a tranquil retirement. Fitting it was to the character of each that Elton should perish by violence in a Persian insurrection, whereas Hanway expired peacefully in his bed at the age of seventy-four. During the latter half of his life, he lived in London, an amiable busybody, occupying himself with innumerable charities and philanthropic institutions. In this period, he poured out a stream of pamphlets on a wide variety of subjects, ranging from the benefits of street paving to the evils of tea drinking. The latter, incidentally, won him the enmity of that inveterate tea drinker, Dr. Johnson, who remarked spitefully that Hanway had "won some reputation by traveling abroad, but lost it all by traveling at home."[29] In the same vein, Carlyle characterized him as "a dull worthy man," but admitted he "was not always so extinct as he has now become."[30] Impervious to criticism, however, the honest bourgeois persevered in his good works, ranging from the reclamation of street walkers to the improvement of the condition of chimney sweeps and from the training of apprentice seamen to the care of foundlings, and in all displaying the same methodical resolution which characterized his steadfast conduct during his Russian and Persian adventures.

Awkward and discursive as was Hanway's account of his journey, its various animadversions were tributary to the main current of his commercial consciousness. Again and again, the towns he passed through were described in terms of their economic activity, rivers were classified according to their navigability, and even a seemingly isolated description of the climate included references to its influence upon maritime and land transport. At the very outset, Hanway professed his intention of recording the commercial practices of the Caspian trade for future times in the event of its reestablishment, and this utilitarian purpose was never very far from his mind. For this reason, he was at his best in such detailed descriptions as the method of ordering and conducting caravans through Russia, and in such passages, the book resembled a sort of Baedeker for commercial posterity. The predominance of practical commercial concerns largely overshadowed the humanitarianism of his retirement. Hence, Hanway showed little sympathy for the conditions of peasant life. As Perry, in an analysis of the backwardness of Russian labor, seemed almost to stumble upon the problem of serfdom, so, too, Hanway included his sole general

[29] James Boswell, *Life of Johnson*, London, 1874, I, 394.
[30] Thomas Carlyle, *Works*, Boston, 1884, IX, 102.

description of peasant tenure in order to explain the prevalence of piracy on the Volga, of interest it would appear, only because it constituted an obstacle to the commerce of that river.

His spirit was sustained throughout his foreign travels by an almost religious conviction of the universal utility of trade. Entrenched in this conviction, he never seriously investigated the consequences of the Anglo-Russian commerce for Russia herself beyond the repetition of contemporary mercantilist dogma. At those rare moments in which he touched the problems of the Russian economy, he insisted upon the favorable balance of gold as ample compensation to Russia for her concessions to the English merchants, but he was much less thorough in his discussion of this benefit than some of his compatriots. Joseph Marshall, for example, expounded its ramifications at some length:

"Let us consider the advantage to Russia, of our paying her a balance of three or four hundred thousand pounds. That balance is paid to a certain number of merchants and dealers at Petersburg and other ports; they pay it to a set of landlords, miners, husbandmen, and manufacturers. These again pay it to all the manufacturers, tradesmen, etc., with whom they deal; and these to a fresh set. Now every art, trade, business, and profession, in the whole empire, come in for an additional income, from this sum, circulating through the mass of industry; and every one of them is essentially the richer. If this circulation could be traced, it would probably be found, that three hundred thousand pounds a year, gained in precious metal, were equal, in general by improvement, to the value of nine or twelve hundred thousand pounds a year."[31]

Certainly, the increase and circulation of specie which resulted from foreign trade invigorated the Russian economy,[32] but other features of this trade tended to qualify the assumed benefits. The exchange of raw materials for consumer goods could do little to stimulate Russian industry.[33] Agrarian production of hemp and flax and even the primitive processing of mineral ores was performed by unskilled laborers who were often little more than slaves. Since the large majority of the profits of this labor went to the serf owners, such a commerce might be supposed to do equally as much to rivet the shackles of slavery as to produce that liberty and individual initiative

[31] Marshall, *op. cit.*, III, 115.
[32] Emile Pernet, *La Politique Economique de Pierre le Grand*, Paris, 1913, p. 17; Gerhard, *op. cit.*, pp. 77-81.
[33] P. I. Lyashchenko, *History of the National Economy of Russia*, New York, 1949, p. 409.

which Britons considered so important to a thriving economy. Furthermore, even these profits but rarely contributed to that primary accumulation of wealth which was the sine qua non of a free capitalistic economy.[34] The profits of the many governmental monopolies were immediately drained off for the support of the huge army, lavish court, and bureaucratic superstructure, whereas those of the landlords were frequently consumed in the purchase of luxury goods originating in foreign lands, all of which, with the single exception of England, enjoyed a favorable balance of trade with Russia. Conscious only of this last, but oblivious to the rest, Hanway delighted in the comfortable assurance of the righteous, almost philanthropic nature of his calling, considering himself, as an English merchant, a sort of benefactor of the Russian people.

In fairness to Hanway, however, it must be admitted that his apparently superficial assumptions were supported by the contemporary climate of opinion. Imports of British gold failed to build up a specie reserve in the imperial treasury, but they helped to underwrite, not only the court extravagances, but necessary governmental expenditures. British purchases of raw materials did not result in proportionate accumulations of capital for reinvestment in production, but they enabled the noble serf owners to support a hitherto unknown scale of existence. In consequence, the politically articulate portion of Russian society came to view the British trade as essential to its well being, and this belief contributed materially to the perpetuation of friendly relations in later times. In 1801, the threat to the incomes of the nobles inherent in the anglo-phobe policies of the Emperor Paul inflamed the discontent leading to his assassination, and a few years later the pressure of similar restrictions in the continental blockade accelerated the rupture between Alexander and Napoleon.[35] In this light, the community of interests which Hanway deduced from the conditions of the Anglo-Russian trade proved to be far more than a figment of a wishful imagination spurred by the vanity of commercial pretentions.

Apart from any question of the correctness of his economic interpretation, however, it was Hanway's conviction of the essential righteousness of his conduct as a British merchant which enabled him to prevail over so many difficulties. By it, his rather commonplace character, endowed only with a methodical intellect, was transformed into a

[34] *ibid.*
[35] W. F. Reddaway, "Macartney in Russia, 1765-1767," *Cambridge Historical Journal*, III, 1931, p. 260.

driving force which surmounted one obstacle after another. A novice to the trade, he overtook a caravan of experienced Armenians and succeeded in conducting his goods across Russia and down the Volga in time to avoid the seasonal immobilization of the navigation of Astrakhan. There, his persistent representations overcame the Governor's objections to an immediate clearance of the British-owned *Empress of Russia*, despite the intelligence that Elton had employed this very ship, in the service of Nadir Shah, to subdue a Caspian province.[36] During the succeeding ten months in Persia, he weathered out a variety of vicissitudes. Isolated from all European contacts in the city of Astrabad, his goods were confiscated by a party of rebels, and he was in imminent danger of either enslavement or assassination. Nevertheless, refusing refuge in disguise or flight, he chose to maintain "his proper character"[37] as a British merchant and by steady address was able to procure not only a convoy of soldiers, but a bill for the full amount of the value of his goods. After a series of betrayals, a critical illness, an attack by pirates, and an absurd episode in which he served as a guard for a Persian harem, he ultimately recovered eighty-five per cent. of the value of his woolens and, investing it in a cargo of raw silk, reembarked for Astrakhan in September of 1744.

Yet all these successes were ultimately brought to nothing by his failure to dissuade the fiery Elton from his Persian engagements. The thoroughly aroused Russian government seemed now to have predetermined the prohibition of the British Caspian trade. The pretext of a long quarantine served to delay further transportation of Hanway's goods until the following spring, and the subsequent confiscation of the British ships brought all traffic to a standstill. Further attempts by the Russia Company to recall Elton proved that his determination was not to be shaken on any account. An offer of a lifetime pension of 2,000 rubles annually, upon condition of his return to St. Petersburg, was ignored, and, even more remarkable, a personal letter from George II to Nadir Shah, written at the request of the company merchants—and what better proof that England was, in fact, "a nation of shopkeepers"?—demanding the return of the renegade elicited the same response. Small wonder that Hanway could not succeed, where English gold and English royalty failed. The impasse continued until 1746, when news reached St. Petersburg that one of Elton's warships had stopped a Russian merchantman for neglecting to salute the Persian flag. It was promptly succeeded by an ukase abrogating Article VIII

[36] Hanway, *op. cit.*, I, 86.   [37] Pugh, *op. cit.*, p. 35.

of the treaty of 1734 and bringing the trans-Caspian trade to an official end. However disastrous the outcome of this episode of Anglo-Russian commerce, Hanway's conscience might yet seek solace in reflecting upon his own creditable share in the Persian adventure.

Throughout both his personal and historical account of the Russian trade, the worthy Hanway reflected the character of that great merchant class with its solid bourgeois virtues which was slowly shouldering aside the rash adventurers, the Captain John Eltons, whose era, in England at least, was passing. He was, at once, a merchant, a patriot, and a devout Christian, yet this triple character blended into one unified personality. The ethics of his Christianity did not seem contradictory to his patriotism and commercial ambitions. The Almighty had selected the subjects of the British nation for His peculiar favorites. The power and prosperity of this nation depended upon her commerce. The righteous merchant served both God and country in the performance of his profession which properly understood, possessed the power "to employ the poor, to banish idleness—the root of all evil, and to increase the riches of the nation."[38] This strange admixture of morality, materialism, and patriotic loyalty formed the triple standard of a vital social philosophy. Upright, practical, persevering, the figure of Hanway has something monumental in it as he marches across Russia. Whether arranging his caravan for a night on the steppes, battling the subterfuges of a hostile bureaucracy, sailing his woolens past the Volga pirates, or carrying his umbrella through the hoots of a London mob he exhibits the stuff of which the British commercial empire was made.

[38] Hanway, *op. cit.*, I, 369.

EXTRACTS FROM: *An Historical Account of the British Trade over the Caspian: with the Author's Journal of Travels from England through Russia into Persia; and back through Russia, Germany and Holland. To which are added, the revolutions of Persia during the present century, with the particular history of the great usurper, Nadir Kouli.*

by Jonas Hanway

CONTENTS

....

I · THE BALTIC CITIES

1. RECEPTION AT RIGA

IT WAS about the 20th of may when I arrived at Riga. The weather was
as hot as ever I remember it, during many years abode in Portugal;
for the sun leaves the horizon only three or four hours, and its reflection
continues even great part of that time; so that, tho' the dews fall,
neither the earth, nor consequently the air, has time to become temperate.

    Here I was received by the British factors with great kindness and
marks of regard. . . . These gentlemen are distinguished by their
affluence and generosity. They gave me a hospitable reception, which
was the more pleasing, as I found myself reserved for the honor of
being a state prisoner. I produced the most indubitable credentials . . .
and also letters of recommendation to the English factors in Riga, by
all which it appeared I was an English factor going to reside in St.
Petersburg. But the governor having received orders that no person
should proceed from thence without express leave from the court . . .
he would not give me a passport, and I was obliged to wait there for
seventeen days. Such is the jealousy, which the neighbourhood of the
Swedes creates in time of war. [1, 49-50]

    I spent this time as agreeably as a garrison and its confines would
permit, but not a little mortified and surprised with the extreme heat.
I was assured, that after the melting of the snow, the earth being
impregnated with the nitre which the snow contains, sometimes
brings to maturity, in six weeks, the rye which has lain in the ground

during the winter; and that wheat has been sown and reaped within the same time. . . .

The river Dwena [Dvina] generally closes about the end of November, and opens again near the middle of March; insomuch that this town has the advantage of St. Petersburg, the Neva being there closed about six weeks longer. When the ice breaks up, it often comes down in such large pieces, and with so vast a weight, as to remove points of land, and form banks, which sometimes remain for several years. This renders it impossible for any standing bridge to be built over the river, but this inconveniency is removed by a bridge of rafts and boards, during the summer season; so that they walk even with the surface of the water. [1, 50-51]

2. ITS CHARACTER AND COMMERCE

The chief commodities here, are hemp, flax, masts, and timber. The quantity of the hemp is generally about . . . six thousand four hundred tons, which is brought down in . . . flat-bottomed boats of fifty to seventy feet long, and twenty to thirty feet broad, made head and stern alike, and steered by oars of about twenty-five feet, of which there is one at the head, and another at the stern.

The Polanders bring a large proportion of these commodities, chiefly from the Polish Ukraine. The flax is brought from Druana and Lithuania. . . . The timber is from those parts of Poland which border on Turkey; great part of that which is fit for masts is two summers in its passage to Riga. This place formerly exported vast quantities of corn for Sweden and other countries; but the system of politics in that country having been for some time repugnant to that of Russia, the town has suffered the inconvenience of a prohibition.

The houses here are made steep in the roof, for better carrying off the water, which is very penetrating when the snow melts. In this they excel the Russians, who have still greater occasion to provide against the like inconvenience. The cellars are used as magazines for flax, and other goods; and the entrance, or first apartment, in most houses, is the coach-house, by which you must pass to the parlour and dining-room. The houses have seldom above two stories, and the streets are narrow. German is the language of the people of Riga, but the peasants in the neighbourhood, and other parts of Livonia, speaks Unduetch, a dialect entirely differing from the German. [1, 51-52]

3. THE COUNTRY TO ST. PETERSBURG

My partner in St. Petersburg, having procured a passport for me, I provided myself with a sleeping waggon, and on the 7th of june, I took post for St. Petersburg. The soil about Riga is sandy, but, after some distance, the country becomes more pleasant. In some places it is champaign, in others the hills diversify the scene. It abounds in wood and corn land, and is well watered. The post horses are exceeding bad, but as the stages are short, and the houses clean, this inconvenience is supportable. . . .

Dorpt [Dorpat, now called Tartu] has the appearance of a superb heap of ruins. Here are the remains of a castle which Peter the Great took from the Swedes in 1704, upon which occasion great part of the town was destroyed by fire. From hence the country near the road is cleared of wood, and in many places well inhabited. I travelled along the banks of the Lake Peipus, which is said to abound in fish. It is one hundred and twenty wersts long, and sixty broad, communicating with the Lake Pscow [Pskov], the borders of which are famous for producing flax. . . .

Narva, which is the capital of Estonia, is not a large town, but stands on a rising-ground, is clean, and well fortified. Its trade consists mostly in flax and timber. . . . The land within twenty wersts of St. Petersburg on the banks of the Neva, is very marshy. From Narva to St. Petersburg is one hundred and forty-six wersts, and the whole distance from Riga five hundred and forty-six. Notwithstanding the several stops I made on the road, together with the bad post-horses, I arrived the fourth day, without much difficulty. [1, 52-54]

II · ST. PETERSBURG

1. AN ELEGANT METROPOLIS

St. Petersburg, which was founded by Peter the Great in the beginning of this century, may at present be considered as the modern and polite metropolis, and the chief residence of the Russian empire; and though so lately a morass, it is now an elegant and superb city, very healthful, and abounding in all the necessaries, and many of the pleasures of life. It was formerly built of wood, but now the use of this material is permitted only in the suburbs.

This city is ranged on both sides of the Neva extending from east to west near two English miles; at the upper end of the north side is the citadel, which is more famous for the number of lives it cost in building than for either its strength or great importance. . . . This city has neither gates nor walls, but the marshy land near it . . . render the access to it extremely difficult for an army. It is divided by several canals, Peter the Great intending to take Amsterdam as his model in building it; but from the reluctance with which it was originally begun by his subjects, who were compelled to build, and likewise from errors in the plan, some part of the city remains intirely unexecuted, and in others the houses are too near the canals. This does not hinder, but there are some regular, broad, and well built streets, and several very noble structures. . . .

These edifices are for the most part of brick, and plaistered over so as to make an elegant appearance, but the work is generally done in a hurry, and the materials not very durable. An Italian architect having been some years since established in Russia, the taste of Italy is adopted in almost all their houses; and though the severity of the climate is so great, they abound in windows much beyond our houses in England. [1, 376-377]

2. THE COURT ENTERTAINMENTS

There are some courts in Europe which seem to adopt this as a principle, that the more money courtiers spend, the less will be their riches, and consequently the greater their dependence. In England we think the richer the subjects, the more able; and consequently it may be presumed, the more willing they are to serve the state. Of all the pompous shows in Russia, the appearance made upon the great duke's marriage, in cloaths and equipage, was the most magnificent, and answered the highest idea that can well be formed of the splendor of any court. A man may travel over the world during a long life, without seeing anything comparable to it. . . .

Here Italian operas and French comedies are acted at the expense of the Empress, into which foreigners who make any appearance, are admitted. . . . Masquerades, balls and concerts are also frequent at court; but the Empress seems to delight chiefly in select companies, at the houses of those persons who are most in her favor. [1, 372-374]

3. THE NORTHERN SEASONS

With regard to the climate of Russia, it is easy to conceive how extremely it differs, even in the several parts of it included in Europe, and still more in their Asiatic dominions. In St. Petersburg, we find that february generally brings a bright sun and clear sky, and the frost being yet very sharp, every object seems to glitter with gems; the nerves thus become braced by the cold; and though the reflexion of the sun from the snow is very strong, yet the eyes are seldom hurt by it. There is no small amusement in riding in sledges, to those who by the length of the winter have in some measure forgot the much superior pleasure which nature presents when she is cloathed in green.

March is often attended with showers, and these with the heat of the sun penetrate the body of the ice, which is generally three quarters of a yard thick on the Neva; being at length rotten, and appearing as a honeycomb, about the end of that month, it ordinarily breaks up, and its motion seems to attract the north-east wind, for the wind generally blows very cold from that quarter.

The gulph of Finland, at the entrance of Cronstadt [Kronshtadt], is seldom free of ice before the end of april; so that the most early ships do not often arrive before the first week in may. This month is frequently very warm, the days being so much lengthened. . . . The nitre contained in the snow invigorates the earth to that degree, and the intense heat of the sun brings on the verdure so fast, that the eye can discover its progress from day to day. Till the middle of july it seems to be one continued day, the sun not intirely disappearing above two hours in the twenty-four. . . . August generally closes the scene; so that we can hardly say there are above three months of summer.

September . . . brings rain and frost; october increases the severity of both; and november always closes up the Neva. Then comes on the season for the speedy and easy conveyances on the snow, which brings fresh provisions to market a thousand English miles by land, as those can witness who have often eat in St. Petersburg the beef of Archangel. In december and january the cold is often very intense, and the poor, who are sometimes overtaken by liquor, or exposed in plains or other open places . . . not infrequently perish with cold. Russia is by no means a proper country for those who delight in rural pleasures, or think a walk in a fine day one of the most elevated joys the heart can receive. [1, 378-379]

III · THE CHARACTER
OF THE ANGLO-RUSSIAN COMMERCE

I. COMFORTS OF THE BRITISH MERCHANTRY

THE BRITISH factors in St. Petersburg are generally well esteemed by the natives of Russia and acquire fortunes which some of them of late years have been wise enough to preserve. They inhabit the best houses on the banks of the Neva, and are hospitable, not to say magnificent, in their way of life, keeping pace with the luxury of men of superior fortunes at home;[39] but the reader who has not been abroad, must observe that the British factories[40] in general make a better figure than those of any other nation, which may be considered as a sort of compensation for the voluntary banishment which they suffer from one of the best countries in the world. This indeed may sometimes be a means of prolonging that banishment, and of creating a fondness to a foreign country, in prejudice of the love which they ought to have for their own; however, this generous way of life gives them an influence and ascendancy among the people with whom they reside, and helps to support the national interest and honor. [1, 367]

[39] The prestige and comfort enjoyed by the members of the Russia Company were remarked by a host of travelers throughout the period. Even the aristocratic Lady Craven expressed her appreciation of their hospitality: "Dans le Ligne Anglais, a quarter of this town, where the English merchants live, I find English grates, English coal, and English hospitality to make me welcome and the fire-side cheerful—I have never been fortunate enough to make any acquaintance in the world of commerce; but if all English merchants and their families are as well informed and civil as those I find here—I should be very glad to be admitted into the city of London as a visitor to enjoy the rational conversation which at the court-end is seldom to be found." A score of years later, Robert Ker Porter extolled the tenacity with which his countrymen clung to their national customs: "In the families of our English merchants resident at St. Petersburg, you may still recal the simplicity of home, in the chastened elegance of their abodes. Their tables, as well as those of other foreign merchants, are always open to their friends; and the warmest hospitality ever ready to welcome all who bring introductions from their correspondents abroad. This truly estimable order of men are held in the highest esteem by the nobles of a metropolis which they so truly benefit and enrich. Many of them possess little paradises on the road leading to Peterhoff, to which their families resort for the hot and short-lived months of summer. Since my arrival I have paid several visits to these charming retreats, where every thing around reminded me of dear England. The house enbosomed in trees, and furnished in the English style; gardens planted in the same taste; and the language and manners of the inmates; all would have persuaded me to forget I was in a strange land." It was John Carr, however, who encountered the most extraordinary instance of patriotic ostentation at these same summer residences. "In the gardens of one of them, I trod with delight upon British ground. An ardent love for his country had induced the hospitable owner, at a great expense, to bring a quantity of English ballast from English ships to cover his walks with." Elizabeth Craven, *A Journey through the Crimea to Constantinople*, London, 1789, pp. 125-126; Robert Ker Porter, *Travelling Sketches*, Philadelphia, 1809, p. 22; John Carr, *Northern Summer*, Philadelphia, 1805, p. 224.

[40] Now obsolete, this term referred to the body of factors or commercial agents.

2. NATURAL COMMERCIAL ADVANTAGES

I shall now make a few general remarks, in regard to the commercial interest of Russia. The productions of the earth, and foreign trade, are acknowledged to be the great sources from whence the riches of every nation proceed: Russia has made great strides in the improvement of her commerce for several years past, enjoying some advantages beyond any other nation: the number and greatness of her rivers open a communication almost to every part of the globe, but particularly within her own extended dominions. As to timber, hemp, and iron, which are the instrumental causes of trade; no country in the world produces a greater quantity, which is a natural consequence of the cheapness of land and labour . . . but if we have occasion for the commodities of Russia, that empire has the great source of her revenues in the trade which this island carries on with her subjects.

Hemp, which twenty years since was hardly worth five rubles . . . of late years has been about twice that value. . . . As they can afford this article in St. Petersburg at six or seven rubles, they will certainly bring enough of it to market so long as they can obtain eight or nine. Iron is also a very improveable article; they have both wood, hands and ore in Siberia sufficient to make a quantity, which would depreciate the value of the Swedish iron, raise their rivalship and competition with the Swedes in this important article of the revenues of that nation, and at the same time greatly augment those of the Russian empire. . . . It is not forty years since the Russians began to open iron mines, and yet in the year 1750 they exported twenty thousand tuns. . . . [1, 368]

3. THE COMMUNITY OF INTERESTS

The ordinary computation of the Russian general export, from St. Petersburg, is three millions, of which the British subjects in Russia take off two, consisting chiefly in hemp, flax, iron, hog's bristles, hare skins, hempen and flaxen manufactures, Russia leather, and other articles. The ordinary imports of the Russians were two millions, consisting in indigo, cochineal, lead, pewter, tin, wrought silks, gold and silver lace, toys, cotton and linnen manufactures, woollens and wines. The Russians receive the ballance in their favor in silver and gold. . . . The consumption of the Russians is so far encreased with their acquisitions by commerce, that they import now more than usual, but the English have still above a million ballance against them.

It seems to be a maxim established in all countries where commerce has made any progress, that the value of exports must exceed that of the imports, for otherwise the ballance must necessarily be paid in money. . . . The augmentation of the revenues of Russia . . . ought to be imputed in a great measure to the increase of her trade for some years past; and the increase of her national wealth to the great annual ballance in her favor, of one million of rubles (220,000 pounds). . . .

The interior trade of Russia is certainly very much augmented, and the commerce they carry on with the Tartars and other frontier nations, is a considerable object; as Russia sometimes receives a large quantity of foreign silver and gold from those nations, in exchange either for her own or foreign productions. I will not undertake, from an impulse of my good wishes, to determine what articles Russia should be cautious of importing; but those of the produce of Great Britain are either essentially necessary to her, or such as she can never suffer by: I speak not of the major part of them, for I think not one article, EVEN OUR ALE, but tends to the good of the Russians; not to mention the great advantages to Russia of the Riga and Narva trade with Great Britain and Ireland. As our Russian trade is well conducted, I shall pass it over, observing only, that in whatever light it is considered, it ought to be a means of establishing a perpetual friendship between this nation and the Russian empire. [1, 369-370]

4. THE FREEDOM OF THE TRADE

Now it is evident that there cannot be a trade where a greater liberty is open . . . than this in question. The Russian markets are always well supplied, each trader pursuing his own inclination to import, and his own opinion concerning the rise and fall of markets, and the opportunities of sale: I have known British houses in St. Petersburg, that for several successive years have had from forty to an hundred bales of cloth remaining over the annual demand. The credit given the Russians is never less than twelve months, unless in small articles, and it is often extended to fifteen and eighteen months, and the prices of goods are as low as possible for the merchant to receive a living profit.

There are no monopolies or exclusive privileges assumed by the Russia Company, nor any rule of conduct established, which has the least appearance of being injurious to this nation; for any natural born protestant subject may, for five pounds, take his freedom of the company, go into Russia, and establish a house of business, under the protection of the British crown. The English merchant may also consign goods to any person who is a native of Russia, or a subject of Great Britain, remembering that the advantage in favor of the British subjects in Russia, according to the 27th article of the treaty of commerce, is about one third part in the customs of soldiers' cloths, (coarse cloth so called) Yorkshires, (a thick coarse cloth), and flannels. Nor is there any restraint with regard to the markets of these kingdoms, for any Russian as well as freeman of the company, may send Russian goods into England; he is only to pay the aliens duty, as established by law ... (which in general terms is provided for in the treaty of commerce). The law of nations, the right of reciprocal protection, and the last article of the treaty do, I apprehend, make the Russians entirely free to trade to this country. Some Russian merchants have actually been here; but finding they could not dispose of their goods in a satisfactory manner, nor live near so cheap as at home, they returned to their own country.[41] [1, 390]

5. TANGIBLE PRIVILEGES OF THE BRITISH MERCHANTRY: THE TREATY

Besides this favor in the customs, the British factors in St. Petersburg esteem it a valuable privilege, that in all cases where they are defendants, particularly that of bankruptcy, their affairs are cognizable by the college of trade, and their books sacred to the inspection of four reputable merchants, appointed by that college. In many cases also, where they are plaintiffs, they apply to the college of trade; but their common suits and demands for money of the Russian merchants, have been for some years transferred to the magistracy.

With regard to the quartering of soldiers in Russia, the British subjects are indulged in a peculiar manner, and no doubt it ought to be deemed a favor, under a military government, to be exempt from it. This privilege however was more sacred and more considerable formerly than of late years. I have myself opposed attempts made by the

---

[41] Several other Englishmen similarly noted the virtual exclusion of the Russians from their own trade. John Richards stated that, "notwithstanding the immense trade of Russia, it is remarkable there are few or no Russians who may be properly termed merchants, nor are there any Russian factors established at the different courts in Europe, except one house lately in Constantinople." Joseph Marshall deplored the fact that "the trade of Petersburg . . . would figure on comparison with many very great marts in all parts of Europe, but unfortunately, that vast commerce is, nine-tenths of it, carried on in foreign bottoms." In explaining this paradox, British observers tended to attribute it to Russian ignorance and inefficiency, like Hanway, failing to mention the countless mercantilist restrictions which the British government, despite the concessions of the commercial treaty, retained in force on all foreign commerce and shipping. John Richards, *A Tour from London to Petersburgh and from thence to Moscow*, Dublin, 1781, p. 28; Marshall, *op. cit.*, III, 113.

officers of the police to oblige me as a tenant to find quarters. I do not know that these attempts have yet succeeded against tenant or landlord, but if the landlord is compelled to find quarters, and the rent is raised on this account, the tenant ought to complain; for we consider it not only as the spirit of the treaty, that British subjects shall enjoy an entire exemption from quarters; that is, that the landlord not being chargeable with it, the tenant shall have his rent so much the cheaper. This must be the sense of the 16th article, or it means nothing; for who can imagine it should be deemed a favor to the British government, that common soldiers may not sit in the compting-house of a British merchant in Russia? [1, 390-391]

6. INTANGIBLE PRIVILEGES OF THE BRITISH MERCHANTRY: REPUTATION

The Russians know very well, that the English were the first that discovered Archangel; that they had an exclusive privilege of trade to Russia in the reign of Queen Elizabeth; that Peter the Great, whose maxims of government are justly dear to them, always shewed a distinguished regard to the English merchants, and even at the time that the politics of the two nations did not entirely coincide, he gave them his royal word, that at all events they might consider themselves as under his peculiar care and protection.... The Russians are also sensible of the political as well as of the commercial interest of the two nations, and consider this country, and I hope will always consider it, as their hereditary friend.

(I remember the compliment made to this nation by the governor of Astrachan, [Astrakhan] a very ingenious man ... speaking to his friends in my presence: "You are to consider," says he, "the English merchants in a different light from those of any other nation trading to this country; they are skilful, generous, humane, upright; they extend their commerce over the whole earth; and every country where they come is enriched by them. The commodities they deal in are necessary, substantial, and of the greatest use to the community; and they take off more of the Russian commodities than all the other nations united.") As our extensive commerce has reached every corner of the earth, the greater our support is at home, the greater must our reputation be abroad. Reputation is certainly no imaginary thing, but must be in some degree productive of good to our commercial interest. . . .

The British houses in St. Petersburg have not only a trade to Great Britain and Ireland, but to Holland, Prussia, Sweden, Holstein, and several parts of Germany; also to Portugal, Spain, and Italy. This has arisen from the connexions of their extensive commerce. . . . There long has been, and I hope ever will be, an honorable distinction abroad, between us and other foreigners, both as Britons and as merchants, not in the esteem of the Russians only, but of all other nations. [1, 391-392]

IV · ST. PETERSBURG TO MOSCOW

1. PREPARATIONS AND DEPARTURE

VERY few weeks had past before my partner, and other factors who were correspondents with Mr. Elton, being alarmed with the complaints of the Russian court, in relation to that gentleman, resolved, that one of them would make a journey to Persia. I then offered my service, which was accepted. . . .

Sir Cyril Wych, at that time his majesty's minister at the court of Russia . . . by a memorial to the great chancellor's office, demanded a passport for me; which was granted. I provided myself with a convenient sleeping-waggon, another for my clerk, and a third for my baggage, also a Russian menial servant, a tartar boy and a soldier: then having received such instructions as were necessary from the factors who were interested in this new commerce, and taken upon me the charge of a caravan of thirty-seven bales of English cloth, I prepared for my journey.

This caravan of cloth making twenty loads, set out the 1st of September. The 10th of that month I followed it, not without some painful apprehensions that though I might probably arrive time enough to obtain a passage over the Caspian into Persia, yet the caravan would be too late in the season. [1, 54-55]

2. EMBARRASSMENTS AND ANXIETY

It is too much the custom in Russia for officers or persons who travel with servants or soldiers, to treat the peasants with insolence. The first charge I gave my attendants, was, to avoid every occasion of dispute, and still more of oppression; that if any insult was offered to them, they should inform me, that I might judge in what manner it ought to be resented.

The rainy and frosty season being already come on, I found the roads extremely bad, especially for about fifteen wersts. The adjacent country to St. Petersburg, would be impassable but for the great care which is taken in mending the roads with timbers and fascines. . . .

On the 11th we found the road better, though the ground about us was marshy. . . . On the 12th we advanced thirty-six wersts to the river Volcoff [Volkhov], which it was necessary to pass. . . . The ferryman finding that I was a merchant, began to be insolent. These boors usually entertain a contemptible notion of their own traders, compared with military people, which they extend to merchants in general. I could not help observing upon this, as upon many other occasions, the obstinate opinion which the peasants had imbibed of the little respect due to merchants, though this barbarity of manners wears off very fast amongst the politer part of the people. The delay and impertinence to which I found myself thus exposed, necessarily called on my soldier to exercise his cane, which soon brought my antagonist to his duty. . . .

The 13th, the darkness of the night, the hard wind and rain, and excessive bad road, obliged us to halt, and sleep in our waggons in the open field, especially as one of them remained till morning stuck in a bog. . . . From the Volcoff, we passed the Msta, near Novogorode [Novgorod] and thence came to Bronitz [Bronnitsy] on the 14th, which is two hundred and thirty wersts from St. Petersburg. . . .

The Russians, though not the acutest lawyers, understand how to torture words, and make them say what was never intended. My poderosnoi [podorozhnaia] (order for horses), by some omission or ambiguity, now left me at the mercy of the post-masters. . . . The 15th. Last night the axle-tree of my own waggon broke: the Russian vehicles, unless made by express commission, are very subject to such accidents. . . . The 16th. By noon we had advanced ninety-nine wersts to Vishneivolochoque [Vyshniy Volochek]. The next day, passing over several branches of the Msta and Twersa [Tvertsa], we reached Twere [Tver, now called Kalinin], where I came up with my caravan of cloth. Great complaints were made by the Iswoshicks [Izvoshchiki] (carriers), of the badness of the roads, insomuch that my fear of not reaching Persia that year encreased; therefore, instead of one horse to each load, I ordered two, and promised to divide something considerable among the carriers, if they exerted themselves to the utmost of their strength and ability. [1, 55-57]

3. TVER

Twere . . . is a very ancient city, but of no beauty; the largest and best structure was then building for the use of civil officers of the government. This place stands on both sides of the Twersa, which runs into, or is rather a branch of the great river Volga . . . so that in this place, as well as in many others, the Volga seems to be a rich mine of gold to the Russian Empire.

Twere is a great rendezvous for merchants who trade to the towns on the banks of the Volga. In the ordinary course of the year, here is not a depth of twenty inches water; but yet in the months of april and may this river receives such vast floods from the melting of the snow as raises the water to ten or eleven feet. Large flat bottomed vessels of two hundred tons take this opportunity of passing to and from Astrachan, and other places; the trade to Persia being sometimes carried on by the same channel. They bring here great quantities of rock salt, caviar, and fish; and carry back bale goods, corn, meal, and all kinds of groceries, performing the voyage in sixteen or twenty days.

The 19th we arrived at Klin, which is a very agreeable place, near a small branch of the river Kliazma [Klyazma]. Passing through other small villages, we travelled eighty-four wersts, and the next day we arrived at Mosco [Moscow], the metropolis of the Russian empire. [1, 60]

4. MOSCOW

On my arrival I was received with great hospitality by Mr. John Tamesz,[42] who by his skill and industry as a merchant and manufacturer, has acquired a great reputation. His fabric[43] appeared as a little town, having about four hundred looms, which employs more than one thousand hands in making sail-cloth, sheetings, ravensducks, and drillings.

Mosco is in the latitude of 50, 40, and is built in some measure after the eastern manner, having not many regular streets, but a great number of houses with gardens. . . . The river Moskwa, [Moskva] which runs through it, and joins the Occa [Oka] near Kolumna [Kolomna] makes many windings, which add a very striking beauty to the city; but in the summer it is in several places shallow and unnavigable. The

[42] Apparently, the son of the Dutchman, John Tamès, who came to Russia in the reign of Peter, enjoying considerable success in the manufacture of sailcloth, table linen, toweling, and fine handkerchiefs. Pernet, *op. cit.*, p. 81.

[43] In eighteenth century terminology, a place where anything is made: a factory.

several eminences, groves of trees, gardens and lawns interspersed, form the most pleasing prospects, and enliven the imagination. The frequent dreadful fires with which this city has been afflicted, have hardly left houses to accommodate the empress's retinue without distressing her people; insomuch, that this princess has been prevented from taking that delight in it which the situation of the place affords. (The removal of the court to Mosco occasions such a conflux of people, that I have been assured no less than eighty thousand passports for Mosco have been delivered in St. Petersburg in the space of a few months.)

The most remarkable thing I saw is the great bell, which is indeed stupendous, and surprizes equally on account of its size, and the folly of those who caused it to be made: but the Russians, for time immemorial, have had a strange ambition of this kind. The bell in question weighing near twelve thousand three hundred and twenty-seven poods [puds], was cast in the reign of the late empress Anne. (Four hundred and forty-three thousand seven hundred and seventy-two lb. English, value at three shillings, is sixty-five thousand six hundred and eighty-one pounds.) The sound of it rather amazed and deafened, than delighted the inhabitants.

The waters of the Moskwa are not esteemed. In some seasons agues are predominant in this city, but in general the climate is good. Being in the heart of the empire, it is the grand residence of that part of the nobility which is not obliged to follow the court; and it is particularly inhabited by the chief merchants and manufacturers. . . .

Before we leave Mosco, it is necessary to observe that there remain many traces of the ancient Russian customs, which are hardly to be seen in St. Petersburg, this last city being in some degree considered as another country: those who have a superstitious reverence for antiquity, look on it also with jealousy mixed with contempt, as being more modern than Mosco. [1, 61-62]

V · THE CONDUCT OF A CARAVAN

1. THE RUSSIAN CARRIAGES

IN RUSSIA, carriages for merchandize are drawn only by one horse. These vehicles are nine or ten feet long, and two or three broad, and are principally composed of two strong poles, supported by four wheels of near an equal size, and about as high as the fore wheels of our ordinary coaches, but made very slight: many of the rounds of the wheels are of a single piece of wood, and open in one part for near an inch; and some of them are not shod with iron.

The first care is to lay the bales as high as the cart will admit, on a bed of matts of the thickest sort. Besides the original package, which is calculated to stand the weather, the bales are usually covered with very thick matts, and over these other matts are laid, to prevent the friction of the ropes; lastly . . . raw cow hides . . . are always best to defend the goods from rain, or from the snow. . . . Each bale is sealed up by the custom-house with a leaden seal, to prevent its being opened on the road, or any of the goods vended in the country . . . when they are intended for Persia. [1, 57]

2. LEGAL RESTRICTIONS AND PRIVILEGES

In St. Petersburg, from whence the British caravans always set out, it is necessary to provide a wipis [vypis] (a custom-house permit), which must be carried to the custom-house of Astrachan, and also passports for the people that attend the caravan. The manner of procuring horses is to agree with one or more poderatchicks [podriad-chiki] (master carriers), who provide for the whole caravan, in the summer season, at the rate of one ruble a pood (thirty-six pounds English) for the carriage from St. Petersburg to Zaritzen [Tsaritsyn, now called Stalingrad], which is near eighteen hundred wersts; and in winter it is only forty copeeks [copecks], (which is equal to nineteen and a half pence per stone of fourteen pounds English, for twelve hundred English miles in summer, but in winter, not quite eight pence per stone). . . . On every agreement of this kind, the crown receives a duty of ten per cent but the carriers are not very scrupulous in regard to the declaration of the exact price. . . .

This duty is by agreement usually paid by the master-carrier . . . and having part of the money advanced, he provides the carriers, and everything necessary for the journey. And here a zapis, (a registered bond), is of excellent use to keep these people in order, for by this they oblige themselves to watch the goods at night, and preserve them as much as possible from fire, water, and thieves; but in the last case, little dependence ought to be made on them, either for courage or for arms. On this account the conductor of the caravan (who with us in the British trade was generally a foreigner) ought to take particular care of this registered bond; for the carriers being uneasy at the restraint it

lays them under, will sometimes attempt to steal it from him while
he is asleep. . . .

The conductors of caravans generally chuse to lodge in villages, a
few miles wide of Mosco. If they come into the city, the goods must
be housed in the Gostinadwore [Gostiniy dvor], (public warehouses)
or pay three copeeks a load, the same as if they had been housed. There
is no necessity to make any stay in this city, except to register the clear-
ances, or to gratify the carriers, who are too fond of the spirit of corn
to pass great towns without their fill of it.

At Novochoperskaja, [Novo-Khopersk] a frontier garrison towards
the Don Cossacks, they examine the Chamatavoi Yerlique [Chuma-
tovoi Yarlyk] (the certificate of customs clearance). . . . The officers,
in order to extort a present, usually make great difficulties; but when
they are reminded, that according to the treaty of commerce with the
British Crown, and the Empress's regulations of trade, a dollar is due
for every hour of illegal detention, they soon become reconciled to
the acceptance of a loaf of sugar, or a few bottles of brandy; and suffer
the caravan to proceed. [1, 57-58]

3. PRACTICAL DIFFICULTIES AND PRECAUTIONS

The caravans . . . in the winter, between St. Petersburg and Mosco
. . . usually travel seventy wersts in twenty-four hours; but from Mosco
to Zaritsen, only forty or fifty wersts: in summer their stages are
shorter. Great part of the last mentioned road being through an uninhabited country, makes the carriers cautious not to jade their horses.
Every time they set out, the conductor ought to count the loads. When
necessity requires that the caravan should be drawn within fences, or
into yards, the heads of the waggons ought to stand towards the door
in a regular order, and a guard, who will keep a better watch than an
ordinary carrier, should be set over it: for want of this precaution,
whole caravans in Russia have been sometimes consumed by fire. It is
most eligible to stop in the field, where the usual method is to form
the carriages into a ring, and to bring the horses as well as the men
within it, always observing to keep in such a position as best to prevent an attack or repulse an enemy. The Khalmucks [Kalmucks or
Kalmyks] on the banks of the Volga are ever ready to embrace an
opportunity of plundering and destroying passengers; therefore, when
there is any occasion to travel on those banks, which should be avoided
as much as possible, an advance guard of at least four Cossacks is of

great use; especially to patrole in the night. It is not often practiced, but I found it indispensably necessary when I travelled on those banks. . . .

A hundred carriages take up two-thirds of a mile in length; so that when no horseman is at hand to spread the alarm, the rear might be easily carried off. They have not even a trumpet, horn, or other instrument for this purpose; they trust in providence, and think any care of this kind unnecessary, though the neglect has sometimes proved of fatal consequence.

By the time the caravans, which set out in the winter, usually arrive at Zaritzen, the Volga becomes very dangerous; for which reason goods are housed there till the waters are open. . . . It must be observed, that to save the shipping season, either on the Baltic or the Caspian sea, it is sometimes necessary to make loads only of fifteen poods [540 pounds] for a single horse. . . . Another way, which I experienced, is to hire double horses to twenty-five poods [900 pounds], which saves many days, and was the cause that my caravan got safe into Persia when another, which set out a week sooner from St. Petersburg, wintered in Astrachan.

It is necessary to send previous advice to Zaritzen, that a vessel may be provided by the time you arrive there. Those vessels which carry three thousand poods (about forty-five tons) are as large as is consistent with safety and despatch to go down the Volga to Astrachan. They cost from sixty to a hundred rubles, (twelve to eighteen pounds), and considering how ill they are put together, sometimes prove very dear. They require fifteen or twenty hands to navigate them, of which half ought to be soldiers, in order to serve as a convoy against robbers: of these I shall have occasion to speak more at large. [1, 58-59]

VI · MOSCOW TO TSARITSYN

1. RICH LAND AND POOR PEASANTS

HAVING repaired our vehicles, and provided such things as were thought necessary, the 24th of September we left Mosco. The weather was now become more soft and pleasant. We travelled southward . . . not far from the western banks of the Occa. The country is hilly, but abounding in arable lands, and adorned with a beautiful variety of groves. . . .

The 25th at night we arrived in Kolumna, eighty wersts from Mosco. This is one of the cities of the best appearance in this part of the world, having many stone and brick buildings, and a good wall: it has also several turrets of a very irregular figure, yet being covered with gilded tin, they make a good appearance. . . .

The 26th, being advanced to Perislawl Rjazanskoi [Pereyaslav-Rya-zanski, now called Ryazan], I found myself in another climate, for the harvest was not yet gathered in. The roads are for the most part very good; the country has not much wood, but is delightfully watered. The poverty of the people is great, as appears by the houses of the peasants, which are covered with straw, in a manner that declares their ignorance even of thatching. . . . I was surprised to behold so fine a country, at the small distance of two hundred wersts from the metrop-olis, with such an appearance of indigence;[44] but some lords are such bad oeconomists, that they defeat their own end, by not only refusing to assist their vassals, but in a great measure obstructing their industry, thro' a rapacious impatience of gain, before the peasants feel the sweets of their labour. Such a conduct must naturally be productive of indo-lence.

The 27th, the weather and the road continued extremely pleasant. . . .

The 28th . . . We were now in an open fertile country, but the people so poor that many of their . . . (cottages) consisted only of one room, about five or six yards square, which is often destined to contain six or eight people of both sexes. The inhabitants, who are not numerous in these parts, are not very reserved with regard to the ordinary conse-quences of such cohabitations. [1, 63-64]

2. THE STEPPE

The 30th, we travelled seventy wersts farther, to the city of Tambove [Tambov], which is a mean place. . . . The peasants complained of the exactions of the officers and soldiers who had lately marched that way for Astrachan and the Persian frontiers.

October the 1st, we entered the Step [Steppe]. The inhabitants who are nearest to it often manure some tracts of land, by burning the grass, which grows to a great length. In places which are not burnt, provender is found even in the winter season; for by scraping away the snow, the cattle feed on the half perished grass. We overtook a caravan of forty

44 In 1769, Marshall, noting the same paradox of the fertility of the land and the poverty of the peasants, drew a provocative comparison: "I remark, that the peasants in this empire, are in general happy, in proportion to the neglect under which the country lies; in the midst of vast wastes and forests they seem to be tolerably easy; but any tracts well cultivated, are done at their expense, and they appear very near on the same rank, as the blacks in our sugar colonies." Marshall, *op.cit.*, III, 166-167.

loads of European goods, going to Zaritzen, the property of Armenian merchants. The 2nd, we arrived at Novochoperskaja [Novokhoperskaya], the proper boundary of Russia, on the river Choper [Khoper], which falls into the Don. This place is the Russian frontier towards the Don Cossacks. [1, 64]

3. THE COSSACKS OF THE DON

The 3rd, we travelled most part of the night on the banks of the Choper, where there are several mills for corn; the country is very thin of inhabitants, and those only on the western banks. . . . I found the people very clean, and well cloathed. The women are gay and comely. . . .

The Cossacks are a species of Tartars, their name signifies freebooters, but in these parts they are civilized, and faithful to the Russian government, which, by an excellent policy, is indulgent to them. Thus they are ready when called on, to attend the Russian army, and bring with them usually each man two horses. Upon these occasions they are well cloathed, and accoutred at their own expense. They receive no pay, except in time of war, when they are actually employed, and then only six rubles a year, with provision and plunder; yet being exempt from taxes, they have no provocation to forsake their masters. They are a very gallant as well as sober people, and some of them are said to possess one thousand sheep, and three hundred cows.

We saw little more, for three days, than land and sky, except for some woods and mountains to the eastward, which gave pleasure in proportion to the absence of other objects. There are prodigious flights of blue pigeons, of which we killed as many as we could consume. The post huts on the Step could not always supply us with a sufficient number of horses, so that where any inhabitants could be found within six or eight miles from the road, we were more than once obliged to send out for them. Passing the Choper and the Don, we advanced, in five days and nights, near five hundred wersts . . . having met with very few inhabitants. At length we arrived at Grigoriskoi [Grigorovka]. . . . Here they take a great quantity of crawfish, especially in spring, at which time the flesh is most esteemed: when they are pounded and mixed with water, the eyes sink to the bottom. Quantities of these eyes are sent into Turkey, and other countries, being well known to be used in medicines. Their houses, or rather huts, are built of oak plank; but so little provident are they of timber, that the bench I sat upon was hewn with an ax, and near three inches thick. Fish and fowl of all kinds are in great plenty. [1, 64-65]

4. THE ABANDONED CANAL

The 9th . . . This morning we arrived under the lines which are thrown up from the Don to the Volga, for the distance of about fifty wersts. The ditch is near fifteen feet deep, but not made entirely square. There is a bank of earth near twenty feet high, with a strong timber rail towards the top. Sentry boxes are placed at certain distances, from which the guard can communicate an alarm to the chief garrison, Zaritzen, which terminates the line on the western banks of the Volga. . . . On this spot also Peter the Great intended to join the Don and the Volga, and the canal was actually begun for that purpose. By this means a communication would have been opened with Turkey, and the Czar might have attacked that empire with ships built on the Volga, where the materials are in great abundance: but this undertaking proved very difficult from the hardness of the soil. Besides as it was found practicable to build ships on the Don, this and other weighty reasons prevented the execution of the design. . . . The sun was yet warm and the weather delightful. . . . On the plains in this neighbourhood, they feed dromedaries, which are not unlike camels. [1, 65]

5. THE TARTARS AT TSARITSYN

Zaritzen is situated in the latitude of 47½, at the distance of one thousand and forty-two wersts from Mosco, on a high bank of the Volga, of which it commands a delightful prospect. The buildings are mean, nor are there many inhabitants: the place is defended by a deep ditch, a rampart garnished with artillery, and a garrison of three thousand men.

In a deep valley, under the south side of this place, is an encampment of Khalmuck Tartars, who are in friendship with the Russians so long as they awe them by their power; for these barbarians do not keep their faith more inviolably than some politer nations. . . . The many violences committed by these barbarians, at length induced the Russian government to compel them to take up their habitations on the banks of the Volga, below Astrachan, where they have a less field for robbery and murder, though here also they transgress. . . .

Having letters of recommendation to Kalzoff, the commandant of Zaritzen, I was kindly received; but upon such occasions it is necessary to present some French brandy, sugar, or the like, as an earnest for protection. Colonel Beausobre and another Frenchman, who was an officer in the Russian service, made acquaintance with me, and were extremely polite and obliging. News was just then arrived, that the inspector of the customs, attended by four soldiers, in coming from Astrachan, had been murdered by the Khalmucks: these French officers however assured me I might go down the Volga without danger, alledging that the Tartars of every denomination were kept in subjection to the Russian government; and that the murder of the inspector and his men, was a consequence of their rashness in attempting to steal some of the Khalmucks children. . . . I was more amazed at such an enterprize, as children two or three years old, had been offered me by the Khalmucks for two rubles a head. [1, 67-68]

VII · LIFE ON THE VOLGA

1. THE RIVER CRAFT

I now employed myself in procuring a proper vessel to convey my caravan to Astrachan, and had the good fortune to find one which had just arrived with four hundred bags of flour. The best proof that she could bear a burthen, was that of seeing her loaded. This however gave me no great satisfaction, for I was extremely shocked to see on what slight embarkations my friends were obliged to trust their valuable effects, in the navigation of a river full of shelves and trees, which accidentally falling into the water, sink, and become as dangerous as rocks; an experience which we had that very summer made by a rich cargo of silk that was much damaged, and in imminent danger of being entirely lost. The reader will imagine that forty rubles (eight pounds) cannot purchase a good vessel; however this price procured the best I could find. Their decks are only loose pieces of the bark of trees; they have no knees, and but few beams: hardly any pitch or tar is used; in place of it are long slips of bark, which they nail over the gaping seams, to prevent the loose and bad corking from falling out. Instead of iron bolts, they have spikes of deal with round heads. The method of keeping them clear of water, is by a large scoop which is suspended by the beam over the well-way, and through a scuttle at a proper height they scoop out the water with great facility. Notwithstanding these vessels appeared as so many wrecks, the trade carried on by means of them is very considerable. The Armenians sometimes load goods on large barks, which are from two to three hundred tons, at the rate of fifty copeeks per bale. [1, 69]

2. THE WATER HIGHWAY

Though I have in several parts of this work made occasional mention of the Volga, yet a river of such consideration deserves a more particular attention. . . . This river . . . is reputed for extent and depth one of the noblest in the world . . . running, according to general computation, near four thousand five hundred wersts before it empties itself into the Caspian Sea. It takes in the river Twersa which comes from Twere; and the Moscwa from Mosco; the Occa from Kolumna; the Kama . . . the Samar [Samara] at Samara, [now called Kuibyshev] with a great number of other rivers. It is of the utmost utility to the greatest part of the vast empire of Russia, not only with regard to commerce, but as it has been the means of reducing the different tribes of Tartars who frequent its borders.

The immense quantities of water which this river receives from others, and from the many hilly countries from whence descend great torrents, particularly when the snow melts in the spring, are the cause of its swelling at different times and places. It begins usually to rise in march, and increases in april and may, continuing above its usual mark, till the end of june; and then it decreases very fast. There is often another rise in september, by autumnal rains; but this is not so constant, nor near so considerable. It varies in different places; at Astrachan it is only seven or eight feet. . . . About Zaritzen, which is above four hundred wersts higher, I saw a mark at about twenty feet . . . and at Casan [Kazan], which is twelve hundred and fifty wersts yet higher, the rise is said to be much greater. As there are so many different climates in the course of this river, the ice breaks up at different times; as at Astrachan about the end of february, and at Casan generally a month later. Here the banks alter almost every year, partly by the force of the current, and partly by the sands which are blown into the river from the adjacent country. The danger arising from these shifting banks is not very great; but they create delays. The common course of the stream can hardly be reckoned above a mile an hour, but in the time of the floods it is generally three miles.

The navigation is very difficult for vessels drawing above five feet water, except in the flood times, when the largest flat-bottomed vessels find sufficient water. I have seen a vessel afloat in the month of october, said to have six hundred tuns of salt and fish aboard: and in some seasons they have barks of greater burthen. The trade from many parts is great and extensive, but from no place more considerable than from Yarislaw [Yaroslavl] and Casan. [1, 93-94]

3. THE SKILL OF THE BOATMEN

The sailors who navigate this river, are remarkable for their dexterity in warping. They have three boats to carry out the warps, which they take in forward; and at the same time they coil the warp from the stern into the boat, while the other two boats are ahead laying fresh warps; for as soon as they have run out one, the end of the other is ready. These vessels sometimes carry from one hundred and fifty to two hundred men, and as their bigness prevents their sailing, except the wind be very fair, they warp thirty English miles in a day against the stream, which, as we have already observed, is sometimes very rapid. [1, 94]

4. THE COMMERCE IN CAVIAR

Besides the vast abundance of fish taken in this river, and sent either salted or frozen to distant parts of the Russian empire, there is considerable commerce carried on in Caviare. The method of preparing this commodity is to take away the stringy part; then to mix it with salt well cleaned and made into brine; and when it is drained from the oily parts and pressed, it becomes of such a consistency as to keep two or three years. The grain is of a darkish grey colour, almost as big as pepper corn, and cuts transparent. In the winter it is sent fresh to all parts of the empire, and is much esteemed by the natives as well as by foreigners, being well known to partake of the nature of oysters. There is also a large quantity made for exportation, which is consumed in Italy and by the christians in the Levant. The Armenians have the skill of preparing it best, and usually make above six thousand poods (about a hundred tuns) every year. In 1749, they brought twenty thousand poods to market. [1, 94]

5. ROBBERS AND PIRATES

It was here [at Tsaritsyn] I had first an opportunity of hearing the history of the Volga and Caspian pirates, particularly of those who commit murders and robberies on this great river. According to the fundamental law of the government in Russia, the people are in a state of vassalage, and one man can call another his property by virtue of his purchase, or by a right of inheritance. According to this law, no vassal can leave the lands of his lord without permission given, and signified by a passport, the term of which seldom extends above a year or two. When the time is expired, the vassal must return home, no matter how far off, or how great his poverty, to renew his passport and receive his lord's commands, unless by any particular indulgence he can obtain a renewal of it by writing to his friends. These passports are generally registered in the towns or villages where the vassal resides, and great care is taken by the police to see this executed: by this means, and likewise, by making it necessary to take passports before they quit the place, the police knows the condition and number of the inhabitants. A register is made also of foreigners residing in every place in the empire, who are obliged to make a report of themselves and their domestics. Hence it comes that there is no country in the world of such vast extent, where thieves and murderers can be more easily discovered, and where they are more frequently apprehended.

Among vast numbers of common people, it is not to be imagined, but by accident or wilful neglect, some of them will violate the law with regard to these passports. Being thus rendered obnoxious to punishment, the worst of them grow desperate; and though the numbers of such persons were much greater in less civilized times than at present, yet many, to this day, turn robbers by land and water, chusing the great rivers near vast tracts of uninhabited countries, where upon occasion they can the more easily escape. The severities of the masters of fisheries . . . also tempt their vassals to turn pirates: whenever they are warmly pursued, or distressed for support, they run their vessels ashore, turn mahommedans, and put themselves under the protection of the Persians. These robbers often go in gangs of thirty, forty, and sometimes eighty persons, in rowboats which carry from twenty to thirty hands: they equip themselves with fire arms, and their general practice is to board immediately; but where a fierce resistance is apprehended, they seldom attack.

The Armenian merchants . . . when the scene of trade was changed from Archangel to St. Petersburg, they went from thence either to Twere or Saratoff, [Saratov] according to the season of the year, and there embarked on the Volga, this being a more easy and cheap conveyance; but the frequency of robberies at length determined them to convey their caravans to Zaritzen, as making so much the shorter tract down the Volga. Few of the Russian merchants transport any cargo of value down this river without a convoy. These robbers appear mostly in the spring, when the banks of the Volga being overflowed, they have a greater field, and can the more easily escape a pursuit. . . .

The Armenians are generally intrepid, and fight bravely in defense of their property, but the bourlacks [Burlaks] (watermen) who navigate the Volga are so extremely intimidated by these robbers, that as soon as they appear, they generally behave like men struck with a panic, and even ascribe to them irresistible power, derived from an infernal spirit. Formerly their custom in these cases was to fall on their faces, as soon as required by the robbers, and suffer them to plunder at pleasure, not daring to look up, lest it should cost them their lives. The master of the vessel, or the merchant, being thus at their mercy, is happy if he escapes with his life; for these villains have seldom any sentiments of humanity to a man of a superior rank; and if he attempts to defend himself in hopes of bringing his people to the charge, he may be sure, if conquered, of being barbarously murdered. . . .

As their cruelties are very great, so is the punishment inflicted on them when they are taken. A float is built, in size according to the number of the delinquents, and a gallows erected on it, to contain a sufficient number of iron hooks, on which they are hung alive by the ribs. The float is launched into the stream, with labels over their heads signifying their crimes; and orders are given to the inhabitants of all towns and villages on the borders of the river, upon pain of death, not only to afford no relief to any of these wretches, but to push off the float, should it land near them. . . . These malefactors sometimes hang thus three, four, and some five days alive. The pain generally produces a raving fever, in which they utter the most horrid imprecations, and implore the relief of water, or other small liquors. [1, 69-71]

VIII · ASTRAKHAN

1. THE VOYAGE FROM TSARITSYN

AFTER giving the necessary instructions with regard to the convoy of my caravan, we prepared for our own voyage down the Volga: for this purpose we bought two boats, to be navigated each by five Bourlacks and my own attendants, with the addition of six soldiers as a convoy. . . .

The wind being at north east, we put off the shore. The stern part of my boat was covered with matts, so that I could sleep in it protected from the weather, which now began to be very cold. I took a part of the soldiers with me, that if by any accident our convoy should be separated from us, we might have some assistance. . . . The 15th, I saw several large water birds, much bigger than swans, which they resemble in their feet and beaks; the Russians call them Dika Baba [dikaia baba, a pelican] (signifies wild old women). They have a very large craw, where they receive a great quantity of food, even a whole fish of a considerable size. They fly, as I saw afterwards on the Caspian, very near to each other, in the form of a semicircle, not far above the water; and having driven the fish together in a body into the shallows, they dart down upon them; this is their only food. . . .

In the spring, the high waters of the Volga not only undermine its banks, but sweep away large trees, so that some creeks of the river had hardly any passage left. When they are open, it is more agreeable to pass through the small branches, than the great channel. As we had hitherto a contrary wind, by the 16th, we advanced no farther than fifty wersts. . . . In many places are high banks, in others it is a flat shore, the breadth varying from a mile to a quarter. Here they had a variety of wild asparagus and many eagles.

The 18th, though we were obliged to lay-by in the night, we advanced ninety wersts, but it was not without danger of being drowned; for our boat had no keel, nor any running tackle, and our watermen were extremely unskilful, insomuch that not being able to let the sail fly, it was a singular providence that a gust of wind had not set us swimming. As we proceeded further, several wrecks appeared on the banks of the river. Great flights of geese and swans were now on the wing, retiring from the approaching severities of this climate, to the warmer regions of Persia. . . .

The 19th, we advanced near ninety wersts. . . . From Zaritzen to Astrakhan, where I arrived this day, very little wood appears on the banks of the Volga. In some parts of the western side, the country is hilly but the soil in several places is rich. . . . [1, 69-73]

2. AN ASIATIC CITY

This city is the metropolis of a kingdom of the same name, situated within the limits of Asia in an island . . . sixty English miles from the Caspian Sea. . . . It was for many ages subject to the Tartars, from whom it was taken by Ivan Wassilowitch, Czar of Muscovy,[45] in 1554; taken by them again in 1668; and again retaken by the Russians. . . .

---

[45] Ivan IV, called "the Terrible" (1530-1584).

It contains about seventy thousand inhabitants, among whom are many Armenians and Tartars of various denominations, with a few Persians and Indians. The manners and customs of all these different people exhibit an epitome of Asia. The city is about two and a half miles in circumference, but including the suburbs, near five miles. It is surrounded by a brick wall in a ruinous condition, being about two hundred years old. . . .

The houses are of wood, and most of them very mean; the higher parts of the city command a prospect of the Volga, which spreads itself here near three miles, giving pleasure and convenience to the inhabitants. In the summer the people are generally sickly, which is owing to the marshy lands near it. The earth being impregnated with salt, which appears on the surface, is extremely fertile, bearing fruit in abundance, the immoderate use of which creates many distempers among the common people. The melting of the snow which creates floods in the spring and the rising of the water in autumn, are also observed to affect the air, and produce sicknesses. [1, 82]

3. GARDENS AND VINEYARDS

This city is surrounded by gardens and vineyards, which lie about two miles from it. These produce almost every kind of garden-stuff known in England, except potatoes, collyflowers and artichoaks; and their orchards furnish them with plenty of apples, pears, cherries, etc. Olearius commends the fruits of Astrachan, but I met with none extraordinary, except the water-melons. . . . The court finds the grapes delicious enough to bear the great expense of land carriage. . . . The wine of Astrachan is also very indifferent. As their summers are generally dry, they are obliged to water their gardens; this is done by large wheels, some of which are moved by horses, others by the wind. These wheels are of a sufficient height to throw the water into the highest part of the garden, from whence it runs in trenches to the root of every tree and plant. The gardens and vineyards are generally watered in this manner, from the middle of may to the middle of september. [1, 82-83]

4. FLIGHTS OF LOCUSTS

Captain Woodroofe, who was for some time at Astrachan, assured me, that from the latter end of july to the beginning of october, the country about that city is frequently infested with locusts, which fly in such prodigious numbers as to darken the air, and appear at a distance like a heavy cloud. . . . Whenever they fall, they eat up everything that is green. In this season, therefore, all the gardeners look out for them, and upon their first appearance endeavour to keep them off, by making as much smoak and as great noise as possible; but, in spite of all their art, these destructive insects, after flying as long as they are able, sometimes fall in their gardens, on the tops of houses, and even into fires. . . .

Woodroofe mentions in his journal, that once in particular, as he was sailing up the Volga to Astrachan, he observed a prodigious cloud of them coming from the west north west. . . . When the locusts falling down, the water was covered with such prodigious swarms of them, that in some places they greatly obstructed the motion of the boat for ten or twelve fathoms together. He says also, that they live for some time under water; for as they mounted on each other's backs, they formed a cluster near three feet diameter, which rolled along by the force of the wind and the rapidity of the current. In this manner they were driven ashore: their wings being dried, they got upon the pasture, and very few were drowned. They lay so thick upon the plain for three days, to the extent of as many miles, that it was impossible to walk without treading on them. When they began to fly, they disappeared in less than half an hour, leaving the plain without a blade of grass. [1, 83-84]

5. TRADE, RESOURCES, AND CROWN MONOPOLIES

The commerce of Astrachan is very considerable, though much diminished by the troubles in Persia, and the frequent revolts and insolent behavior of the Tartars. . . . The foreign trade of the Russians consists in red leather, linnens, woollen cloths, and European manufactures, which they export to Persia, the greatest part for the account of the Armenians. In return they import several manufactures of Persia . . . as silk sashes intermixed with gold, for the consumption of the Polanders; wrought silks and stuffs mixed with cotton; rice, cotton, a small quantity of drugs, and especially raw silk. They also bring rhubarb, but as the government has engrossed this article, private persons are forbid to deal in it, under penalty of death.

About ten miles below the city [Astrakhan] is a small island . . . remarkable for its large storehouses of salt, which is made about twelve miles to the eastward of it, and being brought thither in boats, is conveyed in large flat-bottomed vessels up the Volga. With this all the country is supplied, as far as Mosco and Twere. They dig annually some millions of poods, the exclusive property of which is claimed by the crown, and brings in a considerable revenue; (the revenue of Astrachan is reckoned one hundred and forty to one hundred and sixty thousand rubles, or thirty-three thousand five hundred pounds, of which the greatest part arises from salt and fish,) for the common food of the soldiery, and for the bulk of the people, is bread and salt. In this place also are large fisheries, to which the neighbourhood of the salt works is of great advantage. These extend even to the sea, reaching south eastward as far as Yaeik [Yaik, now called Ural River], and also a hundred miles above Zaritzen. From these fisheries all the country is supplied as far as St. Petersburg: the vessels are loaded with salt fish, and sent away in the spring; but as fresh fish keeps good so long as it is frozen, the winter is no sooner set in, than it is transported by land as far as Mosco and St. Petersburg. The principal sorts are sturgeon, starlett, beluga, and affotra.

The first establisher of these fisheries was Tikon Demedoff,[46] a carrier, who settled there about fifty years ago: his whole fortune then consisted in two horses, but through his industry and abilities, he became the greatest merchant in that country. The crown, which before this time was a stranger to those advantages, has of late years, besides the salt, engrossed some of the fisheries also. [1, 83-84]

IX · THE END OF THE CASPIAN AFFAIR

1. THE FIRST RECEPTION AT ASTRAKHAN: COMPLICATIONS

I was kindly received in Astrachan by Mr. George Thomson agent to the British merchants trading to Persia; and also by the governor, general Wassilie Nikietish Tattischeff,[47] to whom I carried a valuable present on account of the merchants. . . . This old man had been a page to Peter the Great, and having long commanded in those parts, was greatly instrumental in reducing the Tartars: but his genius turned most to literature and commerce; nor was he at all deficient in the arts

[46] Possibly a member of the famous Russian family descended from Nikita Demidov (1665-1720), who began as an ironworker and armorer, but who later became a favorite of Peter the Great.

[47] Vasili Nikitich Tatishchev (1686-1750). A statesman and historian, he had been active in the naïve attempts at constitutional reform in the revolution which placed the Empress Anne upon the throne, and he continued in the administration until his disgrace in 1745. The history referred to is chiefly of interest as an example of the progress of that branch of learning in eighteenth century Russia, but, although now outmoded, it retains some value, because much of the material upon which it was based has since been lost.

of gain. . . . He mentioned . . . that he had been about four and twenty years writing the history of Russia. Upon his recall from Astrachan two years afterwards, he sent me part of that history in manuscript, requesting me to procure a translation; but this by no means suited my convenience. . . .

This old man was remarkable for his socratical look, his emancipated body, which he preserved many years by great temperance, and for keeping his mind continually employed. When he was not writing, reading, or discoursing about business, he played at dice one hand against the other. . . .

I was several times with the governor, whose discourse ran continually on Elton; the sum of it was, "that Nadir Shah, having conceived an high opinion of this gentleman's capacity, had made him presents, and either engaged him for a salary to build ships for him, or required his assistance to superintend such an undertaking . . . as such enterprizes were no way relative to affairs of commerce, they could not but alarm the Russian Court." . . . I confess there was cause of jealousy. . . . Elton had brought us into such circumstances, that it was hardly possible to avoid offending the Empress or the Shah, if not both. I took occasion to remind the governor that . . . in any case it ought not to affect me, who was now charged to take care of the commercial interest, and of that only. Upon this he desired me to deliver a memorial to the same effect, by way of a petition to the chancery.

It was not difficult to foresee the consequences of acquiescing to such an extraordinary demand; though, of the two evils, I thought it the greatest to refuse. . . . Accordingly I delivered the following petition into her imperial majesty's chancery:

The petition of Jonas Hanway, British merchant, sheweth that whereas reports have been spread, that one of the British subjects residing in Reshd, [Resht] has been concerned in affairs ungrateful to the court of Russia; your petitioner is now going into Ghilan [Gilan] to know the truth, and, if necessary, to use his endeavours to dissuade any such subject there engaged in trade, from voluntarily meddling with any other business; and to prevent, as much as possible, the British ships on the Caspian from being employed in any manner not consistent with the treaty of commerce;[48] so that no just

[48] Here, Hanway's account appended the following note: "It must be observed, however, that the treaty made no provision for these ships." This was true, as the Russian government had granted permission for their construction as an additional privilege, only several years after the conclusion of the treaty. Because, rather than in spite of this fact, the imputation that this petition imposed terms not legally binding was insolently self-righteous. Moreover, the Russian consul in Persia reported, and Hanway's experience later confirmed, that one of these, the *Empress of Russia*, the very ship in which Hanway sailed to Persia, had been employed in the

cause may be given to create the least obstruction of the British trade thro' the empire of Russia. And as the season is very far advanced, your petitioner desires immediate despatch may be given to the British ships as soon as they shall arrive, etc. [1, 78-81]

2. THE EMBARKATION FOR PERSIA: SUCCESS

I had spent fifteen days here, in expectation of the arrival of captain Woodroofe[49] from Ghilan, and, observing that the season was far advanced, I determined, so soon as my caravan should come down the Volga, to embark in a Russian vessel; but the 4th of November I received the joyful news of Woodroofe's arrival at Yerkie (the mouth of the Volga) with a hundred bales of raw silk. . . . [1, 86]

We left Astrachan under convoy of the governor's barge with twelve grenadiers. . . . At night we slept within pistol-shot of a Khalmuck settlement. . . . As we advanced within thirty wersts of the mouth of the Volga, we decried a great number of small islands; the whole scene appearing wild and inhospitable. . . .

Being happily arrived at Yerkie, we embarked in the British ship *Empress of Russia*, much delighted to find ourselves in a vessel of good oak, regularly built, well fitted, and probably the only complete ship which till that time had appeared on the Caspian. It was no less a pleasure to see the English flag hoisted, and some satisfaction to receive those common marks of esteem which masters of ships usually pay their merchants when they have any guns. [1, 92-93]

3. THE SECOND RECEPTION OF ASTRAKHAN: FAILURE[50]

The 29th of september, after a passage of thirteen days, we came to anchor at Yerkie: here we were visited by the commander of the guard-ship, who informed us, that if we had any other goods on board but such as were of the produce of Ghilan, and did not declare them, the law made it death to the offender, besides burning the ship and cargo. . . . The Russian consul had represented to the governor of Astrachan,

---

service of Nadir Shah in a punitive expedition upon the Caspian coast, inimical to Russian designs in that area. For Hanway, therefore, to term the request for this petition an "extraordinary demand" is a sterling example of sublime self-assurance.

[49] Captain Thomas Woodroofe, the British commander of the *Empress of Russia*, which he and Elton had built at Kazan with the permission of the Russian government in the spring of 1741.

[50] Hanway's Persian adventures have already been sketched for the reader. After nearly a year's absence and many misfortunes, he had been able to recover eighty-five per cent of the value of his woolens, and, having invested this amount in a cargo of raw silk, he set sail with Woodroofe on September 16, 1744, on the return journey to St. Petersburg.

that there was a plague at Cashan, [Kashan] from whence manufactured Persian goods were wont to be brought into Russia. The
commander having required us to come on shore, we went to a small
uninhabited island, on the east side of the entrance of the Volga. A
fire being made, the surgeon and his attendants took the windward of
us, and demanded to see our breasts . . . and after he was satisfied that
we had no infection, our letters were delivered to him, being first
dipped in vinegar, and dried in the smoak. . . . After we had waited
here with impatience till the 11th of october, in very cold and disagreeable weather, without any supplies of fresh provision; a signal was at
length made by the guard-ship, for us to come on board. Here we had
the mortification to learn, that we were ordered to perform a quarantain of six weeks on an uninhabited island, a little to the eastward. . . .
At length, on the 16th, I received letters from the English agent in
Astrachan, acquainting me that captain Woodroofe's ship and crew
were ordered to perform a quarantain of twelve weeks instead of six.
. . . The whole secret of the affair was, that her imperial majesty's
ministers finding that Mr. Elton was deeply engaged in projects, which
they considered as detrimental to the Russian empire, had given orders
to the governor of Astrachan, not only to prevent any goods going to
the consignment of Mr. Elton; which was naturally considered as a
prelude to the total prohibition of the trade; but also to detain the two
British ships as soon as they should arrive. . . .

The governor of Astrachan, apprehending that I might have something to communicate to him, permitted me to come to the city, on
condition of remaining a week longer in quarantain . . . and without
bringing with me the least part of my cloathes or baggage. . . .

My quarantain being expired, on the 26th the governor of Astrachan
sent me his barge . . . with some of his own cloathe, for I was required
to strip myself entirely naked in the open air; and pass through the
unpleasant ceremony of having a large pail of warm water thrown
upon me. Having gone through this discipline, I embarked. . . .

The 27th, we arrived safe in Astrachan. . . . The next day I waited on
the governor, whose behaviour was now very different from what it
had been twelve months before. . . . I took notice to him, that I found
myself in some disgrace in Russia, on account of my supposed connexion with Elton; though, in reality, we were entirely separated, his
pursuits and mine being of a very different nature. It was plain from
his discourse, that he thought this separation was political only. . . .
I did not appear before him with an empty hand, yet his behaviour was

hardly within the limits of civility. The reproach which I presume he was under for indulging us, had now changed his conduct in such a manner, as if it had been criminal to appear an advocate for our trade. . . .

I passed my hours very disagreeably, being for the second time since I left St. Petersburg, separated from all my cloathes, servants, and conveniences of life, and detained in a civil quarantain; for I was not permitted to depart for St. Petersburg, till the six weeks were expired. . . . [1, 279-281]

4. THE BLESSINGS OF PROVIDENCE: COMPENSATION

The 22nd of november, I obtained permission to depart for St. Petersburg. The Volga was covered with floating ice, insomuch that no boatman would undertake to carry me to Zaritzen; therefore I resolved to travel by land on the western banks of that river. As I had with me but two servants, I thought it necessary to join a caravan, the Khalmucks having lately committed several murders on that road. . . .

The 23d, we lost our way for some hours, the desert being full of hills, and in many places very sandy. . . . On the 28th, the weather grew more severe, and the snow made wheel carriages very laborious. . . . The Volga was now full of floating ice. . . .

On the 1st of december, our company divided, upon which occasion I preferred the party that intended to make the most despatch; this day we travelled seventy wersts . . . and the day following we arrived at Zaritzen.

As the snow now rendered the roads impracticable for wheel carriages, I set my waggon on a sledge. . . . On the 6th, I took my leave of my Russian friends, and departed from Zaritzen attended by two servants. . . . The 7th, the cold weather increased so much, that the frost seized very strong wine which was under my feather-bed. . . . In four days more we had travelled only two hundred and twenty wersts . . . and not without losing our way several times, the snow being yet untrodden. It often happens, particularly on the Yaeik Step, that passengers who do not provide a compass, lose their way and perish. . . .

The 12th, we reached Michaelove [Michailovsk] . . . the grand mart of the Cossack towns. They hold their fair in january, when the merchants of Casan bring woollen and other manufactures, for which the Cossacks exchange the furs of foxes taken near the Don. . . .

The 18th, we advanced forty wersts, passing through many villages surrounded with arable lands, and well watered. The woods which the eye every way meets at certain distances, contribute much to beautify the prospect; but this was no season for rural pleasures. The 20th, these two days we travelled about one hundred and fifty wersts. Upon the road we had frequent opportunities of observing in what manner the peasants render their houses habitable in cold weather. As few of them have any chimneys, the smoak of their stoves is carried out through the windows; but this method leaves so thick a cloud, that 'tis impossible to breathe above two or three feet from the floor, till the wood is burnt to ashes. . . . This being the season that the peasants send their tributes to their lords, the roads were crowded with carts loaded with provisions of every kind.

The 22d, we arrived in Mosco. . . . Here I received letters acquainting me with the death of a relation, by which I reaped certain pecuniary advantages, much exceeding any I could expect from my engagement in the Caspian affair: providence was thus indulgent to me, as if it meant to reward me for the sincerity of my endeavours. . . .

Early on the 1st of january 1745, I arrived in St. Petersburg, having performed the journey from Mosco in about three days and a half. I had been absent a year and sixteen weeks, in which time I had travelled about four thousand English miles by land, through a variety of adventures and accidents, not indeed the most perilous, yet such as loudly called for a grateful acknowledgment of the goodness of providence. [1, 281-287]

X · CREDO

1. FOLLOWERS OF AN HONORABLE CALLING

THOUGH it is common for mankind to look on the commercial intercourse of the world, in no other light than as an employment calculated for the support of life, or a means of amassing wealth; yet if we extend our thoughts a little farther, and take in the numerous connections and dependencies arising from that intercourse, either at home or abroad, we may easily discover that it deserves a high degree of respect, since it tends to promote all the pleasures of humanity; and probably from hence it was, that merchants were called the Honorable of the Earth, when nations were much more ignorant of each other than they are at present. . . .

The merchant whose mind is strong enough to pursue gain without indulging any anxious fears, and without forgetting the more essential duties of life, is in a happy employment, was it only for this reason, that there are but few callings so free and independent. . . . [1, 366]

2. TRAVELERS TO ANOTHER WORLD

Thanks to the goodness of providence, I am now returned into this Happy Island; happy, in spite of all its blemishes, compared with any country that I have yet been acquainted with. Perfect happiness most certainly is not the lot of mortals on this side of the grave . . . there is yet a better country, whither we are travelling, where only the mind can possess an entire satisfaction. . . . Though we grasp the fleeting moments, it is but as to-morrow when a curtain will be drawn over all the glories, as well as the miseries of this world. In the meanwhile, whether we go abroad, or remain at home; enjoy a profusion, or a mediocrity of the gifts of providence, we are travelling to another country. Our noblest science, our highest accomplishment, our supreme felicity, is the knowledge and observance of that compass, whose needle points to our proper home; to those regions, where millions of blessed spirits inhabit; where the eye will be satisfied with seeing, the understanding with knowledge, and the heart with delights, of which this world can give but faint ideas. . . . [11, 64-65]

3. NATIVES OF AN EARTHLY PARADISE

Look round, and survey the noble structures, and the profusion of their useful, their magnificent, their superb appendages, in this great metropolis. Consider the flourishing state of every branch of learning, art, and science. Let us send our thoughts abroad to the numerous regions of the earth, to which our commerce is extended, and from whence such sources of wealth flow in upon us. Let us consider what an increase of riches our American colonies produce, which is so much the more valuable, as it is more independent of the politics of other nations. But, above all, let us contemplate the beauteous face of this island, and the various delights it affords: the noble fabrics, with the several proud monuments of antiquity, in almost every part of England: gardens unequalled by any in the world; mines rich in fuel and useful metals; hills and vallies, rivers and seas, all conspiring to render us rich and happy. The Almighty seems to have made choice of this island as the great granary of Europe and America. He has enabled us also to befriend mankind, in cloathing them in every quarter of the globe. Our wool is computed to near twelve millions when manufactured; this is four times the revenues of one of the greatest empires in the world [Russia] and which now seems to hold the balance of European power.

But when we consider the admirable laws to which we are subject; the good government we are under; and the pure religion we profess, can we forbear exulting in the thought of being born members of such a community; or sending up our prayers in incense of gratitude, to beg that generations yet unborn may enjoy all these good things? [ii, 76-77]

CHAPTER THREE
William Richardson

William Richardson:

HUMANIST SCHOLAR OF SLAVERY

(1768-1772)

WILLIAM RICHARDSON's *Anecdotes of the Russian Empire* revealed impressions of Russia widely divergent from those of his predecessors, Perry and Hanway, and these differences derived not only from the circumstances of his visit, but from the character and background of the man. He was born at Aberfoyle, Scotland, on October 1, 1743,[1] the son of the minister of the little parish. Unlike Perry and Hanway, early apprenticed to the naval and merchant services, respectively, he received an excellent formal education. After a grounding in Latin and Greek in the parish school, he was sent, when only fourteen years of age, to the University of Glasgow. There he showed great aptitude in his studies of language and philosophy and attracted additional attention for his facility at versification, but when he had completed the requirements for the degree of Master of Arts, he undertook the study of theology. Left to his own devices, he would no doubt have taken the cloth and returned, like his father, to spend the rest of his days in quiet dignity as minister of one of the little highland theocracies, but in 1766, after he had completed three sessions, he was granted the favor of an appointment as tutor to the two sons of Charles, Lord Cathcart.

Two uneventful years with his charges at Eton were followed by the single adventure of his scholarly career, for when Lord Cathcart received an appointment as Ambassador Extraordinary to the Court of Catherine II, the young Scot accompanied the Cathcart family to St. Petersburg in the dual capacity of tutor and secretary to His Lordship. After four years in the Russian capital, he again returned to the University of Glasgow in the company of his remaining pupil, William Shaw, later Lord Cathcart, and in the following year, at the instance of the father, succeeded his former teacher in the Chair of Humanity, which he occupied until his death forty-one years later. During this period he wrote and published at intervals a variety of works in addi-

[1] Robert Chambers, *A Biographical Dictionary of Eminent Scotsmen*, Glasgow, 1855, IV, 176.

tion to the *Anecdotes*, including poems, critical essays, particularly on Shakespeare, dramas, periodical contributions, and even a brief biography. In short, with the exception of the Russian episode, an experience almost entirely confined to St. Petersburg and sheltered, as it were, from the real impact of Russian life by diplomatic immunity, his was the career of a man who spent over half a century in the slow moving current of university life.

It is not surprising, in view of the literary education and taste of its author, that the opening pages of the *Anecdotes*, drafted in their final form in 1783, should promise both light and amusing reading. The epistolary style lends intimacy. The language is vivid, and the composition, clear. Each letter represents an integrated unit, and if the reader misses the broad vistas found in the travels of Perry and Hanway, he is spared their rambling digressions and is compensated by glimpses into the life of a glittering court which had not existed in their time. The stylistic deficiencies are rare, as when the author becomes self-consciously literary or yields to that overly sentimental strain in eighteenth-century literature epitomized in the novels of another Richardson. Thus, one letter is devoted to a labored point by point comparison of a Russian winter with a translation of the third book of Vergil's *Georgics*. Another, describing a public appearance by the young Grand Duke Paul, includes the remarks: "I was told that the Empress was present among the ladies; but . . . she did not chuse upon that occasion to be acknowledged as Empress. The mother wished to observe her son. It was the first time he had spoken in public; and the mother's heart must have thrilled with pleasure. I almost wept for joy."[2] In view of the actual relations between Catherine and Paul, the young Scot might have spared himself this emotional disturbance.

Although individually the letters have unity of composition, collectively they cover a wide range of subjects, and some of the letters, as Richardson himself explained in the preface, "are scarcely any other wise related to his subject than that they were written during the time he remained in Russia."[3] Of this sort were several original poems, an account of the abdication of the King of Sardinia, a dissertation on the science of astronomy, and an "Account of a Circassian Princess, the Widow of Donduc Ambo, Chan of the Calmuck Tartars." This last, although it pertained to Russia, was simply a précis of several chap-

[2] William Richardson, *Anecdotes of the Russian Empire*, London, 1784, p. 40.
[3] *ibid.*, p. viii.

ters from the writings of an earlier traveler, John Cook,[4] and, therefore, might have been performed as easily by one who had never
visited Russia at all. These interesting irrelevancies are easily overlooked, however, and the total effect of the book is extraordinarily
pleasing. The appearance of St. Petersburg, the splendor of Catherine's
court, and the person and character of Catherine herself are delineated
in a lively and interesting style. Finally, although the reader is repeatedly reminded of Richardson's felicity of expression, it is soon apparent
that he was far more than a skillful raconteur.

The most interesting portion of Richardson's letters is devoted to the
interpretation and formation of the Russian national character in its
broadest sense, and the quotations below have been selected with this
in mind. Although the original sequence has been somewhat altered,
it was felt that this was of relatively little importance in a collection of
separate "anecdotes," which, having no connecting narrative, were
related by thematic rather than chronological considerations. This in-
terpretive material, by its inclusive scope, is rendered capable of standing alone, nearly independent of all interpolation; but another order of
remarks, which are of secondary but very respectable significance,
would be nearly unintelligible without some understanding of the
background. These mainly regard Russian relations with the rest of
Europe. These relations, commercial, cultural, and political, had been
vastly accelerated since the opening of the century and Richardson's
position in St. Petersburg, Russia's "window to the west," as secretary
to a favored ambassador, gave him great opportunities to make observations on all three.

It is significant of Richardson's mentality that the commercial position of Russia held little interest for him. He referred to it directly only
once in a letter covering but three pages of a four hundred and seventy-
eight page volume. To be sure, these few lines give a compelling idea
of Russia's economic progress, but they give no conception that, since
1750 (the date of Hanway's departure) Russian world trade had doubled, that her trade with England had kept pace, and that the adverse
balance to England, which had tripled in the same period, now
amounted to nearly a million pounds annually.[5] The table of goods
exported from St. Petersburg in the year 1769, which he included in
the letter, he seems to have copied from the files of Lord Cathcart without troubling himself further about it, even to the extent of translating

---

[4] John Cook, *Voyages and Travels through the Russian Empire*, 2 vols., Edinburgh, 1770.
[5] J. J. Oddy, *European Commerce*, Philadelphia, 1807, I, 205.

the value of rubles into pounds. Finally, he never mentioned that remarkable renewal of the Anglo-Russian trade treaty which Sir George Macartney had been at such pains to secure only four years before. This peremptory treatment of a subject which was the absorbing preoccupation of Hanway and, to a lesser extent, of all British travelers, suggests that Richardson included the letter at all only as a concession to the general mercantile interest of the British reading public.

Cultural, as well as commercial, ties with the west had been greatly strengthened since the opening of the century. This had been due in great part to a shift in the political and economic balance of the old Muscovite society. In Peter's time, the tsarism had asserted its despotic control to force the nobility into state service, and Russia had imported not the refinement but the techniques and scientific knowledge of western civilization. Since his death, the strong corporate aristocracy which he had helped to create had forced concession after concession from a series of weak and dependent sovereigns, until Peter III had, in 1762, released it from all obligation to state service. Secure in its political immunities and economic privileges, this idle and irresponsible class now sought to beguile its leisure hours with the literature, fashions, and amusements of western Europe.[6] Operas, plays, balls, masquerades, and other court festivities, all furnished entertainment to the young tutor of Lord Cathcart's household. Richardson reported on a library of 30,000 volumes which, although kept in "bad order" and not very valuable, included a considerable "collection . . . of Russ translations of French, English, and German authors."[7] Many Russians, however, did not require the use of translations. One of Richardson's letters presented a copy of an exchange of correspondence in French between Count Orlov[8] and Jean Jacques Rousseau, in which the former, in the very best taste, offered the philosopher one of his country estates for his private, personal use. Elsewhere Richardson remarked that "among those in St. Petersburg who seek amusement in reading, I find that German literature is much in fashion."[9] He himself fell in with this vogue, and the *Anecdotes* contained the translation of the

[6] V. O. Kliuchevsky, *A History of Russia*, New York, 1931, v, 91-110.

[7] Richardson, *op. cit.*, p. 132.

[8] Count Aleksei Grigorievich Orlov (1737-1808), one of the famous Orlov brothers, who played an important role in the palace revolution placing Catherine upon the throne in 1762. He was alleged the murderer of Peter III, but later he distinguished himself as the commander of the naval expedition against the Turks in the Mediterranean (1770), and he held a lesser military post in the campaigns against Napoleon (1806-1807).

[9] Richardson, *op. cit.*, p. 97.

works of several German authors, including Lessing and Gellert, and the composition of original fables in the manner of the latter. It must have been gratifying for the young Briton to report the warm reception of a group of English players by an audience including not only English merchants, but "Russians and Germans as well" and, on one occasion, the Empress, herself.[10] In general, however, Richardson's visit antedated the English vogue which swept over Russia later in the century, and this was his only report of British influence in the mania for things foreign which gripped Russian society under Catherine.[11]

It was a source of irritation to many British travelers that one of the most prominent characteristics of the Europeanization of the Russian nobility was its slavish imitation of the manners and fashions of France. To be sure, all Europe paid tribute to the superior genius of French wit and polish, but the Muscovite aristocracy committed the most inane excesses in an admiration amounting to idolatry. Macartney commented at length on the "ridiculous imitation of foreign and particularly French manners. . . . In France it is the etiquette of fashion to begin the spring season at Easter and to mark it by dress; the imitative Russian does the same and flings off his winter garments whilst the earth is covered with snow and themselves shivering with cold. It is the peculiar privilege of the noblesse of Paris to have Swiss porters at the gates of their hotels. At Petersburg, a Russ gentleman of any fashion must have a Swiss also, or some tall fellow with a lace belt and hanger which, it seems, are indispensable accoutrements of a Parisian janitor."[12] "Crowds of French adventurers" exploited Muscovite gullibility as tutors, librarians, or mere sycophants in the houses of the nobility. Lord Cathcart suggested that Catherine had been prompted to the founding of her seminary for young ladies by her realization of "the almost impossibility of education, especially for females, and the number of strange low French people, who have made themselves necessary in all families."[13] There are stories of a Finn who, for years, taught his own language for French to eager Muscovite Francophiles, and a tutor who, in excusing his unfamiliarity with the moods of French verbs, explained that he had not been to Paris in some time and that "the modes change

[10] *ibid.*, p. 397.

[11] E. J. Simmons, *English Literature and Culture in Russia, 1553-1840*, Cambridge, Mass., 1935, pp. 73-102.

[12] George Macartney, "An Account of Russia in the year 1767," *Some Account of the Public Life of the Earl of Macartney*, edited by John Barrow, London, 1807, II, 36.

[13] Cathcart to Weymouth, September 26, 1768, *Sbornik*, XII, 371.

there very frequently."[14] In view of all the evidence, Richardson can scarcely be accused of intentional distortion in his delineation of the superficiality of Russian culture.

If the French continued to dominate in the salon, British influence was making itself felt in other aspects of Russian life. The role and prestige of English merchants in St. Petersburg has already been demonstrated. British political and legal institutions, thanks to Montesquieu and Blackstone, evoked the admiration of many of the most educated Russians, the foremost of whom was the Empress herself. British physicians were in demand throughout the entire period. Dr. Dimsdale[15] was summoned to St. Petersburg for the express purpose of inoculating both Catherine and the Grand Duke Paul against smallpox, and John Rogerson, physician to the imperial court, enjoyed a more than professional influence for many years of his residence.[16] Similarly, with the recognition of British maritime supremacy after the Seven Years' War, her seamen were much sought after in Catherine's revitalized fleet, and upon the reduction of the British naval arm

[14] Simmons, *op. cit.*, p. 74. Some thirty years later, when English fashions had somewhat displaced the French, Richardson might have found men of his own country quite as unscrupulous as the Gallic adventurers he despised. In 1804, John Carr remarked: "The education of the young nobility very frequently suffers from the free and unguarded manner in which they received every needy adventurer in the capacity of domestic tutor, principally if he be an Englishman: English taylors, and servants out of livery, and travelling valets, frequently become the preceptors and governors of children. A fellow of this description said one day: 'In summer I be clerk to a butcher in Cronstadt, and in winter I teaches English to the Russian nobility's children.'" John Carr, *Northern Summer*, Philadelphia, 1805, p. 195. Nevertheless, French fashions continued to exert a strong influence upon the Russian nobility, and in 1805 and 1806, Catherine Wilmot even considered them an important diplomatic weapon of Napoleonic policy: "The dress . . . is a bad imitation of the French, and they have universally adopted their language . . . and in the midst of this adoption of manners, customs and language there is something childishly silly in their reprobating Buonaparte when they can't eat their dinners without a French cook to dress it, when they can't educate their children without unprincipled adventurers from Paris to act as tutors and governesses, when every house of consequence . . . has an outcast Frenchman to instruct the heir apparent—in a word, when every association of fashion, luxury, elegance, and fascination is drawn from France . . . a dying squeak against Buonaparte redeems them in their own eyes from this political suicide. Such arrant folly!" "I am . . . convinced that thro' novels, hairdressers, tutoresses, abbés, cooks, and milliners Russia will be revolutionized by France before twenty years roll over their heads." The Marchioness of Londonderry and H. M. Hyde, ed., *The Russian Journals of Martha and Catherine Wilmot*, London, 1934, pp. 194, 216.

[15] E. A. B. Hodgetts, *The Life of Catherine the Great*, London, 1914, pp. 237-250.

[16] Archibald Steuart, *Scottish Influences in Russian History*, Glasgow, 1913, p. 121. Other Scottish physicians mentioned in this work range from Robert Erskine, who, entering the Russian service in 1704, organized and presided over the Chancery of Medicine, to James Wylie, who signed the death certificate of the murdered Emperor Paul in 1801. James Mounsey, the Rogerson already mentioned, Matthew Guthrie, and Sir Alexander Critten were personal physicians of the Empress Elizabeth, Catherine II, Paul I, and Alexander I, respectively, and other Scots who practiced medicine in Russia included John Cook, L. Coulterwood, Dr. Selkirk, Matthew Halliday, and Robert Simpson.

to its peacetime footing, many officers took service in the Russian ships and dockyards. Joseph Marshall, whose visit to Russia was contemporaneous with Richardson's remarked that: "In the docks, they have a great number of carpenters continually at work, among whom are many English, discharged by the government, on the conclusion of the peace in 1763. They meet with great encouragement here, and are much better employed, than if in the service of France or Spain."[17] In conjunction with this influx of British naval personnel, the diplomatic events of Cathcart's embassy witnessed perhaps the most curious episode of Anglo-Russian relations of the entire period and one upon which Richardson's position as Cathcart's secretary might have enabled him to throw considerable light.

For some years prior to Cathcart's arrival in 1768, British representatives had been negotiating, not only for a renewal of the commercial agreement of 1734, but for a defensive military alliance as well. The complementary economic interests of the two countries had been reconciled in the commercial treaty of 1766, but their political aims were far less compatible. On the one hand, the prize of British colonial possessions offered a continual incentive for aggression by the Bourbon powers, and the war thus threatened would inevitably involve a Russia allied to Britain in a continental conflict in which she could hope to gain little. On the other, England, entirely preoccupied with colonial, commercial, and maritime affairs, felt no inclination to contract for the defense of Russia from an attack by Turkey, the only power from which she had anything to fear. While the Anglo-Russian negotiations lingered at this impasse, Britain's sworn enemy, Frederick II, established the basis for mutual cooperation with Catherine, first by accepting in a subsidy treaty the Turkish clause[18] so often rejected by the Foreign Office, and then by conspiring with her for the first partition of Poland, which Conway, the Secretary of State, had described as the least important nation in all Europe from the British standpoint.[19] In view of the British apathy toward both Poland[20] and Turkey, essential British interests were thought to be very little affected, when a skirmish between Russians and Poles, violating the neutrality of the Turk-

---

[17] Joseph Marshall, *Travels*, London, 1773, III, 112.
[18] A. W. Ward and G. P. Gooch, *The Cambridge History of British Foreign Policy*, New York, 1922, I, 122; W. F. Reddaway, "Macartney in Russia, 1765-67," *Cambridge Historical Journal*, III, 1931, 265.
[19] *ibid*.
[20] For a full treatment of the British attitude toward Polish affairs, see D. B. Horn, *British Public Opinion and the First Partition of Poland*, Edinburgh, 1945, particularly pp. 1-13.

ish border, proved the occasion for a declaration of war by the Porte. Nevertheless, the desire to curry favor with Catherine involved the Foreign Office in a strange diplomatic adventure.

Britain had recoiled from accepting the Turkish clause in a formal alliance as a possible threat to her commercial interests in the Levant, but she did not scruple, informally and in secret, to offer important material aid to the Russian war effort. This consisted in the abetting of a Russian naval expedition against the Turks in the Mediterranean, and it appears extraordinary today that British diplomacy which, for the past century and a half, has been occupied in keeping Russia out of the Mediterranean by supporting the Ottoman Empire should have so materially contributed to the contrary issue in 1770. Of the real utility of the assistance there can be no doubt. In the first place, many of the ships had been constructed with the help of British shipwrights. In the summer of 1770, the British ministry, which in 1734 had stipu- lated by treaty that the Russian government should make no attempt to enroll Britons in its service, agreed to permit Admiral Knowles to accept the presidency of the Russian board of admiralty.[21] Again, one of the Russian squadrons which sailed for the Mediterranean in 1769 was commanded by a Scot, John Elphinston,[22] but recently commis- sioned as a Russian vice-admiral. The ships of his squadron, separated by a gale in the North Sea, sought temporary shelter in various English ports until Elphinston was able to collect them for refitting and a safe winter haven at Portsmouth. Setting out again in the following April, they were joined by four English transports, disguised under Russian names, but commanded by British officers. Other Britons held im- portant posts at the Battle of Chesme, where, on July 5, 1770, almost the entire naval power of the Turks was destroyed at one blow. Samuel Greig,[23] who began a distinguished career in the navy during this expedition, was promoted to the rank of admiral for his services on this day, and two of the fire-ships which attacked the Turkish fleet were commanded by the Scots, Dougdale and Mackenzie. It is clear that the

[21] Cathcart to Rochford, November 16, 1770, *Sbornik*, XIII, 151; John Campbell, *The British Admirals*, London, 1818, v, 334.

[22] For a full account of Elphinston's exploits in the Russian Navy, see *An Authentic Narrative of the Russian Expedition against the Turks by Sea and Land*, London, 1772, which offers much additional information of the extent of British assistance; see also, Goodall to Stephens, Septem- ber 3, 1770, *Sbornik*, XIV, 79; despatch no. 35, entitled: "A Summary Account of the Transac- tions of the Russian Fleet from the Time of their Arrival on the coast of Greece in March, 1770, to the Battle of Chesme on the coast of Natolia on the 5th of July following," *ibid.*, p. 81ff.

[23] Chambers, *op. cit.*, II, 537.

success of the entire expedition, which played such an important part in opening the Turkish straits to Russian navigation, depended in large measure on British support.

Whatever its deficiencies as diplomatic strategy, this episode was bound to increase British popularity in Russia. In particular, the influx of such officers into the service of the Russian government tended to promote British prestige. Richardson recorded an instance of this in quoting a letter from Count Rumiantsev[24] to Lord Cathcart. By the marriage of his sister, the Countess Bruce, Rumiantsev had family affiliations with one Scottish adventurer; his letter attested ties of gratitude to another. "I confess I have always been ambitious of having the good opinion of your nation. I had much intercourse with the natives of your country in my youth; and I reckon among them many particular friends. Besides the obligations I owe to the late Mareschal Keith,[25] that is to say, all the knowledge I have in my profession, and consequently all my fortune shall make me, on all occasions, ardently desire to render justice to the merit of Englishmen."[26] Although it is possible from his various fragmentary remarks, and by means of interpolation, to reconstruct the outlines of Russian relations with the west, it is apparent from Richardson's treatment that he had little interest in the subject as such. Ignoring his excellent opportunities to gain an insight into the nature of Russian ties with Europe, he cited only isolated instances in the gratification of some independent interest such as national pride, love of the picturesque, or literary and artistic tastes. They are, on the whole, desultory and unrelated to any general interpretation of the subject.

In his analysis of the character of the Russian nation, on the other hand, Richardson was extraordinarily comprehensive. The epistolary style did not lend itself to strictly systematic treatment. Yet in Richardson's hands, the separate letters provide a skeletal framework for a

[24] Count Pëtr Aleksandrovich Rumiantsev (1725-1796). A Russian general, who distinguished himself in the Seven Years' War and the Turkish War of 1768-1774, he later assisted in the direction of campaigns against the Turks (1787-1791) and the Poles (1794). His sister, the Countess Bruce, was the confidante and favorite of Catherine during the early years of her reign.

[25] James Francis Edmund Keith, a soldier of fortune for twenty years until 1747. For a sketch of his Russian services, see J. H. Burton, *The Scot Abroad*, Edinburgh and London, 1864, II, 161ff.

[26] Richardson, *op. cit.*, p. 318. Other travelers observed similar good effects from the influence of British expatriates. John Carr remarked in 1804: "The intermixture of so many English subjects in the naval and commercial departments of Russia, so essential to their advancement, and consequently to the general interest of the empire, must ever preserve a favorable disposition in that country toward the British nation." Carr, *op. cit.*, p. 184.

really synthetic interpretation of a whole society, taking into consideration, although in varying proportion, economic, intellectual, religious, and political influences. Moreover, he discerned a single unifying principle in all these phases of Russian life and developed it with all the consistency, if not the rigor and completeness, of a Burckhardt. Despite some considerable gaps, Richardson's description and explanation of the Russian national character represented a striking example of the progress which the eighteenth century had made towards the development of the social sciences.

The principles of Richardson's own social philosophy were early revealed in a digression quite unrelated to his analysis of Russian society. Having described the unfortunate circumstances of the subject Finnish minority, he suddenly launched forth into the discussion of an "historical" parallel: "Perhaps circumstances of this sort may account for the character of many modern Jews; and, so long as these circumstances continue, they will always be a separate people.—On the dispersion of that famous nation, many things concurred to keep them distinct from other nations among whom they dwelt and to render them even objects of their aversion. . . . Among the European states, the manners and maxims of chivalry were about to commence: men subsisted by war and agriculture; commerce and manufactures were not held in esteem, but the Jews were neither proprietors of land, nor retainers of great men. They no longer made use of the sword, and subsisted neither by agriculture nor military depredation. Condemned and detested for their origin, their religion, their hatred of Christianity, and its persecution of its Holy Author, they felt that they had no character to lose and betook themselves for subsistence to such employments as the Europeans despised. They earned a livelihood by traffic; and by such occupations as among the Romans, and the northern nations who rose on the ruins of Rome, were never practised but by the dregs of the people. This, therefore, added to the contempt and hatred of their condition, and contributed, by a corresponding process, to render them really base and despicable. . . . They suffered themselves to deserve both contempt and aversion, and not only engaged in employments which were held dishonourable, but acted dishonourably in such employments. They not only practised commerce, but were guilty of fraud. As Europe became civilized, they found that they were enabled by their occupations, both to subsist and become wealthy. Their situation, therefore, however despised by the gentiles, had considerable advantages, which compensated for the contempt they suffered, and reconciled them to their condition. It also ought to be remarked that the opportunity which fraud and deceit gave them of retaliating in some measure the injuries they underwent, as it gratified their resentment, tended to darken their understandings, and hindered them from discerning the atrocity of their conduct.—Upon the whole, of this digression, it may not be improper to remark, that those who enjoy pre-eminence and treat their inferiors with contempt, merely on account of difference of situation, trespass against the interests of society, by compelling men to become worthless. It also may be mentioned, that as situations of this sort are of such powerful, as well as of such malignant influence, if there are persons who, in defiance of them, assert the dignity of human nature by the inflexible dignity of their own conduct, they do honour to the species."[27]

Aside from a certain independent interest, this quotation reveals many of the same characteristics which dominated in Richardson's attitude towards Russian society. His reconstruction of the past, if a trifle overimaginative, showed real historical insight. The political domination of the Romans and their successors, the religious prejudices of the Christians, the economic employments of the Jews, and the ideals of chivalry, all in combination, were held responsible for the peculiar dispersion and isolation of the Jewish people. It is notable that all these were natural forces working in history. "To account for this event from any supernatural cause must be . . . unsatisfactory. It is not probable that God, though He may, for wise purposes, have intended that the Jews should remain in this situation, would chuse to effectuate this by means different from His other operations in the world. . . ."[28] In short, whether or not God worked in history, He, nevertheless restricted Himself to certain rules of conduct which rendered His operations susceptible to the rational analysis of the human mind. Newtonian physics had prescribed certain fixed laws limiting divine activity in the physical universe: now the growing historical science placed similar prohibitions around the area of human society.

The view of man which followed indicated that his nature was neither good nor evil intrinsically but merely the product of social forces operating in time. By them, human nature might be either exalted or corrupted, and Richardson never lost his preoccupation with this moral problem. Good humanist that he was, he always upheld "the dignity of human nature," but the social forces which he examined often produced, instead, human degradation. Coolly objective as an

---

[27] Richardson, *op. cit.*, pp. 93-95.　　　　[28] *ibid.*, pp. 455-456.

analyst of the social determinants which had formed the Jewish character, he was, nevertheless, a rigorous moralist in his appraisal of the historical result. Although he appealed to neither religious nor racial prejudice, he did not hesitate to classify the modern Jews as not only "really base and despicable," but even as "incapable of discerning the atrocity of their conduct." Were it not for the saving grace of his final reminder as to "the dignity of human nature," the whole might be construed as an historical justification of anti-Semitism. This is a harsh sort of tolerance, and, indeed, Richardson's humanitarianism was often tempered with condescension and even with contempt. This paradoxical combination of faith in the social sciences as a means of explaining human behavior with a strict social morality which insisted on condemning it characterized much of Richardson's treatment of the Russian people.

It was his persistent preoccupation with the consequences of the Russian despotism which furnished the thematic unity of his letters. His rather unsystematic, but wide-ranging explorations into various phases of Russian society repeatedly returned to some critical evaluation of despotism, judged always in terms of its human consequences. Richardson's was not the first, but it was the most telling treatment of this theme. In 1767, Sir George Macartney had seen a close correlation between political absolutism and the moral degradation of the Russian people, but he disappointed his readers of a promise to give an analytical exposition of the formation of the national character. After an excellent survey of the condition of the various classes of society, he remarked: ". . . it may be expected that I shall endeavor to trace the cause . . . why the Russians should so long have continued in barbarism, why, though emerging from it for a century past, they still continue the least virtuous and least ingenious nation in Europe." Discarding the influence of climate and largely discounting that of education, he announced: "We shall prove in the following pages that the government has always been despotic, is still despotic, and likely long to continue so. If, then, the form of government can be supposed to influence or rather create the mental qualities and temper of the people, the Russians must remain unaltered as long as the form of government continues the same." Macartney's book contains some of the most entertaining and illuminating passages in the whole literature of the subject, but he never clarified this proposition. Instead it was left to Richardson to articulate Macartney's statement that "the form of government certainly is and will always be the principal cause of the want of virtue and genius in this country, as making the motive of one and the rewards of both depend upon accident and caprice."[29]

It was the capriciousness of despotism which was its most pernicious influence. It was natural that visitors from England, where, ever since Locke, the security of person and property had been regarded as a cornerstone of the whole social edifice, should find this quality of Russian life particularly disturbing. Many, like Perry, commented only that the insecurity of property among the peasants destroyed their incentive to work, thereby injuring the economic prosperity of the country. John Williams went further, observing that this insecurity was a condition embracing all ranks of society, that: ". . . the sovereign of the Russian empire is absolute and despotic in the utmost latitude of these words and master of the lives and properties of all his subjects who, though they are the first nobility . . . may nevertheless for the most trifling offence, or even for no offence at all be seized upon and sent to Siberia . . . and have all their goods confiscated; that the nobility . . . are no less arbitrary and despotic over the lives and property of their vassals, than the sovereign is over them; and that the sovereign is in many respects in a more disagreeable situation than any person in his dominions: . . . a bold and enterprising person who can gain over a party of the guards may in two hours time dethrone the sovereign and overturn the whole system of government."[30] Richardson accepted the wider interpretation of the insecurity of a despotic society and proceeded to make a sweeping application of the principle. In his view, the psychological effects of insecurity colored every aspect of human behavior. The Russian, accustomed to the futility of any reliance on the future, was oriented entirely to the present. This affected his attitudes toward politics, religion, ethics, education, and even his games and amusements. Richardson once went so far as to assert that the peasants had no surnames because "incapable of holding any property, and having nothing but bondage to transmit to their children, such distinction is useless."[31] Yet, if his theory led him to occasional exaggerations and distortions, it brought to his letters an integration which distinguished him from among all the other British travelers.

Although, on the whole, he credited the good intentions of Catherine, the view of her Russia which he presented must have denied the enlightenment of her or any other despotism. His indictment of the

[29] Macartney, *op. cit.*, pp. 45-46.
[30] John Williams, *The Rise, Progress, and Present State of the Northern Governments*, London, 1777, II, 289.
[31] Richardson, *op. cit.*, p. 206.

servile system was the bitterest by any British author, and a comparison with contemporary accounts indicates occasional exaggeration. Nevertheless, it must be admitted that the reign of Catherine was perhaps the blackest in the whole history of serfdom. He was correct in his report that even the formerly free peasants of the Ukraine "have lately undergone a deplorable change, and have been reduced, by an edict of the present Empress, to the condition of her other subjects."[32] Moreover, the status of the peasantry must have appeared even more terrible during "the Golden Age of the Nobility," when the emancipation of that class from all obligations to state service had destroyed the justification for their privileges over the serfs. The system seemed a threat to the young humanist's ideals of the dignity of man. That men, being of his own species, as he put it, should be obliged to live on the level of beasts was intolerable. Paradoxically, however, he insisted that the system had, in fact, made beasts of them, and, perhaps prompted by a sort of morbid perversity, he dwelt upon and magnified the moral defects of the peasantry more than any other Briton.

Richardson was at his best in his analysis of the formation of that despotism which he so despised. As the taste for history spread through the century, more and more of the Russian past found its way into the accounts of travelers. Perry had had only the vaguest conception of pre-Petrine Russia, but Williams, Macartney, and Coxe traced the course of Russian history back to the time of the Christian conversion. They dwelt largely with the recent past, however, and tended to record the births, deaths, personalities, quarrels, and wars of the great rulers to the exclusion of a broad general interpretation. In sharp contrast, therefore, was Richardson's inquiry into the existence of feudalism in ancient Russia. Imaginative and general as it is, it is nevertheless a convincing and stimulating account of a development which is still today shrouded in obscurity. The main characteristics of the social structure he defined as "the supreme authority of the Emperor over the nobility, and of the nobility over their slaves,"[33] and his theory that Russia's geographical exposure to the invasions of Asiatic warrior tribes had a strong influence in the growth of this dual despotism currently enjoys widespread acceptance. Yet even could Richardson's essay be proven largely erroneous, it could not be denied that his

[32] Richardson, *op. cit.*, p. 378; compare G. T. Robinson, *Rural Russia under the Old Regime*, New York, 1932, p. 31.

[33] Richardson, *op. cit.*, p. 371. These words bear a startling resemblance to those used by G. T. Robinson to characterize the outstanding developments of a period of some four hundred years. Robinson, *op. cit.*, p. 25.

breadth of conception, judicious imagination, and use of the comparative method showed a real talent for historical thinking.

Richardson's faith in the verdict of history strongly influenced his attitude towards Russia's future. Through the course of centuries historical forces had been fashioning a despotism which, in its turn, had degraded the intellectual and moral character of its people. He did not believe, with the philosophers of the French Revolution, that the trend of history could be altered in a moment by the application of certain universal rights. The servile system had made brutes of the Russian peasantry, but an immediate emancipation would not restore their humanity, but only loose "twenty million robbers and spoilers" to prey upon society. Freedom for Russia would have to come very gradually, being introduced little by little to those sections of the population which had had some previous historical experience of it. In short, liberty was not a mechanical principle, but a living organism which demanded careful cultivation to grow in foreign climes.

Richardson's conviction that this liberty had hitherto been realized only in England seems always to have loomed in the way of his speculations on the Russian future. Whether his humanitarianism recoiled before the picture of human degradation which Russia appeared to present, or whether the problems of emancipation recalled him to the remembrance of the historical process which had produced the political system he loved, he always retreated from the subject of a potential Russian reformation to a eulogy of the wonderful realities of English government. Perry, employed in the Russian service, had been proud of English technical and scientific achievement, but he had largely identified himself with the Russian ambitions when assessing her riches and discussing her problems. Hanway, the merchant entrepreneur, whose main wish for Russia was the perpetuation of the terms of the commercial treaty of 1734, gloried in the material and spiritual blessings which a wise and merciful God had seen fit to shower upon His "most favored nation." With Richardson, the humanistic scholar, suspended quite apart from Russian life, the religious element largely disappeared, and the British were the choice not of a personal God but of a providential history. In either case, the choice had an element of finality in which the patriotic Briton could take satisfaction. With that same strange mixture of humanitarian and moralist which he had shown in his discussion of the Jews, Richardson turned away from the contaminated Russians toward the people whom the centuries had made virtuous. In these political reflections, Russia served Richardson somewhat as France later served Burke, as the text of the sermon, the hideous example to be avoided by real lovers of liberty. In short, in these passages, Richardson represented an early disciple of that historical nationalism which appeared in England in the latter half of the eighteenth century when the political consciousness of all Europe was being roused by the ferment of the French Revolution.

∴∴∴∴∴∴∴∴∴∴∴∴∴∴∴∴∴∴∴∴∴∴∴∴∴∴∴∴∴∴∴∴∴∴

EXTRACTS FROM: *Anecdotes of the Russian Empire in a series of letters written a few years ago from St. Petersburg.*

by William Richardson

CONTENTS

....

I · THE VOYAGE FROM ENGLAND:
AUGUST, 1768

August 2: I embarked in the evening along with Lord C. and his family on board the Tweed frigate at the Nore.

August 3: Early in the morning the vessel was under sail, the wind very favourable. The Tweed carries thirty-two guns, and, including forty marines, her full complement of men is two hundred and twenty.

August 6: Very stormy. The weather, hitherto, had been remarkably pleasant. This day we entered the Categate [Kattegat].

August 7: The weather fine; the wind favourable. We sailed along the coast of Zeeland. Nothing of the kind could be more delightful than the verdure and the variety of hill and dale, displayed in that beautiful island. In the afternoon we passed a small palace belonging to the King of Denmark . . . built, as I was told, on the very place formerly occupied by the palace of Hamlet's father. In an adjoining garden, the very spot is shewn where the Prince is said to have been poisoned. . . .

August 10: We sailed along the coast of Gottland [Gothland]. . . . The number of islands in the Baltic, displaying a variety of different appearances, constantly shifting and succeeding one another, renders the navigation of that sea, in summer or autumn, remarkably agreeable.

August 11: A very stormy day. At noon we came in sight of Dago, an uncouth, black, and disagreeable island, the first specimen of the Russian dominions. . . .

August 14: We passed the island of Haugland [Hogland]. . . . The coast is mountainous, rocky, and covered with heath. At night we lay at anchor in Cronstadt [Kronshtadt]. . . . In this place are the principal dock-yards of the Russian Empress. The island itself is four miles in length, and two in breadth, and has some wood upon it. The town of Cronstadt is very small and ill-built. It is distant about eighteen miles from St. Petersburg.

August 15: This day we left the Tweed and arrived at St. Petersburgh in one of the Empress' yachts. The weather was very fine, and we had, in sailing along, a full view of the neighbouring coast of Estonia. The palaces of Oranibaum [Oranienbaum] and Peterhof [or Leninsk] have a magnificent appearance to the sea, and the face of the country is agreeably diversified with woods and little hills. The country around St. Petersburg is very woody: so that in approaching it, the steeples and spires which are covered with tin and brass, and some of them gilt, seemed as if they arose from the midst of the forest. [2-14]

II · ST. PETERSBURG: WINTER

1. A COSMOPOLITAN CITY

It is said here, that, except Constantinople, no city in Europe contains a greater variety of strangers than St. Petersburg.[34] In London and Paris you have Europeans of all nations; but you have not, additionally to these, different races of Tartars, Circassians and Armenians. . . . In consequence of the number of strangers in St. Petersburg, many persons speak a variety of different languages: nor would even the ladies think you were calling them bad names, if you were to say they were Polyglots. The English ladies here speak French, German and Russ, and some of them Italian. Their other graces and accomplishments are proportioned to their gift of tongues. [412-414]

2. FURRY COCOONS

Our weather is indeed very severe. You may judge of its severity by our precautions. We have recourse to them, not only in our dress, but in our houses. Our dress, within doors, is the same as during the winter in England. But when we encounter the external cold, our defensive raiment is indeed very grotesque . . . a large fur cap . . . a garment resembling a night-gown, extending from the neck to the heel, made of whatever stuff you please, but lined throughout with the thickest fur. Fur-shoes, having the hair on the outside, are tied over the shoes we commonly wear. Our arms are secured by the long sleeves of the

[34] Macartney also attested the international character of the population of the Russian capital. "Foreigners of almost every nation acquainted with are to be found in Russia, either as established or temporary residents. In the customs house book of Petersburg alone, we observe the names of merchants of every country in Europe: English, French, Hollanders, Austrians, Prussians, Saxons, Hamburgers, Lubeckers, Danes, Swedes, Spaniards, Italians, Greeks, etc., etc." Macartney, *op. cit.*, p. 24.

upper garment or pelisse . . . and our hands by large muffs, which are also used to defend the face. On entering any house, some of the servants immediately untie your fur-shoes, and divest you of your pelisse: nor is it unamusing to see fine gentlemen, adorned with silver and gold, and purple, and precious stones, starting forth from their rough external guise, like so many gaudy butterflies, bursting suddenly from their winter incrustations. [147-148]

3. STIFLING STOVES

In houses of any distinction here, every room is provided with a large stove, reaching from the floor to the ceiling. It is usually made of brick; and is often so adorned with various colours, and with ornaments of brass as to exhibit a very good appearance. From this stove, flues and passages, for conveying the heat around the room, are sometimes constructed within the walls. After the wood is completely burnt down, so that not the smallest particle of flame or of smoke remain, the little iron door by which the fuel was put into its place, but which stood open while the wood was burning, is fastened very close; and, by another aperture in the side of the stove . . . halfway between the floor and the ceiling, the passage by which the smoke enters the chimney is also covered. Thus, the heat, confined entirely within the room, becomes sometimes excessive, and almost insufferable; nor have I ever felt so much warmth in any house in London, as in the houses of St. Petersburg. . . . [148-149]

4. SHINING DARTS

In the coldest and brightest weather, you see an infinite multitude of little shining darts or spiculae, flying in all directions through the sky. They seem to be about a quarter of an inch in length; they have not more thickness than the finest hair; and their golden colour, glancing as they shoot through the deep azure sky, has a great deal of beauty. If the weather were warmer, and if the climate were more genial, and if we had any belief in ancient mythology, we should take them to be an immense multitude of arrows, discharged by some mischievous cupids. Nor would such an explanation be without evidence in the character of the Russians. . . . [53-54]

5. FLYING SLEDGES

When the snow has fallen in its greatest quantity, and the roads are beat smooth, the motion of the sledge is very easy and agreeable. It is drawn in this country by horses, and the swiftness with which they go, even upon ice, is astonishing. The horses here are small, but very nimble and beautiful; and the Russians, in general, are excellent horsemen. Driving in sledges is one of the chief amusements that persons of rank can have without doors in the winter; and accordingly, they endeavour to display their fancy in the form and embellishments of these whimsical carriages. They are quite open, and the most elegant I have seen have the appearance of shells, painted with showy colours; so that the ladies and gentlemen who drive in them resemble Divinities of the sea. Those used by persons of any distinction are drawn by two horses, but those that ply in the streets are drawn only by one. They fly with astonishing swiftness; so that in the space of five or ten minutes you can be transported to any quarter of the city. [54-55]

6. A VIOLENT TRANSITION

Till the beginning of April, the ice was as firm on the Neva as in the middle of January. It broke up a few weeks ago, and announced its departure with a dreadful noise. If climate could have any effect on national characters, the proofs ought to be manifest in Russia. The heats and colds are excessive, and the transition, from one extreme to the other, sudden. A fortnight ago the ground was covered with snow; this day the heat is almost insufferable: at present scarcely a bud appears; but we expect, in a few days, to see the fields and trees invested with verdure.—A short letter, this, you will say, and a short account of a Russian spring. It is so;—but a long description would be unsuitable, when a Russian spring is the subject. [66]

III · THE PORTRAIT OF AN EMPRESS

I. FAIRER THAN HER DAUGHTERS

August 19, 1768: The Empress of Russia is taller than the middle size, very comely, gracefully formed, but inclined to grow corpulent; and of a fair complexion, which, like every other female in this country, she endeavours to improve by the addition of rouge. She has a fine mouth and teeth; and blue eyes, expressive of scrutiny, something not so good as observation, and not so bad as suspicion. Her features are in general regular and pleasing. Indeed, with regard to her appearance altogether, it would be doing her an injustice to say it was masculine, yet it would not be doing her justice to say, it was entirely feminine.

As Milton intended to say of Eve, that she was fairer than any of her daughters, so this great Sovereign is certainly fairer than any of her subjects, whom I have seen. . . . Her demeanour to all around her seemed very smiling and courteous. [19-20]

2. AN IMPERIAL DAY

Nov. 7, 1768: Her Majesty . . . rises at five in the morning, and is engaged in business till near ten. She then breakfasts and goes to prayers: dines at two: withdraws to her own apartments soon after dinner: drinks tea at five: sees company, plays at cards, or attends public places, the play, opera, or masquerade, till supper: and goes to sleep at ten. By eleven every thing about the palace is as still as midnight. Whist is her favourite game at cards. She usually plays for five imperials (ten guineas) the rubber; and as she plays with great clearness and attention, she is often successful: she sometimes plays, too, at picquet and cribbage. . . . In the morning between prayers and dinner, she frequently takes an airing, according as the weather admits, in a coach or a sledge. On these occasions, she has sometimes no guards, and very few attendants; and does not chuse to be known or saluted as Empress. It is in this manner that she visits any great works that may be going on in the city, or in the neighbourhood. She is fond of having small parties of eight or ten persons with her at dinner. . . . When she retires to her palaces in the country, especially to Zarskocelo [Tsarskoe Selo] she lays aside all state, and lives with her ladies on the footing of as easy intimacy as possible. Any one of them who rises on her entering or going out of a room, is fined a ruble, and all forfeits of this sort are given to the poor. You will easily perceive, that by her regular and judicious distribution of time, she is able to transact a great deal of business; and that the affability of her manners renders her much beloved. [23-25]

3. PHILANTHROPIST OR PEACOCK?

I will not yet say anything very positive concerning her character and principles of action. For, she may be very social, and very affable and "smile and smile and"—you know the rest.

I may, however, very safely affirm, that a great number of her actions, so great indeed as to constitute a distinguishing feature in her character, proceed either from the desire of doing good, or the love of fame. If from the last, it must also be acknowledged, that the praise she is so desirous of obtaining, is, in many instances, the praise of humanity. Sometimes, indeed, there is a sort of whim or affectation of singularity, in the manner of conferring her favours, that looks as if the desire of being spoken of, fully as much as the desire of doing good, is the fountain from which they flow. [25-26]

January 1769: I assure you, my dear Sir, I do not find it an easy matter to obtain information. . . . No intelligence of a political nature, but such as the court chuses to communicate; no views of men and manners, and no anecdotes of incidents in domestic life, can be collected from the news-papers. How unlike England! that land enlightened by the radiance of Chroniclers, Advertisers, and Gazetteers. The half of Russia may be destroyed, and the other half know nothing about the matter. . . . [37-38]

I have to contend, too, with another difficulty. I perceive that the same objects are seen in very different lights by different persons. . . . I was lately present at a distribution of prizes to the students educated in the Academy of Arts and Sciences. . . . There were . . . present many ladies and gentlemen of the Court. Count Betskoy began the ceremony by addressing a speech to the Grand Duke, in which he recommended the seminary to his protection. To this His Imperial Highness replied: "As the welfare of Russia shall ever be the object nearest my heart; and as the proper education of youth is of so much consequence in every well-ordered state, it claims, and shall ever obtain, my most constant attention." . . .

I was told that the Empress was present among the ladies. . . .

Tell me now, would not a stranger, on witnessing such a scene, on seeing one of the most powerful Sovereigns on earth and the presumptive heir of this mighty empire so attentive to the welfare and improvement of their people, would he not feel rapture, approve, and applaud? Yet, when I expressed those sentiments, there were persons who shake their heads. . . . This Academy has subsisted for many years, but what have they done? It may be mentioned, with ostentatious pomp, in a news-paper, or by Voltaire, and nothing else is intended. [39-41]

4. EMANCIPATOR OR AUTOCRAT?

November 1768: I was lately present at a meeting of the deputies summoned by the Empress from all the nations of her empire, and who have been assembled to assist Her Majesty in forming a system of legislation. There is something magnificent in this idea: and if she

really intends what she professes, to give equitable laws to all her subjects and dependents, from the Baltic to the wall of China, and from
Lapland to the Caspian, she deserves admiration. . . .

The meeting consists of about six hundred members. They meet in
the palace, where they have one large hall for the whole assembly; and
several adjoining rooms for committees. They consist of representatives
of the nobility, the peasantry, and the inhabitants of towns or cities.
. . . The chief officers in this assembly are a Marischal, who presides;
and a Procureur General for the Crown. . . .

In transacting business, the following method is observed. The Procureur lays before the deputies some principle or subject of law proposed by the Empress, and concerning which they are to give an
opinion. They then adjourn; and the committee to whom that subject
particularly belongs, prepare it for the next general meeting. Then all
the members are permitted to deliver their opinions in a written speech,
and to determine the point before them, by the plurality of votes. But
whatever their determinations may be, it remains with the Empress to
ratify them or not, as she pleases. Two of the subjects lately discussed
in this assembly were, "Whether any but the nobility had a right to
buy lands?" and, "Whether any but the nobility had a right to buy
slaves?"

I have heard that freedom of extemporaneous speaking was allowed
in some of the first meetings of this assembly; but that that being likely
to occasion too much disorder, it was discontinued. At present, it is
expected that no person, unless his views be very well known, shall
deliver a speech without previously consulting the Marischal; and if he
disapproves of it, the orator, though he had the powers of a Cicero,
must keep his speech in his pocket. Indeed, this assembly has no pretensions whatever to freedom of debate, and scarcely any tendency
towards establishing political liberty. The members, in general, are
chosen by the will of the sovereign: by her the subjects of debate are
proposed: she keeps in her own hands the right of ratifying every
determination: and the assembly, convoked by her sole authority, may
be dismissed at her pleasure.[35] [28-31]

[35] Sir George Macartney's remarks on the general policy of Catherine here corroborate Richardson's opinion: ". . . to despotism Russia owes her greatness and her dominions, so that
if ever the monarchy becomes more limited, she will lose her power and strength in proportion
as she advances in virtue and civil improvement. It will therefore always be the interest, and
has ever been the practice of a sovereign . . . to check every improvement where it might tax
his authority, and encourage it only where it is subservient to his grandeur and glory. I am
sensible that the various projects of the present empress may seem to contradict what I have
said above. The fact is that most of her projects are impracticable, and therefore my assertion

IV · FOREIGN AFFAIRS

1. COMMERCE WITH BRITAIN

THE IRON in Siberia is wrought at little expence: the places where it is found are by the sides of large rivers. Provisions are cheap: a sheep may be bought for thirty copics [kopecks] (one shilling), and the rivers are stored with excellent fish. Wood for working the iron is found everywhere in the greatest abundance. Not only so, but the soil in southern and eastern parts of Russia is very fertile. The Ukraine alone, with no other labour than that of plowing, could supply the whole of European Russia with corn. The empire, besides its vicinity to the Caspian, Euxine [Black Sea], Baltic and Northern Seas, is interspersed with lakes and intersected by navigable rivers; these might easily, by means of canals, be made to communicate with one another. Nor is even land-carriage interrupted, or rendered difficult here, as in many other places, by fens and mountains. The natural advantages of Russia, therefore, might render it one of the richest countries in Europe.

Accordingly, even in its present infant state of improvement, the balance of trade has been, of late years, more unfavorable to Britain than formerly. Many such manufactures as were imported by English traders, some time ago, and sold here with large profits, are now wrought in the country. Formerly, the coarse cloth, with which the army is clothed, was brought from England; it is now wrought in Russia. Pewter also was a profitable commodity; but pewter dishes, with earthenware, and even china, are to be had here very good, and manufactured in the country. The silk manufacture at Moscow is in a thriving condition; and Russian linen and diaper are sold in Britain. [259-260]

2. WAR WITH TURKEY

Its Effects on the Empress

June 1769: Indeed, the issue of this war may be of great consequence, not only to the Russian empire, but to the Empress in particular. Her elevation to the throne was not auspicious, and there are, no doubt, many persons in the empire not yet reconciled to her government. Many of the nobility choose rather to reside at Moscow, than with the Court at St. Petersburg. The Russians are in general fickle, and fond

---

loses none of its weight. Besides, should the least inconvenience arise from the execution of them, Catherine, than whom no sovereign was ever more jealous or tenacious of her authority, could suppress them with a nod and overthrow them with a breath." *ibid.*, p. 46.

of change. The Great Duke will soon be of age, and it was understood by many, when the Empress was crowned, that when her son was old enough to reign, she was to resign. An unsuccessful foreign war tends to impair the authority of all despots; and this is the first foreign war she has ever waged. . . . Accordingly, she exerts every effort; and, actuated in this manner, we are not to expect a languid, slow, and protracted contest, but a war of spirited and vigorous operation. [75-76]

The Mediterranean Expedition

January 1769: I need not inform you that the Russian Army is reckoned inferior to none in Europe. It is not, however, on her army alone that the Empress means to depend. At the time that the war is to be carried on with great vigour in Moldavia and the Crimea, some considerable exertions will be made by sea. The command of the great army, to act on the frontiers of Poland and Moldavia, is given to Prince Galitzen, [Prince Dmitri Alekseevich Golitsyn] and it is reported that an English Admiral is to have a considerable command in the fleet intended for the Mediterranean. [49-50]

June 1769: The reduction of Chotzim [Chotzen], it is expected, will be the immediate consequence of Galitzen's victory; and in the mean time a considerable fleet is preparing at Cronstadt, to attempt some important stroke in the Mediterranean or Archipelago. One of the best officers in the Russian fleet, is Commander Greig [Sir Samuel Greig] a native of Fifeshire. His naval abilities are reckoned very great; yet that simplicity and modesty of deportment which usually accompany, and too often veil, the most distinguished merit, may with a people, so fond of shew and glare as the Russians are, and so apt to judge of men, according as they seem to entertain a high opinion of themselves, keep out of sight for a time, and even lessen the value of his abilities.[36] [76-77]

July 1769: A fleet of seven sail-of-the-line, and some frigates, having with them a considerable number of land-forces, and under the command of Admiral Elphinston, will set out, very soon, on an expedition into the Mediterranean. The Admiral is a Captain in the British navy; and, among other important services, conducted the British fleet

---

[36] In the actual event, Greig had no reason to complain that his "simplicity and modesty of deportment" had hindered his advancement in the Russian service. He was eventually promoted to the rank of full admiral and, at his death in 1788, might even be said to have acquired a measure of "show and glare" by his election to the orders of St. Andrew, St. Alexander Nevski, St. George, St. Vladimir, and St. Anne. Chambers, *op. cit.*, II, 537.

through the Straits of Bahama, when the English, in the last war, invaded Cuba. [105]

Defeats, Discontent, and Despotism

July 1769: Since the last accounts I gave you of the war in Moldavia several events have happened, at first favourable, but now unfavourable, to the Russians. . . . The Russian army is so much weakened, and so much alarmed, that they have again . . . repassed the Neister, [Dniester] but this they were not able to effectuate without considerable loss. . . . These things have flattened our spirits. The people are beginning to murmur. Rumours of conspiracies are secretly propagated; several persons, I have heard, either guilty or suspected of treason, have disappeared: but these things are not noised abroad, they are only mentioned in confidential whispers. The people are prohibited from speaking or writing about politics. The Empress tells them, that as her maternal care for her dear people keeps her sleepless by night, and busy by day . . . they have no occasion to give themselves any further trouble about public affairs, than to act implicitly as she directs; and, in order the more effectually to save her dear people from unnecessary labour, she not only exhorts, but actually forbids them to speak, write, or think politics. The spies are busy: the suspected great men are closely watched. For "Not a Thane of them, but in his house she has a servant fee'd." Happy king of England! who may go about with as much security after a defeat, as after a victory; who has no occasion for a board of spies against his own subjects; and may allow his people to speak, write, and think as they please. [101-104]

3. INTRIGUE IN POLAND

A Tottering Throne

January 1769: Count Poniatowsky,[37] the present King of Poland, was, at an early period of his life appointed Envoy from his own country to the Court of Russia. During his residence in that empire, he attached himself to the great Duchess, who is now Empress, and in-

---

[37] Stanislas Augustus Poniatowski (1732-1798), the last king of an independent Poland. He was descended from an ancient Polish line and connected with the powerful Czartoryski family on his mother's side. In 1755, in company with the friendly British ambassador, Sir Charles Hanbury-Williams, he went to St. Petersburg on a diplomatic mission. There, with the blessings of his older friend, he became the lover of the then Grand Duchess Catherine. In 1764, with Russian backing, he was elected to the Polish throne, which he did not finally abdicate until the final partition in 1795, when he returned to Russia. For the Russian embassy, see Earl of Ilchester and Mrs. Langford Brooke, *The Life of Sir Charles Hanbury-Williams*, London, 1929, pp. 303ff.

sinuated himself into her favour. This Princess, possessed of eminent talents, and actuated by an unbounded ambition, having dethroned her husband, who succeeded to the Empress Elizabeth, and having invested herself with the Imperial dignity, resolved to establish her credit at home, and her importance abroad by governing the affairs of Poland. Accordingly, connecting herself with the King of Prussia, and in spite of the efforts of France, Austria, and the Saxon Princes, she advanced Poniatowsky to the throne, hoping, perhaps, that he would cooperate implicitly in her designs, or imagining that he possessed greater abilities than he has hitherto displayed. Surely no prince has had a finer opportunity of distinguishing himself as a warrior or politician.[38] He was celebrated by Voltaire, who also celebrated the King of Denmark, and who celebrates all princes that are free-thinkers and that pay him for his adulation. Yet Poniatowsky, like some others, to whom he has offered incense, has done little credit to his panegyric. He has shewn neither spirit nor patriotism, and is said to be chiefly desirous of amassing treasure . . . and of securing to himself in an independency in some foreign country, should he, like another Stanislas, be forced to abdicate his unmerited dignity. [45-47]

Civil Distraction

June 1769: The whole of Poland is in a state of distraction. There are confederacies and associations of armed men in every quarter; and almost in every quarter there are Russian troops, or such as are inlisted under the royal banner. Of consequence, there are constant encounters; sometimes the one party, and sometimes the other, is successful. These conflicts contribute nothing to the reestablishment of public affairs: they are bloody and barbarous: all the effect they produce is, to extend and diversify the miseries of the country; nor, in any of them that ever I heard of, is there, even in individuals, any such display of conduct, military talents, and heroism, as, independent of their effects, would render them interesting. It is really wonderful, that the present civil war in Poland has called forth in that nation, no gallant spirits to draw

[38] Here Richardson expressed an opinion at variance both with the facts and with the general view. The oppression of the peasants by the nobility and the strife between Catholic and dissenting factions had nearly extinguished all national feeling. The elective monarchy, the absence of a real standing army, and the liberum veto, giving free reign both to the turbulence of the nobility and to the meddling designs of foreign rulers, made the task of the central government all but impossible, and Poniatowski's position far from enviable. Recognition of the decadence of Poland by various British travelers, including Joseph Marshall, John Williams, and William Coxe, helped to incline public opinion in favor of the first partition. Horn, *op. cit.*, pp. 66-77.

upon themselves particular attention, and to rise above the general mass of furious and fierce partizans. No supereminent abilities have appeared among them. How different have been the effects produced by the civil wars both in France and in England! [72-74]

A Principle of Power

October 1770: You will observe, that the great Despots of Europe seem desirous of having small Princes, rather than mighty Potentates, on the frontiers of their dominions. Such neighbours are not so formidable: in case of foreign wars they stand in the way of invasion; and may in time become a part of the neighbouring empire. Perhaps the Sovereigns of Russia would not be sorry to see Finland and Lithuania, no less than the provinces of ancient Dacia, erected into what they might be pleased to term independent Dukedoms and Principalities. "Why," they will say, in the superabundance of their goodness, "ought the Finlanders and the Lithuanians to be subject to the Kings of Poland and Sweden?" [312]

Premonitions of Partition

January 1771: This city, since the beginning of winter, has exhibited a continued scene of festivity and amusement: feasts, balls, concerts, plays, operas, fireworks, and masquerades in constant succession; and all in honour of, and to divert His Royal Highness, Prince Henry of Prussia, the famous brother of the present King. Yet his Royal Highness does not seem much diverted. He looks at them as an old cat looks at the gambols of a young kitten; or as one who had higher sport going on in his own mind, than the pastime of fiddling and dancing.

He came here about the beginning of November, on pretence of a friendly visit to the Empress; and to have the happiness of waiting on so *magnanimous* a Princess; and to see with his own eyes the progress of those immense improvements so highly celebrated by Voltaire, and the French writers, who receive gifts from Her Majesty. As the Queen of Sheba had heard of King Solomon's "acts and wisdom" and "came to see whether she had heard a true report of them in her own land," so also this royal Prince hath come to visit this mighty Princess. . . . But do you seriously imagine, that this creature of skin and bone should travel through Sweden, whence he has come at present, and Finland, and Poland, all for the pleasure of seeing the metropolis and Empress of Russia? Other Princes may pursue such pastime, but the Princes of the House of Brandenburg fly at a nobler quarry. Or, is the King of

Prussia, as a tame spectator, to reap no advantage from the troubles of Poland, and the Turkish war? What is the meaning of his late conferences with the Emperor of Germany? Depend upon it, these planetary conjunctions are the forerunners of great events. Time, and perhaps a few months, may unfold the secret. You will recollect the signs, when you shall hear after this of changes, usurpations, and revolutions. [323-325]

V · ANECDOTES OF THE RUSSIAN RELIGION

I. POMP AND CEREMONY

I CAN OFFER YOU NOTHING very interesting on the article of Religion. You are acquainted with the tenets of the Greek Church. It is pretended that its principles are pure and rational; the practice, I am sure, is different. I may tell you of pompous ceremonies, magnificent processions, rich dresses, showy pictures, smoking censers, and solemn music; but I cannot tell you that the clergy in general are exemplary, or the laiety upright. On no consideration would a Russian peasant omit his fastings, the bending of his body, and the regularity of his attendance on sacred rites: scourge him if you will, yet you cannot oblige him to cross himself with more than three fingers; but he has no scruple to steal or commit murder. Were I not an eye-witness, I could scarcely conceive it possible that men should so far impose upon their own minds, as to fancy they are rendering acceptable service to Heaven by the performance of many idle ceremonies, while they are acting inconsistently with every moral obligation.[39] [59-60]

2. FASTING AND FEASTING

The Russians observe four fasts in the year. Of these, Lent is of the longest duration: and one of the most solemn ceremonies of their religion is performed at Easter, in honour of the resurrection of Christ. . . . The following week is spent in revelry and rejoicing. Hardly any business is done, for the Russians of all ranks and opinions, nobility and peasantry, believers and unbelievers betake themselves with the

---

[39] Quotations condemning the unethical character of Russian religion could be endlessly multiplied, and nearly every British observer would have subscribed to Macartney's terse dictum: "Their piety . . . is reducible to very few rules of duty, the principal of which are: abstinence in Lent, intoxication on holidays, and confession and sacrament at Easter." Macartney, *op. cit.*, p. 32.

utmost licentiousness to the pleasures of the table.[40] They all embrace one another, saying, "Christ is arisen!" and present eggs to one another, painted with various figures, and inscribed with different devices. Some of these devices are religious; some amorous; and some both together: so that it is no unusual thing to see St. Athanasius with a Cross, on one side of an egg; and on the other, a lover falling at the feet of his mistress. Wherever they meet, whether they are acquainted with one another or not, they embrace and give the customary saluta-tion. Nor is it unusual to see two drunken peasants, announcing the glad tidings, embracing, and tumbling into the kennel. In the vacant places of the city, vast crowds assemble, and sing in their flying chairs, and partake of every sort of amusement. Meantime, every person who chuses, goes into the churches, rings the bells as long as he thinks fit, and believes that he is thus glorifying God, or making expiation for his sins. . . . [60-62]

3. A SANCTIFYING GOOSE

At the end of Lent . . . all ranks of people abandon themselves to feasting and rioting: but this they are not permitted to do till the clergy-men of the place visits their houses, and gives them his benediction. It happened that a Priest, having had some dispute with one of his flock, intentionally passed his house, when making his progress through his parish, and omitted giving him the benediction which he had given to the rest of his parishioners. . . . To be obliged to fast, and say prayers, while all his neighbours were feasting and getting drunk, was not to be borne; it seemed still more insufferable to his wife. In all emer-gencies of this kind, the fair sex are good at giving good counsel. Soft-ened by the admonitions of his help-mate, the husband waited upon the Priest; acknowledged his fault; implored his forgiveness, and craved his blessing. But the holy man was inexorable. The suppliant was forced to employ his last resource; it was his corps-de-reserve; a goose, which he had concealed under his cloak. Its eloquence was irresistible; its intercession was powerful; and the effect instantaneous. For immediately, on sight of it, the countenance of the holy man was

[40] The canny Scot, Dr. Cook, realized a handsome profit on Russian gluttony. "After the last service is over, every one resorts to his home and eats and drinks as much as he is able. For eight days the jubilee is universal; with some it lasts longer, which respecting my interest I found convenient, as surfeits seldom go off without the doctor's aid. The fast, which is very strict, continues seven weeks. This is succeeded by a voracious eating and plenty of the strongest liquors, which never fails to bring many to their beds and not a few to their graves." Cook, *op. cit.*, I, 49.

changed; his severity was softened into complacency, and, from the extreme benignity of his nature, he was disposed to grant remission to a repenting sinner, who had given such evidence of his contrition. But one difficulty remained: the Penitent's house was several miles distant; the day was far spent; next day was Easter; and the Clergyman was obliged to attend in church. What was to be done? for it was essential, in giving the usual benediction, that it should be pronounced close by the four corners of the house. But the goose quickened his invention, and seemed like inspiration to the man of God. An expedient was immediately suggested to him.

"Hold your cap!" said he, to the wondering Penitent. He religiously held open his cap. Then the Priest, crossing himself, bending, and holding his mouth over it, pronounced the benedictions and exorcisms, which he would have pronounced at the man's house. "Now," said he, "hold it close; get home as fast as you can, and at every corner of your house, crossing yourself, open a corner of your cap, and my presence may be dispensed with." The man obeyed; thanked God, and got drunk. . . . [63-65]

4. A BLUSHING SAINT

In a country where the worship of images is practiced . . . every one has an image of the sainted person who protects him, and who is honoured accordingly. This image is so placed in the corner of his room as to be the witness of all his actions, and receive humble obeisance as he enters the door. . . . But though the Russians have such sacred witnesses of their conduct, they soon become so familiar with them, as to hazard the performance of any act whatsoever before them; and I have not heard of any but some of the fair sex, who, in cases of irresistible temptation, have thought of veiling with an apron the face of the blushing saint. [207-208]

5. CONSECRATED WATERS

One of the most magnificent ceremonies in the Greek Church, and that which seems chiefly to draw the attention of strangers is, the consecration of the waters. It is performed twice in the year; but the most splendid display of this ceremony is exhibited on the 6th of January, and is performed in commemoration of the baptism of our Saviour. . . . A pavilion, supported by eight pillars, under which the chief part of the ceremony was performed, was erected on the Moika, a stream which enters the Neva between the Winter Palace and the Admiralty. On the top was a gilded figure of St. John: on the sides were pictures of our Saviour, represented in different situations; and within, immediately over the hole that was cut through the ice into the water, was suspended the figure of a dove. The pavilion was surrounded with a temporary fence of fir branches; and a broad lane from the palace was defended on each side in a similar manner. This passage, by which the procession advanced, was covered with red cloth. The banks of the river, and the adjoining streets, were lined with soldiers. . . . The procession then advanced, by the passage above-mentioned, to the Jordan of the day . . . with all their usual parade of tapers, banners, lofty mitres, and flowing robes. . . . No parade of Priests and Levites, even in the days of Solomon, and by the banks of Shiloh, could be more magnificent. After the rite was performed with the customary prayers and hymns, all who were present had the happiness of being sprinkled with the water thus consecrated and rendered holy. The standards of the army and the artillery received similar consecration; and the rite was concluded with a triple discharge of musquetry.

The Russians conceive that the water, thus sanctified, possesses the most singular virtues. Accordingly the multitude who were assembled on the outside of the fence, and the guard surrounding the pavilion, when the ceremony was over, rushed with ungoverned tumult to wash their hands and their faces in the hallowed orifice. What pushing and brawling, scolding and swearing—to get rid of their sins! . . . For they apprehend, that it is not only blessed with spiritual energy, and is efficacious in washing away the diseases of the soul, but is also a sovereign antidote against the malign influences of evil spirits; and may be prescribed with great advantage against the pains and maladies of the body. . . . [332-335]

6. BAPTISMAL IMMOLATIONS

All infants, who are baptised with the water of the sacred orifice, are supposed to derive from it the most peculiar advantages. Parents therefore are very eager, even at the hazard of their children's lives, to embrace the blessed occasion. I have heard that a priest, in immersing a child, for baptism is performed here by the immersion of the whole body, let it slip, through inattention, into the water. The child was drowned; but the holy man suffered no consternation. "Give me another," said he, with the utmost composure, "for the Lord hath taken this to Himself." The Empress, however, having other uses for her subjects, and not desiring that the Lord should have any more in that way at least, gave orders, that all children to be baptised in the Jordan, should henceforth be let down in a basket. [335-336]

VI · RUSSIAN LAW

I. CONTRADICTIONS AND CAPRICE

ALL THE JUDGES are named by the Sovereign, and hold their places only during her pleasure.—In general, the administration of justice has been represented to me as very tedious, and liable to corruption. I have heard, indeed, that the Empress intends to alter the present system; and, if so, it will certainly receive improvement. In truth, the Courts of Justice now mentioned, bear a greater resemblance to a Court of Chancery (Blackstone) than to anything else. The decisions of the judges are neither founded on general principles of equity, nor on established laws. They are founded chiefly on precedents and former decisions. This, as you will easily conceive, renders the issue of a law-suit very doubtful; and, indeed, it frequently happens, that precedents and former Ucases [ukases] may be perfectly applicable to the same cause; and yet in direct opposition to one another. In cases the most familiar that can be thought of, contradictory decrees of different sovereigns, and, sometimes even of the same sovereign, may be appealed to. Thus it is obvious, that, on the present footing, everything depends on the will of the Judge. [229-230]

2. ADVOCATES WITHOUT EDUCATION

Those persons who correspond to counsels or advocates in Britain, are very little respected in Russia. They receive no regular education in the study of law. And how should they, where there is none to study? They are usually such persons as have been Judges' servants, or have had other opportunities of learning the forms of courts and of being acquainted with the precedents or Ucases. Dexterity in the knowledge and application of these constitutes the highest merit. They never plead; but give their advice in the conduct of a law-suit; write the necessary papers; and either in public or private lay the facts before the judges. This last, indeed, may be considered as a species of pleading, since they may represent facts in such colours, as to influence both judgment and inclination. I have heard it surmised, however, by persons, I confess, of acrimony, but not without knowledge, and even experience, that the best service they usually render their clients, is to inform them by what means they may have easiest access to the good-will of the Judges.

The most eminent counsel who practices here at present, had been a shop-keeper, and had involved himself in so many law-suits as to become bankrupt. But though he lost his fortune, he gained knowledge; and the same argumentative disposition that had ruined him as a merchant, advanced him at the bar. [230-231]

3. CHAINED BODIES AND FETTERED MINDS

You questioned me in particular about the punishment of crimes in Russia, and seemed to applaud the plan pursued by the late, and continued by the present, Empress, of substituting slavery, hard labour, and corporal punishment, in place of death. The abolition, or suspension of capital punishments, is, indeed, a very plausible topic; it may soothe our sentiments of humanity, it may please in theory; but in practice it appears very inadequate.[41] Robberies here are frequent and barbarous, and constantly attended with murder. Criminals, I have heard, are prosecuted carelessly; and those who are punished with rigour, are treated with inhumanity. They suffer the knout; that is, they suffer dreadful scourging and dislocation; and though they are not formally put to death, many of them die of the cruel wounds they receive. . . . Those who survive such punishment are very seldom reformed; the disgrace and the infamy they suffer, take away all respect for themselves, and regard for the opinion of others. . . . At any rate, the subjects at least of a free state, ought to be much on their guard how they suffer any such punishment to be substituted in place of capital punishment, as may reconcile the imaginations of the people to the possibility of their being happy, or of their enduring life in chains and bondage. They ought always to believe, nor in adopting such a creed, would they

[41] Richardson was here dealing with one of the most controversial subjects in the literature of British travel in Russia. Coxe and Macartney took his view that the abolition of capital punishment was a great mistake, but John Williams argued the contrary case: "The Empress Elizabeth endeavored to do by her clemency what her father did by laws. . . . When she came to the throne, she promised that no person should be punished with death during her reign, and she kept her promise. Those who were found guilty . . . were condemned to labour in the mines or upon the public works, so that their punishments might be of some utility to the community, an institution which was worthy of the most civilized state. In almost every other part of Europe all who are found guilty of capital crimes are put to death; but others are not by this means deterred from committing the life offences. . . . The terrors of death make a much less impression upon such criminals than the dread of punishment, and of hard labour which they are to suffer every day." Williams, *op. cit.*, II, 98.

suffer any delusion, that slavery is a more miserable condition than death. I have felt less horror in seeing malefactors hanging in gibbets on Bagshot and Hounslow-heath, than in seeing men, beings of my own species, endowed with reason and a sense of justice, doomed to hard labour all the days of their life, bent down with oppression, having their faces inscribed with misery, and their limbs rattling with chains. Crimes are not to be punished by the severest pains we are capable of inflicting, and I hope the natives of Britain will consider chains and bondage, in the face of the public, as a punishment no less barbarous to the mind, than torture to the body. In another view, the effects of such punishments on the minds of a free people must be pernicious; and I should be afraid lest their enduring them for any length of time, were a fatal symptom that their zeal for liberty was waxing cold. There is much thought and penetration in the following sentiment, ascribed by Tacitus to Galgacus, in his celebrated speech before his battle with Agricola: "All the battles, which have yet been fought with various success against the Romans, had their resources of hope and aid in our hands; for we, the noblest inhabitants of Britain, and therefore stationed in its deepest recesses, far from the view of servile shores, have preserved even our eyes unpolluted by the contact of subjection." [232-235]

4. SECURITY FOR NONE, JUSTICE FOR FEW

On reading over what I have written, it seems to me that I might have given you a more complete account of the administration of justice in Russia, by telling you what they have not, instead of what they have. Suffice it to say, then, that they have no trials by jury, and no Habeas Corpus Act. A person accused of crimes may be kept in prison forever; or, if he is brought to trial, he is not tried by his Peers. In other respects, causes need not be numerous and complex. The peasants, who are themselves slaves, will probably have no law-suits. The nobility, merchants, and foreigners alone can have any employment for courts of justice. [236-237]

VII · THE SERVILE SYSTEM

I BELIEVE sincerely that no despot, or, if you like the term better, no absolute monarch ever ruled with more prudence, or studied the welfare of his people with more rectitude of attention, than the present Empress of Russia. Yet it is impossible for a native of Britain, giving an account of this country to an Englishman, not to express such feelings and reflections, as a comparison between the British government, and that of other nations, must naturally suggest. [193]

I. THE SLAVES OF THE NOBLES

The peasants in Russia, that is to say, the greatest part of the subjects of this empire, are in a state of abject slavery; and are reckoned the property of the nobles to whom they belong, as much as their dogs and horses. Indeed, the wealth of a great man in Russia is not computed by the extent of land he possesses, or by the quantity of grain he can bring to market, but by the number of his slaves. Those belonging to Prince Sherebatoff[42] and constituting his fortune, are said to be no less in number than a hundred and twenty-seven thousand.[43] [193]

Insecurity of Property

Every slave pays about a ruble (four shillings) yearly to his owner; and if he be in the way of making money, the tribute he makes is augmented. In general, every Russian nobleman allots to the peasants that belong to him, a certain portion of land to be cultivated by them, the produce of which, excepting what suffices for their own maintenance, is paid to the proprietor. Sometimes those slaves practice trades, or engage in traffic; and all such persons pay a much greater sum yearly to their owners, than is done by the labourer of the ground. In fact, a Russian peasant has no property; everything he possesses, even the miserable raiment that shelters him from the cold, may be seized by his master as his own.—A carpenter, being known to have made some money, was commanded by the rapacious steward of a rapacious Knaez [Kniaz], to give two hundred rubles to his owner. The man obeyed, and brought the money in copper. "I must have it in silver," said the steward. The slave, denying that he had so much, was instantly scourged till he promised to fulfil the demand. He brought the silver, and the covetous superior retained both the silver and the copper.— You will easily conceive, that men in this situation, if they were ever enabled to improve their fortunes, will conceal their wealth and assume an external appearance of indigence and misery. [194-195]

[42] Prince M. Shcherbatov (1733-1790), aristocrat, student of the Enlightenment, and author of a fifteen volume history of Russia from its origins to "the Time of Troubles."

[43] G. T. Robinson estimates that "in 1767, the greatest proprietor of the day owned 44,561 male souls, and perhaps as many females." However, the difficulty of obtaining accurate information somewhat excuses the discrepancy. Robinson, *op. cit.*, p. 29.

Oppression of Person

The owner has also the power of selling his slave, or of hiring his labour to other persons; and, it happens sometimes, that a Knaez, or Boyard, [Boyar] shall give his slave to a neighbouring Boyard in exchange for a dog or a horse. The owner may also inflict on his slaves whatever punishment he pleases, and for any sort of offence. It is against law, indeed, to put any of them to death; yet it happens, sometimes, that a poor slave dies of the wounds he receives from a passionate and unrelenting superior. I have heard, that not long ago a lady at Moscow, the sister of Marischal S——, was convicted of having put to death upwards of seventy slaves, by scourging, and by inflicting on them other barbarous punishments. It was a matter of amusement with her to contrive such modes of punishment as were whimsical and unusual. Such enormity, however, notwithstanding her rank, and the great power which the nobility have over their slaves, was not to pass with impunity. She was tried, was found guilty, and condemned to stand in the market-place with a label on her breast declaring her crime, and to be shut up in a dungeon. But she, who had felt no reluctance in making her fellow-creatures suffer the most inhuman torments, and had even amused herself with the variety of their sufferings, had such a sense of her rank, and such lively feelings of her own disgrace, that pride, shame, and resentment deprived her of her reason. In truth, both the crime and the punishment seem to me strongly marked with the characters of barbarity.

As a Russian peasant has no property, can enjoy none of the fruits of his own labour more than is sufficient to preserve his existence, and can transmit nothing to his children but the inheritance of wretched bondage, he thinks of nothing beyond the present. You are not, of consequence, to expect among them much industry and exertion. Exposed to corporal punishment, and put on the footing of irrational animals, how can they possess that spirit and elevation of sentiment which distinguish the natives of a free state? Treated with so much inhumanity, how can they be humane? I am confident, that most of the defects which appear in their national character, are in consequence of the despotism of the Russian government. [195-197]

Separation from the Land

They often come from distant provinces, and are either employed as domestic slaves, mechanics, or as day-labourers, at Moscow, Petersburg, and other cities. In these cases they must have certificates and a written permit, specifying their names, owners, and the time they are allowed to be absent. When they come to any town, with a view of remaining there, and engaging themselves in any work, the person who employs them must lodge their certificates with the master of the police in the place where they are about to reside. After remaining their alloted time, they must return to their former owners, and must be accountable to them for everything they have earned.—To these practices the Empress alludes in the following passages, in her instructions to the deputies assembled for making laws: "It seems, too, that method for exacting their revenues, invented by the lords, diminishes both the inhabitants, and the spirit of agriculture, in Russia. Almost all the villages are heavily taxed. The lords, who seldom or never reside in their villages, lay an impost on every head, of one, two, or even five rubles, without the least regard to the means by which their peasants may be able to raise this money. It is highly necessary that the law should prescribe a rule to the lords, for a more judicious method of raising their revenues; and oblige them to levy such a tax as tends least to separate the peasant from his house and family: this would be the means by which agriculture would become more extensive, and population more increased in the empire. Even now, some husbandmen do not see their houses for fifteen years together, and yet pay the tax annually to their respective lords; which they procure in towns at a vast distance from their families, and wander over the whole empire for that purpose." [197-199]

2. THE SLAVES OF THE CROWN

The condition of those peasants who are immediate slaves of the crown, is reckoned less wretched than the condition of those who belong to the nobility; and they are of three kinds: The first are those who, having either secretly, or by the favour of a humane superior, been able to procure as much money as may enable them to purchase their freedom, have also the good luck to live under a superior who is equitable enough to free them for the sum they offer. Such persons, and their children, are ever after immediate slaves of the crown. On the same footing are all priests and their children; though the dependence of the inferior upon the superior clergy, is sometimes as grievous as the most painful bondage. Soldiers also, and their children; and this class includes the whole body of the nobility, are immediate slaves of the crown. [199-200]

3. THE DEPRAVITY OF DESPOTISM

You say I will have much pleasure in contemplating the manners and political constitution of a people so different from the natives of Britain. I cannot altogether agree with you. . . . There is some satisfaction in recollecting, that while other nations groan under the yoke of bondage, the natives of our happy islands enjoy more real freedom than any nation that does now, or ever did, exist. In other respects, it is no very pleasing exercise to witness the depression and sufferings of the human race; to contemplate the miseries and manners of slaves! Poor abject slaves! who are not allowed the rights of men—hardly those of irrational creatures! who must toil, undergo hardships, and suffer the most grievous suffering, to gratify the desires or humour the caprice of some oppressive master! Judge of their condition.—From the hour of their birth they are in the power of a rapacious chief, who may sell, scourge, or employ them in any labour he pleases. They have no property, no home, nothing that their proud superior may not seize, and claim as his own. The horse and the bull may chuse their loves, according to their own inclination, a privilege not allowed to the Russians. They no sooner arrive at the age of puberty, when they are often compelled to marry whatsoever female their proprietor chuses, in order, by a continued progeny of slaves, to preserve or augment his revenue. In such families, no conjugal happiness,—no paternal or filial affection can ever exist.[44] Where the husband or wife hate each other, or are indifferent, there can be little fidelity; the husband takes little care of the child; the mother is not always affectionate; the poor, guiltless infant is thus neglected; Nature defeats the purposes of avarice, and a great proportion of their children die in their nonage. Those who survive become little better than savage. In their early years, no tender affections softened or humanized their hearts; none can grow up in an after period; they receive no prejudices or opinions favourable to mankind; and they enter into life as into a den of tigers.

[44] Richardson seems here to have been carried away. It would be natural to assume that the patriarchal nature of Russian society would tend to develop strong family ties, even without the testimony of other observers. John Cook, although admitting the existence of forced marriage, described "the ceremony of marriage and consummation" as being "carried on with as great decorum and modesty as with us, and I never heard but that the men treated their wives with the greatest tenderness and affection. One great occasion why they have young married is that their children may be able, if necessary, to support them in their old age. I am of the opinion there cannot be produced many examples in Russia that children ever did or durst suffer their parents to pine in want whilst they themselves lived in plenty." Cook, *op. cit.*, I, 71. Macartney was struck by "an extreme veneration, obedience, and respect for their parents, few instances of undutifulness or ingratitude to them to be found here." Macartney, *op. cit.*, p. 32.

The guile, the baseness, and the rugged ferocity attributed to slaves, and men overwhelmed with oppression, are chiefly owing to their oppressors. Exposed to the avarice and pride of some haughty superior, who is himself a slave, and who has not in his breast one sentiment of humanity, they have no other defence against oppression but deceit; and feel no other emotion from the treatment they receive, but hatred and deep revenge. It is thus, in accustoming the mind to vicious habits, more than in merely depriving us of our property, and the security of our persons, that despotism is the bane of society. Those poor unhappy men, who are bought and sold, who are beaten, loaded with fetters, and valued no higher than a dog, treated with unabating rigour, become inhuman; insulted with unremitting contempt, become base; and, forever afraid of rapacious injustice, they grow deceitful. [239-241]

VIII · MANNERS AND CUSTOMS

1. THE NOBLE

The Establishments of Tyrants

I CANNOT SAY MUCH for the taste displayed by persons of high rank in Russia, either in their dress, houses, or retinue. They are pompous and tawdry. The equipage of a Russian nobleman deserves particular notice. The great man lolls in a clumsy gilt coach, drawn by six horses, sometimes of different colours, and having the traces of hempen ropes instead of leather. The coachmen and postilions are often in the coarse dress of the peasants, while three or four gorgeous footmen are stuck behind. One or two petty officers ride by the side of the coach, and these are usually attended by a peasant, who is also on horseback; and thus princes and noblemen are dragged to court. . . .

I mentioned to you formerly, that the inferior orders of men in this country are in a state of abject slavery. Nor is it inconsistent with this account to say, that many persons of high rank in Russia live on a footing of easy familiarity with such of their menials as become favourites, and are capable of amusing them with their humour and low wit. All domestic tyrants, from the days of the Greeks and Romans inclusively, treat those slaves who are not favourites with the utmost rigour, and those who are, with a weak unbecoming indulgence.[45]

---

[45] Forty years later, Martha Wilmot, without exploring its ramifications or attempting to understand its cause, noted this same paradox of social fraternization amid political tyranny: "A mixture of familiarity and pride appears to me to be a striking characteristic of this country. 'Tis by no means uncommon to see masters and slaves mingle in the same dance, and

Perhaps in no other country in Europe could you obtain a juster idea of the parasitical character, so frequently displayed by the comic and satirical poets of antiquity. The parasites here are, in general, Frenchmen, whose lively loquacity seems absolutely necessary for the amusement of those great men, to whose tables they have admission. At the same time, if the following representation, in one of the finest satires that any language can boast of, be founded on observation, the circumstance now mentioned is not peculiar to the Russian Princes.

> ... Obsequious, artful, voluble, and gay,
> On Britain's fond credulity they prey.—
> Studious to please, and ready to submit,
> The supple Gaul was born a parasite:
> Still to his interest, true, where'er he goes,
> Wit, bravery, worth, his lavish tongue bestows ...
> Well may they venture on the mimic's art,
> Who play from morn to night a borrow'd part;
> Practis'd their master's notions to embrace,
> Repeat his maxims and reflect his face;
> With ev'ry wild absurdity comply,
> And view each object with another's eye;
> To shake with laughter, ere the jest they hear,
> To pour at will the counterfeited tear;
> And as their patron hints the cold or heat,
> To shake in dog days, in December, sweat. . . .[46]

Besides parasites, many Russians of high rank retain dwarfs in their families, and persons not without shrewdness, who affect folly, and amuse them in the character of buffoons. They also retain a vast number of other slaves, who are employed by them in all manner of whimsical or necessary services. The Countess W—— has in her family several Calmuck women, who are taught to read German and Russ, who read by her bed-side till she falls asleep; and continue reading or talking, without intermission, all the time she is asleep, for, if they did not, the Countess would awake, immediately, not much, I suppose, to the satisfaction of the poor attendants. [218-222]

The Educations of Slaves

I need scarcely tell you, that the Russians are very careless in the edu-

---

visiting at a strange house, I have been more than once puzzled to find out which was the mistress and which the *femme de chambre*." Londonderry and Hyde, *op. cit.*, p. 48.

[46] Richardson is here quoting, apparently from memory, from Samuel Johnson's *London*, a poem adapted from a satire of Juvenal originally aimed at the Greek sycophants who plagued Roman society in his day.

cation of their children. They do not send them to public schools; but have them taught at home under private tutors. These tutors are generally French or Germans, into whose character they make but little enquiry. If their children learn to dance; and if they can read, speak, and write French, and have a little geography, they desire no more. I have seen one of those instructors, who has, in the course of his life, appeared in the different shapes of a comedian, valet-de-chambre, and hair-dresser.—Indeed, I do not wonder at the conduct of the Russians in this respect. Why educate their children? They are to live and die in thralldom; they may be in glory today, and tomorrow sent to Siberia. Why should they train their offspring for any expectations beyond those of the present moment? The citizens of free states alone are inexcusable, if they do not improve their minds to the utmost limits of their capacity. Why quicken the sensibilities, or enlarge the mind of a slave? You only teach him to hate himself. If, however, there was any probability, that, by enlightening the minds of the Russians, they should not only be enabled to discern the abasement of their condition; but also to contrive and execute the means of emancipation, I should heartily regret their present blindness. [222-223]

The Skepticism of Simpletons

After the account I have given you of the taste and literary education of the Russians, you will not be surprised if I tell you, that their religious principles are not very correct, nor in some of them, perhaps, very deeply rooted. A priest came to hear the confession of a great man. "Holy Father," says the Count, "have you a good memory?" "Yes." "Then you remember what I told you at my last confession. Since that time I have had the same temptations from without; the same weakness from within; and here is the same number of rubles." I would not say, however, that the Princes of Russia are much inferior, either in religious or moral improvement, to many great men, even in those states of Europe that enjoy the means of superior knowledge. If I am not much mistaken, there are among them a greater number who affect indifference or disbelief in religious matters, than who really disbelieve.[47] Perhaps, in times of sickness, disgrace, and low-spirits, they have more faith in St. Nicholas, than in Voltaire.

[47] Macartney went even further: "Those of superior rank, who have a better education, especially such as have traveled, and have discovered the absurdity of their earlier principles and have surmounted those prejudices, they have generally stopped at that point and are for the most part skeptics without any religion at all, and commonly without knowing why they are so, taking up their infidelity on trust from those with whom they have chanced to con-

The fair sex in all ages have more sensibility, less of the pride of reason, and I had almost said, more good sense than the men; and accordingly you find fewer among them who affect irreligion. Their notions may be erroneous; this is owing to their instructors: but their dispositions are pious, and they owe this to themselves. Indeed, when I see Russian Princesses, as they sit down to an entertainment, crossing themselves, which they do very gracefully, in testimony of religious gratitude, I respect both their good sense and their piety. [224-226]

2. THE PEASANT

Robustness of Physique

The Russians are tall, robust, and well-proportioned; their teeth are remarkably good; their hair is in general black, and their complexions ruddy. I have scarcely seen any red-haired persons among them; and those who are fair, are not so good-looking as those who are dark-complexioned. Squinting or stuttering are seldom met with; and you see few or none who are either lame or deformed. . . .

The women of all ranks in this country, though very sprightly and very gay, forever dancing, and singing, and laughing, and talking, have not the same pretentions that the men have to good looks, and the graces of external appearance. They have no delicacy of shape; and their complexions are—what they please. For those even in the lowest condition, if they are able to afford it, bedaub their faces with red. Red is the favourite colour here, inasmuch, that the word denoting it in the Russian language, is synonymous with beautiful. . . .

Coarseness of Dress

Their dress, I mean that of the Russian peasants, is very simple, but well suited to their rigorous climate. It consists of skins, coarse woollen cloth, and coarse linen, which they use for shirts or drawers. Their upper garment is a large frock, reaching to their knees, folding over before, and fastened about the middle with a girdle. In the various and glaring colours of the girdle, they sometimes endeavour to display their taste. They have pieces of cloth wrapped in a variety of folds about their legs, and fastened with strings; nor do they seem at all solicitous of exhibiting in this limb any qualities of shape or proportion. Their necks are naked, and exposed to the weather, and, of consequence, they

---

verse abroad or from the few foreign books they have read and following those guides as implicity as others follow the superstitions of their ancestors." Macartney, *op. cit.*, p. 81.

resemble bulls necks. They have long beards and bushy hair; and have their heads covered with worsted or fur caps, rising, for the most part, in a conic form. Every Russian, of what rank soever, usually wears upon his breast, and hanging by a ribbon or string tied about his neck, a small cross of gold, silver, or lead. They receive these crosses from their God-fathers at their baptism; and they never part with them as long as they live. [201-205]

Rudeness of Dwellings

Their houses are made of wood, and constructed in a very particular manner. A number of large trees are stripped of their bark; they are not cut into deals, but are laid close and horizontally upon one another; they are fastened at the end with wooden pegs; and thus, by fixing the end of one tree into another, they constitute the walls. The roof is sometimes of boards, and sometimes thatched. I have heard, that houses of this sort are frequently placed on wheels, so as to be movable from one place to another. The Russians, in constructing their houses, make use of very few instruments. The hatchet is almost the only one in use among them; it serves them even for a saw; and it is wonderful how straight and regularly they can cut with it. They make use neither of the plane, nor of the chisel. I except from this account those who are professed carpenters. [205-206]

Obeisance of Behavior

Two Russian peasants, meeting each other, take off their caps, bow most profoundly, shake hands, wipe their beards, kiss one another, and, according to their different ages, call one another brother or father, or by some appellation that expresses affection. Both men and women in their salutations bow very low. I was much struck with this circumstance; and soon found, that, in their obeisance to the great, and in the worship of their saints, they were early trained to prostration and pliancy of body. Indeed, the servile submission they testify to their superiors, can only be equaled by the haughty usage they meet with in return.

Two Russian peasants, if they should happen to quarrel, seldom proceed to blows; but they deal abuse with great profusion; and their abusive language consists of the basest allusions, and the most shocking obscenity. This can scarcely be exemplified in the manners of any other nation. If ever they come to blows, the conflict has a most ludicrous appearance, they know nothing of the clenched fist of an Englishman; but lay about them most uncouthly with open hands and extended arms. [209-210]

IX · NATIONAL CHARACTER

I. SENSUOUS AMUSEMENTS

I KNOW NO CIRCUMSTANCE by which the national character of any people may more easily be detected, than their amusements. When men divert themselves, they are careless, unguarded, and unreserved: then the heart, and all its latent tendencies, disguised inclinations, and indulged habits, appear. Nor am I acquainted with any circumstance by which national characters are more diversified. The Romans were a less refined people than the Greeks; their amusements accordingly were coarser and more sanguinary. In like manner the diversions of the French and Spaniards mark the difference of their national characters. The pastime of the Spaniards, without doors, is fierce and bloody; nor is the . . . bullfight, of which they are so passionately fond, the amusement of men only, but has its admirers also among the women. Hence, Butler has said of them,

> That Spanish heroes with their lances,
> At once wound bulls and ladies' fancies:
> And he acquires the noblest spouse,
> That widows greatest herds of cows.

Chess, and the other amusements to which a Spaniard has recourse within doors, are certainly very grave and solemn. How different from the gaiety, sprightliness, good humour, and seeming levity of a Frenchman!

The diversions of an Englishman exhibit strength, agility, and a love of exertion. Those of a Russian exhibit sloth, inactivity, and a love of pleasure.[48] The Russians, in their amusements, are indeed extremely social. They assemble in crowds, sing, drink, swing on see-saws, are drawn up and down and roundabout in flying chairs fixed upon wheels, some with a perpendicular, and some with a horizontal motion. In the

---

[48] Macartney also made observations upon the amusements of the Russians. "Though in a northern climate, they have an Asiatic aversion to all corporal activity and manly exercise and scarce form an idea of either beyond the smooth velocity of a sled or the measured paces of a man at court. They have no passion for the sports of the field. Hunting, shooting, fishing, as practiced with us, they are utterly strangers to. Avoiding every recreation attended with exertion or fatigue, they prefer the more indolent amusements of chess, cards, or billiards, in which they are usually extraordinarily proficient. . . . They loll through and sleep away life and wake up to the calls of sensuality and the grosser pleasures." *ibid.*, p. 38.

winter season, they are pushed down ice-hills and glissades. Those ice-hills are raised upon the river, and are constructed of wooden frames. They are very high; so that you ascend fifty or sixty steps on the side behind what is properly called the glissade. . . . The side by which you go down is so steep, as to be just not perpendicular. Upon this, snow having been piled, and water poured, it becomes a precipice of the smoothest ice. In descending, you sit upon a small wooden seat made for the purpose, and generally in the lap of a Russian, who sits behind to direct your course, having his legs extended on each side of you. In this posture you are pushed down the hill, and slide with such velocity, that for some seconds you cannot breathe; and after reaching the bottom, the impulse you have received carries you forward some hundred paces. . . . Skating is not a common diversion, because the ice, where it is not swept, is usually covered with snow. The Russians are also fond of dancing; yet their dancing does not display so much nimbleness, agility, and liveliness, as it expresses the same tainted imagination, which assumes a less seducing and more boisterous form in their quarrels and abuse. [210-213]

2. INFANTILE LEVITY

You will have remarked . . . in the accounts I have given you, that the lower classes here are very social, and much addicted to merriment. They are even infantine in their amusements. Old, bearded boors divert themselves with such pastimes and gambols, as in our grave country we should think too trifling for a child. The truth is, that, beyond the present moment, they have nothing either to think about, or care for; and, of consequence, they are perfectly thoughtless and careless. In the country they live chiefly in villages; when they come to the great towns, many of them having no houses of their own, pass most of their time, when they are not employed in labour, in their cabecks, (public-houses) where they drink, talk, and sing until they fall asleep, and on holidays they assemble together in vacant places in or near the city, for their customary exercises and amusements. Those two circumstances, therefore, namely, their social dispositions, promoted in the manner now mentioned, and their total want of care or concern about the future, give them the appearance of having great sprightliness and good humour; and of possessing no inconsiderable share of enjoyment. Persons of high rank, though their situations must occasion some variety in the circumstances that influence their manners, are subject to the same effects, and exhibit a similar appearance. If you call such enjoyment happiness, or such social dispositions virtuous, you may: I own I cannot agree with you.

Russians of all ranks are most ardent in their expressions of friendship; but I suspect the constancy of their attachments is not equal to the fervency of their emotions. They have more sensibility than firmness; they possess a temper and dispositions, which, properly improved, and with the encouragements held forth by freedom, might render them a worthy, as in some cases, they are an amiable, and, in many, an amusing people.[49] [215-217]

3. SPORADIC ENTHUSIASM

Consistently with this account, the Russians, though they have great quickness in learning the rudiments of art or knowledge, seldom make great proficiency. They soon arrive at a certain degree of excellence; there they remain; they tire; become listless; entertain disgust; and advance no further. In this particular, also, if they enjoy the incitements afforded by a free government, their national character might improve, and they might be rendered capable of more perseverance. After the wishes of novelty cease, men engaged in arduous pursuits, must be carried on by a steady regard to their own interest and honour. Where their honour and interest are not much concerned, how can they persevere? [217]

4. POLITICAL INSTABILITY

They have certainly more sensibility than firmness. They have lively

[49] Macartney's opinion of the Russian national character, although it corroborates Richardson's in many respects, reveals sufficient divergence to justify considerable quotation. ". . . in general, they are lazy in body, indolent of mind, and sensual to excess. Knowing no happiness beyond the gratification of drunkenness and gluttony, they are hospitable, charitable, and good natured. Nay, what may seem incredible to a foreigner, they are humane and can by no means be accused of cruelty. . . . They possess a great deal of natural shrewdness and sagacity and have a strong turn for ridicule, and in their transactions acquit themselves with uncommon cunning and address. . . . Their understanding and penetration are considerably lessened by their superstitious and obstinate attachment to ancient customs. . . . The Russians, however, when properly managed, when soothed by persuasion, allured by profit, or animated by example, become extremely docile, and learn all mechanic arts with surprising facility. They generally pass for being knavish; yet surely they possess a greater share of honesty than we have any right to expect, for, considering the temptations they are exposed to, the abolition of capital punishment, and the very little disgrace for successful villainy and corruption in the highest ranks of people, it is astonishing that any integrity among the commonality should be found at all. They . . . are obedient and submissive to their superiors, and of a servility and politeness to their equals which is scarcely to be paralleled. . . . They are not malicious or vindictive. Their acts of passion seem neither violent nor dangerous. As their resentments are not gloomy nor lasting, so their friendships are not permanent nor warm. Indeed, all the affections of the soul seem weaker in them than in most other nations." *ibid.*, p. 30.

feelings; but, having seldom employed their reason in forming general rules of conduct for the commerce of life, their actions, as flowing from variable and shifting emotions, are desultory, and even inconsistent.

I have heard, for instance, that in confidential conversation, they sometimes indulge themselves in severe and indignant expressions against the present administration of public affairs.—"That they should always be governed by women, or foreigners, or by foreigners exalted they know not how, or by persons of no original eminence, men of yesterday, and who have arisen to dignity by their guilt or base compliances,"—are, on such occasions, the usual topics of their discontent. They work themselves into what they conceive virtuous indignation, or patriotic resentment. They even talk of changes and revolutions: "Things," they will say, "that have happened once, may happen again"; and thus the fervour of their emotion, exhausted in the expression, abates. Other feelings arise, and suggest other convictions.—"The present administration has been successful; laurels have been obtained; public measures have been conducted with spirit and wisdom; they themselves enjoy security; not only so, perhaps they enjoy fortune and honours; how wrong then would it be in them to wish for change; how ungrateful! how guilty! even of treason! they deserve punishment! perhaps it may come upon them! their associates may think as they do! may feel indignation! or fear for themselves! the danger is urgent, and must be prevented." Hurried by this new set of feelings, they repent, confess, and from the deep sense they have of their trespass, betray their friends. On account of this extreme sensibility, unsubdued or ungoverned by reason, it is scarcely probable that the Russians themselves, how much soever they may occasionally express resentment, indignation, or love of liberty, as I have heard some of them do with more violence than any liberty-boy of Brentford, unless some dexterous, insinuating, and steady foreigner take advantage of their temporary transports, shall ever accomplish any great revolution. The chief rulers have penetration enough to discern this defect of character; and though they may be often informed of treasonable speeches, they are nevertheless very much at their ease. At the same time, this feature in the national character of the Russians, shews how necessary it is for their Sovereigns, without incurring the *blame of improper suspicion*, to be watchful over their proceedings, and well acquainted with their secret designs. [244-246]

5. PERSONAL HYPOCRISY

I really believe, that the inconstancy, the deviations from truth, and even perfidy, with which the Russians are sometimes charged,[50] are not so much the effects of determined vice, as of irregular feeling. They may appear wicked, not because they act from perverted principles, but because they have no permanent principles. They never could say to themselves, "*Video meliora proboque, deteriora sequor,*" because whatsoever they do, or even perpetrate, they think they are acting aright; and as they seldom look back on the past, or anticipate the future, they derive little advantage in the culture of their moral principles from experience. They are bearded children; the creatures of the present hour; they will express the most ardent affection in the most ardent language; they will express the most furious rage in the most vindictive terms. But as you need not lay great stress on the advantages to be reaped from their friendship, so you need not be greatly afraid of their inveterate or latent enmity. In moments of extreme good humour, a Russian will make ample promises; he is quite sincere; his feelings at the time interest him in your favour; but those feelings subside; other interests engage his heart; he never meant to deceive you; but his promises are not fulfilled. . . . Rigid virtue may call this double-dealing; but the Russian neither intends deceit, nor thinks his conduct deceitful. [246-248]

6. EMOTIONAL VOLATILITY

In like manner, you may sometimes see persons of the highest rank, even before strangers, engage in violent disputes, particularly if they are playing at cards or billiards; and treat one another at least with impetuosity. Their own language, though they may have been speaking French or German before, becomes on these occasions the vehicle

[50] Typical of such charges is a passage from Lord Cathcart's correspondence with Rochford: "The Russians in general are men of no education or principles of knowledge of any sort, though not without quickness of parts. Some of them have great pretensions, and in such, policy can never deserve a better name than cunning, which may deceive a stranger and embarrass rivals, but never will be able to conduct affairs or gain the confidence of discerning friends." Cathcart to Rochford, March 17, 1769, *Sbornik*, XII, 427. In common with Richardson, Catherine Wilmot saw a similar hypocrisy as the consequence of despotic influences: "I look upon every noble as an iron link in the massy chain which manacles this realm, and as to the individuals amongst them that I have met at Moscow 'tis impossible to be in their company without recollecting that they are subjects under a despotism, for in their judgements *bad* and *good* literally appears to be synonymous with *favour* and *disgrace*. The idea attach'd to what arises from *character* always gives place to *office*, and the exterior of deference can be calculated by the court almanack much better than by the chronicle of friendship." Londonderry and Hyde, *op. cit.*, p. 224.

of their prayers and wishes; and its habits of phraseology seem better suited than those of the western languages, for such *pure* and *respectful* intercourse. In a few minutes after they are as calm as if nothing had happened, and seem to love one another the more for this transient ebullition.

Persons of such irregular sensibility are occasionally very brave, or very dastardly; and so are the Russians. Sometimes the slightest danger appalls them; and sometimes you would imagine that they were incapable of fear or had no sense of danger. This tendency is corrected in their army by the strictest discipline. It is perfectly consistent with this account, that slight enjoyments should raise them to the summit of happiness; and that slight losses, or disappointments, should cast them down in despair. Accordingly, their happiness displays itself in appearances of infantine levity; and their despondency often terminates in suicide. The immediate view of punishment, or the prospect of evil striking their senses, may restrain their emotions; but removed at a distance, or out of sight, it is of little power. . . .

Persons of the character now mentioned, are often fluent in speech, and eloquent in expression. They are also apt to be influenced by the powers of eloquence. Full of sensibility, they enter easily into the feelings of others. Such are the Russians. . . . That Russians of all ranks are fond of music is no less consistent with the foregoing account, than their powers and susceptibility of eloquence. [248-252]

7. UTOPIAN SPECULATIONS

In a word, the defects in the national character of the Russians, seem to me to arise chiefly from want of culture. Were they taught to reflect on the past, and to anticipate the future, they would be led to form maxims and general rules for the direction of their conduct. Reason would then be listened to; and their moral principles would recover their authority. But they will never either reflect or anticipate, till they are moved to those exercises by some prevailing interest; nor can they ever have any such interest, till they have entire security for their persons and possessions. How is this to be done? It is an important problem; and great and immortal would be the glory of that sovereign who would really desire to understand the solution. Immortal would be the glory of that sovereign who would restore above twenty millions of men to the rights of intelligent and rational beings. But is this achievement to be performed by one person, and at once? I believe not. It must be the work of time; and must be carried on by successive changes. To give liberty at once to twenty millions of slaves, would be to let loose on mankind so many robbers and spoilers. Before slaves can receive freedom in full possession, they must be taught to know, relish, and use its blessings. This, however, is to be done gradually; and if it is to be done according to a regular plan, those who have such things in their power, must observe the growth of freedom in those places where it arose spontaneous, and without any previous purpose.—Perhaps, if a despot intended to lay the foundation of a design so magnificent, it would be proper to begin with giving great privileges to commercial and manufacturing towns. It would also be right to restore their rights to such provinces as might formerly have enjoyed some freedom; and of which they might still entertain some fond recollection. I am the more inclined to express these opinions, as some of the Russians, and particularly those in the vicinity of Archangel, who, I have heard, enjoy greater privileges than their brethren, are usually represented as honest, able, and industrious, and indeed, of a character very different from the rest.

But I quit such Utopian speculations; and will only express my wishes, that the small portion of the human race who enjoy real freedom, may preserve and make a proper use of it. [252-254]

CHAPTER FOUR
Sir James Harris

Sir James Harris:

LION IN THE VIXEN'S DEN

(1777-1783)

JAMES HARRIS, member of Parliament in 1770, a Knight of the Bath in 1779, the first Baron Malmesbury and Viscount Fitzharris in 1788, and the first Earl of Malmesbury in 1800, unlike those travelers previously dealt with, was destined, from the very beginning of his life, for membership in the ruling class. He was born in the cathedral city of Salisbury on April 21, 1746, in the house which had been the town residence of his ancestors for two centuries past, and his kinsman, the Earl of Shaftsbury, stood godfather at his christening. His father, James Harris, although not himself a member of the nobility enjoyed a respected reputation in both artistic and political circles. For all that Samuel Johnson had termed him "a prig and a bad prig"[1] his various critical works and particularly his "Hermes," a thesis on grammar, received wide acclaim. Moreover, he joined the Ministry of George Grenville as a Lord of the Admiralty in 1761 and later acted as a Lord of the Treasury until the latter's fall in 1765. As a parent, he consistently employed his influence to advance his only son, and his generosity, guidance, and character exercised a most important influence upon the development of the younger Harris. Even twenty years after his father's death, when, as the first Earl of Malmesbury, he had retired from public life, the son paid him this grateful tribute: "To my father's precept and example I owe every good quality I have; to his reputation and character I attribute my more than common success in life. . . . It was as his son that I first obtained friends and patrons. . . . Once, indeed, placed in a conspicuous and responsible situation, I was anxious to act becomingly in it, and even here I return with pleasure to the same grateful source, for while my father lived, which was during the first twelve years of my public life, the strongest incentive I had to exert

[1] James Boswell, *Life of Johnson*, edited by G. B. Hill, New York, 1904, III, 277.

myself was in the satisfaction I knew he would derive from any credit I might acquire."[2]

Harris's education was typical of that of many young Englishmen of his class and generation. It was extensive rather than intensive, and oriented less toward scholarship than to social polish and influential connections. Beginning at four years of age in a dames' school and, later, in a grammar school in his native Salisbury, he continued his education at Winchester where, as he afterwards admitted, he did pretty much as he liked. In the fall of 1762, his father called him away to London to spend a few months with him after their prolonged separation, and there, as a youth just turning seventeen, young James saw and heard at close quarters many of the leading public figures in the stirring period which marked the close of the Seven Years' War. While this experience matured his mind, the self-conscious sophistication which he derived from it contributed to that condescending attitude which he assumed toward his later studies at Oxford. During two years at Merton College, he confessed that he never saw his tutor "but during a fortnight, when I took it into my head to learn trigonometry."[3] University life was merely an imitation of high life in London with a regular round of evening card parties in the society of "very pleasant, but very idle fellows."[4] As in London, however, Harris formed many friendships, and since these "idle fellows" included such men as Charles James Fox, William Eden, later Lord Auckland, Lord Romney, Lord Nottingham, Sir James Stepney, and Sir Robert Spencer, their acquaintance was to prove not the least valuable part of his schooling.

The foreign phase of Harris's education began in 1765, when he left Oxford to study at the University of Leyden. Here he really applied himself for the first time to political and diplomatic history as well as to mastery of the Dutch language, but he did not neglect the opportunity to improve his social advantages. As the protege of Sir Joseph Yorke, later Baron Dover, and for many years British Minister at the Hague, he was introduced into the society of the capital and received his first impressions of life in the diplomatic service. A year later, he returned to England, but in 1767, he was back on the continent and, in the fashion of the Grand Tour, visited Berlin, Warsaw, the Hague, and Paris. Everywhere his father's connections opened up for him the life of the court circles, and his journals reveal a deepening interest in the

[2] James Howard Harris, 3rd Earl of Malmesbury, ed., *Diaries and Correspondence of James Harris, the First Earl of Malmesbury*, London, 1845, I, p. ix.

[3] *ibid.*, p. xi.   [4] *ibid.*

public affairs of the countries he visited. It is not surprising that on his return to England he should have sought and obtained, through the influence of Lord Shelbourne, a post as Secretary to the Embassy at the Court of Madrid, there to begin a service lasting through thirty of the most eventful years in British diplomatic history.

If family position had freed young Harris from financial worries and brought him social and political advancement, it could not spare him the embarrassments which events had destined for every British diplomat of the period. In the two short decades following 1763 "the first British Empire" was established by one Treaty of Paris and dissolved by another. British prestige abroad fell from its zenith to its nadir. At the close of the Seven Years' War, Edward Gibbon had observed: "Our opinions, our fashions, even our games were adopted in France; a ray of national glory illuminated each individual, and every Englishman was supposed to be born a patriot and a philosopher."[5] Yet only twenty years later, when a second war had cost England her American colonies, destroyed her maritime supremacy, and paraded her spiritual degradation, Horace Walpole wrote to a friend: "You must be happy now not to have a son who would live to grovel in the dregs of England."[6] That this alteration was in good part the consequence of the bankruptcy of British diplomacy could in no wise be expected to lessen its impact upon a patriotic foreign representative.

It was the brilliance of Britain's victory in 1763 which blinded the Foreign Office to the many very real dangers of her position, and thereby created the greatest danger of them all. The general temper is well illustrated in an official dispatch of May 1, 1767, from Conway, Secretary of State, to the Secretary of the Embassy at St. Petersburg. In essence it was simply an extravagant eulogy praising in unequivocal terms England's wealth, her loyal and populous colonies, her military and naval power, and her great and unanimous national spirit.[7] Yet this naive conceit was only one aspect of the general unpreparedness for the mantle of world empire which fell upon Britain's shoulders in 1763. Intoxicated by success, she closed her eyes to the possibility of failure. Dazzled by her colonial acquisitions, she turned her back upon the continent of Europe. Convinced of her maritime supremacy, she

[5] G. Hill, ed., *Memoirs of the Life of Edward Gibbon*, London, 1900, p. 151.

[6] Reginald Coupland, *The American Revolution and the British Empire*, London, 1930, p. 13.

[7] Conway to Shirley, October 9, 1767, *Sbornik*, xii, 310-316. That this letter was, in fact, a representative expression of official policy is stated by Reddaway in his comment that it summarized "in one despatch the basis for a thousand negotiations. It formulated the creed to which every British diplomatist must subscribe." W. F. Reddaway, "Macartney in Russia, 1765-1767," *Cambridge Historical Journal*, iii, 1931, p. 261.

allowed her naval arm, little by little, to fall into a state of disrepair, destined ultimately to lose her the command of the sea at a crucial juncture in the coming war. Endowed with a new determination to govern the American colonies so long left to themselves, she undertook a political problem for which she had neither the understanding nor the administrative machinery. Added to all these pitfalls, her political leaders, divided less by differences of principle than by ambition for power, waged a fierce struggle in Parliament, undermining ministerial stability and political consistency, with results remarked by Sir Andrew Mitchell in 1767: "The recent frequent changes in England have created a degree of diffidence in foreign powers which renders all negotiation both difficult and disagreeable."[8]

In the meanwhile, developments on the continent, unattended in any effective sense of the word by the British government, had isolated her from every power in Europe save Russia. The frustrations of the recent defeat, mutual losses in America, and compatible designs on British possessions in the Mediterranean strengthened the Bourbon "Family Compact" of France and Spain. The rather uneasy Austrian alliance was confirmed by a series of Bourbon-Hapsburg marriages, not only in the Italian possessions but on the throne of France itself. Frederick of Prussia, unalterably estranged from the British government by its desertion of his cause in the recent war, now looked eastward with those territorial ambitions ultimately realized in the First Partition of Poland. Finally, the traditional, if declining French influence in Poland, Sweden, and Turkey seemed to preclude these states from the British orbit. In Russia, alone, a combination of influences promised hope of an effective alliance. Both countries shared a traditional religious hatred of Roman Catholicism. Furthermore, they were connected by the more tangible link of powerful commercial ties. Whereas France had traditionally opposed Russian interests in the border states, England had the precedent of subsidy treaties in 1748[9] and 1755.[10] Finally, in an autocracy such as Russia, the unquestionably Anglophile predi-

[8] A. W. Ward and G. P. Gooch, *The Cambridge History of British Foreign Policy*, New York, 1922, I, 130.

[9] R. Lodge, "An Episode in Anglo-Russian Relations during the War of the Austrian Succession," *Royal Historical Society Transactions*, 4th Series, IX, 63-84; see also his "Lord Hyndford's Embassy to Russia, 1744-1749," *English Historical Review*, January and July, 1931, pp. 48-76, 389-422.

[10] Earl of Ilchester and Mrs. Langford-Brooke, *The Life of Sir Charles Hanbury-Williams*, London, 1929, pp. 303-324; D. B. Horn, *Hanbury-Williams and European Diplomacy, 1747-1758*, London, 1930, pp. 221ff.

lections of Catherine[11] were not to be overlooked, and the Northern System of Count Panin,[12] her Foreign Minister, which sought to create a league of all the Baltic powers, would profit greatly from British maritime and financial strength. For all these reasons, British negotiations in St. Petersburg assumed a very real significance in the complicated web of continental diplomacy throughout this period.

From the outset, British negligence, inconsistency, and refusal to compromise dissipated initial advantages and contributed to deepen the menacing isolation. Ignoring essential Russian interests throughout, the "nation of shopkeepers" stubbornly refused to acknowledge a Turkish attack on Russia as an occasion for invoking the terms of the projected treaty. Their objections were based, not on the wholly justifiable fear that a Russian conquest of the Ottoman Empire would remove an important barrier to Russian encroachments upon the British Mediterranean trade and Indian possessions, but on the premise that such an engagement would prejudice the Porte against the comparably negligible trade of the Turkey Company.[13] In the impasse which this created, Prussia in 1764, and in 1765 Denmark, whose finances could ill afford the subsidy required by Russia, acceded to the Turkish clause, and Panin's Northern League was begun without British participation. Having lost the solid advantages of a formal agreement, however, the British Foreign Office, only five years later, gave valuable assistance to the Mediterranean naval expedition which did much to procure Russia the navigation of the Straits and threatened to establish her as a future rival in the Mediterranean.

In Sweden, too, Panin's requests for assistance were ignored. There (much as in Poland) the constitutional authority of the Diet had opened a huge market for the corruption of its membership by mutually hostile Russian and French agents. Such bribery was extremely expensive, however: Panin confided to Macartney in 1755 that he had spent over half a million rubles (about £130,000), and that even little Denmark had contributed 100,000 rubles to "this cursed Diet."[14] Yet Macartney, whose government, as Secretary of State Conway boasted,[15]

[11] E. J. Simmons, *English Literature and Culture in Russia, 1553-1840*, Cambridge, Mass., 1935, pp. 86-92.

[12] Count Nikita Ivanovich Panin (1718-1783), minister of foreign affairs under Catherine.

[13] Even during the last third of the century, the greatest number of ships engaged in the trade of the Turkey Company in any single year was only 27, as contrasted to the 600 or 700 ships consigned by members of the Russia Company annually. Dietrich Gerhard, *England und der Aufstieg Russlands*, Munich, 1932, p. 99.

[14] Reddaway, *op. cit.*, p. 284.

[15] Conway to Shirley, October 9, 1767, *Sbornik*, XII, 312.

drew a revenue equal to that of the whole Russian Empire from land rentals in the Indian possessions alone, was instructed to point to an expenditure of a paltry £4,000 in Sweden as a claim on Russian gratitude. In her anxiety to maintain control in Sweden during the distractions of the Turkish War, Russia actually withdrew the Turkish clause on the condition that England should conclude a subsidy treaty with Sweden. At this moment, a single stroke would have completed the Northern System, but the Foreign Office decreed that this proposal simply "could not be listened to"[16] on the incredible grounds that the payment of a subsidy "violated the national rule against such measures in time of peace."[17] Then in 1772, French machination assisted Gustavus III to overthrow the constitutional authority of the Diet which Prussia and Russia had formally engaged to maintain both in 1764 and in 1769, but which, in their preoccupation with Turkish and Polish affairs, they were unable to enforce without British assistance. Even Harris shared in the delusions of the Foreign Office in this instance, for in a later commentary upon this event he righteously condemned the Russian failure in Sweden as owing to the fact that "they neglected the advice of friends."[18]

Finally, the British refusal to cooperate in Poland, the third sphere of Russian interest, might have been justified on moral grounds, but analysis of the policy which dubbed the partition merely "a curious transaction"[19] finds indifference rather than moral indignation at the core. Even the single diplomatic success of the period, the renewal of the commercial agreement of 1734, was achieved in the face of oscillations between gross inattention and scrupulous insistence upon detailed points. In actuality, Russian commercial dependence upon England virtually predetermined the outcome, but the conduct of the negotiation was hardly calculated to ingratiate the British interests at St. Petersburg. On three separate occasions, the home government refused to ratify treaties essentially the same as that finally concluded, and in each case the refusal was attended by maddening delays.[20] When Macartney signed the final treaty on August 16, 1766, he had been without instructions for nearly four months.[21] In short, with the exception of those commercial affiliations to which the English mind was always

[16] Rochford to Cathcart, August 25, 1770, *Sbornik*, xix, 57.
[17] Cathcart to Rochford, May 7, 1769, *Sbornik*, xii, 439.
[18] Harris to Suffolk, July 31, 1778, Malmesbury, *op. cit.*, i, 176.
[19] Suffolk to Harris, June 5, 1772, *ibid.*, p. 70.
[20] John Barrow, ed., *Some Account of the Public Life of the Earl of Macartney*, i, 28.
[21] Reddaway, *op. cit.*, p. 277.

so sensitive, the nearly fifteen years of negotiation prior to Harris's arrival in St. Petersburg had served to diminish British influence at a time when events elsewhere in Europe rendered it a matter of crucial importance.

In addition to the discouragement of serving a bankrupt diplomacy, British representatives at St. Petersburg were subjected to many other handicaps. The distance between the two courts greatly increased the difficulties of getting instructions from home, even when the indolence of the foreign secretary was not to blame. In regard to the latter, Sir Robert Murray Keith estimated that he received only one reply for every forty dispatches which he himself sent to the Foreign Office,[22] and Harris consoled himself for the infrequency of his instructions with the reflection that, in any case, he had "never received an instruction that was worth reading."[23] With the greatest good fortune a request for instructions might be answered within six weeks, but when winter had closed the navigation of the Baltic, a much longer time was required. The inspection of the common post rendered it useless as a channel for diplomatic intelligence, and even the use of cipher and special couriers was often unavailing against the machinations of hostile agents who did not hesitate to rob and had been known to murder the dispatch bearers.[24] There were annoying delays at the Russian end as well. The observances of fasts and religious holidays brought all negotiation to a standstill. The real and feigned cumbrousness of Muscovite bureaucracy wrought on the nerves of many an ambassador, while Catherine's close supervision over foreign affairs necessitated many postponements during her absence or indispositions.

Life in the Russian capital had certain marked disadvantages. Its climate and marshy environs made it an unhealthy place of residence. Macartney, who suffered from frequent illnesses, wrote in May, 1767, that no less than fifteen of his acquaintances had died of the climate within three months,[25] and Harris's predecessor, Sir Robert Gunning, was not the first ambassador to request his recall for reasons of health. An additional drain upon the physical strength of the diplomat was

[22] Mrs. G. Smyth, *Memoirs and Correspondence of Sir Robert Murray Keith*, London, 1849, II, 219, 221, 224.

[23] Malmesbury, *op. cit.*, II, 59.

[24] Albert Sorel, *Europe under the Old Regime*, translated by F. H. Herrick, Los Angeles, 1947, pp. 66-67. In the introductory chapter of this book, Sorel makes a searching exposition of the naked principles of expediency which underlay the international relations of this period and shows the extraordinary variety of practices, unchecked by any moral or philosophical scruple, which were employed toward the single end of power to the state.

[25] Reddaway, *op. cit.*, p. 267.

the necessity of participating in the extraordinary festivity of court life. Guy Dickens commented: "The good of the King's service requires that His Majesty should have at the court a Minister in full strength and vigour of his age, as in their way of thinking here they look upon a Foreign Minister not missing a court day, ball, masquerade, play, or any other public diversion, to be the chief and principal objects of his mission; which at my time of life I cannot do. And yet it is absolutely necessary."[26] Lord Cathcart, too, found himself ill-suited to the character of the Russian Court, but for a different reason: "Never having been a card player, and having long since ceased to be a dancer, I was obliged to decline the honour proposed to me of making the Empress's party. . . ."[27] Still another consequence of the parade of the Russian capital was its financial burden. The salary of a British Minister might be sufficient to sustain him amid the austerities of Potsdam, but it was quite insufficient for the Court of Catherine. Sir Charles Hanbury-Williams complained of not being provided with a house: "I therefore had a palace taken for me without a chair or a stool in it. I give £500 a year; and it has already cost me £2,000 to furnish it. . . . The posting of my letters will cost me at least £300 a year, and the accidental expenses of this court are very high. . . ."[28] Sir George Macartney, in a residence of only two years, contracted a debt of nearly £6,000.[29] Even fortified as he was by his vigorous youth, social polish, and independent wealth, Harris was not free from similar embarrassments during his embassy to the Russian Court.

In later life, Harris's achievements were to win him a distinguished reputation both at home and abroad. Not only the honors of a grateful and sympathetic government, but the grudging tributes of his enemies were his reward. Mirabeau described him as both crafty and audacious[30] in reluctant admiration of his subtle machinations in Holland, and, many years after his death, Talleyrand styled him the ablest member of the British diplomatic service in his time.[31] The judgment of history confirms these high praises, but it does not conceal those failings which, in his early life, occasionally offset the advantages which nature and education had bestowed. His personal appearance was impressive. His confident mien and fine head of prematurely white hair won him the nickname of "the Lion"; nor was this entirely a

---

[26] Ilchester, *op. cit.*, p. 314.
[27] Cathcart to Weymouth, August 30, 1768, *Sbornik*, XII, 356.
[28] Ilchester, *op. cit.*, p. 310.   [29] Barrow, *op. cit.*, I, 36.
[30] H. G. R. de Mirabeau, *Cour du Berlin*, London, 1900, II, 13.
[31] Malmesbury, *op. cit.*, p. xix.

misnomer as applied to his character. His courage in the face of adversity was certainly leonine, but his sense of the dignity of his position occasionally bordered on the pompous. His scrupulous conscientiousness in the performance of his duty was assuredly a virtue, but it was combined with a certain priggishness which occasionally distorted his evaluations. His early travels on the continent had imparted a pleasing urbanity to his manners, but coming, as they did, on the wave of British prestige after the Seven Years' War, they tended to make him overconfident of the national reputation. Moreover, the experience of his diplomatic apprenticeship had tended to confirm him in this idea. At Madrid in 1770, when but twenty-four years of age, he had learned of the Spanish expedition to oust a British garrison from the Falkland Islands. In the absence of his superior, Sir James Grey, without any instructions from home, and entirely on his own responsibility, he took so high a tone with the Spanish Minister that a retrocession on the British terms was procured without a war. In St. Petersburg, however, Harris could assume the role neither of the outraged gladiator, demanding redress of grievances, as in Madrid, nor of the indifferent spectator to the Polish partition, as he had done later in Berlin, but was forced to act as the suppliant suitor on behalf of a hard-pressed government sorely in need of the assistance of Catherine. At the Russian Court, it was necessary for "the Lion" to learn the ways of the fox.

The qualities of the diplomat par excellence have been brilliantly described by La Bruyère. "The minister and plenipotentiary is a chameleon, a Proteus. . . . He considers the time, the place, the occasion, his strength or weakness, the genius of the nation with which he treats, the temperament and character of the persons with whom he negotiates. All his views, all his statements, all the refinements of his policy tend to one sole end, which is never to be deceived himself, and always to deceive others."[32] The Thespian character of eighteenth-century diplomacy was foreign to Harris's self-conscious morality. He found it difficult to play the many different roles demanded of an ambassador to the Russian Court. In his intrigues with the then Grand Duchess Catherine, Sir Charles Hanbury-Williams had acted as political advisor, financier, and even, in her affair with the young Poniatowski and later King of Poland, as a sort of procurer. Awkwardly, at first, but with increasing facility, Harris mingled in the intrigues of the Court, employing bribes and secret agents to gain intelligence; yet throughout his Embassy he was unable to predict the course of Russian policy

[32] Sorel, *op. cit.*, p. 13.

or to influence its direction in any but a negative sense. If he showed skill in the art of deceiving others, in his analysis of events, he was often deceived himself.

Perhaps the main defect of Harris's understanding was his academic insistence upon the interpretation of historic trends as permanently fixed principles of international relations. As a patriotic Englishman whose nation had everything to lose by an alteration in the status quo, he viewed with a kind of indignation the principle of change which this idea denied. France had proved herself the traditional enemy of Russia; England, her traditional ally. Therefore, it was indisputable that the Russian and the British interest were unalterably the same. Stubbornly rooted in this conviction, he refused to recognize the advantages which cooperation with France might offer Catherine. During the first two years of Harris's residence, France first mediated a Russian dispute with Turkey in favor of the former and then assisted Russia to arbitrate the Bavarian Succession between Prussia and Austria, both increasing her European prestige and establishing a precedent for interference in German affairs, but Harris continued to deny the advantage of the French connection. In the same period, England, which offered Russia nothing, was overmatched in a conflict with her American colonies, France, and Spain, and yet Harris insisted upon the expediency of an Anglo-Russian connection. His arguments were not totally without force, and, indeed, Catherine would have deplored a crushing defeat of England, but the dogmatic grip in which they held his mind precluded any real understanding of the calculated opportunism which guided Russian policy.

In his irritation at Panin's refusal to admit of his outmoded reasoning, Harris consoled himself with several equally ill-conceived reflections. The enviable Russian preponderance had no solid foundation in systematic policy. Whereas Richardson had deplored the instability and insecurity of Russian life for its brutalizing effect upon the whole people, Harris, whose observations were confined to the Court alone, condemned its political inconsistency not on grounds of humanitarianism but as a menace to that Anglo-Russian alliance which nature, history, and the hostility of the common French enemy had decreed. Unable to read any continuity of action into the history of Russian diplomacy, Harris concluded that the current Russian preponderance rested on "fortuitous concurrences of interests . . . and a kind of preordained good luck."[33] This wholly inadequate explanation ignored

[33] Malmesbury, *op. cit.*, p. 200.

the axiom of the astute Frederick II that: "Fortune and chance are words with no real significance. . . . He whose conduct is best calculated triumphs over those who act with less consistency."[34] Finally, Harris concluded, Dame Fortune was fickle, and a foreign policy which depended upon her must ultimately come to disaster. A time would come when Russia, not England, would be the suppliant. The uncertainty of human affairs might allow this to be a reasonable assumption even in the face of the actual events of the Napoleonic Wars, but the petulance of his language shows it to have been founded upon frustration and envy rather than upon objective speculation.

The turn of affairs in the summer of 1779, as seen by Harris, urgently demanded action. Spain had joined in the war in June of that year. At the same time, various neutral maritime powers, at the instance of France, had renewed their appeals to Catherine to protest the practices of the British navy, which, having declared a paper blockade of the French ports and a wide definition of contraband articles, had been preying upon neutral shipping and taking many prizes. Catherine herself, he was convinced, both from gestures of personal partiality[35] and the tone of various private conversations, favored the English cause, but Panin he judged to be an inveterate enemy. The capricious vacillations of Russian policy could only be accounted for by the sway which intriguers and sycophants held over the Empress. Unaware that, despite the feminine temper which enabled her to enjoy the coquetries of the diplomatic game, Catherine directed a hard-headed and opportunistic policy with a logical consistency denied to his own government, and shocked by the succession of favorites and lovers with whom Catherine amused herself, he judged her a vain and dissolute woman, the slave of her passions, and the tool of flatterers and intriguing ministers who misrepresented the truth in accordance with their private interest. While he chafed at the inactivity of a home government which sent him no instructions, French and Prussian agents, acting through Count Panin, were luring her into an unwitting opposition to her own and the British best interest. It was in this conviction that "the Lion" finally resolved upon a daring and decisive step.

In the face of Panin's hostility, Sir James determined, without instructions or even the knowledge of the Foreign Office, to obtain a

---

[34] Sorel, *op. cit.*, p. 14.

[35] Amongst these had been Catherine's consent to perform the investiture of Harris with the Order of the Bath, conferred upon him on March 20, 1779. The practice of requesting foreign monarchs to confer such distinctions upon a diplomatic representative aimed at the creation of a personal bond between the two.

secret interview with Catherine, in order to propose to her an original plan of Russian assistance. It was first necessary to mingle in that factious personal intrigue which seemed to him so peculiarly to dominate every aspect of the Russian Court. Accordingly, he applied to Prince Potemkin,[36] Panin's chief rival, whose ascendancy his wishes had hitherto opposed, to request the privilege of such a meeting. Potemkin received him sympathetically and, early in July, invited him to his nephew's country house, where the two had a long private conversation. Harris was convinced from past experience that any request for a formal alliance would be met with a flat rejection; moreover, a direct plea for assistance (here speaks the proud Briton) "carried with it an air of solicitation and humility I did not like to assume."[37] His more plausible plan was to suggest to Catherine that she make a strong declaration, both at Paris and Madrid, denouncing a war which threatened such ill consequences to the established political system of Europe and support this declaration by the immediate armament of her fleet. Whereas Potemkin agreed that such a step, while not directly interfering in the course of hostilities, would do much to restore the diplomatic balance among the neutrals in England's favor, he objected that Panin, as Foreign Minister, and Chernyshev, as head of the Admiralty, who would be responsible for the execution of the plan, would find some means to betray its purpose. Harris, showing an astute grasp of practical detail which must have surprised Potemkin, was ready with an answer. Potemkin himself might draw up the declaration and bring it to Panin as coming from the Empress. As for Chernyshev, Catherine had merely to follow her own precedent of the last war, when she had settled all matters of equipment, not with the chief of the Admiralty, but with the officer who was actually to command at sea. Potemkin agreed, promising to obtain the interview at the earliest possible date, and the first bastion had been carried.

Through the dry language of Harris's official dispatch, it is possible to perceive the excitement of the following weeks. Almost daily for a fortnight he drove to the summer palace at Peterhof from his neighboring villa, eagerly marking every sign of favor in Catherine's behavior. On the evening of July 22, there was a masquerade in honor of

[36] Prince Grigori Aleksandrovich Potemkin (1739-1791), Russian field marshal, who rose to immense power from a lowly rank in the army by virtue of Catherine's favor. After a short period as her lover, he contented himself with arranging Catherine's further amours and devoted himself to official business, patronizing the arts, and heaping up incredible wealth. He was still in the zenith of his power when apoplexy claimed him at the age of fifty-two.

[37] Harris to Weymouth, September 20, 1779, Malmesbury, *op. cit.*, p. 213.

the Grand Duchess and, as usual, Sir James played cards at the Empress's table. Afterwards, she retired, presumably to bed, but a short time later, Korsakoff, her guardsman lover, singling out Sir James from amidst the crowded ballroom, led him a back way to a private dressing room, the scene of his critical rendezvous with the great Empress. Catherine, charming and a trifle arch, listened attentively, appearing at the same time, sincerely anxious for the British cause, wary of involvement in the war, and attracted to the prestige value of the declaration. In the end, she requested a written outline of the project and dismissed the British courtier. The interview had intensified, rather than dispelled the suspense, yet as he groped in the darkness "through the intricate passages back to the ballroom,"[38] Harris was excited by new determination.

Having once embarked upon this totally unauthorized venture, "the Lion" employed every means at his disposal for furthering its progress. On the morning after the interview, he gave into Potemkin's hands the written draft of his proposal. On the following evening, dining with the Empress in a small company, he was encouraged by a few whispered words from the monarch. Soon afterwards, however, he suffered his first disappointment in the secret intelligence that Catherine had requested Panin's opinion of the project. By a further effort, his secret agents[39] were actually able to procure for him a draft of the objections which Panin intended to raise. These he attempted to counter in another written paper given in through Potemkin, but in actuality they were largely unanswerable. The Russian Minister pointed out that a defeat of England would not upset the political system of Europe, but only restore the balance of power as it had been established at Aix-la-Chapelle in 1748, that Harris's scheme did not have the support of the Ministry, and that the Ministry itself was about to fall.[40] Panin enjoyed an additional advantage by being able to work behind the scenes during a two weeks' religious fast which excluded Harris

[38] *ibid.*, p. 218.

[39] Although Harris, in the progress of his embassy, made an increasing number of references to secret agents and informers, he was scrupulously careful to avoid the use of their names. Undoubtedly, one source of intelligence was Catherine's personal physician, the Scot, Dr. John Rogerson, who was known to be in the British employ. Other British expatriates, too, occasionally served their native country, and, besides these, there was a host of intriguing adventurers, a sort of "diplomatic freemasonry," who were always ready to procure or to sell intelligence. Simmons, *op. cit.*, pp. 73ff.; R. G. Albion, *Forests and Sea Power*, Cambridge, Mass., 1926, pp. 195ff.; Sorel, *op. cit.*, pp. 63ff.

[40] In October of 1779, Weymouth was succeeded by Stormont as secretary of state for the northern department in the third of the six ministries which divided the power during Harris's embassy.

from all contacts with either Catherine or Potemkin. This and succeeding delays in the face of the approaching winter, closing the Russian ports to navigation, finally eclipsed all hope of the execution of the plan until the following spring, but it was not until September 20 that Harris, admitting temporary defeat, informed the home government of the independent course which had been determined by his decision of nearly three months before.

Harris's unflagging efforts throughout the winter revealed his hope of ultimate victory. In at least one respect, the obtaining of the whole-hearted support of his government for his plan, he was markedly successful. On November 5, a letter from George III to Catherine, written at Harris's recommendation, outlined every feature of his proposal and requested its execution.[41] It is a striking instance, rarely seen in this period, of prompt and cordial compliance by the home government with the wishes of a foreign representative. At the same time, Harris tried to conciliate the irritation of ship seizures by the British navy. On December 31, he gave in to Panin a written promise that not only the ships of the regular navy, but also privateers would no longer interfere with any Russian navigation on the Baltic. Although he maintained a wary eye upon the secret operations of French agents, he was assured by Potemkin that the Empress was most favorable to the English cause. At last, an opening offered itself when the Spanish seized a Russian corn ship, sold its cargo, and maltreated its crew. Catherine immediately drafted a strong protest to both France and Spain, and Harris rejoiced. His advantage was further improved by the intelligence that a British cruiser had previously stopped the same Russian ship and immediately released it with courteous deference, but before he could make use of this news, Potemkin sent for him. With the unexpected suddenness of a comedy farce the blow fell. Potemkin professing the most "impetuous joy" triumphantly announced that the fleet was to be armed and sent out to defend the neutral rights of Russian shipping. This was in reality no more than the Armed Neutrality which the French had advocated the preceding year, but Potemkin gaily insisted, over Harris's helpless objections, that it was really intended against the Spanish and that it would help England by drawing off at least twenty ships of the line from the Bourbon forces. Harris was unconvinced, but summoned what grace he could to thank his Russian friend and withdrew to dispatch the news to his government. The ceaseless activity of seven months had ended in disaster.

[41] Malmesbury, *op. cit.*, pp. 228-229.

Uncertain for a long period as to the real consequences and intentions of the naval armament, Harris paid the closest attention to the developments of the following weeks. A Declaration of Neutral Rights was dispatched to all the courts of Europe. This explicitly stated the principle that neutral ships made neutral goods and with cruel irony cited the terms of the English Commercial Treaty of 1766 for the definition of contraband goods. Since this did not include naval stores, the British maritime strategy of throttling their shipment to her enemies was entirely undercut. As one after another of the neutral powers joined with Russia in the Armed Neutrality, increasingly large supplies of essential hemp, timber, and other naval stores reached France and Spain, in neutral bottoms, thereby exercising a decisive effect on the course of the war.[42] By the autumn of 1780, English action had forced Holland to join with France, and thenceforth Dutch ships, which previously had been able to traffic nearly unmolested between Russia and the Bourbon countries, were again the legitimate prey of the British navy, but it was too late. The surrender at Yorktown in 1781 demonstrated the vulnerability of a Britain without maritime supremacy.[43]

It is difficult to assess the real intent of the declaration of Armed Neutrality. Harris saw it as the consequence of a court intrigue by which Panin, gaining a temporary ascendance over Potemkin, was able to pervert to his own ends Catherine's genuine desire to assist England.[44] This interpretation grants too little to the intelligence of Catherine, which Harris consistently underrated. Catherine did not wish to see England utterly vanquished, and she may even have intended originally to fall in with Harris's proposal, but she never allowed her personal predilections to interfere with the dictates of self-interest, and there were good reasons why a great English victory would be equally obnoxious to her. Her designs on the Crimea were not, as Harris thought, a chimera, and a war between the western powers which weakened all participants increased her relative strength.[45] Harris had argued that, in the event of American independence, France would purchase naval supplies from America rather than Russia, but the American colonies, as a source of naval supplies, were manifestly far more dangerous in the hands of England, Russia's best customer, than independent of her. In general, Catherine leaned toward England at

[42] Albion, *op. cit.*, pp. 182-194.
[43] *ibid.*, pp. 309-311.
[44] W. H. Trescott takes essentially the same view. J. B. Scott, ed., *The Armed Neutralities of 1780 and 1800*, New York and London, 1918, pp. 72ff.
[45] George Soloveytchik, *Potemkin, a Picture of Catherine's Russia*, London, 1938, pp. 204-205.

those periods when she appeared threatened by a total defeat, but toward France whenever the British arms were successful. Therefore, Rodney's victory at Cape St. Vincent, which she pretended to hail with such enthusiasm, was in all probability fatal to Harris's project. He never perceived the importance of the Crimean objective, which might have clarified his other thinking. Like Macartney,[46] his contempt for Russian commercial ability made the idea of a Russian trade into the Mediterranean preposterous and unthinkable, and he ignored its implications for Catherine's foreign policy as a whole. In a sense, the declaration of Armed Neutrality was a self-conscious declaration of commercial independence from England not unlike that of her colonies on the other side of the world. In the years which followed, Catherine's Russia entered into a series of commercial agreements with other nations including Denmark, Austria, France, Sicily, Portugal, Turkey, and Poland,[47] and although British commercial practice continued to engross the majority of the Russian exports, her half century of exclusive privilege was at an end.

It would be impossible to trace out in this small space the diplomatic complexities which attended the whole of Harris's embassy. The selections from his official and diplomatic correspondence included below have been designed to illustrate the nature of his problems rather than to narrate the events of these years. Although his efforts were unflagging, one disappointment followed another, and while it is questionable whether even the most perfect understanding of the real intentions of Catherine could have succeeded in the face of the swift march of events, his predictions of their course repeatedly proved false. For example, the Russian swing away from Prussia and toward Austria was attributed entirely to Catherine's personal inclinations toward Joseph II and repugnance for the character of Frederick the Great and his nephew. The mercurial Potemkin remained a mystery throughout.[48] To professional reverses were added many personal problems: the death of his adored father, the departure of his wife and children because of illness, and the breakdown of his own health. His letters reveal a growing despair at his failures; frustrated, uncomprehending,

---

[46] Macartney dismissed Catherine's commercial ambitions with lofty condescension: "Barbarous as they are and ignorant of those arts which improve the understanding . . . I have little apprehension either from their experiments in commerce or their efforts at navigation. Like children they are allured by every new idea, pursue it for a moment, and then abandon it." Reddaway, *op. cit.*, p. 280.

[47] Gerhard, *op. cit.*, pp. 130-137.

[48] For a detailed account of the personal relations between Harris and Potemkin, see Soloveytchik, *op. cit.*, pp. 190-248.

homesick, ill and alone, he was sustained only by that spirited patriotism which always remained a dominant trait of his character. In Russia, as throughout his foreign service, it provided the consolation of his darkest hour: ". . . if a long residence abroad kept me for a while distant from my family and friends and distant from my native country, it did not estrange my love and affection for either. On the contrary, it afforded me many and most striking reasons to value and cherish them still more. . . . An Englishman who, after a long absence from England, returns to it with feelings and sentiments partial to other countries and adverse to his own, has no real mind, is without the powers of discernment and plain easy comparison, and has not title to enjoy the superior moral, political, and local advantages to which he is born, but of which he is unsensible and unworthy."[49]

Moreover, from despair new hope was born. Paradoxically, Harris became the advocate for England of that same opportunism which he had affected to despise in Russia. New alliances were to be based, not upon outworn historical precedents and traditions, but in conformity with the actual stresses and strains of the revised continental balance. A new era was dawning for the country he represented. Political faction, formerly so harmful, was to be largely obviated under the new leadership of Pitt. Rid of the troublesome problems of governing the independent American colonies, England was to derive even greater profits from an increasing commerce with them. On the other side of the world, the establishment of a governor-generalship in India (1786) brought to Britain the consciousness of being an Asiatic power, aware, as never before, of the Asiatic designs of Russia. "Splendid isolation" was at an end. Finally, England was on the verge of a great industrial expansion which all the diplomatic wizardry of Catherine would never be able to match. Improved road and canal transportation, the expansion of coal mining, and the introduction of the steam engine heralded a new era, and Napoleon was to discover to his cost what a valuable weapon of international conflict a thriving economy could be. In short, if the diplomatic bankruptcy of the two decades prior to 1783 could be proved a logical consequence of a national preoccupation with the development of its industrial and commercial techniques, it might be assessed a wiser course than the cunning but expensive manipulations, which under Catherine, sapped the vitality and resources of an overburdened people.

[49] Malmesbury, *op. cit.*, p. xii.

EXTRACTS FROM: *The Diary and Correspondence*

by Sir James Harris

CONTENTS

··

I · FIRST IMPRESSIONS

1. JOURNEY FROM DANZIG TO KÖNIGSBERG [NOW CALLED KALININGRAD], DECEMBER 3, 1777[50]

WE FOUND the roads very bad before we got there [Danzig], but they
have been still worse since: for these last four days we have had one of
our wheels in the Baltic, and, as there blew a very strong westerly wind,
I was almost afraid sometimes we should be wrecked. One wheel thus
placed, and the other in the deep sand, we have never advanced above
twenty miles a day. Unfortunately we have neither frost nor snow to
afford us a better prospect as we proceed, and the weather is perversely
fine and mild, I still hope to be in St. Petersburg in a fortnight, although we have 700 miles to go. . . .

   As we went along the coast to-day, we passed by two wrecks, one a
very fresh one, near enough for us to walk into and examine it; and
off the harbour of Pillau we saw a large vessel which was driven ashore
last night, and not likely to be got off. The night before last we were
lighted by a noble aurora borealis; the brightness of the waves, which
often washed our carriage, the immense extent of barren shore and sea
this fine phenomenon discovered to us, made it a very romantic scene;
it would have been more pleasing if our horses had not failed us, and
forced us to lie in the sand till near one in the morning. . . . [133-134]

2. CIVILITIES OF THE COURT, ST. PETERSBURG, JANUARY 16, 1778

   Prepared even as I was for the magnificence and parade of this Court,
yet it exceeds in everything my ideas: to this is joined the most perfect

---

[50] All dates of the letters and dispatches in the following selections are according to the
Gregorian calendar, first adopted in the Catholic countries in 1582 and in Great Britain and
her colonies in 1752. The old Julian calendar, maintained in Russia because of Greek Orthodox
suspicions of all Catholic customs, had lost eleven days in the eighteenth century, through its
failure to recognize a minor discrepancy in the astronomical year.

order and decorum. The Empress herself unites, in the most wonderful manner, the talents of putting those she honours with her conversation at their ease, and of keeping up her own dignity. Her character extends throughout her whole administration; and although she is rigidly obeyed, yet she has introduced a lenity in the mode of government to which, till her reign, this country was a stranger.

The character of M. de Panin, her First Minister, is too well known for me to enlarge upon it; he is civil to me beyond expression, and I always find his doors open to me. The Foreign Ministers here are few in number: I have found in several of them old acquaintance, and experienced civilities from them all. I have been several times at court since my first audience, and have always been distinguished by her Imperial Majesty. . . .

Mrs. Harris and my sister were prevented going to court immediately on their arrival by a total destruction of their wardrobe, occasioned by the negligence of the captain in whose ship the boxes came. This loss is severely felt in a country where every article of this kind is constantly dear and scarce; but more particularly so at a moment when the festivities on the birth of the young Prince Alexander Paulowitz increase the demand.[51] Since that, a very severe head-ache prevented Mrs. Harris going the day that was fixed, and Sunday now remains for the ceremony of her presentation. The Russian ladies have been exceedingly civil and attentive in assisting her to repair her loss, and she is by their help, enabled to appear completely equipped in a Russian dress. [139-140]

3. INFLUENCE AND CHARACTER OF COUNT PANIN, FEBRUARY 6, 1778

I am too recently arrived to have formed any connexions I can rely on, and am too well acquainted with the national character of this people, not to mistrust any tenders I may have had, either of friendship or of service. I felt, therefore, that if in conveying his Majesty's sentiments to the Empress, or in obtaining hers, I made use of any collateral or indirect influence, I exposed myself to the greatest hazard of being betrayed, and consequently acquiring, on my outset, the reputation of an intriguing and uncandid negotiator. . . . It is, moreover, evident, that nobody but Count Panin has materially the Empress's ear in the

[51] Harris had been accompanied both by his younger sister, Catherine Gertrude, and by his wife, Harriet Mary, second daughter of Sir George Amyand, who was to bear him two children in St. Petersburg. The accident which kept her from the festivities upon the birth of the future Alexander I must have seemed particularly confining to a bride of but six months.

discussion of foreign affairs, and that the others who approach her never interfere but in the disposal of home employments and the distribution of honours. It might, indeed, be fairly supposed that there are some who, from the free access they have to her person, and from the great predilection she shows them, might, in certain moments, bias her opinion; but they are chosen from that set of men the most averse to public business, or to any serious reflections, and are so munificently provided for by their Imperial Mistress, that it is impossible ever to catch their attention by any pecuniary emoluments, however considerable.

The addressing myself, therefore, directly to Count Panin appeared to me as the only channel left open. In doing this, I endeavoured as much as possible to consult the character of the man; great good-nature, great vanity, and excessive indolence, are the marked features of it. He joins to these, a wonderful desire of being thought open and frank, and, in discoursing on business, aims, though unsuccessfully, at all the dignity of the First Minister of, what he thinks, the first empire in the world. I should not do him justice if I did not add that he is beyond the reach of corruption, and in all transactions where he moves alone, he acts with integrity and honour. [140-141]

4. FURTHER CIVILITIES, FEBRUARY 13, 1778

The day Russel arrived, as I was driving through the streets of this town in a sledge with the Spanish Minister, he, in conducting it, contrived to run against the pole of a coach in so violent a manner as to give me two large cuts in my neck and one in my lip; my right wrist was also considerably strained, and I was very near being deprived of both my tongue and hand at a moment when I was in much want of both of them. As, however, I immediately washed the wounds (for they almost deserve that name) with brandy and water, and have since kept all surgeons from interfering, I was well enough the next day to go to Mons. Panin, and now have only two large patches on my throat. I do not mention all this as a fact by any means worthy your notice, but because, in consequence of it, Her Imperial Majesty sent the lieutenant of the police to me in order that I should help him to discover and bring to punishment the coachman concerned, and has since published a *ukase*, prohibiting all fast driving in the streets. On my first appearance at Court afterwards, both the Empress and Grand Duke were remarkably attentive in their inquiry; all which attentions, as they certainly are paid to the character I hold, I thought it might not be unpleasant for you to hear. . . .

I have not been here long enough to write with any degree of precision on the several characters which compose the Court and first society here. Great luxury and little morality seem to run through every rank. Flattery and servility characterize the inferior class, presumption and pride the higher one. A slight but brilliant varnish covers in both the most illiterate and uninformed minds. Their entertainments, their apartments, and the number of their domestics, are quite Asiatic; and what is very odd, though perhaps very natural, although they imitate the foreigners in everything, and have (I speak of the higher class) neither customs nor character of their own, yet, generally speaking, a stranger is ill received when he comes among them. I, however, am very far myself from laying this imputation at their door, since I have experienced, as well as Mrs. Harris and my sister, every possible civility from them. [148-149]

5. FETES IN HONOR OF THE INFANT ALEXANDER, MARCH 18, 1778

Besides the sumptuous fetes of the principal nobility upon the late joyful occasion, (the last of which at Prince Potemkin's cost 50,000 roubles,) the Empress was pleased to give one in the course of the Carnival, the magnificence and good taste of which surpassed everything that can be conceived. The dessert at supper was set out with jewels to the amount of upwards of two millions sterling; and at the tables of Macao, (a game much in vogue here at present,) besides the stake in money played for, a diamond of fifty roubles' value was given by Her Imperial Majesty to each of those who got *nine*, the highest point of the game. One hundred and fifty diamonds were distributed in this manner. None but Russians of the highest rank were honoured with an invitation to this party; but for some days after foreigners and others were admitted to a sight of this most beautiful decoration of jewels, which was equally extraordinary for the elegance of the design, as for the costliness of the materials. [153-154]

II · OBSTACLES TO NEGOTIATION

1. INDOLENCE AND VANITY OF THE RUSSIANS

February 24, 1778, to Suffolk:[52] I confess that it is more for the sake of endeavouring to obey my instructions to the utmost, rather than

[52] Henry Howard, 12th Earl of Suffolk (1739-1779), secretary of state, member of the North ministry from 1771 until his death in March 1779.

from any hopes of success, that I leave nothing untried to recall this Court to a sense of its real interests, by discovering to them the imminent dangers that surround them,[53] and which, if they have not recourse to their natural ally, will shake, if not crush, the very foundations of their empire. The thorough conviction, however, the Empress is under of her being invincible, the supineness of her Ministers, and the continual dissipation of those who more immediately surround her, and, above all, the idea they are prejudiced with, that we want them more than they want us, will, I fear, prevent anything I can advance taking effect; and that, till the blow is felt, they will never be persuaded that their ideas, as well of their own situation as of that of the other Powers of Europe, are greatly erroneous. [151-152]

March 31, 1778, to Hugh Elliot:[54] The extreme indolence and dissipation of the Minister [Panin] makes him ready, at all times, to believe everything which tends to gratify his ease, and prevent trouble. The incredible vanity of the Sovereign gets the better of her fine parts; she is willing to give credit to any assertion that she supposes to be in consequence of her own greatness and power. The remoteness of their situation makes them forget the *cause* when the *effect* is felt; and although since this reign several events have happened which ought to have roused them to a sense of their situation, their credulity still remains in its full force. It is for this reason that they receive cordially the friendly offers of the French Minister; and although I cannot think they will suffer them to be the affected mediators of a pacification with the Turks, yet they have admitted the Bourbon Ministers here to a greater degree of confidence than they ever should have known at this court. [156]

May 12, 1778, to Sir Joseph Yorke:[55] The Empress . . . has not that ardour for business she was used to be famous for, yet she still will not be biassed by her ministers; these, particularly Count Panin, neglect,

[53] At this period, a disagreement between Turkey and Russia as to the interpretation of the terms of the Treaty of Küchük Kainarji seemed to threaten the outbreak of a new war. Vergennes, in his anxiety to maintain peace on the continent of Europe, in order that France might devote her full attention to her English rival, offered his secret and effective mediation to secure an accommodation with the Porte.

[54] Hugh Elliot, English envoy extraordinary at Berlin from 1777 to 1782, brother to Sir Gilbert Elliot, later the Earl of Minto. The latter was connected to Harris by his marriage to his wife's elder sister.

[55] Sir Joseph Yorke, a friend of Harris's father, had befriended young James on his first journey to Holland in 1765, and they continued in correspondence throughout the remainder of the former's life. Harris had received news on April 4 of a declaration from France that she would trade with the Americans as an independent people and would protect that trade by force, if necessary.

beyond conception, the duty of their offices. Subalterns do the same as their superiors, and the business of this great empire does itself. The effects of it are visible; confusion and imperfection are to be found everywhere. Great expenses, and nothing to show for them. The army in a state of decay; their navy incomplete and ill-equipped; their political system inconsistent, languid, and such as, if pursued, must ultimately reduce this immense mass of power to that state of Asiatic insignificancy from which it so lately emerged. . . .

The natural and necessary allies of this country are neglected. Those interested to diminish its greatness and power are listened to. One general erroneous system reigns throughout the whole; and, unless some sudden light breaks in upon them, or an unexpected stroke revives them to their senses, nothing good or great can be expected from them. [161-162]

May 27, 1778, to William Fraser:[56] The friendship of this country partakes of its climate,—a clear brilliant sky, with a cold freezing atmosphere; all words, and no deeds; empty professions, and shuffling evasions. It is a political, though not a moral consolation, that their incongruous conduct proceeds from the erroneous opinion they have of the rise of their own power, and the declension of ours. . . .

Although in my public capacity I have a tolerable degree of patience, yet it requires more than ever fell to the share of mortal minister to converse with people who, in the midst of business and distress, are supine and insensible, and who will neither hear a reasonable question, nor give a reasonable answer. You will not credit me when I tell you Count Panin does not devote more than half an hour in the twenty-four to business; and that Mr. Oakes, having been robbed of a considerable sum of money, found the *Lieutenant de Police*, the first magistrate of the empire, and whose power is immense, at seven o'clock in the morning, playing at *la Grande Patience*, with a dirty pack of cards, by himself! [169-170]

2. INDECISION AND INATTENTION AT HOME

May 12, 1778, to Sir Joseph Yorke: I . . . (speaking to your Excellency with perfect confidence), am instructed to propose an alliance, and have actually given in a project; as, however, it is word for word the same as that so often rejected, I have little hopes of its being admitted in its present shape. I have powers to mould it anew, and, as I think

[56] Under-secretary to Lord Suffolk in the Foreign Office.

the terms are urgent, shall, in inferior points, take upon myself a decision, which, from the great distance of the two capitals, I trust, will be allowed me; I wish I did not think I saw a want of this decision at home. . . . [161]

May 27, 1778, to his father: The appearance of irresolution and indecision in England has a sensible effect on the Continent, and, till we give stronger proofs of our being in a vigorous and nervous system, we must not expect essential assistance or support from any of our friends on this side of the water. I always impute a great deal to the virulence and inconsiderate conduct of Opposition, but this alone could not reduce our national reputation so low as it now is. I am convinced by experience that this evil is not felt at home in a direct manner, and of course it is not attended to. The evil exists, nevertheless, and its effects are not the less dangerous from being slow. I have often held this language to men in high office; but some parliamentary job, or a reason equally good, has always prevented their paying attention to what I said. The remedy now will be difficult: the disease is grown to its height, which, if taken in time, might have been easily prevented. [171]

III · STATE OF THE RUSSIAN EMPIRE, JULY 1778

July 31, 1778, to Suffolk: The immense extent of the Russian empire, and the security of its frontiers, doubtless render it a desirable ally, and almost an inaccessible enemy. The various articles of commerce the rest of Europe must necessarily fetch from hence, and the very few which this country need receive from them, insure its independence and wealth. Russia, therefore, incontestibly stands very high among the European powers; but it may be controverted whether it can come up to the high reputation it enjoys, or to the superiority it assumes. The advantages just mentioned are merely the effects of situation; they existed before this people were civilized, and will remain with them if they ever should return to that state of barbarity from which they so recently emerged.

To give an empire pre-eminence abroad, its political system should be uniform, wise, and steady. To make it respectable at home, fixed rules of interior policy should be established, and their administration should be secure and uncorrupted. I must confess, my Lord, since my residence here, my researches after such a system and such rules have been fruitless; and it is in vain that I have attempted to discover on what those high-flown encomiums of this government, which every-where met my ear, are founded. . . .

A mistaken lenity, arising either from fear or indolence, has sub-verted the great purposes of law and justice. The great men oppress their inferiors wantonly; the inferiors pilfer and steal in security. From a conviction of this remissness, and from the specious pretense of the cruelty of their lords, we have seen a rebellion break out in the heart of the empire; which, had it been led by men of judgment or courage, would have shaken it to its foundations.[57] No troops were ready to make head against it; a panic had seized half the country; and the same spirit of sedition which animated Pugatscheff,[58] had infected the rest. He was within a few days' march of Moscow, and the Court was near retreating to Riga, when, from want of resolution and conduct, he was defeated, and tranquillity restored to the empire. The sparks of dis-content, however, are not yet extinguished; and it is much to be appre-hended, that, in case of any national calamity, they would blow out afresh. . . .

In opposition to these facts, we may place the establishment of several colonies of emigrants from Germany, the institution of many useful seminaries for the youth of both sexes, and a very great generosity and munificence.

The code of laws, sketched out by the Empress herself in really a masterly manner, have never yet been digested; it remains as a deposit at the Academy, and many reasons render it being put in execution impracticable.

Such, I can venture to assert, is the real state of this empire. A thriv-ing commerce and increasing revenue, owing to its unexhausted re-sources, and the progress of civilization in its remoter quarters, would, under a wise administration, very soon restore it to its force and vigour. The vanity of the Empress, however, throws an obstacle in the way of this amelioration: having been taught by flatterers that Russia is the greatest empire in the world, and confirmed in this idea by the most fortunate successes, she never can be brought to see the situation of her country in its true light, till some great event calls upon her to stand forth; she then will feel her inability of acting that superior part she

---

[57] Harris was handicapped as an observer of social conditions within the interior of Russia by his preoccupation with diplomatic and international developments. To characterize the dis-content of the peasantry against the tyranny of the nobles as a "specious pretense of the cruelty of their lords" bears no relation to the facts.

[58] Yemelyan Ivanovich Pugachev (1744-1775), Cossack leader of the great rebellion which raged intermittently from 1773 to 1775.

assumes, and from conviction will perceive the necessity of treating her friends with more attention, and her enemies with less levity, than she has hitherto done. [175-178]

IV · THE INTERIOR OF THE COURT, AUGUST 1778-JANUARY 1779

August 21, 1778: The new favourite [Korsakoff] is very much on his decline. There are several competitors for his employment: some supported by Prince Potemkin; some by Prince Orlow[59] and Count Panin, who now act together; and some solely from the impression their figure has made on the mind of the Empress. Both parties unite to prevent the success of these independent men, but she seems strongly disposed to choose for herself. . . . As the small remains of decency kept up when I first came have totally disappeared, I should not be surprised if, instead of one favourite, we should see several; and that the effects should by that means hasten the evils which even otherwise must inevitably fall on the empire. [178-179]

September 8, 1778: I have very good reason to believe that in a few days the present favourite will be discarded, and that he will be succeeded by a Secretary in Count Panin's office, by name, Strackhoff, a young man of character, but who . . . nobody ever considered as a candidate for this eminent post. He was noticed, for the first time, at a ball at Peterhoff [Peterhof], the 28th June, and he owes the great fortune to which he is so near being raised, to the free and unbiassed choice of the Empress. . . . If the connexion lasts, and becomes consistent, it must end in the fall of Potemkin: Count Panin's party and interest will increase; and, if he continues to abide by the Orlows, it may produce the most salutary effects to this empire. [179-180]

September 25, 1778: I mentioned to your Lordship . . . the return of Prince Potemkin into favour. He attempted, as long as he could venture, to oppose the choice of the intended favourite, and tried every means his cunning and ascendant over the Empress suggested to him. He dared even to threaten, and held the most unbecoming language; when, finding no effect from this behaviour, but that she determined to abide by her plan, he changed his tone to the most submissive possible; he begged and obtained pardon, and offered his services towards bringing it to bear in the most decorous and expeditious manner. . . .

[59] Prince Grigori Grigoryevich Orlov (1743-1783), brother of Count Aleksei Orlov. He was one of the first and probably the favorite of all Catherine's lovers and a leader in the conspiracy which placed her on the throne.

Count Panin has observed and still observes, on these occasions, the greatest propriety of behaviour; he affects to be above all Court intrigue, resolved, I believe, not to interfere till he is sure of doing it efficaciously. [180]

October 2, 1778: Contrary to the expectation of everybody, Count Alexis Orlow arrived here last Wednesday. His coming has spread great consternation among the favourites of the day, particularly as he has been already closeted, more than once, with the Empress. Potemkin affects outwardly the highest good-humour and indifference. I had the honour last night of playing at the Empress's table, where both these gentlemen assisted, and it is beyond the powers of my pen to describe to your Lordship a scene in which every passion that can affect the human mind bore a part; and which were, by all the actors, concealed with the most masterly hypocrisy. Count Alexis has been remarkably civil to me, and assured me he was as sincere a friend to England as his brother, and not so indolent a one. Indeed, my Lord, I am at a loss to account for the remarkable civilities I receive from the Empress, the Grand Duke and Duchess, and from the chiefs of the different parties. [181]

October 16, 1778: The following conversation I can vouch to be authentic. . . . Soon after Alexis Orlow's arrival, the Empress sent for him, and after the highest encomiums on his character, and the strongest expressions of gratitude for past services, she told him she had now one to require of him, of more importance to her repose than any she had yet asked him. "Be friends," said she, "with Potemkin; prevail upon that extraordinary man to be more circumspect in his conduct, more attentive to the duties of the great offices he fills; to endeavour to conciliate to himself friends, and not, in return for the regard and friendship I have for him, to make my life a continued scene of misery. . . ." The Empress here burst into tears; Orlow withdrew, but returned in a few minutes . . . saying, "I know, Madame, beyond a doubt, that Potemkin has no real attachment for your Majesty; that he consults in everything his own interest alone; that his only superior talent is cunning; that he is gradually endeavouring to divert your Majesty from business, and lull you into a state of voluptuous security, in order to invest himself with the sovereign power. . . . If you choose to get rid of so dangerous a man,[60] my life is at your devotion; but if you mean to temporise with him, I can be of no use to you. . . ." The

---

[60] It will be remembered that Count Aleksei was rumored to have "gotten rid of" Catherine's husband, Peter III.

Empress was much affected at this extraordinary speech; confessed her belief of all he had said of Potemkin; thanked the Count in the strongest manner for his zealous offers, but said she could not bear the thoughts of such harsh proceedings; acknowledged an alteration in her own character, and complained of her health being essentially affected. . . . [184-185]

November 10, 1778: The interior of the Court every day affords a fresh scene, and the Empress's good sense and fine parts are destroyed by the eternal plagues Potemkin and her favourite create for her. Alexis Orlow is silent, and although he is treated with the most cordial distinction, yet his last conversation is not forgot. . . .

I am treated still with the most uncommon civilities. Whether it is because they foresee they shall want us, or whether they may expect, by this means, to prevent my writing what I see and hear, I cannot pretend to say. [186]

February 9, 1779: The interior of the Court for this last fortnight has afforded, and still continues to afford, one constant scene of disorder and intrigue. The Empress having expressed her intention of changing her favourite, many competitors entered the lists. Strackhoff's friends were in great hopes . . . but his own want of conduct, joined to his obstinacy, has rendered their schemes abortive, and it is probable Her Imperial Majesty would have fixed upon Lewaskow, [Levashov] Major of the Semenossky [Semenovsky] guards, if a young man, by name Swickosky, patronised by Madame Bruce,[61] and put forward by her as a successor to Korsack, had not stabbed himself through disappointment. The wound is not mortal, and though great pains have been taken to conceal from the Empress the real motive of this rash action, yet it has given her the greatest uneasiness, and will probably be the cause of Korsack's remaining in his post till the spring is further advanced. Potemkin and Madame Bruce now no longer act in concert; and so jealous is the Prince of the power this lady has acquired over his Imperial Mistress, that he is doing his utmost to supplant her. . . . Madame Bruce having unfortunately conceived a violent passion for Korsack, will facilitate him very much in the execution of this project. Should he succeed, the small remains of decency and decorum which still are outwardly observed at Court will totally disappear, and every hope of the Empress's being reclaimed vanish. [195-196]

---

[61] Countess Bruce, the wife of a descendant of the Scottish adventurer of the reign of Peter I and sister to the great general, Count P. A. Rumiantsev, was Catherine's confidante during the early years, but later lost her favor.

V · STATE OF THE RUSSIAN EMPIRE,
JUNE 1779

I. ITS FORTUITOUS PREPONDERANCE

June 4, 1779, to Weymouth:[62] The lead this Court takes in all the great transactions of Europe . . . and at the same time the supineness and insufficiency of its administration, are facts so seemingly incompatible, that, in a future day, they must appear incredible. To those who live out of Russia, and who only can form their judgment of it from the great events its interference and weight everywhere produce, it must appear as if it was conducted with superior judgment, and defective in no one essential point of its government. On the other hand, to those who reside in this Empire, and who perceive the unaccountable and imperfect manner in which all their plans are traced, and the improper instruments selected for their execution, it must be a matter of astonishment that they do not fail in everything they undertake. That they have not, is evidently the work of chance; a fortuitous concurrence of interests, a state of confusion and anarchy, in which Russia was less involved than any other European power; and, if I may venture to say, a kind of preordination of good-luck which attends every operation of this Court, has not only saved it from the most imminent dangers, but raised it to a degree of greatness and power beyond that which even the ambition of its Sovereign could ever expect to attain. That these events arise from the cause I mention, and that Russia is at least in the momentary possession of this preponderance, are facts I am satisfied your Lordship will readily admit. . . . The permanency of this superior influence is a matter of much greater doubt; and, in order to enable your Lordship, as far as lies in my power to calculate its solidity and duration, I shall trouble you with a . . . description of the character, temper, and principles of those who direct the Empire. [199-200]

2. THE RULERS: POTEMKIN IN THE ASCENDANT

The Empress herself, long before she took the reins of the Empire into her hands, had prepared her mind to govern; with very fine parts, she employed the many leisure hours she had when Grand Duchess, in laying in those materials which made the seven or eight first years of her reign one of the most brilliant periods in the Russian history.

---

[62] Thomas Thynne, 3rd Viscount Weymouth, 1st Marquis of Bath (1734-1796), secretary of state from 1768 to 1770 and, again, from 1775 to 1779.

She then governed systematically, judiciously, and with dignity. We must date her first political error, from the moment she admitted His Prussian Majesty to assume such a weight in her councils. Soon after this followed the fatal division of Poland, the revolution in Sweden, and since, all those unnatural connexions and impolitic measures we have witnessed. . . . Her Court, from being conducted with the greatest dignity and exterior decorum, has gradually become the scene of depravation and immorality. Their progress has been so rapid, that, in the short term I have resided here, the manners and habits are most essentially changed. There is now no hope of her being reclaimed; and, unless a miraculous gleam of light breaks in upon her, at a time of life when it is almost too late to correct, we must not expect any favourable change either in her public or in her private conduct.

Prince Potemkin rules her with an absolute sway; thoroughly acquainted with her weaknesses, her desires, and her passions, he operates on them, and makes them operate as he pleases. Besides this strong hold on her, he keeps her in constant dread of the Grand Duke, and has convinced her . . . that he is the only person who can discover in time, and protect her against, any undertakings in that quarter. He contrived, with infinite art, to destroy everything his most dangerous enemy, Count Alexis Orlow, said. . . . By following the same line of conduct, he has created a degree of distrust and contempt towards the other members of the Government. . . .

Count Panin, for whom the Empress never bore a cordial affection, now is become the object of her aversion; he, on his side, though so high in office, may be considered to go as great lengths in opposition, as, in such a country, a man can venture. . . . [200-202]

3. THE EASTERN CHIMERA

Prince Potemkin himself pays little regard to the politics on the West of Russia; his mind is continually occupied with the idea of raising an Empire in the East: he has so far infected the Empress with these sentiments, that she has been chimerical enough to christen the newborn Grand Duke, Constantine; to give him a Greek nurse, whose name was Helen; and to talk in her private society, of placing him on the throne of the Eastern Empire. In the meanwhile, she is building a town at Czarsco-Zelo [Tsarskoe Selo] to be called Constantingorod. . . .

I am fully satisfied . . . that we have nothing to expect from this Court in the common course of negotiation. The leading men here are too rich for corruption, too headstrong to be persuaded, and too ignorant to listen to plain truth and conviction. . . . They are led by the impulse of the moment, by the immediate prospect fortuitous incidents afford them. The present reigning idea (and it carries away all others) is the establishing a new Empire in the East, at Athens or Constantinople. The Empress discoursed a long while with me the other day on the ancient Greeks; of their alacrity and the superiority of their genius, and of the same character still being extant in the modern ones; and of the possibility of their again becoming the first people, if properly assisted and seconded. . . . I mention this, my Lord, . . . with a view of hinting to your Lordship that, if His Majesty should stand in indispensable need of assistance from this quarter, the only means of obtaining it is, by encouraging this romantic idea. She is now so warmly bent on it, that such a conduct, dexterously managed, would give us the firmest hold of this Court; and as its execution, whenever seriously planned, would instantly appear impracticable, we need not be apprehensive of having engaged ourselves too far in an unpleasant transaction. [203-205]

VI · FLUCTUATIONS AND PERPLEXITIES, JUNE 1779-JUNE 1780

I. PERSONAL FAVOR OF CATHERINE

June 3, 1799, to his Father: I have the good fortune to have made myself not disagreeable to the Empress. She notices me much more than any of my colleagues; more, indeed, I believe, than any stranger is used to. She admits me to all her parties of cards, and a few days ago carried me with only two of her courtiers to a country palace, where she has placed the portraits of all the crowned heads of Europe. We discoursed much on their several merits; and still more on the great demerits of the modern portrait-painters, since in the whole collection, except one of our two eldest Princes done by West, there is not a single picture that has either design, colour, or composition. She calls this place *la Grenouillière*; and it was for it that Wedgwood made, some years ago, a very remarkable service of his ware, on which a green frog was painted. It represented the different country-houses and gardens in England. This, also, we were shown; and this led us to a conversation on English gardening, in which the Empress is a great adept. From this we got to Blackstone, where she soon led me out of my depth; as I believe she would many a Circuiter, being most perfectly mistress of our Laws and Constitution. This distinction from the Sovereign insures me the good-will and civilities of her subjects; and, indeed . . . they carry these civilities to a degree of troublesome excess. [198-199]

2. INSIDIOUS PRACTICES OF THE FRENCH

September 20, 1779, to Weymouth: The present Chargé d'Affaires, le Chevalier Corberon . . . though he has a very moderate capacity, has, by being used to the country, got access to all the valets de chambre and inferior agents in the Russian houses, who, being chiefly French, and having, some of them, great weight with their masters, very often conjured up evil spirits where I least of all expected them. [225]

November 5, 1779, to Weymouth: I have undoubted intelligence of the Frenchman I before mentioned being authorized to spare no money, either to obtain information, or to procure friends to his Court. He has an immense credit in Reimbert's house, and though he does not yet, nor perhaps ever will, appear in the best company, yet he has already got admission into the several clubs, and into many private houses of this capital. He has been indiscreet enough to boast of having wherewithall to buy Prince Potemkin, and, with that arrogance inseparable from his nation, talks of nothing less than uniting this Court with France. [229]

3. THE ENIGMA OF THE EMPRESS

March 3, 1780, to Stormont:[63] The Empress, on coming into the room yesterday evening, immediately said to me, in a whisper, ". . . I give you this ball and entertainment on account of Rodney's successes.[64] Under this roof," said she, referring to the rules of the Hermitage, "frankness and sincerity should ever dwell; I cannot, therefore, conceal from you my satisfaction on this occasion, though I express it to you not as Empress of Russia to the English Minister, neither must it make part of your ministerial despatches, but merely as a friend of England speaking to a good Englishman." She honoured me afterwards with her conversation almost the whole of the evening; and, when my colleagues and the rest of the company went to sup with the Grand Duke

---

[63] David Murray, 7th Viscount Stormont, 2nd Earl of Mansfield (1727-1796), secretary of state, who had joined the North ministry in October 1779. This dispatch is dated one week after that in which Harris reported his first inklings of the Armed Neutrality, the ultimate outcome of which was, however, shrouded in mystery.

[64] The reference is to Rodney's victory off Cape St. Vincent on January 10, 1780, in which he took or destroyed six of eleven ships-of-the-line.

and Duchess, permitted me to partake of her own very frugal repast, which was served on a card-table, without attendants or spectators of any kind. If these distinctions and marks of good-will, both from the Sovereign and her principal favourite, cover any insidious and false design, the intrigue is too artfully concerted for me to unravel it; and if, in my descriptions of the sentiments of this Court, I deceive your Lordship, it is because I myself am most egregiously deceived. [244]

4. A BRIBE FOR POTEMKIN[65]

April 11, 1780, to Stormont: If, on further inquiry, I should find, as I almost suspect, that my friend's fidelity has been shaken, or his political faith corrupted, in the late conferences by any direct offers or indirect promises of reward, I shall think myself, in such a case, not only authorized but obliged to lure him with a similar bait; since, if he ever should be brought to act under Prussian influence . . . every hope of success here will be cut off, and the tide will turn powerfully against us. . . . You will be pleased to recollect that I have to do with a person immensely rich, who well knows the importance of what is asked, and whose avidity, not necessity, is to be paid. He will require, perhaps, as much as Torcy proposed, but without success, to Marlborough.[66] [252]

5. PERSONAL ATTACKS

May 5, 1780, to Stormont: The personal attacks on me are carried to a ridiculous length. Letters from Potzdam [Potsdam] assert that my whole conduct is disapproved at home; that I act from my own head, without orders; and that I do not possess the confidence of any of my superiors. The Russian Minister here [Panin] too says, that from my connexion with Prince Potemkin, and by having obtained indirect means of getting at the Empress, I had put false notions into her head . . . that my behaviour is more like a partisan than a Minister, but that he will make me feel the folly of my conduct, by disgracing me both here and at home. I can, however, assure your Lordship, that I have never been deficient to Count Panin in any shape whatsoever; that, while he is

---

[65] In the factious intrigue of the court, which principally concerned the rivalry of Count Panin and Prince Potemkin, Harris had, by this time, thrown in his lot with the latter, whom he frequently termed "my friend." However, his suspicions were now aroused by a series of conferences between Potemkin and the Prussian minister.

[66] M. de Torcy, minister of Louis XIV, is reported to have offered two million francs to the Duke of Marlborough at the Hague in May 1709, to bring him to the French interest.

thus stabbing me in the dark, he receives me every day in his house with the strongest appearances of cordiality and regard. . . . [259]

6. DISSENSION AT HOME

June 1780, to Keith:[67] Be assured the Empress loves us *as a nation*, and though she has a little spice of the Opposition in her character, yet she will never do us half so much harm as those profligate rascally patriots at home, who, in times like these, are abandoned enough to add to foreign wars, domestic broils and discontents.[68] I think, to curse them must be a merit in the sight of the Lord. I dread the iniquitous temper they have raised, more than twenty combined fleets; since I am fully convinced that we should, if unanimous and true to ourselves, beat them all. [272]

7. FIRST REQUEST FOR RECALL

June 26, 1780, to Stormont: The doubts I had of Prince Potemkin's fidelity being shaken, have indeed disappeared. . . . But he is of a complexion to be influenced ever by the impulse of the moment, and to be wrought upon by what strikes his fancy and imagination, without consulting his judgment and reason. He, besides, is not of a character to persist in a uniform predilection, either for the same person, or the same cause; and the most trifling incidents may create a sudden and total alteration in every part of his conduct. On the other side, I have the strongest confirmation of the opinionative systematic hatred of Count Panin, whose inveteracy against England, after brooding ten or twelve years, now breaks forth with all the acrimony of an enemy who has been forced so long to wear the mask of a friend. . . . With such a friend and such an enemy, I have much to fear, and little to hope. . . . By being without the confidence of any one, having lost every means of getting at the Empress, and certain that everything I say or do will be misconstrued and invidiously applied, every step I attempt to take must be productive of mischief and harm; and, instead of retrieving, I shall effectively destroy the remnant of our interests here. . . . I submit it entirely to your Lordship's judgment and opinion, to decide whether it would not be infinitely important for His Majesty's service that I

[67] Sir Robert Murray Keith, envoy extraordinary and minister plenipotentiary at Vienna from 1772 to 1792.

[68] Lord George Gordon, in a vigorous protest against the removal of political restrictions on the small Catholic minority, had instigated a series of riots in London, resulting in considerable damage to the city and the death of twenty-one persons.

should be removed from hence, to have a Minister named less obnoxious to Count Panin, and who, by making a discreet use of the road I have opened, and taught by my experience, may do His Majesty that service, which it was my greatest and sole ambition to effect, but to which my abilities and zeal have been found inadequate. [275-276]

VII · THE ARMED NEUTRALITY

I. GREIG: ITS ILLEGALITY

May 26, 1780, to Stormont: I would willingly hope that Her Imperial Majesty has been struck by a very manly representation and voluntary act of friendship of Admiral Greig. As soon as he read the Declaration, and saw the grounds on which the instructions were to be made, he collected the various sentences which had been pronounced last war in the Archipelago by the Russian Tribunal instituted for that purpose, and at which he frequently presided, on Neutral ships. After proving in the clearest manner that they confiscated and condemned Turkish property wherever they found it, and the only prizes they made were such property aboard Neutral ships, he gave in the whole to Count Czernicheff, signifying that, as a faithful and affectionate servant of the Empress, he thought himself obliged to set before her eyes, that, if she carried her present measures into execution, she would act in direct contradiction to herself. The Count, not from a regard to us, of which he has not a spark, but from the apprehension he is under that the ships will not be found fit for ocean service, and that, if they sail, he shall be disgraced, certainly gave this paper to the Empress, and as she has the highest notion of the Admiral's capacity and integrity, his decision may operate strongly with her. Though I live in the most intimate friendship with him, he never mentioned to me this fact till it was done, and the merit of it is wholly his own. He assured me, and he spoke in the name of all his countrymen, that, if ever the Empress should require of them to serve in a manner hostile to us, they would, to a man, quit her service. [264-265]

2. ORLOV: ITS INGRATITUDE

February 13, 1781, to Stormont: I have been always attentive to cultivate the acquaintance of the Orlows, and . . . I have hitherto had the luck of living on the best footing with them. . . . In this I am greatly facilitated by their very liberal character, and from their being well-wishers to England from principles of patriotism and sound reason. Count Alexis, the most enlightened and the most active of his family, though out of favour, has still great weight whenever he speaks to the Empress. . . . Yesterday he informed me of a discourse that passed between them on Monday. It arose from her having asked him, on Saturday, why on his late travels he did not visit England, and his having replied, before a large circle, that he was ashamed to show himself in a kingdom to whom Russia was under so great obligations, at a moment when the Russian fleet was sailing with a view to act in direct opposition to its most essential interests; that, if he had appeared in London, he must have expected his old Mediterranean acquaintance would have turned their backs on him; and, when the Empress endeavoured to prove away what he had said, he, still talking aloud, and before the company, entered into a detail of our friendly conduct during the late Turkish war, to which he himself had been a witness, and to which he said he owed the little glory he had obtained . . . that his political sentiments had ever been the same; that he considered the French as a faithless, false nation, enemies to her and to her Empire; that if their conduct was changed, yet their designs were not . . . that the English were, he granted, *less polite* than the French, but much *more sincere*; that they were the only true and useful friends Russia could have, and that if she was indifferent to the esteem and regard of a nation like ours, she ought not to be so to the loss of its good-will and friendship. . . . [335-336]

3. HARRIS: ITS INEXPEDIENCY

February 18, 1782, to Hugh Elliot: The permanent interests of the state are sacrificed to those of the moment. That wise system of policy, so essential to Europe in general, so advantageous to Russia, and so salutary to Great Britain, is forgotten. What may happen, never is adverted to; and the great point is to take immediate advantage of what does happen, without considering whether it is at the expense of a friend or a foe, without reflecting upon its instantaneous effects or consequence. To establish an active trade in a country where there are neither ships, sailors, ports, nor merchants, is the phrenzy of the hour.

The means used to effect it are not less erroneous than the attempt itself is impossible. An universal Free Navigation is to be crammed down the throats of all the Maritime Powers; privileges, which, if they belonged to Russia alone, might be serviceable to her, are to be granted promiscuously to every one; and, while the greatest pains are taking to make the Russian merchants *carriers*, encouragement is given to all her neighbours by the Empress herself to become *carriers*, and she stifles with one hand what she cherishes with the other. . . . It is in vain to remind her how contradictory the principles of her famous Convention are to her own conduct in the last Turkish war; how contrary they are to the established doctrines of the *droit des gens*;[69] how detrimental they are to one of the belligerent Powers, and how advantageous to the others: in a word, how very *unneutral* her Armed *Neutrality* is. . . .

Reasonings . . . on the present situation of Europe, of the very great importance it is for the Northern Powers, for their own sake, to observe a conduct different from that they hold, meet the same fate; or, if they are answered, it is by recrimination, by entering into an examination of the insulary system we have pursued since the Peace of Paris, and by charging us with all the evils brought down upon us. Awake to our errors, and asleep to their own, they seem to think themselves authorized to trifle away their own preponderance and ours, because ten years ago we did not choose to enter into views of which we knew neither the beginning nor the end. . . .

The English, I say, cannot be brought to deviate from their national character in their transactions. . . . They complain when they think themselves injured; they remonstrate when there appears a manifest partiality for their adversaries; and they cannot be brought to acknowledge as infinitely wise what their common sense tells them is infinitely absurd. Thus, therefore, are we become unpopular; "our nation is degenerated, our Ministry is corrupt, insufficient, and unfriendly, and it is not safe for any one to join their cause to ours." [421-423]

4. THE RUSSIAN FLEET: ITS INSTRUMENTALITY

June 23, 1780, to Stormont: The fleet sailed from Cronstadt [Kronshtadt] at five o'clock Wednesday evening with a fair breeze. . . . I sent down a person of confidence to attend to everything which passed. He is returned, and assures me that the confusion and hurry which preceded its sailing, could only be equalled by the discontent and dejection of the men and officers when under sail; that the commanders are as strongly impressed with these sentiments as their subalterns, and go

---

[69] An examination of the facts proves this statement to be sheer nonsense. Nearly every maritime nation, including England, had varied its definition of contraband repeatedly through the years. Expediency was and remained the basic issue, and, although England generally supported the view that naval materials constituted contraband of war, they had not been defined as such in the commercial treaty with Russia in 1766. Albion, *op. cit.*, pp. 187-194.

with the utmost reluctance on an expedition which promises neither glory nor profit. The crews, though complete, are not sea-faring men, and have a sickly cadaverous look. The ships are well-rigged and make a fine appearance; but their timbers are old, and not sound, and they would be ill able to resist a hard gale on the ocean, or a well-directed broadside. Such are the remarks of a sensible accurate observer. [274]

VIII · FLUCTUATIONS AND PERPLEXITIES, SEPTEMBER 1780-JULY 1781

I. REJECTION OF THE PRINCE OF PRUSSIA[70]

September 8, 1780, to Stormont: His Royal Highness the Prince of Prussia arrived here on Wednesday evening. . . . The interview between him and the Empress, which took place yesterday morning with great ceremony and etiquette, was, I believe, very little satisfactory to either. He appeared to her heavy, reserved, and awkward; and her reception struck him as cool, formal, and unpromising. [285-286]

September 26, 1780, to Stormont: Your Lordship will perceive, from the manner in which the Prince of Prussia passes his time, how little progress he makes; the greatest pains were taken yesterday to induce the Empress to have an entertainment at Court, but she absolutely refused it. On Sunday she broke off abruptly her card-party, and, as I was sitting next to her, gave me clearly to understand, that it was from her being worn out by the heaviness of the Prince of Prussia, who sat on the other side of her. [287]

October 3, 1780, to Stormont: His Royal Highness is endeavouring to bring over Prince Potemkin, and, if possible, to obtain through him a more favourable reception at the latter end of his residence: I however do not believe that he is likely to succeed; neither, if he did, that even Prince Potemkin has influence enough to overcome the aversion the Empress has conceived for him. After insinuating, by every kind of means, that it would be agreeable to her if he would fix his departure for an early day, she at last has ordered her private Secretary to tell Count Panin, very plainly, that he must contrive to get him away soon, as she felt if he stayed much longer she might say something rude to

---

[70] The rise of the Austrian interest at St. Petersburg after Joseph II's visit to Russia rendered Frederick II most uneasy, and it was in the attempt to regain his influence with Catherine that he dispatched his nephew, the later Frederick William II, to St. Petersburg. Catherine's brusque treatment of him was, in reality, based upon political considerations, and it is typical of the personal diplomacy which so frequently bewildered Harris.

him. . . . In public she treats him with a coolness and reserve quite foreign to her character, and never speaks to any of his suite. At the masquerade on Friday, and at Court on Sunday, he did not play at cards with her; it is the more remarkable, as, to make room for me on my coming after she was set down, she made Prince Bariatinsky give me his place. While she is behaving with this very unusual neglect to the Prussian party, she is paying the most marked attention to everything which regards the Court of Vienna. [287-288]

October 6, 1780, to Stormont: I am certain . . . that nothing less than a miracle can now make any alteration in the behaviour or sentiments of the Empress towards the Prince Royal. . . . Tuesday, at Mons. Nariskin's, Master of the Horse, she neither played, nor asked him to sup at her table; to which she admitted none but myself, her favourite, and Prince Potemkin. Yesterday, at the masquerade, she appeared under the mask, and immediately on her coming in took me to accompany her through the apartments, saying, "Ne me quittez pas de toute la soirée; je vous ai fait Chevalier, et je veux que vous me défendiez contre les ennuyeux." She stayed from seven till ten, and took not the smallest notice of the Prince, or any of his followers; not indeed scarce of any one but Lady Harris and myself. Your Lordship may easily guess how these distinctions alarm my enemies, and create envy and jealousy in my colleagues. I feel myself most unfortunate that, while I enjoy these distinctions in such an uncommon degree, I cannot derive from them the only advantages I am solicitous about. . . . [289]

2. FOREIGN CORRUPTION

December 24, 1780, to Stormont: Your Lordship can conceive no idea of the height to which corruption is carried in this country, of the exorbitancy of the demands, or of the barefacedness with which they are made. The French, the Dutch, and even the Prussian Ministers are most profuse on this article; and the first, I am certain, has expended (to very little purpose indeed) immense sums since his arrival. He has furnished money to the two first-cousins of Count Panin and the Vice-Chancellor, to purchase houses to the amount of four or five thousand pounds each; every subaltern expects his fees, and these fees are according to the exigences of the times. The Duke of Courland spends £20,000 yearly here, and may boast of having amongst his pensioners, Count Panin, Count Czernicheff, Count Ostermann. Your Lordship may be satisfied that I shall be as economical as possible, but I must pay for every piece of intelligence I get, and my informers know how important it is for me to receive it in time and with accuracy. [321]

3. DEATH OF THE ELDER HARRIS

February 2, 1781, to Sir Joseph Yorke: The very severe domestic loss I have sustained by the death of my father, will, I am sure, appear to your Excellency a very valid excuse for not immediately acknowledging your letter. . . . I was indeed as much prepared for this event as I well could be; but, if such preparation took off from the pain of a sudden shock, it has not diminished that heartfelt affliction not in my power to suppress, and which, from the excellency of the character of him I am lamenting, reflection at least for a while must increase. [331]

4. INTRIGUES OF PANIN[71]

May 4, 1781, to Stormont: Count Panin is at last fixed in his resolution to go into the country. He has asked and obtained from the Empress leave of absence for three months, and is hastening his departure as much as possible: his friends disapprove the step he is taking; and the Prussian, French, and Dutch Ministers consider themselves as left without a chief. My hopes, however, do not rise as theirs sink; and I fear his genius will not less prevail when he is absent than when he is present. The means by which he carries his points are so concealed, his operations so covered and so slow, that it is indifferent whether he directs them near, or at a distance. . . . I am assured the principal motive of His Excellency's hastening his departure is to avoid the storm that will break upon him. . . . He well knows that no sentiments, either of displeasure or of favour, are of long duration in the Empress's mind, and relies that this matter will be made up and forgotten before his return. [360-362]

5. ADMISSION OF PRUSSIA

May 11, 1781, to Stormont: I dined on Wednesday with Prince Potemkin . . . and as soon as his company left him, he talked upon the

---

[71] In the desire to consolidate the Austro-Russian friendship, Catherine and Joseph had determined upon the marriage of the Archduke Francis (the later Emperor Francis II of Austria), Joseph's nephew, to the Princess of Württemberg, the sister of Maria Fyodorovna, wife of the Grand Duke Paul. In order to frustrate this move, Panin, in the Prussian interest, had conspired with Frederick II for the secret betrothal of this Princess to the Prince of Prussia. The inevitable rage consequent upon Catherine's discovery of this perfidy was what Panin wished to avoid by absenting himself from St. Petersburg, and it was Harris's hope that the revelation of this intrigue would utterly destroy the Prussian interest.

interests of our two Courts. . . . He assured me that the Empress . . . was heartily tired of the Armed Neutrality, and was now as desirous to see its end, as, not long ago, she was eager in setting it a-foot. It will appear strange to your Lordship, after hearing this language on Wednesday from a person so perfectly acquainted with the sentiments of his Sovereign, and who certainly did not endeavour to deceive me, that on Thursday I was told from unquestionable authority, that His Prussian Majesty had again applied to be admitted into the Northern League, and that the Empress had not only acquiesced in it, but given orders for the document necessary for his admission to be drawn up immediately. . . . Unless we may attribute this conduct to what my friend told me, and that she really considers the Armed *Neutrality* as an Armed *Nullity*, we must look for its explanation in that singular levity of temper of which every day affords me fresh and painful instances. [364-365]

6. INFLUENCE OF POTEMKIN

May 18, 1781, to Stormont: I understand that the new favourite, Morduinoff [Mordvinov], who has for a long time back performed the duties of his office, will in a few days be admitted to the honours of it, and the present titulary one, Landskoy [Lanskoi], resign to him his apartments in the several palaces. These revolutions are moments when the influence of my friend is without bounds, and when nothing he asks, however extravagant, is refused. I wish I could prevail on him to employ them, once in his life, in a manner honourable to himself and beneficial to his country and his friends and not misuse them by adding to a fortune already preposterous. . . . [366]

May 25, 1781, to Stormont: I understand my friend proposes to make use of the unbounded power these moments will give him, in obtaining not less than 700,000 roubles for himself, and of course more dignified objects will be forgotten, or postponed to a day when his attempts to succeed will be in vain. [366-367]

7. THE AUSTRO-RUSSIAN ALLIANCE

June 9, 1781, to Keith: The Treaty so nearly concluded is broken off, and though the interests of the two Courts remain the same, and the avowed inclinations of reciprocal and invariable regard of the two Sovereigns are supported by the strongest professions, yet the main point is wanting, and, by the deficiency of a solemn and public engagement, full scope is given for the intrigues of their respective ill-wishers to operate; and instead of looking forward to that pleasing prospect this wise connexion offered us, we may now be thankful if the storm does not get blacker.

It is impossible to say what determined the Empress's final opinion on this occasion. . . . Her irresolution has been remarkable, and I do not add a syllable to the truth, when I say, that she varied in her decision not less than *four* times. . . . [367-368]

July 6, 1781, to Keith: It is in the greatest confidence, and under the seal of the most profound secrecy, that I inform you that the Treaty between the two Imperial Courts is signed by letter by the two Sovereigns. It was executed nearly about the 15th of June. . . . It is known to no one here, and I must entreat of you . . . not to betray any sign of being acquainted with it. . . . I am most anxious to learn from you what can be the Emperor's views on having such a singular and unexpected complaisance for the Empress.[72] She is now, I may say, passionately attached to him, and the Prussian interest is fallen forever. [375]

8. MORE FOREIGN CORRUPTION

July 6, 1781, to Stormont: I obtained the information of the conclusion of the Treaty from the confidential Secretary of Mons. Besberodko.[73] I trust I shall keep him to myself, since I have lost almost all my other informers by being outbid for them by the French and Prussians. This is the more painful to me, as I am convinced that I appear very profuse in the article of Secret Service money, and that His Majesty has every reason to expect such services as he receives from me at a much cheaper rate: but the increasing and avid corruption of this Court is not to be conceived; and my enemies, not only because they divide the expense amongst them, but because their respective Courts pour in money upon them, have a great advantage over me. They are also much more adroit at this dirty business than I am, who cannot help despising the person I corrupt. [374]

9. DECLINE OF POTEMKIN

July 6, 1781, to Stormont: The fluctuating history of this Court

[72] The final signature of this most important treaty was delayed by a dispute upon a point of diplomatic protocol, as to whose name, Catherine's or Joseph's, should stand first in the treaty. It was quite unexpected that Joseph, Holy Roman Emperor, should have given in on this point to the relatively recent Romanov pretensions to the imperial title.

[73] Vice-chancellor, ultimate successor to Panin, and, for long thereafter, an influential advisor to Catherine.

affords new matter for every messenger I despatch; it never was more extraordinary than at the present moment. The Empress grows every day more suspicious and hasty: tenacious to a degree of her own power, and obstinately attached to her own opinion, she is jealous or displeased with almost every one that approaches her. From being the most easy and pleasing Mistress to serve, she is become the most difficult; and her domestics, as well as her Ministers and favourites, feel this singular change in her disposition. It makes itself so sensibly felt, that several of the leading people of the State have asked, or mean to ask, their dismission. . . . My friend, too, who is more exposed to the effects of this revolution in her temper than any one, has, I have good reason to believe, expressed to her his earnest desire of throwing up his many employments; and it was not till he received the flattest refusal, that he desisted from his solicitations . . . and, indeed, if anything could make me suppose he had it in contemplation to leave the Court, it is the loads of ready money he is heaping up, by selling his estates, horses, and jewels, and which looks as if he either wished, or was apprehensive he should be forced to retire, and that it was wise to place in time a large capital in some foreign funds. [372-373]

10. OSCILLATIONS OF THE COURT

July 25, 1781, to Stormont: I never believe anything here till it has actually taken place. . . . It is impossible for me to send you a picture of it, that would not before it got to your hands totally lose its likeness; and it is not to be wondered that its operations and conduct are so incomprehensible to your Lordship, when I, who am on the spot, and whose attention is turned on that single object, am in a perpetual puzzle, and never when I go to bed can venture to say what will be the humour and intention of the Empress when I rise. [382]

IX · POTEMKIN

1. HIS TRIUMPH OVER PANIN

September 18, 1781, to Stormont: On Thursday last . . . the Vice-Chancellor received an order signed by the Empress, that it was her pleasure that he should do alone all the business of the Foreign Department; that all acts and rescripts relative to it should be signed by him; that he should report to her what the Foreign Ministers said to him, and his answers to them; that the foreign correspondence should be addressed to him, and the answers written in his name alone.

SIR JAMES HARRIS (LATER, THE FIRST EARL OF MALMESBURY)

PRINCE GRIGORI ALEXSANDROVICH POTEMKIN

This very singular and humiliating exclusion of Count Panin was resolved on by the Empress about a week ago, but she kept her resolution secret till his arrival, making it, if possible, by this means, still more disgraceful for him. As it was quite unexpected here, and as most people supposed Count Panin too artful and too well informed a man to return to certain disgrace and shame, it has caused a very considerable sensation; and, as a very large number of dependants are included in his overthrow, there is as much murmuring as can be ventured to be shown in a Government like this. . . .

I had yesterday much conversation with my friend on this subject. He affects to disapprove the harshness of the measure, though he admits the equity of it. . . . He advised me . . . to keep up an appearance of living perfectly well with Count Panin and (what I certainly shall do) to avoid any expression of triumph or of insult at his disgrace: he added, (and his words made a deep impression on me,) "You know the fickleness of this Court; he may be restored to his places, and, if you treat him with attention during his disgrace, he will then be ashamed to act against you in so glaring a manner as he has hitherto done." . . . I am indeed convinced he does not love Count Panin, and that he was originally instrumental to his disgrace; but he loves Mons. Besberodko and his set still less, and sees with the greatest jealousy and uneasiness the progress they make. My fears all along have been, and still are, that he will endeavour to raise Count Panin in order to sink them; and that, to answer the purposes of a dark Court intrigue, he will forget the more essential interests of his friends. [390-391]

2. HIS STRANGE REVERSAL

November 20, 1781, to Stormont: The Empress now remarkably distinguishes the French and Prussian Ministers, and on Sunday evidently sought an opportunity of talking with the latter, in a way not to be overheard. Till now, she has always treated Mons. de Verac [the French Minister] with great coolness, and expressed a dislike to him; yet for these last three Court days she has excluded me and named him, for her card party, and I know speaks well of him in private.

There is not the least doubt that Prince Potemkin has obtained these distinctions for them; neither, however incredible it appears, that he is in secret intelligence with Count Panin, and that it is probable that, after having produced his disgrace, he will attempt gradually to restore him to favour. It is equally evident that he is adverse to the Austrian cause, and only watches an opening, which the natural levity of the

Empress's character must soon offer, of opposing it. This revolution in his behaviour and principles must be attributed partly to the inconstancy of his disposition, partly to the artful and intriguing disposition of Count Panin, but principally to a strong jealousy he entertains for the Secretary [Besberodko] and his party. [411-412]

3. IN THE FRENCH INTERESTS

November 27, 1781, to Stormont: I shall now, according to my promise, give your Lordship an extract of several communications I have had with my friend. He began by his usual preface of lamenting the alteration in the Empress's character; that she was directed either by her own whims, or by some invisible hand, which his penetration could never discover; that he could effect nothing, and that, thus circumstanced, it was particularly hard he should be charged with the odium of every obnoxious or unfavourable measure. . . . He then with great art touched upon the frequent visits Count Goertz [the Prussian Minister] and the Marquis de Verac made him, and which he well knew could not escape my notice. He said, the first had negotiated with him the purchase of horses in the Ukraine to remount the Prussian cavalry . . . that as for the Marquis de Verac, he was a man of so very insignificant a character, that he supposed his visits could not have given me any umbrage . . . that he came to him . . . to promote the settlement of a Mons. Antoine, who wished to establish a French house at Kerson [Kherson]; and, with a view probably to divert me from having any serious ideas on these subjects, Prince Potemkin exercised a talent he possesses very completely, and counterfeited so inimitably a dialogue between himself, the French Minister, and French merchant, that it was impossible not to lose sight for a while of the very interesting matters on which we were talking.[74] . . . He is actuated by motives above the reach of my faculties. [412-414]

[74] If Harris had better understood the Russian designs in the Black Sea and the Mediterranean, he would not, perhaps, have regarded the report of the conversation between Verac, Antoine, and Potemkin as a mere ruse of the latter to distract his attention. Actually, Antoine had approached the Russian government with a scheme for exporting Russian naval stores through the Dardanelles in French ships flying the Russian flag, and, although this did not accord with Catherine's ambitions for an independent Russian commerce, Antoine, in 1785, succeeded with much difficulty in getting a cargo of masts to France over this route and thereby demonstrated the practicability of a new commerce which grew steadily until its interruption by a second Russo-Turkish war in 1787. With a second peace, however, trade resumed. By 1802, it had increased fifty-fold from the volume prior to the opening of the Black Sea and had clearly manifested to British diplomats and merchants that Russian aims in the Mediterranean were something more than chimerical. Gerhard, *op. cit.*, pp. 117ff.; J. J. Oddy, *European Commerce*, Philadelphia, 1807, I, 167.

4. IN THE BRITISH INTERESTS

June 21, 1782, to Fox:[75] Prince Potemkin . . . arrived[76] at midnight on Tuesday, and immediately wrote me, in his own hand, the following concise, but expressive note: "Vive la Grande Bretaigne et Rodney; je viens d'arriver, mon cher Harris; devinez qui vous écrit, et venez me voir tout de suite." I was with him in an instant, and, after hearing from him the most friendly and cordial assurances, and such as I had been accustomed to in the best days of our connexion, I entered with him on business. . . . I succeeded beyond my expectations; he entered warmly into my ideas, joined issue in all I said, and promised me immediate and effectual support. I passed the greatest part of that night and yesterday in his company, during which time he frequently went up to the Empress, and ever returned in the highest spirits; he constantly made me fresh reports of her regard for England, of her esteem and approbation of its Ministers; and though our conversation naturally wandered, in so many hours, from one subject to another, yet he ever brought it back to our successes, on which he spoke with an enthusiastic satisfaction that, till now, I thought none but an Englishman could feel.

Various collateral circumstances leave me no doubt of his sincerity. If you ask me, why this sudden change? I shall be at a loss for a reply. It is certainly not attributable to any efforts of mine, neither is it to be deduced from any system he wishes to pursue. It must be sought for in the character of this very extraordinary man, who every day affords me new matter of amazement and surprise. Our conversation took place immediately on his coming off a journey of three thousand wersts, which he had performed in sixteen days, during which period he had slept only three times; and besides visiting several estates, and every church he came near, he had been exposed to all the delays and tedious ceremonies of the military and civil honours, which the Empress had ordered should be bestowed on him wherever he passed, yet he did not bear the smallest appearance of fatigue, either in body or mind, and on our separating I was certainly the more exhausted of the two. [446-447]

[75] Charles James Fox (1746-1806), an Oxford acquaintance of Harris and a former member of the North ministry. At this time, he was secretary of state for foreign affairs under the Marquis of Rockingham, a position which he resigned shortly afterwards in the face of opposition from a fellow cabinet member, Lord Shelbourne. He regained this post for a short time in 1783 in the coalition ministry of the Duke of Portland.

[76] Potemkin had been making a preliminary reconnaissance of the situation in the southern provinces prior to the operations which were to result in the ultimate occupation of the Crimea.

X · DARKNESS

1. ESPIONAGE

November 1, 1781, to Stormont: I have ever been apprehensive I should have appeared profuse in my expenditure of secret service money. When the late Lord Suffolk afforded me a discretionary power to dispose of it, I then declined it, flattering myself that, having passed three years in Spain and five at Berlin, with a tolerable degree of success and reputation, without having had recourse to a practice repugnant to my character, I should likewise have been able (particularly as I was at what I thought a *friendly* Court) to have gone on here on the same footing.

I, however, soon discovered my error; I found the intelligence I obtained imperfect or false; that I could conciliate to myself no dependants; *that I was surrounded by spies, and had none*; and that, instead of getting at the secret of others, I was in danger of being betrayed myself.[77] . . .

The entire sum shall be provided for out of my private fortune, if the Treasury, under the pretext of its being unreasonable, should disavow the permission I have received from your Lordship. But I serve a gracious and indulgent Master, who, I am sure, would not wish to recompense my faithful services for fourteen years by distressing a fortune my foreign life has already so considerably reduced.[78] [396-397]

2. SECOND REQUEST FOR RECALL

May 20, 1782, to Fox: I must end this letter by one piece of advice, of the propriety of which I am much surer than of any I have hitherto given; that whatever is to be done, would be better done through any other man than through me. Besides the many reasons I have already given you, I am *used*, if I may be allowed the word. New faces and new habits are recommendations here, and mine have been too long before their eyes. [440]

---

[77] Harris elsewhere remarked that there was no person in his household too lowly for his enemies to bribe, in order to obtain a sight of his papers or the temporary possession of his keys. Whenever he left his secretary alone in his office, he used to lock him in, not because he distrusted his integrity, but because he feared that, carelessly leaving the door of the room open, he might afford access to scheming secret agents.

[78] In a private letter to Fox, Harris stated that his professional expenses had exceeded his compensations by £20,000 in his fourteen years in the diplomatic service.

3. THE LOSS OF FOX

August 2, 1782, to Fox: It was with very great concern that I learnt yesterday by a letter I received from Mr. Fraser, that you had resigned the seals on the 4th instant.

No Minister ever, in so short a time, did so much for his country as yourself. Your resignation cannot be sufficiently lamented.... You had restored to us confidence and consideration on the Continent, and I had begun to flatter myself that five years' anxiety and disappointment would have been terminated by a moment of the most complete satisfaction I could feel as a servant of the public: as such, therefore, I cannot too sensibly express my concern at being deprived of your instructions and advice; they cannot, in my esteem, be replaced.

I trust that what I expressed to you as *my wish* [his recall] will soon be complied with: if it should not, I shall think myself justified in signifying it as my *intention*. [456]

4. THIRD REQUEST FOR RECALL

August 27, 1782, to Grantham:[79] Whoever is fated to negotiate here must have as much patience as prudence; be active himself, yet submit to procrastination in others; have sinews not to be shaken by anxiety and disappointment. He must not negotiate by rule, or observe the precepts of Wickfort; he must watch the temper of the day, catch the lucky moment as it flies, strike while the iron is hot, negotiate by assault, if I may be allowed the expression, and never expect to carry his point by regular approaches.... The distance between London and Petersburg, and the necessity of writing for orders, make this very difficult for an English Minister.... I am worn out, *usé*. A new face, new manners, new flatterers, are necessary here; and though my long residence may, for some reasons, have made me fit for this post, yet the methods I have been compelled to employ to obtain my knowledge and experience have laid me open to so much personal animosity, that in all essential points I am become absolutely disqualified for it. [463-464]

5. MINISTERIAL BLUNDERS

August 27, 1782, to Grantham: I am compelled to say, that the principal cause of my failure was attributable to the very awkward manner

[79] Thomas Robinson, 2nd Baron Grantham (1738-1786), whose younger brother married Harris's sister. He joined Lord Shelbourne's ministry as secretary of state for the foreign department in July 1782, and resigned upon the formation of a coalition government in April 1783.

in which we replied to the famous Neutral Declaration of February 1780. As I well knew from what quarter the blow would come, I was prepared to parry it. My opinion was, "If England feels itself strong enough to do without Russia, let it reject at once these new-fangled doctrines; but if its situation is such as to want assistance, let it yield to the necessity of the hour, recognize them as far as they relate to Russia alone, and, by a well-timed act of complaisance, insure itself a powerful friend." My opinion was not received; an ambiguous and trimming answer was given; we seemed equally afraid to accept or dismiss them. I was instructed secretly to oppose, but avowedly to acquiesce in them; and some unguarded expressions of one of His Majesty's then confidential servants [Lord Hillsborough], made use of in speaking to Mons. Simolin, in direct contradiction to the temperate and cordial language that Minister had heard from Lord Stormont, irritated the Empress to the last degree, and completed the dislike and bad opinion she ever entertained of that Administration. Our enemies took advantage of these circumstances; they heaped coals of fire on our heads, and . . . by making her believe that the work of their cabals was a measure which would immortalize her, and which we alone opposed, so wrought on her passions, that what a few civil words would have done away in the beginning, will now be an everlasting and dangerous thorn in our side. [461]

6. MISTRUST AND BETRAYAL

August 27, 1782, to Grantham: I can clearly remark that the Empress doubts the stability of the present Ministry, suspects that farther changes may take place, and, in common with all other foreigners, has not an idea what is meant by Opposition and Resignations: To explain it to them would be explaining snow to an African Prince. . . .

You may be curious to know what I call *infamous accusations*, and why I might have apprehended *infamous attacks* from Count Panin. He accused me (and made the Grand Duke actually believe it) of having attempted to set fire to the Russian Fleet. He accused me of a design of poisoning the Grand Duke and Duchess and their children, by endeavouring to persuade them that some geraniums, and other equally inoffensive plants I had sent the Grand Duchess, were venomous. He who can forge such lies might have put into my salad some herbs less innocuous than geraniums; and the supposing him capable of it, cannot be imputed to an uncharitable disposition.[80] [465-466]

[80] That Harris should actually express the fear of poisoning by Count Panin reveals the extent

7. LONELY ISOLATION

September 17, 1782, to Grantham: It is a cruel thing to be far removed from one's old connexions, and it is in vain I look round me here for an acquaintance of longer standing than the date of my first audience; my cook and one *valet de chambre* excepted, I have nothing near me which I ever saw before I came into this country, unless I may reckon a coat of Virginia cloth of Castilian memory.[81] [469]

8. ETERNAL SUSPENSE

October 26, 1782, to Sir John Stepney:[82] We are here, seemingly, on the eve of a great event; everything looks as if a crisis was drawing near; indeed, I have so often waited for this crisis, so often thought it at hand, and so often been disappointed, that I may say of myself,

> "Expectat dum difluat amnis, at ille
> Labitur et labetur in omne volubilis ævum."

I remember in Spain a grandee's wife, who thought herself with child for ten years running, and regularly called out every four or five months for the midwife. I think we are somewhat here in the same situation, and till I see the infant I shall doubt the pregnancy. [475-476]

XI · AND A GLEAM OF LIGHT

I. THE EASTERN CHIMERA AGAIN

August 16, 1782, to Grantham: The scene here is materially changed. ... Both the Dutch and general Mediations are no longer the primary

---

to which his nerves had been wrought upon by these personal attacks. The accusation of his incendiary designs upon the Russian fleet, which he now coupled with these sinister forebodings, had formerly been the subject of light banter in a letter from Hugh Elliot, who wrote Harris on July 6, 1780: "We have for some days been told of a most heinous attempt you made to burn the Russian fleet. . . ." James Howard Harris, the 3rd Earl of Malmesbury, ed., *Letters of the First Earl of Malmesbury*, London, 1870, I, 469.

[81] Lady Harris and her two children had been forced to leave St. Petersburg for reasons of health in the summer of 1781. What consolation they had been to Sir James during his stormy embassy may be gleaned from a letter to Hugh Elliot in 1780: "Now for a word on this country: you know its extent, its high reputation—nothing but great deeds are done in it. The monarch is an arrant woman—a vain, spoilt woman. . . . The men in high life, monkeys grafted on bears; and those in lower, bears not inoculated. Religion, virtue, and morality, nowhere to be found; honour cannot be expressed in this language. There is no reward for good actions, . . . no punishment for any crimes. The face of the country in this neighborhood is a desert; the climate never made to be lived in. . . . You will naturally suppose living here not very comfortable; but I am sure of good society at home." Countess of Minto, ed., *Life and Letters of Sir Gilbert Elliot*, London, 1874, I, 62-66; Countess of Minto, ed., *A Memoir of the Right Honourable Hugh Elliot*, Edinburgh, 1868, pp. 214-215.

[82] New minister at Berlin and former Oxford acquaintance of Harris.

objects; nearer concerns employ the Empress's thoughts. . . . A *Turkish war*, if it happens . . . will open a new order of things, in which I think we can be no losers. [457]

August 27, 1782, to Grantham: The events to which the present disturbances in the Crimea may give rise are so important, that I have made it my duty to endeavour to obtain every possible information I could relative to them. . . . The strictest secrecy, under pain of the severest punishments, is enjoined to those who, from their situations, may receive orders on this subject, which is itself discussed in a private correspondence between the Emperor and Empress, without any of their Ministers being consulted. . . .

I can, in great confidence, assure your Lordship, that the Emperor has answered, that he was not only ready to comply with what was his duty as an ally, but that she might employ him to the whole extent of his faculties . . . and from this moment the Empress, instead of fearing a Turkish war, began most ardently to wish for one.

The Empress looks forward to the chimerical idea of establishing an Eastern Empire. The Emperor (supposing him sincere in his assurances) has views wiser and more practicable. He aims at the acquisition of Bosnia and Servia, and other parts of the Turkish empire adjacent to, and formerly belonging to, the kingdom of Hungary. [466-467]

November 15, 1782, to Grantham: The military operations in the East are at last begun, and news is received that the deposed Khan, under the protection of M. Samoiloff, at the head of a very trifling body of troops, but supported by a very considerable corps who are at hand, has entered the Crimea without resistance . . . and a few days will probably bring accounts of his being reinstated in his dignity; in the possession of which, however, he will remain no longer than till the more extensive views of Her Imperial Majesty . . . develop themselves.

Dreading the effects new taxes, laid on merely for the sake of forwarding a plan of speculative ambition, and in which the welfare of the state is not in the remotest degree concerned, might produce in the minds of her subjects, she does not choose to apply to them, although none in Europe are so lightly charged as they are. She well knows that there is no possibility of raising money in her empire, where there are neither bankers, nor considerable merchants, nor monied men of any description; and, under this dilemma, which . . . was not thought of till it was felt, she is going to have recourse to two of the most pernicious methods which could be devised for raising an immediate supply. To debase her coin, already so beneath its supposed value as to have sunk the exchange, in profound peace, lower than it was ever known in the midst of war, and to augment her bank-bills. [479-480]

December 6, 1782, to Grantham: I agree entirely with your Lordship, that even a defection on the side of the Emperor would not check the Empress in her career, and that she is now fully persuaded that single she can accomplish her vast views on the Ottoman empire, which I am inclined to think become every day more extensive, and of course more visionary. [485]

December 20, 1782, to Grantham: The Empress really begins to waver in her opinion; and, either through fear or from reflection, inclines to contract her views of aggrandizement into a much narrower space than she at first allowed her imagination to trace out. . . . The numberless examples which appear in the course of my correspondence of the Empress's mutability, and of her failure of resolution in the hour of trial, would, perhaps, alone be sufficient to account for this change. [488-489]

January 3, 1783, to Grantham: The Empress, I really believe, would, if left alone, be satisfied . . . but, besides the unremitting instigations of Prince Potemkin . . . the Emperor is now by far the keenest of the two for the carrying into execution a project which, when first suggested to him by the Empress, he thought to be idle and visionary. [491-492]

June 6, 1783, to Fox: News is arrived of Prince Potemkin being about a day's journey from Kerson, and in about a week accounts may be expected of his having entered the Crimea. He has asked for more artillery. . . . He seems determined to force the Turks to a rupture. . . . The Empress thinks herself equal to any undertakings against the Turks, and treats their preparations with much less attention than they deserve. She depends on *us* and on the Emperor to keep the Bourbon Courts quiet. . . . [516]

2. THE REQUEST FOR AID

February 28, 1783, to Grantham: A messenger has been despatched from hence, with orders for Mons. Simolin to sound Admiral Rodney, and to try every possible means to induce him to enter into the Russian service, and, in case he should decline, to use his utmost endeavours to engage Admiral Hood or Commodore Elliott, or some other officer of high rank and high reputation; and, if any of these gentlemen should accept the offer, he is instructed to apply immediately for leave from His Majesty that they should be permitted to serve the Empress. He is also instructed to look out for officers of an inferior rank, and to spare no pains nor offers to prevail upon them to come over. [505]

3. THE DECLINE IN HEALTH

April 11, 1783, to Maddison, Under Secretary: I never complain without a cause, neither do I ever give way to imaginary evils; but I feel such a perceptible decrease of my health almost every hour, that it would be staying to certain perdition were I to pass another autumn here. [510-511]

April 11, 1783, to Grantham: I am still confined to my house, and my health is so essentially impaired, that I am compelled, though reluctantly, to repeat, that an immediate removal into a more temperate climate is indispensably necessary for me. [511]

June 10, 1783, to Fox: The autumn is the perilous season for me; I cannot break in upon it without exposing myself to an almost certain illness; I trust, therefore, I may be allowed to fix my departure for the 15th August, *eventually*, for, should such important business be then in agitation as to make my longer stay essential, you may depend, in that case, that every other consideration whatsoever shall give way. [517]

4. THE PROMISE OF THE FUTURE

May 4, 1783, to Fox: I ... am fully persuaded that England, by *waiting patiently*, and by taking proper advantage of the incidents which must arise, may soon form very eligible and advantageous connexions, and enter into these connexions in the most respectable manner, not by seeking them, but by being sought for. [514]

July 11, to Keith: I foresee every day more clearly the hour approaches when, by a little prudence and well-timed address, we may entirely recover our Continental importance. [519]

September 5, 1783, to Fox: My endeavours have all tended to establish and consolidate a system of confidence and cordiality between the two Courts, in order to prepare the way for the proposition of an Alliance on some future day; but at the same time to be careful, not to be so gratuitously profuse in my assurances as to lead the Empress into a belief that we should follow her into all those ambitious excesses which from an over-encouragement she might be disposed to commit.

The manner in which the Russian Ministers have behaved towards me greatly facilitated the conduct I was to observe. It is no very difficult task to repay confidence by confidence . . . nor to obtain the friendship of those who are desirous of cultivating ours. . . . The Empress herself in her reply to the short speech I made her in my audience of leave . . . in the most forcible words she could employ, authorized me to declare to my Royal Master, that nothing could be more acceptable to her than the knowledge of his amicable sentiments, nor anything more sincere and cordial than those she entertained for him.

My successor will have a smooth and pleasant road to walk in. . . . The conduct of this Court speaks, at this moment, very evidently for itself. Their expressions are sincere, partly because they want us, partly because experience has served to open their eyes. The Empress will perhaps never condescend to own it, but I am fully convinced that she feels the impropriety of her conduct during our late war, and that, by her partiality to our enemies, she has done herself as well as us a material injury. [525-527]

CHAPTER FIVE
William Coxe

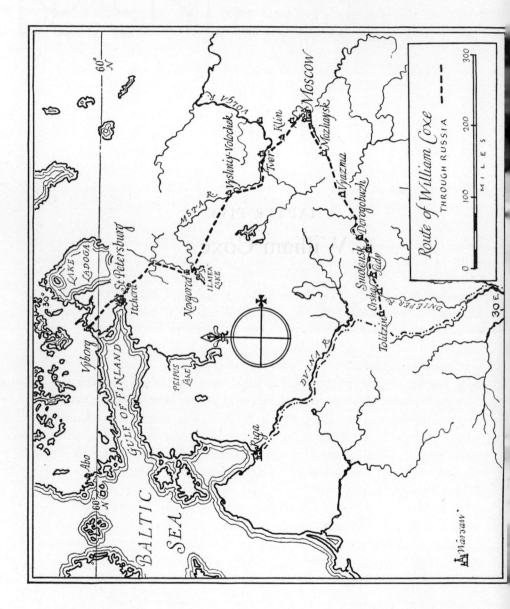

Route of William Coxe
THROUGH RUSSIA

MILES
0   100   200   300

William Coxe:

TUTOR ON TOUR

(1778-1779)

THE career of Archdeacon Coxe might logically entitle him to consideration in several different lights. A tolerant conservative, unconcerned with the religious controversy of his time, he was nevertheless a respected representative of the Anglican clergy for more than half a century. He distinguished himself as both an historian and a biographer.[1] His chronicle of the House of Hapsburg remained a standard work in England until the latter part of the Nineteenth Century; his life of Robert Walpole represented a new trend in the development of the biographical art;[2] and, along with it, his lives of Marlborough and Horace Walpole and memoirs of the Pelham administration are still valuable guides to students of the period.[3] Finally, his accounts of his various travels and, particularly, of his journey to Russia are among the best known of their kind for the whole century.

At the outset, however, it is important to consider Coxe, neither as clergyman, historian, biographer, nor even as the famous travel author he was later to become but, in the light of the immediate function which brought him to Russia, as the traveling tutor of a young nobleman completing his education with a Grand Tour upon the continent. As such, both he and his pupil represented a new class of visitors to Russia. Perry, Hanway, and Harris had each, in his way, pursued some tangible object and even Richardson, whose visit was less purposefully motivated, had not sought travel for its own sake. Now, there appeared a new class of travelers, composed of men of independent wealth and leisure time who came to Russia not to seek their fortunes but to satisfy their appetites. These were the tourists of the Eighteenth Century, and

---

[1] S. A. Allibone, *A Critical Dictionary of English Literature*, Philadelphia, 1902, I, 442.

[2] D. A. Stauffer, *The Art of Biography in Eighteenth Century England*, Princeton, 1941, I, 244, 324.

[3] *Memoirs of Horatio, Lord Walpole*, 3rd ed., London, 1820; *Memoirs of the administration of the Right Honourable Henry Pelham*, London, 1829; *Memoirs of John, Duke of Marlborough*, 2nd ed., London, 1829; *History of the House of Austria*, 2nd ed., London, 1820; *Memoirs of the Life and Administration of Sir Robert Walpole*, London, 1789.

whether they sought the pleasures of the court, the indulgence of idle curiosity, or the rewards of self-instruction, their main business was not business but pleasure.

The intangible values of continental travel had long been recognized by Britons. Conscious of England's position as a cultural backwater, Elizabethan courtiers who had crossed the channel to study the languages, letters and political state of contemporary Europe had been the pioneers of the Grand Tour. Their seventeenth century counterparts tended to confine their travels to France where they acquired the cavalier graces of dancing, riding, fencing and that wit and polish which were nearly indispensable at the Gallophile court of the Stuarts.[4] With the eighteenth century various influences contributed to swell the numbers of the young nobility sent to Europe to complete their educations. Beginning with the War of the Spanish Succession, periodic conflicts multiplied contacts with the continent.[5] The gradual reconstruction of Germany after the havoc of the Thirty Years' War and the abatement of that religious intolerance which had rendered all contact with Catholicism obnoxious to many Englishmen opened up new areas for exploration. The growing profits of the great commercial expansion financed the luxury of travel for an ever larger number, and young Britons beat a track across France to Italy and back through Switzerland, the Rhineland, Germany, or the Low Countries. Finally, as the completion of the Grand Tour became a sort of badge of class, the rising merchantry invaded the precincts of aristocracy and purchased its distinctions for their sons. By 1785, the flood had so increased that Gibbon relayed from Lausanne a report that over 40,000 of his countrymen had been on the continent in the summer of that year.[6]

The traveling tutor had long been and still continued to be a piece of the traditional impedimenta of the Grand Tour, but his utility diminished as the increasing popularity and accessibility of the Tour diluted its educational purposes. Improved travel facilities encouraged a more extensive itinerary which allowed proportionally less time for quiet residence and study. Moreover, the value of firsthand experience of foreign nations seemed to have been lessened by the increasing number of British publications on continental Europe and by the establishment of chairs of modern history in Oxford and Cambridge. A growing national pride exalted all things English and discredited foreign ways

[4] Chare Howard, *English Travellers of the Renaissance*, New York, 1913, pp. 113ff.
[5] W. E. Mead, *The Grand Tour in the Eighteenth Century*, Boston, 1914, p. 103.
[6] *ibid.*, p. 104; Howard, *op. cit.*, pp. 178-205.

WILLIAM COXE

GEORGE, LORD HERBERT

(LATER, THE ELEVENTH EARL OF PEMBROKE)

and values. As a result, the Tour frequently degenerated from a quest after the fruits of a superior civilization to a compound of sightseeing and dissipation. Many an English lordling dashed across Europe, rendering lip service to cultural values by his desultory inspections of Pompeiian ruins or Florentine galleries, yet scarcely mingling in the society of the natives, for which he expressed contempt, except to indulge his tastes for strong drink, the gaming table, or less savoury forms of intemperance. The companionship of such a youth was scarcely attractive to a man of discrimination or taste, and the character of tutor tended to decline with that of his high-spirited young patron. A letter from Lady Elizabeth Craven in Petersburg gives an inkling of the traveling governor's problems. "A little Latin and Greek in the schools of Westminister and Eton, and a great deal of vulgar rioting, make our young men a strange mixture of pedantism and vice, which can only produce imprudence and folly. Thus tutored, at sixteen, they [are] turned upon the hands of some unhappy man, who is to present them at foreign courts, with no other improvement or alteration in the boy's head than that of their hair being powdered and tied behind."[7] Horace Walpole showed less sympathy for the "booby governors," whom he described contemptuously as that "animal still more absurd than Florentine men or English boys."[8]

In the midst of this decadence of the Grand Tour as an educational medium, William Coxe proved exceptionally well qualified as a traveling tutor. He was born in Picadilly on March 7, 1747,[9] and, as the son of the Physician to the King's Household, came of a family of sufficient wealth and social standing to procure an excellent education. At the age of six, he was transferred from the grammar school at Mary-le-bone to Eton, which he attended until 1765. He then enrolled in King's College, Cambridge, where he applied himself assiduously and twice received the Bachelor's Prize for his Latin dissertations. In 1771, he took deacon's orders, motivated less, it would appear, by any burning religious convictions than by the prospect of the respectability, security, and quiet tenor of life which were the common lot of the Anglican clergy. It is not surprising, then, that he should have left his newfound curacy at Denham only a few months later in favor of a position as tutor to the young Marquis of Blandford, six-year-old son of the Duke

[7] Elizabeth Craven, *A Journey through the Crimea to Constantinople*, London, 1789, p. 126.

[8] Mead, *op. cit.*, p. 122.

[9] Except where elsewhere specifically noted, biographical data on William Coxe may be found in the following: *Gentlemen's Magazine*, II, 1828, 86-89; *Annual Register*, 1829, pp. 227-235; Allibone, *op. cit.*, I, 442.

of Marlborough. At Blenheim, the ducal estate, where he was shortly after granted the dignity of Chaplain, he spent the next four years, dividing his time between the famous library and the leisurely discharge of his clerical duties. In 1775, however, the Duke recommended him to his sister, Lady Elizabeth Pembroke, as a proper tutor to her son, George, just turning sixteen, for whom a continental tour was then in prospect.[10] The Earl and Lady Pembroke were well pleased with the respectable and scholarly young clergyman, to whom, in his turn, the engagement seemed to promise not only powerful patronage for future advancement in the church but also an opportunity for travel and study well calculated to indulge his intellectual appetite. Hence, it was readily agreed that William Coxe should accompany George, Lord Herbert, when, late in 1775, he embarked from England upon his European travels.

The plan of the tour was as exceptional in that period as the character of the tutor, for it aimed at all those social, intellectual, and physical accomplishments which were the equipment of the well-rounded man. Over a five year term its itinerary was to include the Low Countries, the Germanies, Switzerland, Poland, Russia, Sweden, Denmark, the Italian peninsula, and France. By means of the Earl's connections, the travelers were to meet the best society in every capital, but the trip was to be no mere court procession. Long periods of winter residence were to be devoted to serious study. A weekly curriculum drawn up in Strassburg included lessons in French, Italian, Latin, and Greek, geography, history, mathematics, fortifications, astronomy, experimental philosophy, readings among the English poets, Blackstone, Beccaria, and Voltaire, and, finally, lessons in music and drawing. Resident experts were hired to assist the instruction. Moreover, it was not to be expected that the Earl, internationally known as an authority on military equitation, should allow his son's physical education to be neglected. For this purpose, he had appointed as a third member of the party, a young protégé, Captain John Floyd, who was to supervise Lord Herbert not only in riding, but in shooting, swimming, tennis, fencing, dancing, and even billiards.

The sincere anxiety of both parents and tutor for the execution of this ambitious program is revealed in the regular correspondence maintained throughout the son's absence. The variety of their concerns

---

[10] The details of the subsequent tour and the relationship between Coxe and the Pembroke family are contained in a lively and interesting correspondence. Sidney Charles Herbert, ed., *Henry, Elizabeth and George, 1734-1780*, London, 1939.

appears to have been nearly limitless ranging from the selection and sequence of reading material to the choice of a mouth-wash recipe. In a single letter, Lord Pembroke cautioned his son against drinking, gaming, the wearing of lace, and the company of young French officers, while recommending to him the use of heavy shoes and flannel socks for tennis, regular dental inspection, and the continual rereading of Voltaire. He concluded with a reminder to "just cut, without shortening the tips of the hair all over and grease thoroughly the second day of every new moon."[11] But it was Lady Pembroke who attained the ultimate in parental solicitude when explaining her preference that Lord Herbert should winter in Vienna prior to any travel in Italy. In March 1776, she wrote to Coxe: "In Italy they scout every idea of decency and morality and will give him very much too little trouble, and I suppose it will be very natural that he should form great prejudices and partialities for the place and people where he first falls in love in ever so small degree, and the turn he takes then may remain very very long, if not forever. This will be the case probably by the time you are established in your next station, and as this is a rather difficult subject for me to talk upon I had better quit it for the present. I will only add that certainly the very best thing that can happen to a young man is to fall desperately in love with a woman of fashion who is clever, and who likes him enough to teach him to endeavour to please her, and yet keep him at his proper distance."[12]

"The triumvirate," as Lord Pembroke affected to call them, spent nearly three years on the continent prior to their arrival in Russia. Two quiet winters at Strassburg were passed in studies interrupted only by a summer tour of Switzerland. In October of 1776, Coxe was able to make a lone pilgrimage to Avignon to visit the last home of his idol, Petrarch, and the tomb of Laura. In April 1777, the trio kept a rendezvous with Lord and Lady Pembroke at Ostend, after which they took a leisurely course for Vienna, passing through the principal cities of the Low Countries and the various courts and capitals of the German states. The great of every locality accorded them civilities in passage and at the Austrian capital, the name of Joseph II was added to that of Frederick the Great in the list of their royal acquaintances. The festivities of Vienna rather distracted Lord Herbert's attention from academic pursuits, but Coxe employed his additional leisure in preparing for publication an account of his travels in Switzerland. Late in the following July, they set off for a tour of the Baltic countries, and after a short

[11] *ibid.*, pp. 51-53.   [12] *ibid.*, pp. 70-71.

visit with King Stanislas in Warsaw, they entered Russia from Poland on August 19, 1778.

Their route through Russia gave them a wider experience of the country than any of their predecessors since Hanway. The trip from Smolensk to Moscow lay through little traveled country, later to be made famous in history by the main army of Napoleon. The days over rough roads with meals of coarse peasant fare and nights upon the floors of peasant huts were succeeded by the hospitable and splendid entertainments of the Moscow nobility. The courtesy of the governor of the province, Prince Volkonski, enabled Coxe to meet both Müller,[13] the famous Russian historian, and Desnitski, a former student of the University of Glasgow, and the "Father of Russian jurisprudence."[14] After two weeks, they set out again for St. Petersburg at a leisurely pace inspecting the points of interest on the way. They had not originally intended to make a long stay in the Russian capital, but apparently its attractions, paraded for them by James Harris, delayed their departure until February of 1779. In the intervening four months, they were again accorded every courtesy, and Catherine herself even went so far as to answer in her own handwriting a list of questions submitted to her by Coxe on the state of the Russian prisons.[15] Within the rather ample limitations of the time and space of this journey, no traveler could have reasonably desired better opportunities to observe and understand the nature of a foreign country.

At St. Petersburg, Coxe took a step which is interesting for the light which it sheds on both the character of the tutor and the influence he enjoyed with his pupil. On October 27, he wrote to Lady Pembroke "desiring permission to return to England, because it is disagreeable to me to travel any longer with Captain Floyd. I esteem him very much and have a great regard for him: but our tempers do not agree, and when people quarrel together, the best thing they can do is separate."[16] Floyd seems really to have had a rather disagreeable manner. Prompted, perhaps, by his gratitude for the patronage of the Earl, he proved himself overzealous and opinionated in the supervision of Lord Herbert's

[13] Gerald Frederic Müller (1705-1783), historian and traveler, born in Westphalia. He was invited to Russia from the University of Leipzig by Peter the Great. With the exception of visits to Germany, Holland, and England, he spent the remainder of his life there, traveling widely, particularly in Siberia. His historical researches and organization of archival material rendered valuable service.

[14] E. J. Simmons, *English Literature and Culture in Russia, 1553-1840*, Cambridge, Mass., 1935, pp. 93-94.

[15] William Coxe, *Travels*, London, 1803, II, pp. 218-220.

[16] Herbert, *op. cit.*, p. 125.

crowded curriculum. This quality had jarred both the tolerant clergy-man and his young pupil. A possible clue to another area of tension is a notation in Floyd's journal upon crossing the Niemen on August 16. Floyd remarked: "I swam over."[17] A traveling companion who insisted upon indulging a whim for performing feats of strength in passage must have been rather a trial for the scholarly tutor. On the other hand, a certain pedantry in Coxe's manner was apt to aggravate impatient tempers. James Harris, while allowing his good qualities, did not forget "some bad national impressions he made here and many very tiresome moments his interrogatory disposition exposed me to."[18]

Young Lord Herbert, however, manifested a strong partiality for Coxe and requested of his family that Floyd should be recalled. Lord Pembroke, although he desired Coxe to remain with his son, was too chary of this protégé's feelings to recall him while the other remained. Therefore, although Coxe continued with the party through Sweden and Denmark, on their arrival at Vienna in June of 1779, after many vacillations he finally determined to return to England and took his leave of Lord Herbert shortly thereafter. The loyalty and affection he had inspired in his pupil are attested in a letter from Lord Herbert to Sir Robert Murray Keith. "With regard to Coxe and Floyd, that is arranged to the dissatisfaction of all parties. . . . I think I told you that Coxe and Floyd, though both good men, were not formed to live together, and that it is much the same with regard to Floyd and me. Now it is arranged that Coxe, who was of great use to me . . . and with whom I lived on perfect good terms, leaves me, and Floyd who wished exceedingly to return on account of his military occupations, remains with me, a person with whom I cannot, unfortunately, be two minutes without some disagreement and who cannot be of any use to me as Coxe was. . . ."[19] That this gratitude was not short-lived is attested by the later kindnesses and patronage of Lord Herbert; that it was at least in some degree merited is evidenced by the high quality of the publi-cations which were the consequence of their association.

It was not until 1784, five years after his return to England, that Coxe finally brought out the *Travels into Poland, Russia, Sweden, and Denmark*. In the interim, he had already enjoyed considerable success with several other publications: a revised and enlarged edition of his Swiss travels in 1779, *An Account of the Russian Discoveries between Asia and America* in 1780, and *An Account of the Prisons and Hos-pitals in Russia, Sweden, and Denmark* in 1781. His newest work, how-

[17] *ibid.*, pp. 124-125.   [18] *ibid.*, p. 381.   [19] *ibid.*, p. 208.

ever, far surpassed its predecessors in popularity. It went through six English editions within twenty years besides translations into French and other languages.[20] The experiences of later life enabled Coxe to revise and enlarge the successive editions in several ways. Another winter in St. Petersburg in 1784-1785 as tutor to Samuel Whitbread provided material for several new chapters. An indirect consequence of his marriage in 1803 to Elinore, the widowed sister of Stephen Shairp,[21] consul general at St. Petersburg, was the inclusion in his final edition of much valuable information on the Anglo-Russian commerce. Similar personal contacts and his continuous reading in French and German as well as English authors enabled him to add or amend, frequently in footnotes or appendices, various statistical data. Finally, as death claimed Catherine, Potemkin, Prince Grigori Orlov, and the famous general, Suvarov, he was able to interpolate certain biographical sketches which tact had previously suppressed.[22] These periodic accretions tend to give the final edition a patchwork quality, but they permitted Coxe to enlarge the scope of the book even beyond its original formidable size and, either by correction or confirmation, to improve the very high order of scholarship which it represented.

Even in its original form, however, despite the fact that the author himself hailed it as the first "systematic" treatment of the subject, the book lacked organization because it lacked unity of perspective. At different times, the author stood at three separate distances from his subject matter. Like any other tourist keeping a journal, he recorded his immediate personal impressions of the landscapes he saw, the towns and cities he visited, and the persons and personages he met on his travels. As a traveling guide, however, he assumed a more distant vantage point, adding to those observations of his immediate experience much additional information culled indirectly from books, documents, or secondary sources. Finally, he occasionally stepped still further back

[20] D. S. von Mohrenschildt, *Russia in the Intellectual Life of 18th Century France*, New York, 1936, pp. 196-197.

[21] The son of Walter Shairp, consul general from 1776 to 1787, he was one of the secretaries to Sir James Harris during his embassy and was left in charge at his departure. He was himself consul general from 1796 to 1807 and wrote many interesting and informative reports on the state of Russian commerce. Dietrich Gerhard, *England und der Aufstieg Russlands*, Munich, 1932, pp. 45, 68ff., 77, 80, 121ff., 144, 146, 423ff.

[22] Sir James Harris seems to have been the restraining force here. He wrote to Lord Herbert in January 1780: "Coxe has written me a letter full of questions; I have answer'd his letter, and some of these questions, and I have added a piece of advice and that very seriously not to print anything that could give umbrage here; he with all his admirable qualities, distinguishes so little between what is to be said, and what is to be secret, that I fear he will promiscuously publish all he knows." Herbert, *op. cit.*, p. 382.

from the Russian scene in passages which attempted, independently, to treat various aspects of the economic, political, and cultural life of Russia. Each of these three positions with their three separate functions, played a significant part in the composition of the whole.

In his personal reactions to his Russian experiences, Coxe revealed a ready and cheerful complaisance. Most striking are his favorable comments on the entertainments, taste, and polish of the Russian nobility. Unlike such predecessors as Perry and Harris, in his character as a tourist he was independent of Russian society on every ground save that of its entertainment value and was, therefore, freed of the nervous tensions which had operated so strongly on their judgments. He had stated his attitude in a letter to Lady Pembroke written only two months after his landing on the continent: "I am not at all surprised, that his Lordship is not over inclined to like the French. . . . He sees at once that all their compliments mean nothing, and that when they seem your greatest friends, they care little about you. And yet I think he may carry this a little too far; for in a foreign country no one can expect or indeed wish to make friends, but to get agreable acquaintance."[23] Lady Elizabeth Craven, another tourist in Catherine's Russia, admitted a similar suspension of moral judgments in her relations with its society. "I am assured that the Russians are deceitful. It may be so, but as I do not desire to have intimacies, I am much better pleased to find new acquaintances pleasant and civil than morose or pert. Wit and talent will always be objects of importance to me. I have found them here, and I shall be sorry to quit them."[24] Coxe, like Lady Craven, assured by many letters of introduction of an hospitable reception by the now thoroughly Europeanized Russian nobility, reflected the same favorable impression of them, and praise of the charm and cordiality of this class was characteristic of tourist accounts from this period.

If Coxe stood on common ground with his fellow tourists in appreciation of the elegancies of Russian life, he distinguished himself by his tolerance of its inconveniences. John Richards refused even to enter a peasant hut on the entire journey from St. Petersburg to Moscow,[25] and the internationally traveled Lady Craven, shivering with cold throughout her stay in the capital, declared "comfort" a word understood only in England.[26] Indeed, similar reactions were characteristic

[23] *ibid.*, p. 66. [24] Cravan, *op. cit.*, p. 133.

[25] John Richards, *A Tour from London to Petersburgh and from thence to Moscow*, Dublin, 1781, p. 49.

[26] Cravan, *op. cit.*, p. 120.

of the whole body of English travel literature, and in some cases, as with Smollet in France, the narratives read like a petition of grievances against the innkeepers, restaurateurs, and postmasters on the route.[27] Coxe encountered, recognized, and described many discomforts and annoyances, but without the narrow petulance of many of the others. One of the most frequent causes of complaint was the evasiveness and dishonesty of the Russian masters of post horses and English travelers often advised their successors to procure the services of a soldier to enforce promptness and fair dealing by means of a cudgel. With good reason, Coxe recommended the same procedure, but without flamboyant railing at the national character. On an occasion when the lack of such a military companion lengthened an easy day's journey to a difficult one of three, he remarked philosophically: "Obstacles continually occur in foreign countries, unforeseen by those who are not sufficiently acquainted with the manners of the natives, and an ignorance of the most trivial circumstances which better information might easily have obviated produces considerable embarrassments."[28]

In addition to the tourist narrative which ran along the route of the journey, observing, noting, and describing the persons and places Coxe encountered, the book, like the traveling tutor, whose function was that of a human Baedeker, frequently paused to explain the character and history of the various points of interest. In these passages the reader can imagine the scholarly Coxe delivering incidental lectures to his young charge as they went their round of the sights. Nearly every town occasioned its historical digression; every tomb demanded a biographical sketch of the monarch or patriarch it commemorated. By this means, Coxe managed to include a remarkably complete, but notably unsystematic history of the Russian people. Moreover, the range of the subject matter was extraordinary. The sight of the murals in a Greek Orthodox church gave way to a discussion of the origin of Italian painting. The cold of the climate led to a description of the experiment of freezing mercury. Zoological and botanical phenomena, the mechanical operation of the locks and canals of the inland waterways, the finances of the government, the origin of the Russian alphabet, the state of the mines, and the progress of the theater, all passed in review. It is in consequence of these somewhat pedantic digressions, abounding in footnotes, that modern critics, while admitting Coxe's accuracy, have condemned the dryness of his style. Nevertheless, Lord Herbert cer-

---

[27] Constantia Maxwell, *The English Traveller in France, 1698-1815*, London, 1932, pp. 77-96.
[28] Coxe, *op. cit.*, I, 221.

tainly enjoyed his tutor's incidental lectures, and the many editions of
the *Travels* attest the popularity of their literary counterpart.

In the selections below, these discursive passages drawn, as they are,
rather from Coxe's reading of the accounts of other travelers, scholars,
and historians than from his direct experience, have been largely
omitted, but a brief consideration of them will help to clarify that view
of history which influenced the third order of his observations about
Russia: the analysis of its social, economic, and political structure.
Throughout the eighteenth century, it is in their evaluations of the
success or failure of Peter's reforms that western accounts of Russia
provide a barometer for the mental climate of their authors. Coxe discussed the reforming Tsar in many telling passages, but their burden
is always the same. "We must readily allow that he considerably reformed and civilized his subjects; that he created a navy, and new-
modelled his army; that he encouraged the arts and sciences, promoted
agriculture and commerce, and laid the foundation of Russian grandeur. . . . If Peter failed in enlightening the mass of his subjects equal to
his wishes, the failure was occasioned by his own precipitate temper,
by the chimerical idea of introducing the arts and sciences by force,
and of performing in a moment what can only be the gradual work
of time: by violating the established customs of his people, and, in contradiction to the dictates of sound policy, requiring an immediate sacrifice of prejudices sanctified by ages."[29]

With a calm objectivity that distinguished him from his predecessors, he assessed the achievements of enlightened despotism. Unlike
Harris, he admitted without rancor that the military reorganization of
the empire had made Catherine "the arbitress of the north and the
mediatrix of Europe."[30] Moreover, the forcible transfer of the capital
to St. Petersburg had improved commercial advantages and polished
the minds and manners of the nobility. Nevertheless, in the sharp
line which Coxe drew, both here and elsewhere, between those aims
which could and those which could not be accomplished by despotic
power, he avoided the pitfalls of the cult of enlightened despotism and
anticipated much of the political philosophy of Burke's *Reflections*.
Arbitrary laws backed by brute force could not reform a clergy or
enlighten a whole people. Nevertheless, Coxe, an educated Anglican
clergyman, did not, like Perry or Richardson, sneer at the superstitious
ignorance of the priesthood or repeat malicious anecdotes of their
obscurantism. In the sixty-eight years since Perry had written his

[29] *ibid.*, II, 62.　　　　[30] *ibid.*, II, 27.

State of Russia, continuous progress in the field of the social sciences had widened the perspective of history, and in this perspective much of the impatience with the slow evolution of civilization had been dissipated. Coxe recognized, as Perry had not, that European influences had been at work in Russia long before the reign of Peter the Great, and he also realized how limited had been the scope of their operation upon the mass of the Russian people. However, it was just because he did not overburden the mechanism of enlightened despotism with exaggerated hopes of immediate reformation that he did not lose faith in its ultimate effectiveness.

In his analysis of the laws, culture, and social structure of Russia, Coxe repeatedly demonstrated his modified faith in the role of enlightened government, even under a despotism. With Richardson, he believed that political freedom, technical and commercial proficiency, the arts and the sciences were delicate plants, not easily uprooted and grown in foreign soils, but he felt that the careful cultivation of a wise leadership might help to overcome the difficulties. History, indeed, proved it. Many Russians had already imbibed improvements from their western neighbors: the natives of Archangel from their commercial conections with England, the army from its military struggles with Sweden, and the nobility from its cultural ties with the west in general. Moreover, Catherine was everywhere at work, modifying and improving institutions, much as Perry had described Peter, but with a finesse denied to the latter. New laws and, perhaps even more important, an improved education were in process of development. With a kind of hard-headed optimism, Coxe examined contemporary institutions with an eye, not for their logical consistency, but for their utilitarian value. If the military table of ranks and precedents was often ridiculous, at least its operations guaranteed the spread of the all-important privilege of holding land. This same optimism combined, perhaps, with his admiration of the Russian nobility blinded him to the real miseries and oppression of the Russian peasantry, so blackly painted by his contemporary, Richardson. He never mentioned them as motivations in an otherwise excellent description of the Pugachev rebellion. To be sure, security of person and property was a necessary prerequisite to any pretensions to civilization, but this could and, indeed, of necessity, must only gradually be introduced into Russian society. On the whole, Coxe's suspicions of "the speculative theorist" did not admit of those sweeping generalizations which provided the brilliance and thematic unity of Richardson's interpretation. Of the two, both fine scholars, it was Richardson, far more than Coxe, who employed historical analysis of the past to explain the character of present Russian society, but he always shrank from the obligation of placing it in the context of a continuing history. For this reason, the picture he drew was often static because it lacked a primary element of human reality, a relationship to future time. It was in this sense that Coxe's *Travels* best justify their modern reputation, for, with all their ponderous pedantry and attention to detail, they constantly depicted the Russian people in the process of growth.

EXTRACTS FROM:

Travels in Poland, Russia, Sweden, and Denmark.

by William Coxe

CONTENTS

....

I · FIRST IMPRESSIONS: SMOLENSK

I. THE ROAD TO SMOLENSK

August 20, 1778: We entered Russia at the small village of Tolitzin, [Tolchin] which in 1772 belonged to Poland; but is now comprised in the portion of country ceded by the late partition treaty. . . . From Tolitzin, through the new government of Mohilef [Mogilev], the road was excellent, and of considerable breadth, with a double row of trees planted on each side, and ditches to drain off the water. . . . The country from Tolitzin to Lady is waving and somewhat hilly, abounds with forests, and produces corn, millet, hemp, and flax. In the largest villages we observed schools and other buildings, constructing at the expence of the empress, also churches with domes, intended for the Polish dissidents of the Greek sect, and the Russians who chuse to settle in the country. . . .

We took up our quarters [at Lady] at the post-house, where we procured a comfortable apartment. These post-houses, which frequently occur on the high-roads of Russia, are mostly constructed upon the same plan, and extremely convenient for the accommodation of travellers: they are large square wooden buildings, enclosing a spacious court-yard; in the center of the front is a range of apartments intended for the reception of travellers, with a gateway on each side leading into the court-yard; the remainder of the front is appropriated to the use of the post-master and his servants, and the other three sides of the quadrangle are divided into stables and sheds for carriages, and large barns for hay and corn. We were agreeably surprized, even in this remote place, to meet with some English strong beer, and no less pleased to see our supper served in dishes of Wedgwood's ware. The luxury of clean straw for our beds was no small addition to these comforts. Calling for our bill in the morning, we found our charge as reasonable as the entertainment was good. . . .

The country was undulating and hilly, and more open than usual until we arrived within a few miles of Smolensko [Smolensk]; when we plunged into a thick forest, which continued almost to the gates of the town, without the intervention of a single village, or scarcely of a single cottage. [1, 143-146]

2. THE APPEARANCE OF SMOLENSK

Smolensko, though by no means the most magnificent, is by far the most singular town I have ever seen. It is situated upon the river Dnieper, and occupies two hills, and the intervening valley. It is surrounded by walls thirty feet high and fifteen in thickness, the lower part of stone, and the upper of brick. . . .

In the middle of the town is an eminence, upon which stands the cathedral; from whence I had a most picturesque view of the town, interspersed within the circuit of the walls, with gardens, groves, copses, fields of pasture and corn. The buildings are mostly wooden, of one story, (many no better than cottages) excepting here and there a gentleman's house, which is called a palace, and several churches, constructed of brick and stuccoed. One long broad street, which is paved, intersects the whole length of the town in a straight line; the other streets wind in circular directions, and are floored with planks. The walls, stretching over the uneven sides of the hill . . . their antient style of architecture, and grotesque towers; the spires of churches shooting above the trees, which are so numerous as almost to conceal the buildings from view; the appearance of meadows and arable ground; all these objects blended together exhibit a scene of the most singular and contrasted kind. On the further side of the Dnieper, many straggling wooden houses form the suburbs, and are joined to the town by a wooden bridge. As far as I could collect from vague information, Smolensko contains 4,000 inhabitants; it has no manufactures, but carries on some commerce with the Ukraine, Dantzig, [Danzig] and Riga. . . . [1, 146-147]

3. DIVINE SERVICE

Having occasion for a new passport and an order for horses, we called upon the governor, in company with a Russian student, who spoke Latin, for our interpreter. The governor being at church, we repaired to the cathedral, and waited until the conclusion of divine service.

The cathedral is a stately building. . . . The inside walls are covered with coarse paintings representing our Savior, the Virgin, and a variety of Saints, which abound in the Greek calendar. The shrine, or sanctuary, into which only the priests are admitted, is separated from the body of the church by a screen with folding doors, and ornamented with twisted pillars of the Corinthian order, richly carved and gilded.

The worship seemed to consist of innumerable ceremonies: the people crossed themselves without ceasing, bowed towards the shrine and to each other, and even touched the ground with their heads. The bishop of Smolensko performed the service; he was a venerable figure, with white flowing hair and long beard; he was dressed in rich episcopal robes, and had a crown on his head. The folding doors were occasionally opened and closed with great pomp and solemnity, whenever the bishop retired within, or came forth to bless the people. At the conclusion of the service, the doors being thrown open, the bishop advanced with a chandelier in each hand, one containing three, and the other two lighted candles, which he repeatedly crossed over each other in different directions; and then waving them towards the congregation, concluded with a final benediction. These chandeliers, as I am informed, are symbolical; one alludes to the Trinity, and the other to the two natures of Christ. [1, 147-148]

4. THE GOVERNOR

At the end of the service, we presented ourselves to the governor, who, to our surprize, received us with an air of coldness, which made such an impression on our interpreter, that he could not utter a single word. At length, a gentleman in the governor's train accosted us in French, and inquired our business. Informing him that we were English gentlemen who desired a passport, and an order for horses, he told us with a smile, that the plainness of our dresses had raised a suspicion of our being tradesmen; but he was not ignorant that English gentlemen seldom wore lace or swords on a journey. . . . He then whispered to the governor, who instantly assumed an appearance of complacency, and testified an intention of complying with our request. [1, 148]

5. THE BISHOP

This matter being adjusted, the bishop joined the company. . . . He addressed us in Latin, and invited us to his house. He led the way; and we followed with the rest of the company to a commodious wooden building adjoining the cathedral. On entering the apartment, the governor and Russian gentlemen kissed his hand with great marks of respect. After desiring all the company to sit, he distinguished us by particular attention; observing, with much politeness, that our company gave him greater pleasure, as he had never, since his residence at Smolensko, received a visit from any Englishmen, for whose nation he had the highest respect. During this conversation, a servant spread a cloth upon a small table, and placed upon it a plate of bread, some salt, and some flowers: another followed with a salver of small glasses full of a transparent liquor. The bishop blessed the bread and the salver with great solemnity, and then took a glass. . . . Every one being served, the bishop drank all our healths, a compliment which the company returned with a bow, and instantly emptied their glasses: we followed this example, and found the liquor to be a dram of cherry-water.

This preliminary being settled, we resumed our conversation with the bishop, and asked several questions relative to the ancient state of Smolensko. He answered every inquiry with great readiness; gave us a concise account of the state of the town under its antient dukes, and informed us that their palace was situated on the spot now occupied by the cathedral. . . . After half an hour's agreeable conversation, we took our leave, greatly pleased with the politeness and affability of the prelate.

Our interpreter then conducted us to the seminary, appropriated for the education of the clergy, in which the Latin, Greek, German, and Polish languages are taught: the priest who showed us the library talked Latin. [1, 148-149]

6. THE JUDGE

In the afternoon, the Russian gentleman, who so obligingly relieved us from our embarrassment before the governor, kindly paid us a visit, and invited us to dine with him on the following day. We accepted his invitation, and waited upon him at two, the usual hour of dining: he was a judge, and lived in a wooden house provided by the court; the rooms were small, but neatly furnished. The company consisted of the judge, his wife, and sister, all of whom talked French: the ladies were dressed in the French fashion, with much rouge; they did not curtsy; but their mode of salute was to bow their heads very low.

Before dinner, *liqueurs* were handed about; each lady took a small glass, and recommended the same to us as favourable to digestion. The table was neatly set out, the dinner excellent, and served up in English cream-coloured ware. Besides plain roast and boiled meats, several Russian dishes were introduced; one of these was a sallad composed of mushrooms and onions, and another the grain of green corn, baked and moistened with sweet oil. Before we rose from the table, our host, calling for a large glass, filled a bumper of champagne, drank it off to our health, and then handed the glass round.

"This is an old custom," he said, "and was meant as an expression of regard: the age is now grown delicate, and the free effusions of hospitality must be suppressed by ceremony; but I am an old-fashioned man, and cannot easily relinquish the habits of my youth."

After dinner, we adjourned to another room, and played two or three rubbers of whist. Coffee and tea were brought in, and a plate of sweetmeats was handed round to the company. At six, we took leave of our friendly host, and returned to our inn, if it may be called by that honourable appellation. [1, 149-150]

7. THE INN

This inn, the only one in the town, was a wooden building, in a ruinous state, formerly painted on the outside. The apartment which we occupied had once been hung with paper, fragments of which here and there covered a small portion of the wainscot, a patchwork of old and new planks. The furniture consisted of two benches and as many chairs, one without a bottom, and the other without a back; a deal box served the purpose of a table. We were inclined to conjecture that there was a heavy tax upon air and light; for all the windows were closed with planks, except one, which could not be opened, and could scarcely be seen through, on account of the dirt. . . . It may perhaps appear surprizing, that a town like Smolensko should contain no tolerable inn; but the surprize will cease when we reflect that few strangers pass this way; that the Russians carry their provisions, and either continue their journey during the night, or are accommodated in private houses. [1, 150-151]

II · THE JOURNEY TO MOSCOW

I. THE ROUTE: SMOLENSK TO VYAZMA

August 25: We quitted Smolensko, crossed the Dnieper over a wooden bridge into the suburbs, and pursued our journey through a valley of fine pasture watered by the Dnieper, spotted with underwood, and terminating on each side in gentle eminences clothed with trees. . . . Near Slovoda, a large straggling village, where we stopped for a few hours during the darkness of the night, we again crossed the Dnieper on a raft formed of trunks of trees tied together with cords, and scarcely large enough to receive the carriage, which sunk it some inches under water: this machine was then pushed from the banks until it met another of the same kind, to which the horses stepped with difficulty; and the distance of the two rafts from each other was so considerable, that the carriage could scarcely be prevented from slipping between them into the river.

The second post from this primitive ferry was Dogorobush [Dorogobuzh], built upon a rising hill . . . some of the houses, lately constructed at the empress's expence, were of brick covered with stucco, and had the appearance of palaces when contrasted with the meanness of the surrounding hovels. . . .

From Dogorobush we proceeded 24 miles to a small village called Zaratesh, where we thought ourselves fortunate in being housed for the night in a tolerable hut, which afforded a rare instance of accomodation in these parts, a room separated from that used by the family. . . .

August 27: Our route the next morning, from Zaratesh to Viasma [Vyasma] lay through a continued forest, occasionally relieved by the interventions of pastures and corn-fields. . . . We then mounted a small eminence to the town, which makes a magnificent appearance. . . . At some distance the number of spires and domes rising above the trees, which conceal the contiguous hovels, would lead a traveller unacquainted with the country to expect a large city, where he will find only a collection of wooden huts. . . . [1, 151-152]

2. THE ACCOMMODATIONS: PEASANT HUTS

The cottages . . . are of a square shape; formed of whole trees, piled upon one another, and secured at the four corners with mortises and tenons. The interstices between these piles are filled with moss. Within, the timbers are smoothed with the axe, so as to form the appearance of wainscot; but without are left with the bark in their rude state. The roofs are in a penthouse form, and generally composed of the bark of trees or shingles, which are sometimes covered with mould or turf. The peasants usually construct the whole house solely with the assistance of the hatchet, and cut the planks of the floor with the same instrument, in many parts being unacquainted with the use of the saw: they finish the shell of the house and the roof, before they begin to cut the windows or doors. The windows are apertures of a few inches square, closed with sliding frames, and the doors are so low as not to admit a middle-sized man without stooping. These cottages sometimes, though very rarely, consist of two stories; in which case the lower apartment is a store-room, and the upper the habitable part of the house: the stair case is most commonly a ladder on the outside. Most of these huts are, however, only one story; a few of them contain two rooms; the generality only one. In some of this latter sort I was frequently awakened by the chickens picking the grains of corn in the straw upon which I lay, and more than once by a less inoffensive animal. [1, 153]

3. THE TRANSPORTATION: PEASANT COACHMEN

The peasants at every post were obliged to furnish us with horses at a fixed and reasonable rate, which had the ill effect of rendering them extremely dilatory in their motions; and as our only interpreter was a Bohemian servant, not perfectly acquainted with the Russian language, his difficulty in explaining, joined to their backwardness in executing our orders, occasioned delays of several hours for a change of horses. The peasants acted in the capacity of coachmen and postillions; they always harnessed four horses a-breast, commonly put eight, and sometimes even ten horses to our carriage; as the stages were for the most part twenty, and sometimes thirty miles, and the roads extremely bad. They seldom used either boots or saddles, and had no sort of stirrup, except a rope doubled and thrown across the horse's back. . . . The method of driving was not in a steady pace, but by starts and bounds, with little attention to the nature of the ground: the peasants seldom trotted their horses, but would suddenly force them into a gallop through the worst roads, and sometimes as suddenly check their speed upon the most level surface. A common piece of rope served them for a whip, which they seldom had any occasion to use, as they urged their horses forwards by hooting and whistling like cat-calls. . . . From the wretched harness, which was continually breaking, the badness of the roads, the length of time we were always detained at the posts before we could procure horses, and other impediments, we were seldom able to travel more than forty or fifty miles a day; although we commenced our journey before sun-rise, and pursued it till it was dark. [1, 154-155]

4. THE ARRIVAL: MOSCOW

The road for some way before we came . . . to Moscow was a broad straight avenue cut through the forest. The trees which composed these vast plantations, set by the hand of Nature were oaks, beech, mountain-ash, poplar, pines, and firs mingled together in the most wanton variety. The different shades of green, and the rich tints of the autumnal colours, were inexpressibly beautiful; while the sublime, but uniform expanse of forest, was occasionally relieved by recesses of pastures and corn-fields.

August 30: The approach to Moscow was first announced at the distance of six miles by some spires over-topping an eminence at the extremity of the broad avenue cut through the forest; about two or three miles further we ascended a height, from whence a superb prospect of the vast city burst upon our sight. It stretched in the form of a crescent, to a prodigious extent; while innumerable churches, towers, gilded spires and domes, white, red, and green buildings, glittering in the sun, formed a splendid appearance, yet strangely contrasting by an intermixture of wooden hovels. . . .

It is the largest town in Europe; the circumference within the rampart, which encloses the suburbs, being 39 versts, or 26 miles; but it is built in so straggling a manner, that the population in no degree corresponds to the extent. . . . Moscow contains within the ramparts 250,000 souls, and in the adjacent villages, 50,000.

If I was struck with the singularity of Smolensko, I was all astonishment at the immensity and variety of Moscow, a city so irregular, so uncommon, so extraordinary, and so contrasted, never before claimed my attention. The streets are in general exceedingly long and broad: some are paved; others, particularly, those in the suburbs, formed with trunks of trees or boarded with planks like the floor of a room; wretched hovels are blended with large palaces; cottages of one story stand next to the most stately mansions. Many brick structures are covered with wooden tops; some of the timber houses are painted, others have iron doors and roofs. Numerous churches present themselves in every quarter, built in the oriental style of architecture; some with domes of copper, others of tin, gilt or painted green, and many roofed with wood. In a word, some parts of this vast city have the appearance of a sequestered desert, other quarters, of a populous town; some of a contemptible village, others of a great capital. [1, 156-160]

III · THE SOJOURN AT MOSCOW

1. AN HOSPITABLE RECEPTION

September 1: This morning we received a card of invitation from Count Osterman,[31] governor of Moscow, to dinner, for the 22d of August; but, as it was the 1st of September, our servant, who took the message, came laughing into the room, and informed us, that we were invited to an entertainment that was past: he had endeavoured, he added, to convince the messenger of the mistake; but the man insisted that the ensuing day was the 22d of August. It was indeed a natural mistake in our servant, who did not know that the Russians still adhere to the old style, and as he had passed the 22d of August in Lithuania, it is no wonder that he was surprized at finding it so soon again at Moscow. . . .

Nothing can exceed the hospitality of the Russians. We never paid a morning visit to any nobleman without being detained to dinner: we also constantly received general invitations; but, considering them as mere compliments, were unwilling to intrude ourselves without further notice. We soon found, however, that the principal persons of distinction kept open tables, and were highly obliged by our resorting to them without ceremony. . . . [1, 164-166]

2. A SOCIAL CALL

The house of count Orlof[32] is situated at the extremity of one of the suburbs, upon an elevated spot, commanding a fine view of the vast city of Moscow and the neighbouring country; many separate buildings occupy a large tract of ground. The offices, stables, manage [manège, riding school], and other detached structures, are of brick; the foundation and lower story of the dwelling-house are built with the same material; but the upper part is of wood, neatly painted of a green colour. (Wooden houses are by many persons in this country supposed to be warmer and more wholesome than those of brick and stone, which is the reason why several of the Russian nobility chuse that part of their house, which they inhabit themselves to be constructed of wood.) We carried a letter of recommendation from prince Stanislaus Poniatowski, the king of Poland's nephew, to the count, who received us with great frankness, and detained us at dinner. . . .

---

[31] Probably of the family of Count Andrei Ivanovich Osterman (1686-1747), German-born statesman who entered the Russian service under Peter the Great. He was minister of foreign affairs for the Anglo-Russian commercial treaty of 1734.

[32] Aleksei Grigorievich Orlov (1737-1809).

The count seemed to live in the true style of old Russian hospitality, and kept an open table, abounding with a great variety of Greek wines, which he brought from the Archipelago. One dish, served on his plentiful board, was extremely delicious, and only inferior to our best venison; it was a quarter of Astracan [Astrakhan] sheep, remarkable for the quantity and flavour of the fat.

There was music during dinner, which generally made part of the entertainment at the tables of the nobility. We observed also another usual instance of parade; numerous retainers and dependents were intermixed with the servants, but seldom assisted in any menial office: they occasionally stood around their lord's chair, and seemed greatly pleased whenever they were distinguished by a nod or a smile. [1, 171-172]

3. AN UNARTIFICIAL ARMENIAN

In this train was an Armenian, recently arrived from Mount Caucasus, who, agreeably to the custom of his country, inhabited a tent pitched in the garden, and covered with felt. His dress consisted of a long loose robe, tied with a sash, large breeches, and boots: his hair was cut, in the manner of the Tartars, in a circular form; his arms were a poignard, and a bow of buffalo's horn strung with the sinews of the same animal. He was extremely attached to his master; and when first presented, voluntarily took the oath of fealty, and swore, in the true language of Eastern hyperbole, to attack all the count's enemies; offering, as proof of his sincerity, to cut off his own ears. . . . He examined our clothes, and seemed delighted with pointing out the superiority of his own dress in the article of convenience; he threw himself into different attitudes with uncommon agility, and defied us to follow his example; he danced a Calmuc dance, which consisted in straining every muscle, and writhing the body into various contortions without stirring from the spot: he beckoned us into the garden, took great pleasure in showing us his tent and his arms: and shot several arrows to an extraordinary height. We were struck with the unartificial character of this Armenian, who seemed like a wild-man just beginning to be civilized. [1, 172-173]

4. AN ACT OF MAGNIFICENCE

Count Orlof, who is fond of the manage [manège, horsemanship], is esteemed to possess, though not the largest, yet the finest stud in Russia, and he was so obliging as to gratify our curiosity by conveying us to his country-house, at the distance of fifteen miles from Moscow. He conveyed us in his own carriage drawn by six horses. . . . An empty coach, with six horses, ranged two by two, followed for parade. He was attended by four hussars, and the Armenian accoutred with his bow and quiver, who continually shouted and waved his hand with the strongest expressions of transport. . . .

The greater part of the stud was grazing in the plain: it consisted of fine stallions, and above sixty brood mares, most of which had foals. The collection was gleaned from the most distant quarters of the globe; from Arabia, Turkey, Tartary, Persia, and England. . . . Amongst these, he chiefly prized four horses . . . of the true *Cochlean* breed, so much esteemed in Arabia, and seldom seen out of their native country. . . .

I cannot forbear to mention in this place an act of almost Eastern magnificence, which this visit afterwards occasioned. One morning in the ensuing winter, at Petersburgh, one of the finest among the Arabian horses, which Lord Herbert had greatly admired, was sent to him, accompanied with the following note:

"My Lord, I observed that this horse pleased you, and therefore desire your acceptance of him. I received him as a present from Ali-Bey. He is a true Arabian of the Cochlean race, and in the late war was brought by the Russian ships from Arabia to me while I was in the Archipelago. I wish he may be as serviceable to you as he has been to me; and I remain, with esteem, your obedient servant,　　Count Alexey Orlof . . ."　　[1, 173-174]

5. A BOXING MATCH

At the close of an entertainment, which the count gave us at Moscow, he introduced us to the sight of a Russian boxing-match, which is a favourite diversion among the common people. We repaired to the manage, where we found about three hundred peasants assembled. They divided into two parties, each of which chose a chief, who called out the combatants, and pitted them against each other; only a single pair were allowed to engage at the same time. . . . When any combatant felled his antagonist he was declared victor, and the contest ceased. . . . Both parties were highly interested in favour of their respective champions, and seemed at times inclined to enter the lists in their support; but the first appearance of dispute, or growing heat, was checked by the count, who acted as mediator: a kind word, or even a nod from him, instantly composed all differences. When he appeared desirous to put an end to the combats, they humbly requested his permission to honour them with his presence a little longer; upon his assent, they bowed their heads to the ground, and seemed as pleased as if they had received the highest favour. The count is greatly beloved by his peasants, and their stern countenances melted into the most affectionate softness at his approach. [I, 174-175]

6. THE ESTATES OF THE NOBILITY

We could not avoid feeling extreme satisfaction at observing that the English style of gardening had penetrated even into these distant regions. The English taste, indeed, can display itself in this country to great advantage, where the parks are extensive, and the verdure, during the short summer, uncommonly beautiful. Most of the Russian nobles have gardeners of our nation, and resign themselves implicitly to their direction. . . .

The Russian nobles display a great degree of grandeur and magnificence in their houses, domestics, and way of living. Their palaces at and near Moscow are stupendous piles of building, and I am informed that their mansions, at a distance from Moscow and Petersburgh, are upon a still grander scale; where they reside as independent princes, like the feudal barons in early times, have their separate courts of justice, and govern their vassals with almost unlimited sway. [I, 175-177]

IV · MOSCOW TO ST. PETERSBURG

1. FROM MOSCOW TO TVER

WE QUITTED Moscow on the 14th of September, traversed a gently rising country, partly open, and partly overspread with forests, passed the night at the village of Parski [Parskoye], in a peasant's cottage, as usual, and changed horses the next morning at Klin. . . . Near it, we observed a saw-pit, which, in this country, was too rare an object not to attract our notice. Beyond Savidof we crossed a rivulet, and soon afterwards reached the banks of the Volga, which we coasted to Gorodna. The next morning the springs of our carriage being ready to start, and one of the wheels in a crazy state, we left it to the care of our servants, and hired the carts of the country, called *kabitkas*, which we filled with hay. After a considerable degree of jolting, we arrived at Tver, which is magnificently situated upon the elevated banks of the Volga. [II, 1]

2. THE CITY OF TVER: RECONSTRUCTION

Tver is divided into the old and new town; the former, situated on the opposite side of the Volga, consists almost entirely of wooden cottages; the latter was scarcely superior; but in 1763, being destroyed by a dreadful conflagration, has risen with lustre from its ashes. The empress ordered a regular plan of a new town to be sketched by an eminent architect, and enjoined that all the houses should be re-constructed in conformity with this model. She raised, at her own expence, the governor's house, the bishop's palace, courts of justice, the new exchange, prison, and other public edifices; and offered to every person who would build a brick house a loan of £300 for twelve years without interest. The money advanced on this occasion amounted to £60,000; and one-third of this sum has been since remitted. The streets, which are broad and long, issue in a straight line from an octagon, in the centre: the houses are of a brick stuccoed white, and form a magnificent appearance. Part only of the new town was finished: when completed, it will consist of two octagons, with several streets leading to them, and intersecting each other at right-angles; and would be no inconsiderable ornament to the most opulent and civilized country.

There is an ecclesiastical seminary at Tver, under the inspection of the bishop, which admits 600 students. In 1776, the empress founded a school for the instruction of 200 burghers' children; and in June 1779, an academy for the education of the young nobility of the province. [1, 2-3]

3. THE GOVERNMENT OF TVER: COMMERCE

Tver is a place of considerable commerce; and both the Volga and the Tvertza [Tvertsa] were covered with boats. It owes its principal trade to the advantageous situation, near the conflux of the two rivers, which convey all the goods and merchandize sent by water from Siberia and the southern provinces towards Petersburgh. . . . The number of barges which passed by the town in 1776 amounted to 2,537; in 1777, to 2,641, and the average number is generally computed at 2,550. . . . These boats are only built for one voyage, and on their arrival at Petersburgh, are sold for fuel.

I have already mentioned the prodigious waste of wood arising from the custom of forming planks with the axe. To prevent this practice, which was no less usual among the shipwrights than among the peasants, orders were issued by government, that each vessel, passing Tver, in which was one plank fashioned with a hatchet, should pay a fine of £6. In consequence of this decree the officer, who levied the fine, collected the first year £6,000, the second £1,500, the third £100, and the fourth nothing. By this judicious regulation the use of the saw has been introduced among the Russian shipwrights, and will probably in time recommend itself to the carpenters and peasants.

The rising spirit of commerce has added greatly to the wealth and population of the town. It contains at present 10,000 souls, and the number of inhabitants in the government of Tver has increased in a surprising degree: a circumstance which shews the advantages arising from the new code of laws. Tver was the first province in which that code was introduced, and has already experienced the beneficial effects of these excellent regulations. . . .

Vishnei-Voloshok [Vyshniy Volochok], one of the imperial villages enfranchised by the empress, and endowed with considerable privileges, has already reaped many benefits from its new immunities. The inhabitants, raised from the situation of slaves to that of freemen, have shaken off their former indolence, and caught a new spirit of emulation and industry: they have turned their attention to trade, and are awakened to a sense of the commercial advantages possessed by the place of their abode. The town is divided into regular streets, and is already provided with a large range of shops and warehouses, which line each side of the canal. All the buildings are of wood, excepting the court of justice erected at the charge of the empress, and four brick houses belonging to a rich burgher. During our stay at Vishnei-Voloshok, we did not fail to examine, with great attention, every part of the celebrated canal. . . ."[33] [1, 3-6]

4. SIGHTS AND SOUNDS

In this part of our journey, we passed numberless herds of oxen, moving towards Petersburgh; most of them were driven from the Ukraine, the nearest part of which country is distant 800 miles from the metropolis. During this long progress the drivers seldom enter any house; they feed their cattle upon the slips of pasture on each side of the road, and have no other shelter in bad weather than the foliage of the trees. In the evening the still silence of the country was interrupted by the occasional lowing of the oxen, and carols of the drivers; while

---

[33] The canal of Vyshniy Volochok was the final fulfilment of John Perry's dream of linking the Baltic and Caspian Seas by water. Its history, construction, and operation were described in detail by Coxe in a separate chapter. Coxe, *op. cit.*, vol. II, pp. 356-359.

the solitary gloom of the forest was enlivened with the glare of numerous fires, surrounded by different groups of herdsmen in various attitudes. [II, 9-10]

In our route through Russia I was surprised at the propensity of the natives to singing. Even the peasants who acted in the capacity of coachmen and postilions, were no sooner mounted than they began to warble an air, and continued it, without the least intermission for several hours. But what still more astonished me was, that they performed occasionally in parts; I frequently observed them engaged in a kind of musical dialogue, making reciprocal questions and responses, as if chanting (if I may so express myself) their ordinary conversation. The postilions *sing* from the beginning to the end of a stage; the soldiers *sing* during their march; the countrymen *sing* amid the most laborious occupations; public-houses re-echo with their carols; and in a still evening I have frequently heard the air vibrate with the notes of the surrounding villages. [II, 14]

5. THE SLOW MARCH OF PROGRESS

As we approached Petersburgh, and nearer the civilized parts of Europe, the villagers were better furnished with the conveniences of life, and further advanced in the knowledge of the necessary arts, than those who fell under our notice between Tolitzin and Moscow. The planks were less frequently hewn with the axe, and saw-pits, which we had long considered as objects of curiosity, oftener occurred: the cottages were more spacious and convenient, provided with larger windows, and generally had chimnies; they were also more amply stored with household furniture, and with wooden, and sometimes even earthen utensils. Still, however, their progress towards civilization is very inconsiderable, and many instances of the grossest barbarism fell under our observation. [II, 13]

6. THE APPROACH TO ST. PETERSBURG

Our coach being much shattered by the bad roads, we left it at Novogorod [Novgorod], and continued our journey in *kabitkas*, the common carriages of the country. . . . The road, made of timber, and as straight as an arrow, ran through a perpetual forest, without the least intermixture of hill or dale, and with few slips of cultivated ground. Through this dreary extent, the gloomy uniformity of the forest was only broken by a few solitary villages at long distances from each other, without the intervention of a single house. . . . About ten miles from Itchora [Izhora] we suddenly turned to the right, and the scene instantly brightened; the woods gave way to cultivation, the country began to be enlivened with houses, the inequalities of the timber road were succeeded by the level of a spacious causeway equal to the finest turnpikes of England, the end of each verst was marked with superb mile-stones of granite and marble, and a long avenue of trees was closed at the distance of a few miles with a view of Petersburgh, the object of our wishes, and the termination of our labours. [II, 23-25]

V · ST. PETERSBURG

I. AN IMMENSE OUTLINE

IN WALKING ABOUT this metropolis I was filled with astonishment on reflecting that so late as the beginning of this century, the ground on which Petersburgh now stands was a morass occupied by a few fishermen's huts. The first building of the city is so recent as to be almost remembered by persons now alive; and its gradual progress is traced without difficulty. . . . [II, 28]

Succeeding sovereigns have continued to embellish Petersburgh, but none more than the present empress, who may be called its second founder. Notwithstanding, however, all these improvements, it bears every mark of an infant city, and is still "only an immense outline, which will require further empresses and almost future ages to complete."[34] [II, 30]

2. THE NORTHERN THAMES

The views upon the banks of the Neva exhibit the most grand and lively scenes I ever beheld. That river is in many places as broad as the Thames at London; it is also deep, rapid, and as transparent as crystal; and the banks are lined with handsome buildings. On the north side the fortress, the Academy of Sciences, and Academy of Arts, are the most striking objects; on the opposite side are the Imperial palace, the Admiralty, the mansions of many Russian nobles, and the English line, so called because the whole row is principally occupied by the English merchants. In the front of these buildings, on the south side, is the Quay, which stretches for three miles, except where it is interrupted by

[34] This quotation from Sir Nathaniel Wraxall is only one of many instances in which the scholarly Coxe cited the works of other travelers.

the Admiralty; and the Neva, during the whole of that space has been lately embanked by a wall, parapet, and pavement of hewn granite; a magnificent and durable monument of imperial munificence. The canals of Catherine and of the Fontanka, which are several miles in length, have been recently embanked in the same manner, and add greatly to the beauty of the metropolis. . . .

I have frequently viewed with surprize the process employed by the Russian workmen, in smoothing the granite. They batter the stone with an iron hammer edged with steel; the quantity which flies off at each stroke, is almost imperceptible; but by repeatedly striking the same place, the prominent parts are worn away, and the stone becomes smooth. [II, 31]

3. CORDIALITY TO FOREIGNERS

The nobles of Petersburgh are no less than those of Moscow distinguished for hospitality to foreigners. We were no sooner presented to a person of rank and fortune, than we were regarded as domestic visitants. Many of the nobility keep an open table, to which the first invitation was considered as a standing passport of admission. The only form necessary on this occasion, was to make inquiry in the morning if the master of the house dined at home; and if he did, we presented ourselves at his table without further ceremony. The oftener we appeared at these hospitable boards, the more acceptable guests we were esteemed, and we always seemed to confer, instead of receiving a favour. . . .

Several of the nobility also receive company every evening in the most easy manner: the parties usually meet at seven; some sit down to whist, macao, loo, and other games; some converse, others dance. Amid the refreshments tea is handed round no less frequently than in England. At ten supper is brought in, and the party generally breaks up between eleven and twelve. It is no exaggeration to say, that, during our continuance in this city, not one evening passed but we had it in our power to attend an assembly of this sort; and had we always frequented the same, we should always have found the greatest cordiality of reception. From these circumstances, perhaps no metropolis in Europe, excepting Vienna, is rendered more agreeable to foreigners than Petersburgh. [II, 57-58]

4. THE FESTIVE BOARD: THE NOBILITY

The tables are served with great profusion and taste. Though the

Russians have adopted the delicacies of French cookery, yet they neither affect to despise their native dishes, nor squeamishly reject the solid joints which characterize an English repast. The plainest, as well as the choicest viands, are collected from the most distant quarters: I have frequently seen at the same table sterlet from the Volga, veal from Archangel, mutton from Astrachan, beef from the Ukraine, and pheasants from Hungary and Bohemia. The common wines are claret, Burgundy, and Champagne; and I never tasted English beer and porter in greater perfection and abundance. Before dinner, even in the house of persons of the first distinction, a small table is spread in a corner of the drawing room, covered with plates of caviare, dried and pickled herrings, smoked ham or tongue, bread, butter, and cheese, together with bottles of different *liqueurs*; and few of the company of either sex omitted a prelude of this kind to the main entertainment. This practice had induced many travellers to relate, that the Russians swallow bowls of brandy before dinner.[35] What are the usages of the vulgar in this particular I cannot determine; but among the nobility I never observed the least violation of extreme sobriety. . . . The usual hour of dining is at three; and the entertainments are mostly regulated according to the French ceremonial; the wine is circulated during meals, and the dishes are no sooner removed than the company retire into another room, and are served with coffee. Nor do the gentlemen, as in England, continue wedded to the bottle, while the ladies withdraw into a separate apartment. [II, 57-58]

5. THE FESTIVE BOARD: THE PEOPLE

On the 6th of December we were witness to a very singular entertainment given to the public by a Russian, who had acquired a large fortune by farming, during four years only, the right of vending spirituous liquors. On surrendering his contract, he gave, as a proof of his gratitude to the lower class of people, by whom he had enriched himself, a feast near the garden of the summer-palace . . . announced by hand-bills distributed throughout the city . . . which commenced at two o'clock in the afternoon. A large semicircular table was covered with all kinds of provision, piled in different shapes, and in the greatest

---

[35] Coxe may here be referring to the comments of an earlier and less reliable author: "Brandy is their favourite liquor, and the quantity some will drink is inconceivable. At entertainments, the master or mistress presents you with a glass of wine or brandy, which holds from one to two quarts which you are under the necessity of drinking, though you should drop down intoxicated." Richards, *op. cit.*, p. 96.

profusion. Large slices of bread and caviare, dried sturgeon, carp, and other fish, were ranged to a great height, in the form of pent-houses and pyramids, and garnished with craw-fish, onions, and pickles. In different parts of the grounds were rows of casks full of spirituous liquors, and still larger vessels of wine, beer, and quass. Among the decorations, I observed the representation of an immense whale in pasteboard, covered with cloth and gold or silver brocade, and filled in the inside with bread, dried fish, and other provisions.

All sorts of games and diversions were exhibited for the amusement of the populace. At the extremity of the grounds was a large square of ice well swept for the scaters; near which were two machines like the swinging vehicles at Bartholomew Fair. One of these machines consisted of two cross-beams fixed horizontally to a pole in the center by means of a pivot; from the ends of the beams hung four sledges, in which people seated themselves, and were turned round with great velocity; the other had four wooden horses suspended from the beams, and the riders were whirled round in like manner. . . . Beyond these were two ice-hills. . . . Two poles, above twenty feet in height, were also erected, with colours flying; and at the top of each was placed a piece of money, as a prize for those who could swarm up and seize it. The poles, being rubbed with oil, soon froze in this severe climate; many and tedious were the attempts of the various competitors in this slippery ascent to fame. The scene was lively and gay; for above 40,000 persons of both sexes were assembled on the occasion. . . .

It was preconcerted, that, on firing a rocket, the people were to drink a glass of spirituous liquor, and, on the discharge of a second, to begin the repast. But the impatience of the populace anticipated the necessity of a second signal; and the whole multitude was soon and at once in motion. The whale was the chief object of contention: within the space of a few minutes he was entirely divested of his gaudy trappings, which became the spoils of his successful invaders. . . . They rent him into a thousand pieces, to seize the provisions with which his inside was stored. The remaining people . . . were employed in uncovering the pent-houses, and pulling down the pyramids. . . . Others crowded around the casks and hogsheads; and with great wooden ladles lapped incessantly wine, beer, and spirits. The confusion and riot, which soon succeeded, is better conceived than described; and we thought it expedient to retire. . . .

But the consequences of this feast were indeed dreadful. The cold had suddenly increased with such violence, that Fahrenheit's thermometer, which at mid-day stood only at 4, sunk towards the close of the evening to 15 below freezing point. Many intoxicated persons were frozen to death; not a few fell a sacrifice to drunken quarrels; and others were robbed and murdered in the more retired parts of the city, as they were returning late to their homes. From a comparison of various reports, we had reason to conclude, that at least 400 persons lost their lives upon this melancholy occasion. (The following day I counted myself no less than forty bodies, collected in two sheds near the place of entertainment.) [II, 98-100]

VI · SCIENCE AND THE ARTS

I. THE ACADEMY OF SCIENCE

THE EMPRESS CATHERINE, with her usual zeal for promoting the diffusion of knowledge, took this useful Society under her . . . immediate protection; she altered the court of directors greatly to the advantage of the whole body; corrected many abuses, and infused a new spirit into their researches. By her particular recommendation, the most ingenious professors visited the various provinces of her dominions; and as the fund of the Academy was not sufficient to supply the whole expence, the empress bestowed a largess of £2,000. . . .

The persons engaged in these expeditions were ordered to pursue their inquiries on the different sorts of earths and waters; on the best methods of cultivating the barren and desert spots; on the local disorders incident to men and animals, and the most efficacious means of relieving them; on breeding cattle, and particularly sheep; on the rearing of bees and silk-worms; on the different places and objects for fishing and hunting; on minerals; on the arts and trades; and on the indigenous plants to form a *Flora Russica*. They were particularly instructed to rectify the longitude and latitude of the principal towns; to make astronomical, geographical, and meteorological observations; to trace the course of the rivers; to take the most exact charts; to describe with accuracy the manners, customs, dresses, language, antiquities, traditions, history, religion; in a word, to gain every information which might tend to illustrate the real state of the empire.

In consequence of these expeditions, perhaps no country can boast, within the space of a few years, such a number of excellent publications on its internal state, natural productions, topography, geography, and history; on the manners, customs, and languages of the different people, as have issued from the press of the Academy . . . and it may not be an exaggeration to assert, that no society in Europe has more distinguished itself for the excellence of its publications. [II, 241-242]

2. THE ACADEMY OF ARTS

The scholars are admitted at the age of six, continue until they have attained that of eighteen; and are instructed in reading, writing, arithmetic, the French and German languages, and drawing. At the age of fourteen they are at liberty to chuse any of the following arts, divided into four classes. 1. Painting, in all its branches of history, portraits, battles, and landscapes; architecture; Mosaic; enameling; etc. 2. Engraving on copper-plates, seal-cutting, etc. 3. Carving in wood, ivory, and amber. 4. Watch-making, turning, instrument-making, casting statues in bronze and other metals, imitating gems and metals in compositions, gilding, and varnishing.

Prizes are annually distributed to those who excel in any particular art; and from those who have obtained four prizes, twelve are selected, who are sent abroad at the charge of the empress . . . during four years. There is a small assortment of paintings for the use of the scholars; and those who have made great progress are permitted to copy the pictures in the imperial collection. There are also models in plaster of the best antique statues in Italy, all executed at Rome, of the same size with the originals, which the artists of the Academy were employed to cast in bronze. We observed several finished pieces of drawing, painting, and sculpture, which had much merit, and seemed to predict the future improvement of the arts in Russia.

Though this institution is admirably calculated for promoting the liberal arts, and deserves the highest encomiums, we must not be surprised on considering the small effects which have hitherto flowed from this endowment. The scholars, for the most part, make a considerable progress during their continuance in the academy, and many improve themselves abroad. It is remarkable, however, that the persons of the greatest merit often settle in other countries; or, if they return, soon sink into an indolence, which appears almost national. The cause of this failure seems to proceed from the little encouragement which they receive from the nation in general. The sovereign may rear artists, like foreign plants in a hot bed, at a prodigious expence, and by constant cultivation; but unless the same care is continued when they are brought to maturity, they will sicken by neglect. And it is impossible even for a monarch, however inclined to protect merit, or for a few of the nobility who follow such an illustrious example, to diffuse a love for the works of art among a people who must first imbibe a degree of taste, which can only be acquired by experience; and if those who excel are not distinguished, they cannot feel that noble spirit of emulation which excites to excellence. As the nation, however, is gradually drawing towards a higher state of civilization and refinement; these institutions must be productive of more extensive and permanent effects. [II, 257-258]

3. THE AGRICULTURAL SOCIETY

The Free Oeconomical Society, or the Society for the promotion of Agriculture, at St. Petersburgh ... is chiefly supported by the voluntary contributions of its members, whose number, in 1781, amounted to 179. The assembly meets regularly once a week, when the papers on agriculture and similar subjects are read. Those which are thought worthy of publication are printed at the expence of the empress, for the profit of the society. The work is sold at a low price; and twelve copies are forwarded *gratis* to the governors of each province, to be distributed in the several governments. . . .

The society gives annual prizes, consisting of gold and silver medals, or money, sometimes to the amount of £140, for the best solutions of certain questions relative to agriculture, and for improvements in husbandry. The empress, in the true spirit of this institution, sends several young men into England, to study practical agriculture. They are chiefly recommended to Arthur Young, Esq.,[36] who has distinguished himself by many excellent works on various branches of husbandry; and who was elected, in the most honourable manner a member of this society. [II, 258-259]

4. THE PROBLEM OF NATIONAL GENIUS

Some authors, in considering the small advances made by the Russians in the arts and sciences, when compared with the progress of the more enlightened nations in Europe, have erroneously attributed this deficiency to the effects of climate, or to an innate want of genius. The latter assertion scarcely deserves a serious refutation; for all intellectual improvement must arise from culture, and the greater or less degree of

---

[36] Arthur Young (1741-1820), English traveler and author, who wrote extensively on agricultural affairs. In 1793, his high reputation won him the secretaryship of the newly created Board of Agriculture.

knowledge must ultimately depend upon the greater or less degree of instruction. . . .

With respect to the objection, that the genius of this nation has been fettered by the intense cold climate,[37] it may be remarked, If climate has an invincible effect on mankind, where shall we draw the line of the greatest intellectual ability? . . . Is the influence of climate uniform or casual? If uniform, why is modern Greece no longer the seat of arts and learning? . . . If the effects of climate are casual, they are then counterbalanced by other circumstances; and it ceases to be a positive criterion of distinction.

Many impediments arise from the government, religion, and, particularly from the vassalage of the peasants, which tend to check the diffusion of the arts and sciences, without the necessity of having recourse to a supposed want of genius, or to the effect of climate. [II, 279-280]

VII · THE MARINE AND COMMERCE

I. MARITIME PROSPECTS

Russia produces every article necessary for the construction and equipment of ships, which are built chiefly at Cronstadt [Kronshtadt], Petersburgh, and Archangel. . . . But though Russia, since the beginning of this century had made surprising exertions in the marine, and rapidly become more powerful at sea than the neighbouring kingdoms in the North; yet, in naval affairs, she must be considered still in her infancy, being principally indebted to the English, as well for the construction of her ships, as for the manoeuvring and disciplining her fleet. Many circumstances indeed concur in retarding the progress of her maritime strength. . . . 1. It is obvious that Russia does not possess a single port on the ocean, excepting that of Archangel, which is of no use but in a commercial light; as well on account of its great distance from the other European seas, as because the navigation round the North Cape of Lapland . . . is only open in the midst of summer. 2. . . . Russia, excepting the late acquisitions on the Black Sea, the desolate shores round Archangel and of the Frozen Ocean, and the inhospitable regions of Kamtchatka [Kamchatka], can boast no greater portion of maritime country than what lies between Wiburgh [Viborg] and Riga; a mere

---

[37] Although she had presumably read Coxe's book, Lady Craven was heartily in accord with this objection: "Alas, sir, eight months of winter; and the horrid cold I feel, must congeal the warmest imagination; poets and painters require verdant lawns; and the flowers of fancy must fade and die, where spring is not to be found." Craven, *op. cit.*, pp. 124-125.

point for so large an empire, and rendered less valuable by bordering on the Gulf of Finland and the Baltic; inland seas without tides, when compared with the ocean scarcely superior to lakes, and inaccessible for at least five months in the year. 3. The third cause is a deficiency of experienced seamen. Government, indeed, retains in its pay about 18,000 sailors, most of whom have never served: a few in time of peace make annual cruizes into the Baltic, or perhaps as far as the English Channel; others are employed in the summer season in navigating the vessels laden with merchandize from Cronstadt to Petersburgh. But such nurseries as these are by no means sufficient; nor can the deficiency be supplied, in case of an immediate war, from private vessels; for Russia has scarcely any merchant ships, which is chiefly owing to the state of vassalage, and the strict laws that prevent the natives from quitting their country without a licence. . . . In a word, no kingdom, without distant colonies, considerable fisheries, and an extensive seacoast, to familiarize the inhabitants to the dangers of the ocean, is likely to acquire such a marine as to become formidable to the great naval powers of Europe. [II, 309-311]

2. MODE OF THE ANGLO-RUSSIAN COMMERCE
AUGUST 1801

By the kind communication of a friend, well versed in the Russian commerce, I am enabled to subjoin a statement of the mode in which the British trade is principally conducted. . . . A foreigner who imports goods into Russia, must sell them to Russians only, and at the port where they arrive, none but natives being allowed to send merchandize into the interior of the empire for sale. . . .

From the month of November, till the shipping season in May, the Russians, who trade in hemp, flax, tallow, bristles, wax, oil, hides, iron, and many other articles, (except manufactures and linens) either come themselves to St. Petersburgh, or employ agents to sell their goods to foreigners, to be delivered according to agreement, in May, June, July, or August. The payments are made according to the circumstances of the sellers and buyers; and sometimes the buyer pays the whole amount, in the winter months, for the goods which are to be delivered in the summer or autumn. . . . The manufacturers and dealers in linens usually come to St. Petersburgh in March, and sell their goods for ready money.

The foreign goods were formerly almost entirely sold on twelve months credit, and some on a still longer term; but lately, several articles, such as coffee and sugar, are sold at St. Petersburgh for ready money; still, however, the interior is supplied with foreign goods on credit, and most of the woollen trade in St. Petersburgh is carried on by allowing the Russians a long credit with the goods. Many, I might almost say all the Russians, who buy goods on credit of foreigners, for the supply of the interior, have no other connections or trade with St. Petersburgh, than merely coming there once or twice a year to purchase goods on credit, which having accomplished, they set off with the goods, and the foreigner neither sees nor hears of them again till the bills become due. By the laws of Russia, none but merchants inscribed in the guilds are allowed to trade; and in case any person not inscribed (that is, a peasant) contracts a debt for more than five roubles, he cannot be prosecuted, nor is he liable beyond that sum. Notwithstanding this law, a great many peasants do trade, and actually purchase goods of foreigners on long credit. . . .

It will be evident that to conduct an extensive commerce on this systeme requires considerable intelligence, an intimate acquaintance with, and unlimited confidence in the native merchants. Nothing can reflect more honour on the Russians, as a commercial people, than that the British merchants are in constant habits of intrusting to them the immense sums employed in the trade with that country, without any security beyond a personal knowledge. [II, 321-324]

3. THE ARTELS

Another circumstance connected with the British trade is too curious to be passed in silence. Every mercantile house in St. Petersburgh employs certain men, called, in the language of the country, Artelschicks [Artelshchiki], who are the counting-house men, and employed by every merchant to collect payment on bills, to receive money, as well as in many instances to pay it in very considerable sums. . . . There being no bankers in Russia, every mercantile house keeps its own cash; and as the payments between merchants, and for bills of exchange, are made entirely in bank notes of no higher value than five, ten, twenty-five, fifty and one hundred roubles, most of them are in so tattered a state, as to require several hours to count over a sum of two or three thousand pounds; this business is performed by artelschicks, and very few instances have occurred of loss by their inattention. . . .

These Russians are mostly natives of Archangel and the adjacent governments, of the lowest class, are often slaves, generally of the crown; and the only security of the merchant arises in some degree from the natural reluctance of the Russian to betray confidence reposed in him; but in a much greater from the nature of their association, which is called an Artel.

An Artel consists of a certain number of labourers, who voluntarily become responsible, as a body, for the honesty of each individual. The separate earnings of each man are put into the common stock, a monthly allowance is made for his support, and at the end of the year the surplus is equally divided. The number varies in different associations from 50 to 100; . . . these societies are not bound by any law of the empire, or even written agreements; nor does the merchant restrain them under any legal obligation; yet there has been no instance of their objecting to any just claim, or of protecting an individual whose conduct had brought a demand on the society.[38] [II, 325-326]

4. THE COMMERCE OF THE BLACK SEA

Many speculations have been made concerning the extent and value of the traffic which Russia is likely to establish in the Black Sea, and the revolution which it may effect in the commerce of Europe, by transferring part of the Baltic trade to the ports of the Mediterranean. In consequence of this change, it is asserted, the southern provinces will find a vent for their superfluous productions; the Russian vessels will open a profitable trade with Crim Tartary, with the Austrian provinces at Kilia-Novo, with the Turks at Constantinople, and with the Greeks in the Levant. The iron of Siberia, the corn, hemp, and flax of the Ukraine and contiguous provinces, will be sent from the havens of the Black Sea, through the Dardanelles, to supply the ports of the Mediterranean; and thus France and Spain will be furnished with naval stores by a cheaper and more expeditious navigation than through the Baltic and the Northern Ocean. . . .

To encourage her subjects to engage in this branch of traffic, the empress has lessened the duties of import and export, and contributed

---

[38] The artel, like the village mir, was an ancient institution the exact character of which is difficult to define. A cooperative society, based rather on voluntary than on patriarchal ties, it frequently resembled a sort of peasant craft guild, enjoying its greatest success in the early part of the Nineteenth Century. As with the mir, so, too, with the artel, the present Russian government has attempted to use ancient institutions to further a modern communist program, and the term is now applied to the cooperative farming unit. B. H. Sumner, *A Short History of Russia*, New York, 1943, pp. 116, 230, 344; John Maynard, *Russia in Flux*, New York, 1948, p. 28.

towards forming a Russian house, or company, trading to the Black Sea. . . . Since that period, besides several Greek vessels, which sailed from the Sea of Azof [Azov] and the Euxine [The Black Sea], under Russian colours, and were allowed to pass the Dardanelles, a Russian ship, manned with seamen in the service of government, and laden with salted beef, took its departure, in 1780, from Kherson, for the port of Toulon; and soon afterwards, five others, freighted with iron, made successful voyages to the Archipelago; also four small vessels, and a fifth of 400 tons just launched, laden with hemp and tobacco, were expected to sail from Kherson for France, in November 1781.

Such, in 1781, was the infant state of that commerce, which some authors have described as capable of producing an immediate revolution in the trade of Europe; and in this, or in a still more fluctuating state, it will probably continue, as long as the Turks retain the dominion of their own seas. For that jealous people will either openly oppose, or clandestinely obstruct, the progress of the Russians, and will never readily give a free passage through the Dardanelles to a powerful rival, though they consented to it in the humiliating peace of 1774. Perhaps these claims, urged on one side, and evaded on the other, will engender perpetual dissentions, and will not be finally terminated but by a series of obstinate and bloody wars. Meanwhile, the trade cannot for a considerable period be extensive, which depends on such casual circumstances as the coalition and rupture of rival and neighbouring powers. [II, 338-348]

VIII · THE LAWS

I. THE PENAL SYSTEM

ACCORDING to the present penal laws, offenders are punished in the following manner. Persons convicted of high treason are either beheaded or imprisoned for life. Felons, after receiving the knoot, have their nostrils torn and their faces marked, are condemned for life to work in the mines of Nershinsk [Nerchinsk]. Petty offenders are either whipped, transported into Siberia as colonists, or sentenced to hard labour for a stated period. Among the colonists are included peasants, who may be arbitrarily consigned by their masters to banishment.

All these persons are transported in spring and autumn from different parts of the Russian dominions. They travel partly by water and partly by land, are chained in pairs, and fastened to a long rope. When the whole troop arrives at Tobolsk, the governor assigns the colonists who are versed in handicraft trades, to different masters in the town; others he disposes as vassals in the neighbouring country. The remainder of the colonists proceed to Irkutsk, where they are distributed by the governor in the same manner. The felons are then conveyed to the district of Nershinsk, where they are condemned to work in the silver mines, or at the different forges. [II, 214]

2. ABOLITION OF CAPITAL PUNISHMENT

Travellers, who visited Russia before the reign of Elizabeth, uniformly concurred in relating the various modes of public executions and in reprobating the severity of the criminal laws. But though we may join with every friend to humanity in rejoicing that many of these dreadful punishments no longer exist, yet we cannot assent to the high encomiums passed on the superior excellence of the penal code since the edict of Elizabeth, which is supposed to have totally annulled capital condemnations.

From this suppression of capital punishment in all instances excepting treason, Elizabeth has been represented, not only by the lively Voltaire, but even by the sagacious Blackstone, as a pattern of legislative clemency. Though the infliction of death for offences which ought not to be capital, is too frequent in many countries, yet Elizabeth's modification of the criminal laws is perhaps no less exceptional, in point of policy and expedience, than illusive, in regard to its supposed lenity.

For should we even erroneously imagine, with some authors, that ... during the space of forty years, *not one criminal suffered death* throughout the vast empire of Russia, surely this lenity to the most atrocious crimes must be considered as extremely injurious to society. As a denunciation of death is to the generality of mankind, the most formidable prevention of crimes, the removal of this salutary terror withdraws a material safeguard from the lives and property of worthy citizens, and diminishes that security which they have a right to claim from the protection of the laws.[39]

The most benevolent person will probably entertain no extraordinary

[39] In a footnote, Coxe opposed Voltaire's opinion that permanent slavery was a more effective punishment than death, not, as Richardson believed, on account of its brutalizing effect upon society, but because, on the contrary, even "if we could devise a punishment more terrible than death, this new punishment, in order to work its effect on vulgar minds, ought to be inflicted within the reach of vulgar observation, and not in the remote region of Siberia. For can we suppose that the lower class of mankind, who are governed by their senses, receive any strong impressions from the casual report of sufferings endured at a great distance?" Coxe, *op. cit.,* II, 215-216.

veneration for this boasted abolition of capital punishment, when he reflects, that though the criminal laws of Russia do not *literally* sentence malefactors to death, they still consign many to that doom through the medium of punishments, in some circumstances, almost assuredly, if not professedly, fatal. . . . It is therefore evident, that capital penalties are virtually retained, although the chief utility resulting from the terror of death is considerably diminished. [II, 214-217]

3. ABOLITION OF TORTURE

Although the sovereign is absolute in the most unlimited sense of the word; yet the prejudice of the Russians in regard to the necessity of torture (and a wise legislator will always respect popular prejudices, however absurd) was so deeply rooted by immemorial usage, that it required great circumspection not to raise discontents by an immediate abolition of that inhuman practice. Accordingly, the cautious manner in which it was gradually suppressed, discovered as much judgement as benevolence. In 1762, Catherine took away the power of inflicting torture from the wayvodes, [voevodi] or inferior justices, by whom it had been shamefully abused. In 1767, a secret order was issued to the judges that whenever they should think torture requisite to force confession, they should lay the general articles of the charge before the governor of the province for his consideration; and all the governors had received previous directions to determine the case according to the principles laid down in the third question of the tenth chapter of instructions for a code of laws; wherein torture is proved to be no less useless than cruel. This, therefore, was a tacit abolition of torture, which has been since formally and publicly annulled. [II, 217-218]

4. THE NEW CODE

Catherine II . . . in 1767, summoned deputies to Moscow from every part of her extensive dominions, and having appointed commissioners for composing a new code of laws, delivered to them her Grand Instructions, written by her imperial majesty in the true spirit of genuine legislation. In conformity to these instructions, the first part of a new code appeared in 1775, and the second part in 1780, and it has been received in many of the new governments into which the Russian Empire is divided. . . .

The empire, divided by Peter the Great into nine extensive governments, is now distributed into a larger number, each upon an average

containing only from 3 to 400,000 males. One or more of these governments is superintended by a *namestnick* [namestnik], or lord lieutenant, and each has a vice-governor, a council, civil and criminal courts
of judicature, some of whose members are appointed by the sovereign,
and the others chosen by the nobles. By this institution Catherine has,
in some instances, circumscribed her prerogative, by diminishing the
power of those tribunals which were only dependent upon the crown,
or transferring it to the nobles, and investing them with many additional privileges with respect to the administration of justice. By introducing likewise into each government superior tribunals, whose decision is final, she has prevented frequent appeals to the imperial colleges
at Petersburgh and Moscow, which were attended with considerable
expence and delay. By establishing or separating the different boards
of finance, police, etc. from the courts of law, which before impeded
each other by meeting in the same place, she has facilitated the despatch
of business, and rendered the administration of justice more speedy.
She has increased the salary of the judges, who, from the narrowness
of their income, were exposed to almost irresistible temptations from
bribery. . . .

To these regulations must be added the abolition of torture . . . the
appointment of regular physicians and surgeons in various districts,
at the expence of the crown; the foundation of schools, and the establishment of new seminaries for those intended for the holy orders;
the erection of new bodies corporate with additional immunities, the
grant of freedom to numberless vassals of the crown; and the means
taken to facilitate the emancipation of the peasants. But of all the plans,
none is more useful and praise-worthy than the establishment of
schools in every government, formed on the most comprehensive scale
and liberal principles. [II, 222-223]

5. THE EFFECTS OF CATHERINE'S PROGRAM

Such are the outlines of these excellent institutions. How far, or in
what degree, they may operate upon a people so widely dispersed, and
of such different manners and customs, can only be proven by time
and experience. But though they may fail in producing *all* those
advantages which the speculative reasoner might expect, yet they must
be attended with most beneficial effects; as sufficiently appears from
the flourishing state of those provinces in which they have been already admitted. If it be allowed that many evils have been reformed,

and many improvements introduced, it cannot at the same time be supposed that the national manners should be suddenly changed, or that the most absolute sovereign can venture to shake those fundamental customs which have been sanctioned by ages. It is surely sufficient if the abuses are remedied, as much as can be expected in such a country; where the vast disproportion of rank and fortune, and the vassalage of the peasants, render it extremely difficult, if not impossible, to establish at once an impartial administration of justice.

Russia, with respect to the vast mass of people, is nearly in the same state in which the greater part of Europe was plunged during the 11th and 12th centuries; when the feudal system was gradually declining; when the unbounded authority of the land-holders over their slaves was beginning to be counter-balanced by the introduction of an intermediate order of merchants, when new towns were continually erecting, and endowed with increasing immunities, and when the crown ventured to give freedom to its vassals. [II, 224-225]

IX · THE SOCIAL STRUCTURE

1. THE FAILURE OF PETER'S REFORMS

MUCH HAS BEEN WRITTEN concerning the great civilization which Peter the Great introduced into Russia; that he obliged the people to shave their beards, and relinquish their national dress; that he naturalized the arts and sciences, disciplined his army, created a navy, and made a total change throughout his extensive empire. We may readily admit the truth of this eulogism with respect to his improvements in the discipline of his army and the creation of a navy; for these were objects within the reach of his persevering genius: but the pompous accounts of the total change which he is said to have effected in the national manners, seem the mere echoes of foreigners, who never visited the country, and who collected the history of Peter from partial information. For though a nation, compared with itself at a former period, may have made a rapid progress toward improvement; yet, as the exaggerated accounts which I had heard and read of the great civilization diffused throughout the whole empire, led me to expect a more polished state of manners, I must own I was astonished at the barbarism in which the bulk of the people still continue. I am ready to allow that the principal nobles are as civilized, and as refined in their entertainments, mode of living, and social intercourse, as those of other European countries. But there is a wide difference between polishing a nation, and polishing a few individuals. The merchants and peasants still universally retain their national dress, their original manners, and, what is most remarkable, the greater part of the merchants and burghers of the large towns, even the citizens of Petersburgh and Moscow, resemble, in their external appearance and general mode of living, the inhabitants of the smallest village; and, notwithstanding the rigorous edicts issued by Peter I, the far greater number still wear their beards; being scarcely less attached to that patriarchal custom than their ancestors, when the fine for mutilating a finger was rated at 1s. 3d.; that for cutting off the beard, or whiskers, at 4s. 10d.

In fact, the peasants, who form the bulk of the nation, are still almost as deficient in the arts as before the reign of Peter, although the sciences have flourished in the capital. But the civilization of a numerous and widely dispersed people is not the work of a moment, and can only be effected by a gradual and almost insensible progress. [II, 226-227]

2. THE NOBILITY

Emptiness of Titles

In Russia, as in the Oriental governments, there is scarcely any distinction of ranks among the nobility, excepting what is derived from the service of the sovereign. Even the eldest sons of those persons, who have been raised to the most considerable honours and highest employments, excepting the advantages which they undoubtedly retain of facilitating their promotion by a ready access to court, do not derive any solid benefits from their birth, like those which the peers of England, the grandees of Spain, or the dukes, who are peers of France, enjoy from their hereditary descent. The importance of a noble family of large property and official honours, is almost annihilated on the death of the chief; because his property is equally divided among his sons; and because titles, although allowed to be hereditary, do not, independent of the sovereign's favour, contribute much to aggrandize the possessors: that of a prince, a count, or a baron, conveying in themselves little personal distinction, unless accompanied by a civil or military employment.[40] [II, 227-228]

[40] Both Charles, Lord Whitworth and Sir James Macartney had noted the indistinct and unprofitable character of the privileges attaching to Russian titles. Since both had begun life as commoners, there is some irony in the tone of condescension which they affected; yet it was a natural reaction among Englishmen to take pride in the nobility, which their system of primogeniture had maintained in all its ancient vigor. By contrast, the Russian nobility often

Military Precedence

Although the law of Peter I, which compelled each nobleman or gentleman, under pain of degradation, to serve in the army, was abolished by Peter III; yet the effects still subsist. No one under the rank of a major is permitted to drive more than two horses; under that of a brigadier, more than four: a nobleman of the highest fortune and distinction, who has never been in the army, is not allowed, excepting by the special permission of the crown, to use in the capital a carriage drawn by more than one horse; while a merchant may have two. There are various methods, however, of procuring military dignity, and the privileges annexed to it. Amongst others, a chamberlain, for instance, to the sovereign, *ranks* as a major-general; the office of a secretary, in the different departments of government, confers the *rank* of an officer; and the contributor of a certain sum to the foundling-hospital at Moscow, obtains the *rank* of a lieutenant. . . . But, however ridiculous those promotions may appear, yet they are founded on the principles of the soundest policy; for as, by a decree of Peter the Great, every officer is noble during his life, and the children of a staff-officer are classed among the nobility, any institution tending to increase the number of this order of men, who alone are entitled to possess land, cannot fail of being highly beneficial to society. [II, 229]

3. THE CLERGY

The Monks

The principal wealth of the church is centered in the monasteries, which formerly had estates to the amount of £400,000 per annum. . . . The empress has annexed these church-lands to the crown, and in return grants annual pensions. . . . Soon after this regulation, many of the monasteries were suppressed; and the members in those which were spared, were considerably reduced. . . . The abolition of monasteries must be acknowledged a beneficial circumstance in most countries; yet one evil is to be apprehended from it in Russia: they were the only seminaries of education for those persons designed for the sacred function; and the monks are, if I may so express myself, almost the sole proprietors of the learning which subsists among the clergy.

presented very sorry specimens, and, even in the last years of tsarist Russia, itinerant peddlers bore openly and legitimately the title of kniaz or prince. Charles Whitworth, *An Account of Russia as it was in the Year 1710*, Strawberry-hill, 1758, pp. 32ff.; George Macartney, "An Account of Russia in the year 1767," *Some Account of the Public Life of the Earl of Macartney*, edited by John Barrow, London, 1807, II, 5ff.

But, most probably, the ill effects which may be expected from the suppression of some convents, will be compensated by the improvement introduced into the administration of those which are continued, and by the schools lately established in various parts of the empire for the education of ecclesiastics. [II, 230]

The Parish-Priests

The parochial clergy, who may, and ought to be, the most useful members of society, are in Russia, the refuse of the people. It is literally true, that many of them cannot even read, in their own language, the Gospel which they are commissioned to preach; but deliver from memory the service, a chapter of the New Testament, or part of a homily, which they repeat every Friday and Sunday. (This shameful ignorance is certainly less common than formerly; as the bishops are more cautious in ordaining such improper persons.) Nor is it in the least surprising that some are so illiterate, when we consider the scanty maintenance which they derive from their profession. Besides the surplice fees, which in the poorest benefices, amount to £4 per annum, and in the most profitable, to but £20; they have only a wooden house, scarcely superior to that of the meanest among their parishioners, and a small portion of land, which they usually cultivate with their own hands.... If they, who ought to enlighten others, are so ignorant, how gross must be the ignorance of their parishioners! In no instance, perhaps, has the empress contributed more towards civilizing her people, than by instituting seminaries for the children of priests, by endeavouring to promote among the clergy a zeal for liberal science, and to rouze them from that profound ignorance in which they are plunged....

I cannot forbear mentioning, that, during the five months we passed at Petersburgh, and in our daily intercourse with the nobility and gentry, I never once saw in company a single person of the sacred profession. It must be allowed, indeed, that the parish-priests are, for the most part, too low and ignorant to be qualified for admission into genteel societies; while the dignitaries, being a separate order, and restrained by strict regulations, reside chiefly in their palaces within the monasteries; and contract an aversion, perhaps an unfitness, for social intercourse. This general character of the Russian hierarchy does by no means comprehend all the individuals; as some of them, with whom I occasionally conversed, were men of liberal manners and enlightened understandings. [II, 231-232]

4. THE MIDDLE CLASS

Encouragements to Growth

Peter, who during his travels, perceived the utility of a third estate for the purposes of commerce, made many regulations with this view, which, though excellent in themselves, yet not being adapted to the state of property in Russia, did not answer the end proposed. Among these regulations, he endowed some free towns with certain privileges, which were afterwards augmented by Elizabeth. But these privileges were confined to Petersburgh, Moscow, Astracan, Tver, and a few other great provincial towns; and all the inhabitants, even merchants not excepted, were not distinguished from the peasants, in two instances, which are considered in this country as indelible marks of servitude: they were subject to the poll-tax, and to be draughted for the army and navy. Catherine has exempted the body of merchants from these two instances of servitude, has increased the number and immunities of the free towns, and permitted many of the crown-peasants, and all free men, to enroll themselves, under stipulated conditions, in the class of merchants or burghers.

The merchants are distributed into three classes. The first comprehends those who have a capital of 10,000 roubles; the second those who possess 5,000; and the third, those who are worth 500 . . . all persons who chuse to enter themselves in any of these classes are exempted from the poll-tax, on condition of paying annually one per cent. of their capital employed in trade to the crown. . . .

This alteration in the mode of assessing merchants is advantageous both to the crown and to the subjects; the former receives, and the latter cheerfully pay, one per cent. of their capital, because they are exempted from the poll-tax, and are entitled to additional immunities. It is also a just impost, as each merchant pays according to his fortune. . . . With respect to the general interests of the nation, it is a master-piece of policy; it excites industry, by holding up to the people a principle of honour, as well as of interest, to be derived from the augmentation of their capital; and affords an additional security from arbitrary impositions, by pledging the good faith of government in the protection of their property. It is likewise productive of another essential public benefit, by creating, as it were, a third estate, which, as it increases in wealth, credit, and importance, must by degrees acquire additional privileges and gradually rise into consequence.

The burghers form the second division of this order: the term burgher is applied to all inhabitants of free towns, who declare that they possess a capital of less than £100. . . . They possess many privileges superior to the peasants; but are distinguished from the merchants by being still subject to the poll-tax, and to enrollment in the army or navy.

Under this third order must be included all the other free subjects of the empire; namely, those slaves who have received liberty from their masters; those who have obtained their dismission from the army and navy; the members of the Academy of Arts, and of other similar institutions . . . and, lastly, the children of all these freemen. All these persons have permission to settle and trade in any part of the empire, and may enroll themselves, according to their capital, among the burghers or merchants. By these wise regulations, the number of persons above slaves will gradually increase, and must in time form a very considerable order of men, as soon as they shall acquire the right of possessing land. [II, 233-235]

Beneficent Influences

The most honest and intelligent persons of this order are the inhabitants of Archangel and its environs: they are mostly able to read, write, and cast accounts;[41] many of them are much employed at Petersburgh, by the members of the British factory, to superintend their warehouses, and they have the general character of faithful and industrious servants. It may, perhaps, be difficult to account for the peculiar circumstances which have concurred to render the inhabitants of the town and environs of Archangel more intelligent than the other Russians, unless the following cause should be thought sufficient. Archangel, from the time of its first discovery by the English . . . was, during a considerable period, the great emporium of Russia; many of the inhabitants, therefore, being connected with foreign merchants, who required great exactness in their dealings, were gradually trained to business. By a kind of local enthusiasm and traditional instruction, they have continued to distinguish themselves among their countrymen, by ac-

---

[41] Of the intelligence of the Russian merchants, in general, John Carr remarked in 1804: "The consummate knowledge which the Russian shopkeeper possesses of the most complicated calculation, and the entangled caprices of that chameleon-colored goddess who presides over the exchange, is absolutely astonishing. If he cannot write, he has recourse to a small wooden frame, containing rows of beans, or little wooden balls, strung upon stretched wires, and with this simple machine he would set the spirit of Necker at defiance." This observation is particularly impressive in contrast with Perry's sovereign contempt for the abacus. John Carr, *Northern Summer*, Philadelphia, 1805, p. 163.

quiring the rudiments of arithmetic, and by a diligent discharge of their trust. [II, 235]

5. THE PEASANTS

Of the Crown and of the Nobles

The peasants of Russia are generally serfs, or slaves, and may be divided into, 1. Peasants of the crown. 2. Peasants belonging to individuals.

1. The crown peasants inhabit the imperial demesnes; and probably comprehend, including those belonging to the church lands . . . about the sixth part of the Russian peasants. They are immediately under the jurisdiction of the imperial officers or bailiffs. Although liable to great exactions, by the tenure of their subjection from these petty tyrants, yet they are much more secure of their property; and being under the protection of the sovereign, any flagrant instances of oppression are more easily made known and redressed. Many of these vassals, in particular districts, have been enfranchised, and permitted to enroll themselves among the merchants and burghers; and the whole body will gradually receive more privileges, as the spirit of humanity and policy penetrates further into these regions.

2. Peasants belonging to individuals are the private property of the landholders, as much as implements of agriculture. . . . With respect to his own demands on his peasants, the lord is restrained by no law. He is absolute master of their time and labour. . . . Any capital which they acquire by their industry, may be seized, and there could be no redress; as, according to the old feudal law, which still exists, a slave cannot institute a process against his master. [II, 235-237]

Technical Education and Legal Improvement

The mode adopted by many landholders with their peasants, reminds me of the practice among the Romans. Atticus, we are told, caused many of his slaves to be instructed in the art of copying manuscripts, which he sold at a very high price, and raised a considerable fortune. On similar principles some of the Russian nobility send their vassals to Moscow or Petersburgh, for the purpose of learning various handicraft trades; they either employ them on their own estates, let them out for hire, sell them at an advanced price, or receive from them an annual compensation for the permission of exercising their trade for their own advantage.

In regard to the lord's authority over their persons, according to the antient laws, he might try them in his own courts of justice, or punish them without any process, he could inflict every species of penalty excepting the kñoot, order them to be whipped, or confined in dungeons; he might send them to houses of correction, or banish them into Siberia; or, in short, take cognizance of every misdemeanour which was not a public offence. . . . By the new regulations, this enormous power is reduced by restrictions more consonant to the humane principles which distinguish all the regulations of the empress, and the right of inflicting punishment is lodged, where it ever ought to be, in the hands of the public magistrate. Abuses, however, still subsist; but must, in time, yield to the influence of such salutary institutions. . . .

Although the sovereign cannot alter the fundamental state of property, by conferring on the peasants, as individuals, privileges which might infringe those of the nobles; yet she has alleviated their condition by issuing several laws in their favour. By allowing free peasants to settle in any part of her dominions, and enroll themselves among the burghers or merchants, according to their respective capital. She has given a stability to their freedom, and afforded the strongest incitements for the exertions of industry. She has repealed those oppressive laws, which forbade, in certain districts, all peasants to marry without the consent of the governor of the province, or the wayvode of the town, who usually exacted a present from the parties. [II, 237-239]

The Bar to Civilization

I am far from asserting, that inhumanity is the general characteristic of the Russian nobility; or that many persons do not treat their vassals with the utmost benevolence. I am also well aware, that several peasants are in such a flourishing condition as to have accummulated very considerable capitals without dread of exaction; and that some even possess landed estates under their masters' names. But if we consider the unhappy pleasure which too many feel in tyrannizing over their inferiors, we have every reason to conclude, that the generality of boors must be still cruelly oppressed. How then can a country be said to be civilized, in which domestic slavery still exists?

The vassals who work for their masters, generally receiving their maintenance, or being accommodated with a small portion of land, always enjoy in sufficient abundance the common necessaries of life; and usually spend their earnings in clothes or spirituous liquors. Those who, in contradiction of this general rule, save the profits of their labour, or trade, conceal as much as possible an acquisition of fortune. . . . The practice of hiding money is common in all countries of the East, where property is not well secured; and where the people, through dread of exactions cannot even venture to use the riches which they have acquired. . . .

From this general review of the various inhabitants in Russia, it may be perceived, that, though proceeding towards civilization, they are still far removed from that state; that a general improvement cannot take place while the greater part continue in absolute vassalage; nor can any effectual change be introduced in the national manners until the people enjoy full security in their persons and property. [II, 238-239]

CHAPTER SIX

Robert Ker Porter

Robert Ker Porter:

COURT PAINTER OF PANORAMAS

(1805-1807)

···

THE MOST OBVIOUS POINT OF DIFFERENCE between the life of Robert Ker
Porter and those of his predecessors lies in the fact that it began in 1780.
Although only thirty odd years younger than Richardson, Harris, and
Coxe and their contemporary for yet another thirty, he spent his forma-
tive and impressionable years in quite another world. Within the span
of his life, three separate, but connected revolutions, the French, the
Industrial, and the Romantic, gathered sufficient momentum to alter
the complexion of the social order from the decadence of the Ancien
Régime to the first flowering of the Victorian Era. To be sure, this
process had had its roots deep in the eighteenth century, and it was not
complete with his death in 1842. Moreover, in 1805, upon his arrival in
Russia, only its first implications had been felt. The economic changes
seem never to have dawned upon Ker Porter's consciousness. The political principles of the French Revolution, although they shook all Europe, had not yet been confirmed; and the romantic movement had
manifested only its first faint stirrings. Nevertheless, the seemingly sudden transition from a world in repose to a world in flux could not but
affect the temperament of a sensitive and impressionable young man.

The biographical accounts of Ker Porter's early life are concerned
rather with the intimate influences upon his personality and mental
development, than with statistical data of his parentage, academic
education, and physical peregrinations. Even the exact date of his birth
is uncertain, and, although his parents are known to have been well
connected, members of the Porter family having been noted as far back
in English history as the Battle of Agincourt, their Christian names
seem nowhere to be mentioned. His father, a younger son of an Irish
branch of the family, was serving as a surgeon with the Enniskillen
Guards at the time of his death in Robert's infancy.[1] Finding herself

[1] See the account of Anna Maria Porter, S. A. Allibone, *A Critical Dictionary of English
Literature*, Philadelphia, 1902, II, 1644.

in straitened circumstances, his young widow left her elder son, James Ogilvie, under the care of a grandfather in England and removed with Jane, Robert, and Anna Maria to Edinburgh in her native Scotland, where were to be found the best educational facilities within her modest means.[2] From his earliest remembrance to young manhood, Ker Porter was surrounded by the affectionate companionship of his mother and sisters, and it is peculiarly fitting, therefore, that the narrative of these formative years should be found only in association with the accounts of the sisters with whom he shared his innermost thoughts.

Although all three proved to be precocious scholars,[3] non-academic influences were of greater importance than formal education in shaping the bent of their minds. Until her death at eighty-seven, Mrs. Porter remained the spiritual center of her devoted family. From her, they acquired a remarkable degree of social charm, and she early encouraged their literary and artistic aptitudes, which she imbued with an abiding love of natural beauty. A second important quality of their later creative lives derived from another childhood source. Listening with rapt attention to the legends and ballads of ancient Scottish heroes from the lips of servants and neighborhood story-tellers, young Robert and his sisters imbibed a keen enthusiasm for tales of chivalry and valor in the long ago. Many years later, Jane directly translated her recollections of this experience into her widely acclaimed and still popular novel, *The Scottish Chiefs,*[4] and all three long retained a passionate interest in the echoes of a romantic past. This was both widened and deepened several years later with their removal to a town in the north of England. There, in the episcopal library which their mother's connections opened for them, they read, as Jane later described it, "from sunrise to sunset in a total abstraction from everything else. History and biography, from the Sacred Scriptures to Plutarch's *Lives,* from the blackletter chronicles of England to Rapin and David Hume, and all poetry connected with the events they told of, from Greece's Homer to our British Shakespeare, from the Ballad of Chevy Chase to that of our

[2] A. K. Elwood, *Memoirs of the Literary Ladies of England*, London, 1843, ii, 276.

[3] Little Anna Maria, at the age of only six, was accorded the title of *dux*, or head of her school, over girls more than twice her age. *ibid.*, ii, 279.

[4] It is an interesting coincidence that the Porter children were the occasional playmates of young Walter Scott in this period, and he is said later to have admitted to George IV that *The Scottish Chiefs* first suggested to him the idea for his Waverly novels. Although Professor Gerould has chosen to regard this as a pleasing fiction of Jane's ego, the publication of her novel in 1809 antedated that of *Waverly* by five years. Allibone, *op. cit.*, ii, 1646; G. H. Gerould, *The Patterns of English and American Fiction*, Boston, 1942, pp. 185-186.

soul stirring Rule, Britannia—this was the food with which we loved to nourish the favourite meditations of our mind. . . ."[5]

About 1790, young Robert entered upon a formal apprenticeship in that art in which he was later to incorporate the budding interests of his youth. Taking up residence in London, his mother enrolled him in the Academy of Arts under the auspices of the famous painter, Benjamin West. The new arrangement expanded the boy's horizons, but in no wise altered the intimacy of the little family, who continued to share both social and artistic experiences. Around Mrs. Porter's "unpretending tea table" gathered many prominent figures of the day: the former military and naval companions of the father as well as the literary friends of the mother: Sir Sidney Smith, the hero of Acre, whose deeds the young artist was later to commemorate in paint, as well as Mrs. Hannah More and Mrs. Elizabeth Hamilton. During this period, all three young Porters, gaining creative inspiration from their close contact, contributed to an unpretentious and shortlived periodical, *Quiz*. It was Ker Porter's meeting with Thaddeus Kusciusko which prompted Jane to write her widely read novel, *Thaddeus of Warsaw*, and the character of her brother is said to have furnished the model for the hero of Anna Maria's *The Village of Mariendorf*. Similarly, the brother frequently accepted his sisters' suggestions for the subjects of his paintings. Hence, throughout an adolescence when most other young men of good families were away at boarding schools or universities, Robert Ker Porter continued in a ripening intimacy with the mother and sisters who had been the earliest companions of his childhood.

During this same period, the precocious youth was developing in another medium a style which bore many striking resemblances to his sisters' literary efforts. In 1793, the Royal Society had distinguished him along with his fellow student and near neighbor, William Turner.[6] No doubt, the romantic landscapes of the latter appealed to him, but the "big brush" and sweeping panoramas of Henry Ashton Barker, a suitor of his elder sister, exercised an even stronger attraction.[7] He enjoyed a moderate success with several altar pieces, but both his own temperament and the genius of the troubled times drew him away from ecclesiastical subjects toward the composition of historic landscapes, combining a sensitivity to nature with the romance of heroic deeds. The British storming of the island of Seringapatam in distant India, where

[5] Elwood, *op. cit.*, II, 278.

[6] A. J. Finberg, *The Life of J. M. W. Turner*, Oxford, 1939, p. 22.

[7] J. L. Roget, *A History of the "Old Water-Colour" Society*, London and New York, 1891, I, 102.

French intriguing had stirred up native unrest, spurred the energies of the artist to an ambitious venture. The wholehearted critical and popular acclaim which immediately greeted its completion was the first step to a reputation which was ultimately to secure him the position of historical painter to the court of the Emperor Alexander I of Russia.

The pen of Jane Porter later recalled both the execution and the reception of this creative adventure: "The historical picture of the taking of Seringapatam was painted by my dear brother Robert at the age of nineteen. It was two hundred and odd feet long . . . I remember, when I first saw the vast expanse of vacant canvas stretched along, or rather in a semicircle, against the wall of the great room in the Lyceum where he painted it, I was terrified at the daring of the undertaking. I could not conceive that he could cover that immense space with the subject he intended, under a year's time at least, but—and it is indeed marvelous!—he did it in SIX WEEKS! . . . when it was completed, my brother invited his revered old friend Mr. West (the then president of the Royal Academy) to come and look at the picture, and give him his opinion of it, ere it should be opened to the public view. . . . He went over from the Lyceum, on the morning on which he had called to see my brother and his finished painting, to Somerset-house, where the committee had been awaiting his presence above an hour. 'What has detained our President so long?' inquired Sir Thomas Lawrence of him on his entrance. 'A WONDER!' returned he, 'a WONDER OF THE WORLD!—I never saw anything like it!—a picture of two hundred feet dimensions, painted by that boy KER PORTER in six weeks! and as admirably done as could have been done by the best historical painter amongst us in as many months!' "[8]

Thomas Dibdin, a literary friend of the family, vividly described the furor of the first public exhibition: "The learned were amazed, and the unlearned were enraptured. I can never forget its first impression upon my own mind. It was as a thing dropt down from the clouds— all fire, energy, intelligence, and animation. You looked a second time, the figures moved, and were commingled in hot and bloody fight. . . . You longed to be leaping from crag to crag with Sir David Baird, who was hallooing his men on to victory! Then, again, you seemed to be listening to the groans of the wounded and the dying—and more than one female was carried out swooning. . . . The public poured in by hundreds and by thousands for even a transient gaze—for such a sight was altogether as marvelous as it was novel. You carried it home and did

[8] T. F. Dibdin, *Reminiscences of a Literary Life*, London, 1836, I, 144-145.

nothing but think of it, talk of it, and dream of it. And all this by a young man of NINETEEN!"[9] This vast turbulent panorama, created by a sort of tour de force, with its emotional unrestraint, its appeal to the exotic charm of the Orient, and its shocked fascination with violence, strikingly anticipated the character of later romanticism. When the same Dibdin reminiscing over the span of the years, typified the painter's landscapes as such haunts "where the corsair of Byron and the pirate of Scott might alike resort for the meditation of more mischief"[10] he strongly suggested another aspect of his identity with the current of romanticism.

Despite all the violence of their emotional impact, however, Ker Porter's paintings remained strangely conventional in their moral tone. Like his sisters, he applied the ethical standards of the upper class Briton to his lurid subject matter. The profession of arms was, after all, an honorable one, and if his great battle pictures portrayed the shocking brutalities of war, they nevertheless presented noble heroism triumphant. Certainly, no true Englishman could argue the moral rectitude of commemorating British victories whether against the heathen hordes of Seringapatam, the Napoleonic forces at Acre, or the flower of French chivalry on the field of Agincourt. Moreover, Ker Porter's art was consciously didactic: "Painting, like poetry, recalls the past; and if the epic poem teaches true greatness in describing it, why may not the historic picture inculcate the same, by showing, even to the eye, examples of the virtue? Such use of the arts ennobles them, and very properly places the muses amongst the gods."[11] There is nothing here of a Byronic preoccupation with evil, but that the generation whose ethical climate Ker Porter breathed should be drawn to the contemplation of the warrior hero rather than of the philosopher king is some indication of the distance which lay between it and that of Richardson, Harris, and Coxe.

It was at some point in the year 1804 that Ker Porter received the compliment of an express invitation from Alexander I to come to Russia, but he seems to have hesitated in his acceptance. The preceding year, his astonishing success had enabled him to purchase a captaincy in the Westminister Guards,[12] and it is likely he yearned for a role in those martial dramas which his brush had been describing. The lull of British military operations, both during the short-lived Peace of Amiens

[9] *ibid.*, pp. 143-148.   [10] *ibid.*, p. 147.
[11] Robert Ker Porter, *Travelling Sketches*, Philadelphia, 1809, p. 247.
[12] *Gentlemen's Magazine*, 1842, p. 89.

and after England's independent resumption of hostilities, affording
no prospect of action, the frustrated hero apparently determined to
postpone his military ambitions and sailed in August 1805 for St. Petersburg, where, ironically enough, at that very moment were being completed those negotiations which were to lead to the campaigns of the
Third Coalition. He spent nearly two and a half years in the Russian
Empire, during which time he completed a set of large canvases ideal-
izing the achievements of Peter the Great and designed to be hung in a
new Admiralty building in St. Petersburg. Considering the astonishing
speed with which he had painted his first panorama, however, these
artistic efforts doubtless imposed but little on his leisure. The imperial
patronage and the personal attentions of the royal family secured him
admission to the houses of the greatest nobles, and dividing his time
between St. Petersburg and Moscow, he availed himself fully of his
opportunities to engage in the festivities of both capitals. These years,
in the enjoyment of imperial beneficence and in the society of the cosmopolitan nobility of a friendly nation, could not but delight a romantic youth in the full flush of health and vigor, but to render his
happiness complete, he fell madly in love with the beautiful Maria
Feodorovna Shcherbatov, a princess and daughter of one of the oldest
families in Russia.

Throughout his residence, his impressions of events, persons, and
the scenes which met his eyes were recorded in a voluminous correspondence with his family in England. When, on his return in 1808,
portions of the letters were selected and published under the title,
Travelling Sketches in Russia and Sweden, they were allegedly addressed to an unidentified "dear friend." However, the logic of the
internal evidence makes it clear beyond a reasonable doubt that these
same letters were, in fact, originally addressed to one or both of his
beloved sisters. Indeed, this is just such a correspondence as might have
been expected of their relationship. There is little attempt at systematic
organization and almost no evidence of scholarship. Ker Porter seems
to have had no real acquaintance with Russian history, and he falsely
idealized his portrait of Peter the Great. To picture him as "the sun,
from which alone has irradiated every science that now blesses this
country"[13] was, perhaps, a pleasing fiction, but to attribute the sobriety
of the contemporary nobility to the "exertions and example"[14] of a
man of Peter's intemperance was to distort the facts beyond all recognition. Finances and commerce nowhere entered his consideration and

[13] Porter, *op. cit.*, p. 135.   [14] *ibid.*, p. 95.

the desultory statistical data were reduced to a minimum. With the
natural ego of one who knew that his innermost thoughts would be
understood and appreciated by his audience, he continually emphasized
his own personal impressions of every object, occasionally referring,
though anonymously, even to his affection for the Princess Shcherbatov. Fortunately for the present effect of the work, his artist's eye
produced many of the finest word pictures in British travel literature,
and it is this quality in combination with the recurrent intrusions of
his romantic imagination which most strongly distinguish him from
his fellow travelers of the century.

It was his subjective attitude which gave Ker Porter that peculiar
sense of living in historical time which is first seen with him. Perry,
too, had witnessed an epoch of transition, warmly enlisting both his
sympathies and his self-interest, but his rationalism rejected the soaring
imagery which, for Ker Porter, made vibrant personal realities of current events. Hanway had given a detailed historical account of the
commercial relations in which he had, himself, played a role, but he
looked backward upon it as a closed chapter of his life. Richardson
and Coxe, for all their differences, had alike been insulated from Russian life and events. Harris had dealt with the native stuff of history,
but although in his intimate reflections he often pictured himself as an
actor in the drama, the stage is small by comparison with the epic
panorama in which Ker Porter placed himself. In his romantic imagination, his personal destinies were intimately intertwined with those of
the political and military giants of the age. His fate was being decided
upon the battlegrounds of Europe and in the cabinets of emperors.
Indeed, this proved to be far more than a romantic conceit, for it was
the disaster of Friedland, the Franco-Russian compact at Tilsit, and
the consequent rupture with Britain which forced him to leave St.
Petersburg in 1807 and to defer for four years his marriage to his beloved princess. Robert Ker Porter lived at a time when the strands
of so many lives were interwoven into a great trans-European web
that a violent motion in any part was sufficient to set the rest vibrating.

This general character of the times combined with the circumstances
of the young artist's visit to form the most favorable impressions of the
Russian Emperor. Both his professional life and the success of his
amour depended upon the good will of Alexander, and Ker Porter had
been on his way from Moscow to obtain the imperial consent for his
intended match when the Emperor was suddenly called to the front.
His personal charm and fine appearance were bound to appeal to the

aesthete in the young Briton, and he was not alone in his admiration. To nearly all Europe, the enlightenment of Alexander had shone forth like a sun from behind the dark cloud of Paul. His liberalism promised relief to the oppressed serfs of his own country and the tyrannized nations of Europe alike. To Englishmen, particularly, the reversal of Paul's policies was welcome. Diplomatic relations were restored almost immediately at Alexander's request, and an expedition of Cossacks which the Anglophobe Paul had dispatched against India was recalled.[15] Within three months, the issues which had divided the two nations in the Armed Neutrality of 1800 had been settled, and commercial activity was resumed. The political alliance of the Third Coalition completed the union of the two nations, and even after the fiasco of Austerlitz, Alexander's hostility toward Napoleon did not cease. Even with the Treaty of Tilsit, although the majority of Englishmen reviled the treachery of the Tsar, Ker Porter's romantic devotion to his idol remained unshaken.

It was not merely personal friendship, but the imaginative projection of personal emotions which evoked Ker Porter's hero worship. His tributes, if not consciously weighed, were not awarded to those who failed to stimulate a romantic interest. The death of Pitt, his health broken by cares of state, as Britain's political leader through twenty of the stormiest years of her history, elicited no mention in the correspondence. His transports were reserved for the glorious naval commander, Nelson, slain in the hour of his greatest triumph on the deck of his flagship. In a letter of November, 1805, interrupted by the arrival of the tragic news, he described his emotions: "Days have elapsed since I could return to this paper. An event indeed! great and momentous to the whole world! . . . Nelson, our brave, our invincible Nelson is no more! Heaven, then, in the moment of victory, took from England her never failing hope. Dear has our country paid for the glory of Trafalgar. . . ." Displaying his belief in the didactic virtues of history, he explored the lesson of Nelson's greatness in an inflated passage and concluded with a burst of patriotic exaltation. "What a summons to deeds of honour to generations yet unborn! . . . Let the balls come: if they strike, it is for thousands your life is given. VICTORY! safety to your country, the preservation of relations, friends, countrymen, all are in that word!"[16]

[15] A. A. Lobanov-Rostovsky, *Russia and Europe, 1789-1825*, Durham, North Carolina, 1947, pp. 67-68.
[16] Porter, *op. cit.*, pp. 110-111.

In the character of his patriotism, Ker Porter differed widely from his predecessors. Coxe had maintained a nearly unique objectivity in this respect, and Perry's patriotism had been largely confined to a justifiable pride in the superiority of British techniques. Hanway had pompously proclaimed that divine sanctions protected the material blessing which accrued from British mercantile supremacy. Harris, whatever his natural prejudices, had claimed to found his preference for England over other nations on "plain easy powers of comparison and discernment." Richardson, the most like Ker Porter in the lyricism of his eulogies, repeatedly and most brilliantly emphasized what all, including Ker Porter, recognized, namely, the preeminent importance of security of person and property for the happiness and improvement of a people. Ker Porter, however, did not rely upon rational or rationalized justification to explain his spontaneous affection for his native land. With a sentimentalism generated through years of national peril, he expressed a sort of romantic devotion to his country, based on a chivalrous loyalty, as personal and as distinct from reason as the love of a knight for his lady. "Blest England. Where'er I go I still think on my country, as a lover of the dear mistress he has left behind. Many he may behold fairer and more richly attired, but still, the heart, the heart! the amiable qualities which produce confidence and comfort, do they not make him indeed exclaim!

'Where'er I go, whatever lands I see,
My soul untravell'd still returns to thee.' "[17]

This romantic patriotism did very little to prejudice Ker Porter's view of Russia, but both personal circumstances and historical influences tended to slant his perspective of Russian society. On the one hand, they inclined him to a sympathetic approach to the aristocracy. Himself descended, through a younger branch, from noble ancestry, he felt no social inferiority. Indeed, he was destined later to be the recipient of no less than four different orders of knighthood.[18] Moreover, his own affiliations in Russia, particularly his betrothal to Princess Shcherbatov, completed his sense of identification, and in his idealization of the aristocracy, his own vanity did not suffer. Historically, the climate of

[17] *ibid.*, p. 118. This seems to be a misquotation of the opening lines of Oliver Goldsmith's *The Traveller*:

> "Where'er I roam, whatever realms to see,
> My heart untravell'd finally turns to thee. . . ."

[18] In 1807, he was created a knight of St. Joachim of Württemberg; in 1813, he received an additional knighthood from the Prince Regent; in 1819, he was awarded the Lion and Sun of Persia; and, in 1832, William IV created him a knight commander of the Hanoverian Order.

reaction to the French Revolution encouraged this tendency. French émigrés mingled with the upper classes of every European capital, and the future Louis XVIII himself had established his exiled court at Mittau under the protection of Alexander. Contacts with these victims of the revolutionary storm and the natural alarm of the upper classes of other nations had helped to formulate a growing consciousness of class and a sense of an international aristocracy, sharing a common culture, ethical code, and mode of life. Therefore, it was easy for Ker Porter to see his hospitable friends of the Russian nobility, brethren in arms against the common enemy, as a gallant and chivalrous order. On the other hand, these same influences acted to produce rather unfavorable impressions of the Russian peasantry. The young painter saw relatively little of the peasants' world, and he apparently both accepted and uncritically repeated anecdotes and descriptions of them by nobles professing the liberalism of their sentiments. The characteristic attitude of his rather desultory treatment of the lower orders was one of pitying condescension, but occasionally, as when he labeled them "canaille," his language smacked rather of the French émigré than of the British liberal.

Historical influences and external circumstances help to explain Ker Porter's distinctive attitude towards Russian society, but the clue to those traits which most strongly differentiate him from his fellows must be sought deeper within his individual personality. The recurrent interpolation of aesthetic criteria as having independent value is a unique feature of Ker Porter's reactions. Thus, every English traveler had, in one way or another, remarked "much useless labour to regret" in the primitive techniques of the rude gangs of Russian workmen they had seen, but it was the painter alone who observed that "setting aside utility, these groups add to the picturesque of the scene."[19] It is the use of the word, "picturesque," which provides the key. Life viewed merely as a series of pictures is removed not only from utilitarian, but from all other immediate considerations. The distance between the observed and the observer hangs like an invisible curtain separating the two. Even Ker Porter's rather precious humanitarianism was not always proof against this barrier, and he admitted having been transfixed with laughter at the spectacle of his servant raining blows upon the back of a landlord.[20] It should be noted that somewhat superficially and by no means exclusively practical considerations are largely confined to discussions of the Russian army, in some

[19] Porter, *op. cit.*, p. 18.   [20] *ibid.*, pp. 148-149.

degree, the shield of England. In great measure, however, the *Travelling Sketches* is no more than the title implies, a somewhat disconnected series of magnificent surface representations.

These sketches derive their vitality from a sort of aesthetic and refined hedonism. At first glance, Ker Porter, by virtue of his position in the imperial employ, would seem to have been rather more integrally connected with the fundamentals of the social structure than many of his predecessors, but his work was in reality a private affair between himself and a subject long dead. His real affiliations were social and romantic, in the conventional sense, and, therefore, within ethical barriers and the limitations of common sense, the pleasure-pain principle had a wide rein. It was this which endowed the main content of his pictures. The luxurious entertainments of the nobility made his senses reel. The beauty and charms of the ladies enchanted him. The appearance of the country and the action of the seasons stimulated his creative imagination. These, therefore, he reproduced with a glowing and romantic imagery. But where some quaint or curious usage of the peasants failed to make them picturesque, he was revolted by their unloveliness. Like Richardson, but with an emphasis on the aesthetic rather than the moral plane, he felt almost a personal affront in the image of their brutality. Unlike him, he repeatedly failed to analyze the broader social aspects of the scenes which greeted his eyes. Throughout the major portion of his sojourn, Ker Porter remained primarily a painter, rather than an analyst of Russian life.

Under the circumstances, it is not surprising that no systematic interpretation of Russia should emerge from the work as a whole. In this connection, it must be remembered that system was not the aim of the intimate family correspondence upon which the book was based; but neither should it be forgotten that the comparable variety of Richardson's letters received thematic unity from an active social conscience. Intermittently, Ker Porter applied the political and social dogmas of his countrymen to conditions in Russia, but his indignation at the spectacle of domestic slavery or the wide contrast in the status of noble and peasant was dissipated by a characteristic historical dilettantism. Thus, having drawn the parallel of the establishment of a contemporary Russian noble to that of a medieval English baron, his mind relaxed into passive speculation: "I find it no unamusing train of thought to pursue the progress of different nations through various stages of civilization, till I can with ease point out the periods in each when their customs and manners have exactly paralleled. Thus the present manners of some countries are only correspondent with what were the manners of a neighboring nation a century ago. And so I go on, when I have nothing else to do, making the world pass before me, as we whirl about its effigy on a globe, with our finger."[21] The ideas here stated, if pursued to their logical conclusion, might have suggested a broad philosophy of history, including a specific interpretation of the Russian role therein. They implied that all the nations of the world were progressing by a sort of mechanical process toward the same absolute goal, the same type of civilization, and that Russia, a cultural anachronism, was following inexorably in the track of the western leaders. The implications of these concepts were immense, but Ker Porter declined to pursue them, preferring instead to use them merely as a key to idle, but pleasurable daydreams, and thereby betraying himself simultaneously as an hedonist, a romantic, and a dilettante.

[21] *ibid.*, p. 176. With greater energy, but with equal lack of system, Ker Porter's Irish acquaintance, Catherine Wilmot, remarked the same anachronism of Russian culture in the life of Europe: "Russia is but in the 12th century. Yes! I know all about the luxury of Moscow and the civilization of Petersburg, but have you ever seen a clumsy romping ignorant girl of 12 years old with a fine Parisian cap upon her head? So seems to my eye this imperial realm. The cloister'd ignorance not only of the 12th but of the 11th century is the groundwork of this colossal region and 5 or 6 centurys will no doubt produce the same effects here they have in other parts of Europe; but time must disengage the ligaments which bind the plant before it strengthens and expands into a self supported standard. More sudden means would bend it to the earth, and so of Russian political liberty and civilization!" The Marchioness of Londonderry and H. M. Hyde, *The Russian Journals of Martha and Catherine Wilmot*, London, 1934, p. 223.

EXTRACTS FROM: *Travelling Sketches in Russia and Sweden*

by Robert Ker Porter

CONTENTS

....

I · ST. PETERSBURG: STREET SCENES

1. A SNOWY METAMORPHOSIS

How CHANGED is the face of nature since last I addressed you! all is
frozen; and covered with the chilling snows of winter. If the city
astonished me when under the glowing tints of an autumnal atmosphere, how much more striking does its present pale silvery light make
it appear!

Now, *indeed, this is Russia*! every sensation, every perception, confirms the conviction. The natives have suddenly changed their woollen
kaftans, for the greasy and unseemly skins of sheep. The freezing power
which has turned every inanimate object into ice, seems to have thawed
their hearts and their faculties: they sing, they laugh, they wrestle;
tumbling about like great bears amongst the furrows of the surrounding snow. In fact, this season, so prolonged with them, seems more
congenial with their natures than their short but vivid summer. . . .

Where are now the expanded waters of the Neva? The gay gondolas
and painted yachts? The myriads of vessels and boats continually pass-

ing and repassing? All have disappeared: one bleak, extended snowy plain generalizes the views: and scarcely a trace is left to convey an idea that a river ever glided through the heart of this imperial city. The roofs of the palaces, public buildings, and private houses, are shrouded in the same pale garb. But no objects are so strangely beautiful as the trees which grow in several divisions of this metropolis; when divested of their leaves, the repeated coats of snow thickening on their branches, form them into the appearance of white coral encrusted with brilliant diamond dust. . . .

Cold to the Russians, seems to be what heat is to the torpid animal, for Petersburgh at this moment presents a prospect of much greater bustle and activity than during the warmer months. The additional multitudes, spread in busy swarms throughout every quarter, are inconceivable: sledges, carriages, and other *traineau* vehicles, cross and pass each other with incredible velocity. The sensation excited in the eye by the swift, transitory movement of so many objects upon the unbroken glare of the snow, is painful and blinding: and you might as well determine to fix your sight upon a particular ant (at the demolition of its little world), as upon one of these figures when beholding them from a height. From the fortress tower for instance; where I have just been beholding a scene as extraordinary to an English eye, as it is undescribable and amusing. [88-90]

2. THE SLEDGES

The sledge is precisely a pair of colossal skates joined together. On these (according to the taste of the owner) is erected the most agreeable and convenient carriage which either his purse may afford or his situation claim. The sledges of the humbler order are solely formed of logs of wood bound together with ropes into the beforementioned shape: on this is an even surface of plank or matting, for the accommodation of themselves or loads. . . . The sledges which succeed the drojcka [droshky] (the St. Petersburgh hackney coach), are generally very neat, yet always gaudy, being decorated with red, green, gold and silver, with strange carved work and uncouth whirligigs of iron. Their interior is well bespread with *damp* hay, for the benefit of the hirer in order to keep his feet *warm*. . . .

The sledge carriage of a prince, or nobleman, is uncommonly handsome. All its appointments are magnificent; and never out of harmony. In it we behold the genuine uncontaminated taste of the country: no bad imitations of German or English coach work are here attempted; all is characteristic; and a picturesque effect, peculiarly its own, is produced by the vehicle itself, its furs, its horse, their trappings, and the streaming beards of the charioteers. . . .

The horses attached to this conveyance are the pride of the opulent. Their beauty and value are more considered than the sledge itself. The excess of vanity amongst the young officers and nobility here, consists in driving about two animals whose exquisite elegance of form, and playfulness of action, attract the attention of every passenger. The form of these horses is slight and Arabic, possessing the grace of an Italian greyhound with a peculiar lightness and looseness of pace. One only, is placed in the shafts which never alters its pace from a rapid trot: the other is widely traced by its side; and is taught to pace, curvet, and prance, in the most perfect taste of a finished manège. Their tails and manes are always of enormous length; a beauty so admired by the Russians that twenty horses out of thirty have false ones. . . . The harness of these creatures is curiously picturesque, being studded with polished brass or silver, hundreds of tassels, intermixed with embossed leather and scarlet cloth. These strange ornaments give the trappings an air of eastern *barbaric* splendor, perfectly consonant with the animal's shape. However, as every carriage in Russia (even should it be built in the excesses of the British mode), is drawn by horses thus romantically caparisoned, the union is sometimes monstrous: and I have often felt the contradiction so forcibly, as to remind me of an absurd sight I once saw at home. It was an Indian chief in a London assembly. He was decorated with chains, shells, and tiger's teeth, while all the spruce, powdered *beaux* around him were in the extreme of European *costume*. [90-91]

3. THE FAIR ON THE FROZEN NEVA

To strangers, accustomed to the various changes produced in men and things by the influence of intense frost, nothing appears more wonderful or note-worthy than that part of the city dedicated to the sale of frozen provisions. Your astonished sight is there arrested by a vast open square, containing the bodies of many thousand animals piled in pyramidical heaps on all sides. Cows, sheep, hogs, fowls, butter, eggs, fish, are all stiffened into granite.

The fish are attractively beautiful; possessing the vividness of their living colours, with the transparent clearness of wax imitations. The beasts present a far less pleasing spectacle. Most of the largest sort being skined, and classed according to their species; groups of many hundreds are seen piled up on their hind legs against one another, as if each were making an effort to climb over the back of its neighbour. The motionless apparent animation of their seemingly struggling attitudes (as if suddenly seized in moving, and petrified by frost), gives a horrid life to this dead scene. Had an enchanter's wand been instantaneously waved over this *sea* of animals during their different actions, they could not have been fixed more decidedly. Their hardness, too, is so extreme, that the natives chop them up for the purchaser, like wood; and the chips of their carcases fly off in the same way as splinters do from masses of timber or coal.

A hatchet, the favourite instrument of the country, is used in the operation; as indeed it is generally applied to every other act of ingenuity or strength. Sometimes to things so nicely delicate, that if the boors were taught to write, I have little doubt but their pens would be made and repaired with it.

But to return to the market. The provisions collected here are the product of countries many thousand versts beyond Mosco. Siberia, Archangel, and still remoter provinces, furnish the merchandize, which during the frost's severity is conveyed hither on sledges. In consequence of the multitudes of these commodities, and the short period allowed to the existence of the market, they are cheaper than at any other part of the year; and are therefore bought in large quantities to be laid up as winter stock. When deposited in cellars they keep good for a length of time.

At certain hours every day the market, while it lasts, is a fashionable lounge. There you meet all the beauty and gaiety of St. Petersburgh; even from the imperial family down to the Russ merchant's wife. Incredible crowds of sledges, carriages, and pedestrians, throng the place: the different groups of spectators, purchasers, venders, and commodities, form such an extraordinary *tout ensemble* as no other city is known to equal.

During this mart of congealed merchandize, affecting scenes often occur. . . . Whenever a new levy is made for the army, a given number (according to the state's necessity) is taken from every five hundred slaves capable of bearing arms. Most of the villages have been thus deprived of some of their inhabitants; and it is with the affectionate hope of again seeing their different relatives, that many very aged men accompany these frozen caravans. . . . Ignorant of any particular corps, and only conscious that it is a *soldier* they seek, under the liveliest impressions of expectation and affection, they momentarily look for the blessing of again embracing a son, a brother, or some other near and beloved kinsman. Actuated by similar feelings, hundreds of soldiers (after their military duties are over for the day) are seen going from group to group, searching for their own parents amongst these patriarchal strangers. . . . Nothing can be more affecting than to witness their joyful meetings: fathers embracing their sons, brothers their brothers. But . . . the heart saddens while listening to the impatient inquiries of many, who are soon deprived of their dearest hopes, by the information that another country contains their offspring; perhaps another world. [100-102]

II · ST. PETERSBURG PORTRAITS: NOBLE AND PEASANT

I. THE NATIVE APPAREL

THE NOBILITY of both sexes, when not enveloped in pelisses, appear in our fashions, only a little more *à la Française*. But it is in the dress of the peasant, the simple covering with which the unsophisticated native of the snows of Russia shields himself from the cold, that we find the characteristic garb of these northern regions. The head is protected from the inclemency of the weather by caps of velvet and fur. . . . A long kaftan of blue or brown cloth, reaching below the knees, fitting close to the shape without any cape, and crossing diagonally the breast (being fastened with cylindrical buttons of brass or white metal till it reaches the bottom of the waist) is the body's covering. Round the waist is a sash of crimson worsted net, like those worn by British officers. In this they place their gloves, or if they be labourers, their hatchets. . . . Their shirts and trowsers are of coarse linen striped with either red or blue. Thick swathes of rags are rolled about their legs to keep out the cold, over which they pull a pair of large and ill constructed boots. Those who do not arrive at the luxury of these leathern defences, increase the swathings to such a bulk by wrappings and cross bandages, that their lower extremities appear more like flour sacks than the legs of men. When thus bulwarked, they stuff them into a pair of enormous shoes, made very ingeniously from the bark of the linden tree. . . . This style of dress appertains to the commonalty alone, and it is curious to observe how closely it resembles that worn by the

English in the reign of Richard the Second. . . . Any one who has considered the old tombs in our cathedrals, or has studied the costume to be seen in many illuminated manuscripts extant, will not doubt of the fact, but immediately perceive that the peasantry of Russia in the nineteenth century, are contemporaries in fashion with those of England in the fourteenth. [92-93]

2. THE WOMEN

The Peasants

Alas! this race of the lovely sex are such contradictions to their usual appellation, that I fear you will think me a very uncivil commentator. However, judge for yourself. They are generally stunted, clumsy, round faced, small featured, and sallow complexioned. The latter defect they strive to remedy by a profusion of paint of various hues, which they daub on with as little taste as art. [93-94]

The Ladies

The fair of this metropolis are not in general very formidable rivals to those of other capitals which I have visited. There are some very fine women, but the majority have small claims to the title of beautiful. Their features are rather of the Kalmuc [Kalmuck] cast; and from the sedentary habits they acquire, nature soon allows the rose of their charms to blow into too full luxuriance. Like exotics in a hothouse, the artificial heat brings them to untimely maturity; and they fade away, even at the moment when we expect to find them at their highest bloom. But it is only their exterior which thus changes. At the age of thirty, or thirty-five, the face may be withered, the figure overgrown; but still youth is in the mind and the heart; and conversing with these charming women, you soon forget that she who discourses with the wit of Thalia or the grace of Erato, does not also possess the beauty of Venus as well as her tenderness. [98]

3. THE LIFE OF A NOBLE

The usual pastimes of the nobles, when they are not pursuing military exercises, or employed in offices of state, are the carriage or the sledge during the morning. They dine at half past two o'clock, and after that either sleep for a couple of hours (for they do not sit long at table) or play at games of cards, of which there are a great variety; billiards is also a frequent amusement. . . . The evening produces the theatre, or assemblies at their own houses, when, either cards are again resorted to, or a light dance exhilarates the scene, to which the company who prefer sitting, play on the pianoforte and harp. Various little pastimes, such as forfeits, the magic music, etc. etc. are brought forward. And thus wit and innocent mirth carry on the hours till supper is announced. This meal is generally too luxurious for the health and beauty of those who draw round the table. Soups, fish, roast, and boiled meats, and savoury dishes, fill the groaning board. Good appetites are seldom wanting; and thus, both mentally and bodily recreated, or rather, over-burthened, do the parties betake themselves to rest; their stomachs fevered with the richest foods, they lie down in bedrooms where an artificial heat, like that of a hothouse, ferments their digestion, leaving them at waking pale, languid, and spiritless. This is the common mode: but where experience has opened the eyes of some, and travel informed others, such injurious customs are set aside; and we behold, as in England, the blooming cheek of a Hebe rising brightly with the morn; and the athletic form of manhood moving with all the freshness of health, all the elasticity of youthful vigour. [109-110]

4. THE DEATH OF A PEASANT

St. Petersburgh . . . is by no means unhealthy. The air is uncontaminated by pestilential vapours, as care is taken to drain the swamps; which otherwise, with the Augean additions from the *cleanliness* of the lower inhabitants, might prove dreadfully noxious. The police manages all this with admirable diligence; and *maugre* the natural love which the *canaille* seem to have to wallow in an uncleansed stye, I never saw a race more healthy than the common people are in Russia; and were it not for their excessive use of brandy, I believe the rigour of the climate, and their constant exercise, would prolong their days to an almost patriarchal date. . . . [199-200]

Drunkenness is nowhere to be seen but with the lower ranks; and they, like the swine in the gospel, have so potently imbibed the foul fiend, as to be carried headlong to their destruction. During the chilling blasts of winter . . . , it is then that we see the intoxicated native stagger forth from some open door, reel from side to side, and meet that fate which in the course of one season freezes thousands to death. . . . After spending perhaps his last *copeck* in a dirty, hot *kaback* or public house, he is thrust out by the keeper as an object no longer worthy of his attention. Away the impetus carries him, till he is brought up by the opposite wall. Heedless of any injury he may have sustained by the shock, he rapidly pursues the weight of his head, by the assistance of his treacherous heels, howling discordant sounds from some incoherent Russian song; a religious fit will frequently interrupt his harmony, when crossing himself several times, and as often muttering his *gospodi pomilui*, "Lord have mercy upon us!", he reels forward . . . and then he tears the air again with his loud and national ditties: staggering and stumbling till his foot slips, and that earth receives him, whence a thousand chances are, that he will never again arise. He lies just as he fell; and sings himself gradually to that sleep from which he awakes no more. [95-96]

5. CONTRASTING TEMPERS

These latter people, who are usually slaves to the crown or the nobles, are universally good-natured, and possess a wonderful ingenuity and quickness of apprehension. At present their shrewdness is so apparent in bargains, that if in making any, you do not compel them to give written articles of agreement, you may be sure of being cheated in every possible way. . . . I can also pay them the compliment of registering their Spartan mode of action, as a dexterous theft in the way of over-reaching, is regarded by them as the very triumph of their genius. [95]

The nobility of Russia are honest, frank, and hospitable. A something about them still exists which reminds you that Muscovy and England first shook hands in the days of our good queen Bess. There is a hardihood, at the same time, a courtliness of demeanour, that recalls to recollection the prowess of sir Francis Drake, the gallantry of sir Walter Raleigh. What Elizabeth was to England, Catherine the Second was to Russia: the effects remain: after the flower is cropt and laid in the tomb, its fragrance survives and embalms the surrounding atmosphere. [108]

III · THE COMPOSITION OF AN EMPIRE

1. THE HUMANITY OF A STATE: THE FOUNDLING HOSPITAL

THE EMPEROR is hourly expected. When he arrives, you shall have my sentiments of this amiable and idolized monarch. Meanwhile, I will interest you in the virtues of the illustrious widow of his predecessor, the good dowager empress.

How can I do it better than by giving you a sketch of an institution which reflects the highest honour upon its august patroness? . . . The hospital in question was instituted forty years ago. . . . It is designed for the reception of foundlings. The number of little deserted souls now within the walls of this blessed asylum at St. Petersburgh, is nearly six hundred. . . .

The infants (arranged in wards and classes according to their age), are watched during the helpless period of existence with maternal care. When their mental and bodily powers are capable of useful occupation, they are instructed in such arts or employments as may render them advantageous to that state which is so justly entitled to their filial gratitude. The girls are taught first to make the different parts of their habiliments; then to manufacture fringe, lace, and an exquisite embroidery, which is used on court dresses, funeral palls, and sacerdotal robes. The boys are made alert in tayloring, shoemaking, and similar occupations of public utility. By this means the capital is supplied with industrious mechanics of both sexes: by this means the humanity of the state turns private indiscretion into national benefit; and not only thousands of innocent creatures are preserved in existence, but many, many a parent is saved from the most horrid of crimes. [114-115]

2. THE SUB-HUMANITY OF A SPECIES: THE WET NURSES

This excellent charity is not only furnished with unexceptional superintendents for the advanced classes, but anxious care is taken to supply the infants with the nourishment allotted to them by nature. For this purpose, great numbers of hale, stout women; who have newly become mothers, are brought from the villages of Ingria and Finland, in droves like milch cows; who (after their health is ascertained) are distributed over the hospital.

In my life I never saw such wretched, humiliating specimens of human nature! their odious appearance struck me the more horribly when I remembered that they were of the *angelic* sex. Imagination cannot paint their strange costume, their stupid countenances; the sallow mahogany-coloured flesh of their uncouth flabby persons, their settled vacancy of stare, and complete nonentity of expression. The duty marked out for these poor creatures to fulfil, is the loveliest and most interesting one in which a woman can appear: but here, alas! disgust is the only feeling excited. While surveying them, I could not help making a comparison between their aspects and the wet nurses of England. The latter, all health and roses; their eyes beaming a simple philanthropic affection over the little helpless being thus succoured; their persons firm as marble; and their whole air vouching for their imparting the riches of a good constitution to the child whom a mother's inability, perhaps, has consigned to their care. . . .

If (as it is said) the temper, propensities, and constitution are transmitted by our *lacteal* food, they who have been thus subsisted will make but heavy members of society. . . . Yet perhaps the inconveniences may not be very great; as the destined pursuits of these oddly-nurtured mortals seldom require either very laborious or very brilliant exertions of the mind. [115-116]

3. THE CANKERS OF GENIUS: MILITARISM AND SLAVERY

Owing to the peculiar constitution of this empire, the arts and sciences are, in general, but secondary objects in the minds of the natives. The nobles deem no profession honourable but that of arms. Ambition would be thought to stoop, if it sought any celebrity from excelling by the chissel, the pencil, or the pen: hence, the finest talents among the highborn are never directed towards any of these points. Military glory is all their aim: and, if it chances to be united with the spontaneous growth of any milder genius, it is well; the possessor is pleased, and his friends delighted; but no fame accrues from classical endowments. The study of the arts and sciences is left to slaves; or at best, to slaves made free: and they, unhappy men! from being descended from that contemned race, can never, by any exertions of their own, or by the conclusive appeal of appropriate actions, assert the inherent nobility of the heavenly gifted mind. Slavery is a taint that can never be erased: and thus the generous ambition of genius is cankered at the very root. [108-109]

4. THE SINEWS OF STRENGTH: PATRIOTISM AND THE MIDDLE RANK

The domestics in every family being slaves, they as much belong to their lord, as the chairs and tables of the house; and are, in general, treated too much like mere pieces of furniture. While they do their duty it is well; they are quietly used according to their appropriate service; but as fellow creatures they are seldom considered. . . .

This system is so abhorred by the benevolent Alexander, that he takes every opportunity of buying the estates of the nobles, and immediately giving freedom to the peasants. By this generous policy he removes the yoke from their necks, and brings forward into freedom and occasions of earning an honest and independent subsistence, a race of men who will soon form themselves into the most useful part of the body politic; that middle rank, which is the sinew of a nation's strength, the source of her riches, and the guardian of her glory.

We need only turn our eyes to England to see the proof of this. Look at her wealthy yeomanry, her merchants as princes; and her commons sitting at the helm of state, and equal in power with the nobility, guiding it in safety and honour through all the shocks of contending empires! . . .

Though, judging of the fate of nations by their determination and means of resistance, little fear is to be entertained for the independence either of England or of this country. The same *amor patriae* is paramount here, which so surely guarantees the freedom of our native island. Usurpation is held in equal detestation, while so amiable a monarch as Alexander fills the imperial throne. [117-119]

IV · COURT SKETCHES

I. PORTRAIT OF THE EMPEROR

HAVING been presented to this interesting personage, I cannot but give you a sketch of his figure and manners. . . . He is mild in his demeanor, gentle in his motions, and particularly graceful in his address. The goodness of his heart shines forth in his eyes, and the sweetness of his temper ever embellishes his lip with a smile. So great is his benevolence, that not a day passes without bringing forward some instance of his attention to the welfare and comfort of his people; and his lenity in punishing criminals is so forbearing, that in all cases the most tender mercy waits upon his justice. His figure is handsome and elegant, his air, affable and engaging; and his countenance ever expresses his benignity of his mind. His height is about five feet, eleven inches. He is fair with blue eyes; and his complexion, though not florid, is beaming with health, and most interestingly tinged with the hue of a military life.

On our first presentation, according to the etiquette of this court, the Emperor passed forward, only bowing to the strangers. But after that formal ceremony was once over, at every other levée he converses with all the dignified freedom which sits so gracefully upon persons of his rank; and more particularly captivates in him, from the intelligence and amiable interest of his manners. [119-120]

2. A BANQUET OF THE SENSES

Since the return of its invaluable monarch, St. Petersburgh has been a scene of continued gaiety. And as it is also the opening of the new year, a time of extraordinary festivity in Russia, there is no end to the *fêtes*, feasts, and rejoicings.

Amongst them all, I must not omit describing an evening which I lately passed at the Winter Palace. The entertainment given there was a public masquerade; where from the imperial family, down to the Russ tradesman, all ceremony was suspended. This immense winter residence (of which the Hermitage forms only a very small part) was thrown open: every saloon, gallery, and corridor blazed with chandeliers. The dome of the grand hall of Saint George shone like a crystal heaven. Indeed, in the luxury of light no country is so lavish as Russia. . . .

The crowd and heat of the masquerade was almost unbearable (fifteen hundred persons having received tickets of admission); and when involved in a vortex where mingled many of the *unpurified* natives, the more refined were unable to form an antidote to the effluvia. Otto of roses [attar of roses] and the most costly perfumes, were breathed in vain through this motley and steaming group. . . . At eight o'clock the masquerade was filled to suffocation; and about an hour afterwards the imperial family entered . . . they passed through every chamber, to the gratification of the multitude, mingling without reserve amidst the lowest of their subjects. . . .

After remaining more than two hours in the assembly, the imperial family withdrew into the Hermitage. This department of the palace being sacred to them and their party, became literally a heaven to retire to, from the bustle, heat, and offensive vapour of the purgatory we had left . . . and here was spread a court supper, that in splendor and taste well accorded with the graces of the imperial family which adorned the banquet. The theatre of the Hermitage . . . was adapted for the occasion in a style exquisitely beautiful and novel. . . .

In the first place, the pit was boarded level with the stage. On this platform were placed tables, in all the pride of an imperial banquet, richly lighted and royally spread for feasting. The festooned curtain common to theatres, was here made of gold tissue, forming resplendent draperies, glittering with fringes of cut glass. Immediately behind this façade, rose drapery of the same magnificent materials in form of a Turkish tent; from the centre of which hung a lustre whose numberless crystal pendents produced a constellation of light. Over this fell a veil of spun glass, woven into transparent network like lace, through which played the prismatic colours with indescribable brilliancy; cords and tassels of glass in various festoons, crossed each other amongst the draperies; beneath which stood a circular bower of rose trees in full blow and fragrance. A range of arches . . . were tastefully ornamented with arabesque devices; and their openings filled up with a film of spun glass *apparently* finer than cobweb; on which were painted in opaque colours, sylphic figures, which thus seemed floating in the air. Unseen lights were so ingeniously placed as to reflect from this glassy gauze, producing such an effect as the sun's rays on a light falling shower.

When the whole of this enchanted spot was illuminated, it might well have been mistaken for a diamond mine, destined for the banquet of genii. Nay, the charm was completed by the sound of music from a hidden instrument, which united in itself the characters of the organ and Eolian harp. . . . These soft, melodious breathings issued from the thicket of rose trees, and finished the magical effect of this *Arabian night* like scene. . . . The banquet of the senses was before me; and around, the lovely Houris with the peerless Cadige at their head! You must forgive my being a little in the superlative upon a subject so excessive in all the luxuries of eye, ear, taste, and smell. [120-124]

V · THE ARMY

1. THE GRANDEUR OF AN EPITAPH

HERE LIES SUWARROFF![22] A more comprehensive epitaph could not have been chosen. On these words meeting the eye, his greatness and extraordinary life rush at once upon the mind; and we feel, from this sublime appeal, the whole force of his character. . . . Many instances might be brought, to show how happy the Russians are in this kind of short, natural, and Spartan expression. On a medal, struck in the reign of Catherine II, in honour of a great victory, and presented to the officers and soldiers who distinguished themselves in the battle, this was written under the emblems of conquest: I WAS THERE. . . . The simplicity of this style is great as the empire, and strikes like its own gigantic

---

[22] Aleksandr Vasilyevich Suvorov (1729-1800). Beginning as a private in the army, he ultimately became one of the greatest of all Russian generals. His services in the Seven Years' War, in the rebellion of Pugachev (1773), against the Turks (1774, 1787-1792), and against the Poles (1794) won him the rank of field marshal. His greatest successes, however, were in driving the French from Italy in the War of the Second Coalition (1798-1799).

rocks. Polish it with the refinements of art, and though ornament may be acquired, its sublimity would be lost. Such a mode of speech proves a certain grandeur in the minds of the people. Greatness is perceived at once; and . . . what men easily feel and readily admire, they are not far from imitating. [55-56]

2. THE HARDIHOOD OF THE HORSES

The troops which first strike the eye of a stranger on entering St. Petersburgh, are the Cossacs [Cossacks]; and certainly more curious objects cannot be imagined. Their persons, air, and appointments, and the animals on which they are mounted, seem so totally at variance, that you can hardly suppose a reason for so unequal a union. The men are robust and fit for service: their horses appear completely the reverse: mean in shape, and slouching in motion, every limb speaks of languor, and every moment you expect to see them drop down dead under their heavy burthen: but so false are these shows, that there is not a more hardy animal existing; it will travel incalculable journeys, and remain exposed to the heat or cold, day and night, without manifesting any sense of inconvenience.

These little rugged beasts never, like our *war horses*, know the luxury of a snug stable and a well littered bed, nor ever enjoy the comfort of a currycomb or whisp of straw. Their sustenance is of the most scanty sort; but, in spite of toil and rough fare, they endure all with unabated strength; and are thus, of all animals, the best fitted for a soldier's life. Indeed, when I consider their training, and also that of the Russian soldiers in general, I cannot but prefer the simplicity of their wants to the comparatively luxurious habits of our army. [131-132]

3. THE UTILITY OF THE COSSACK UNIFORMS

Their dress is military and useful; consisting of a close dark blue jacket, and very large full trowsers, under which they wear drawers and boots. Their head is covered with a high black cap of sheepskin: a red bag hangs from its top ornamented with a chain of white worsted lace and tassals: a red stripe, rather broad, runs along the outside of the trowsers, as well as a cord of the same colour around the cape and sleeves. A single row of buttons closes the jacket at the breast. A broad leather belt, containing cartridges, and to which is suspended a light sabre, confines their waists. Their principal weapons are a pike about eight feet long, and a pair of pistols. A black belt crosses their left

shoulder, to which is attached a sort of tin cartouch box, holding ammunition, and surmounted with a ramrod. An uncouth saddle is bound
on the horse, somewhat like a doubled pillow, under which is a square
piece of oil cloth painted in various colours. . . . [133-134] The custom
of loading military uniforms with expensive and needless ornaments
is certainly wearing out, . . . and much rejoiced will every true soldier
be, when he sees the army in general more usefully and less gaudily
appointed. . . . The most soldierlike and serviceable dress I have met
with in any country is that of the Cossacs, for it includes every thing,
(excepting more appropriate arms), which is requisite in cavalry. . . .
[139-140] Some of the men wear moustachios, and some dispense with
that fierce appendage. Such is the dress of one order of the Cossacs.
[134]

4. THE DISCIPLINE OF THE RECRUITS

Recruits . . . are so well and rapidly disciplined by means of the cane,
that the change from a clumsy blundering boor, to that of a neat active
soldier, is generally as instantaneous as that from one of his native
winters to all the beauties of spring. He is brought up from his . . .
village, with his beard and hair in the trim of nature; clad in sheep-
skins, linden shoes, and walking with all the trudging awkwardness
of unrestrained habit. A very short period changes his aspect entirely.
His beard is sheared off, his hair bound into a regular *queue*; and by
way of making it grow in a more martial form, it is shaven from the
forehead over the ears and halfway from the back part of the head. A
regimental greatcoat is put upon his person: he is booted, and set
upright on his legs, at his peril not to lose his position. Thus then he is
metamorphosed, and ere long has all the air of a soldier, completely
getting rid of every relic of what he once had been. [180-181]

5. THE HEROISM OF AUTOMATONS

I am not yet sufficiently intimate with my subject to give you a just
opinion of what may be all the virtues of a Russian soldier. The officers
are in general full of high military honour; and, if we admit obedience
to be the first qualification in the private, and no attempt to argue the
propriety of any order received, to be the second, then certainly the
Russian soldiers possess those excellences in full perfection. Taken
from a state of slavery, they have no idea of acting for themselves when
any of their superiors are by; hence, they are as ready to receive all
outward impressions as a piece of clay in the modeller's hands; and that

the hands of their modellers are not very idle, they daily feel on their heads and shoulders enforced by the cane.

Though humbled, the spirit of this hardy race is not subdued. It shows its latent manly powers in the field against the enemy: for there is not a braver set of men anywhere than the Russian soldiers. The frequent wars between them and the Persians and Turks, who are such fierce combatants, gives them a wild ferocity in action, and accustoms them to the determination never to give way. This temper they carry into other countries, as the campaigns of Suwarroff and Bagration so gloriously testify. [140]

VI · TRAVELING SKETCHES: ST. PETERSBURG TO MOSCOW

I. A TRAVELING CRADLE

The vehicle we purchased for ourselves was a *Kabitka*; a well contrived and snug machine. . . . Its form is simple, being nothing more than a large wooden cradle, fixed on a double keel or skate of the same material, strongly shod with iron. Our trunks were placed at the head and foot; and filling the intermediate space at the bottom with hay, mattrasses, pillows, and other soft accompaniments, we wrapped our persons in pelisses, furred boots, caps, etc. and laying ourselves prostrate, side by side, in the bed we had made, were ready to sally forth in as regular a northern array as any veteran of the Russian winter. . . . We soon arrived at the barrier gate, and producing our credentials to the officer on guard, were allowed honourable passage; and again putting our cattle to their speed, pressed forward towards the next stage with a swiftness incredible. We saw that our horses were like those of the Cossacs, of bad appearance, but radical worth; and reclining in our cradle, committed ourselves to their guidance with feelings of confidence and ease most luxuriously delightful. [142-143]

2. THE ROADSIDE VILLAGES

Most of the villages consist of one street only, pretty wide, presenting to the eye a row of gable ends, resembling the ancient towns in Britain. In the wall, are windows of four panes of glass, with curious carved ornaments a-top; and on their shutters (which open outwards) a variety of flowers, stars, and strange devices are painted in the rudest taste, and often blended with gilding. The national admiration of painting and sculpture is everywhere manifested on the façades of the cottages. The latter is certainly the best executed; and in some of their wild carvings frequently may be discovered the germs of real talent. Every house has a gallery or ballustrading below, besides the roof projecting from the face of the building, to defend its inmates from the sun during summer, and the weather in the severer season. I understand that no habitations are cooler than these during the hot months, nor any warmer through the whole of the cold. A sort of double gate separates each from its neighbour, and leads into a large courtyard filled with sheds, old kabitkas, and other carriages of the country; besides an accumulation of dirt, rotten straw, jaded horses, pigs, and other nuisances; completing a museum of nastiness scarcely to be found in any other civilized spot on the globe. [144]

3. A SNOWSCAPE

No idea can be formed of the immense plains we traversed, unless you imagine yourself at sea, far, far from the sight of land. The Arabian deserts cannot be more awful to the eye, than the appearance of this scene. Such is the general aspect of the country during the rigours of winter; with now and then an exception of a large forest skirting the horizon for a considerable length of way. At intervals, as you shoot along, you see openings amongst its lofty trees, from which emerge picturesque groups of natives and their one-horse sledges, whereon are placed the different articles of commerce, going to various parts of this empire. They travel in vast numbers, and from all quarters, seldom fewer than one hundred and fifty in a string, having a driver to every seventh horse. The effect of this cavalcade at a distance is very curious; and in a morning, as they advance towards you, the scene is as beautiful as striking. The sun then rising, throws his rays across the snow, transforming it to the sight into a surface of diamonds. From the cold of the night, every man and horse is encrusted with these frosty particles; and the beams falling on them too, seem to cover their rude faces and rugged habits with a tissue of the most dazzling brilliants. The manes of the horses, and the long beards of the men, from the quantity of congealed breath, have a particularly glittering effect. [145]

4. A LAUGHABLE SPECTACLE

Our unlucky barouche, after a variety of disasters in its journey, here [at Tver] broke fairly down. . . . After much bungling we at length got the vehicle mounted on its skates; and I inquired of the landlord his demand for the share he had in the repairs; he coolly asked *thirty rubles*! ... At this moment my servant came up. ... He inquired what was the matter. I told him the extortion of the man, and that I wanted to beat him down. "I'll beat him down!" cried he, catching the poor wretch by the beard and laying upon his shoulders, with all his might, an immense bludgeon large enough to be called a club. As the terrified host swung round at the arm's length of my doughty champion, the blows fell like hail upon his back, while he kept bawling out: "twenty, fifteen, ten, etc." till he reduced his demands to the more reasonable sum of two rubles. On this cry, like the last bidding at an auction, the appraiser was satisfied, and the hammer fell. The poor battered wretch was released; and bowing with a grateful air to his chastiser, turned to me. Almost killed with laughing at so extraordinary a sight, I paid him his rubles. I was no less amused at the stupid indifference with which the standers by regarded the whole transaction. ... The bow he made to my triumphant valet entertained me as much as any thing, ... and I was so convulsed with laughter at the oddity of the group they formed, and the whole was performed in so short a time, that I declare I had not power to stir from the spot or speak a word; and so for once allowed the ridiculous to get the better of my humanity. [148-149]

5. A PEASANT INTERIOR

One room is the habitation of all the inmates. ... One quarter of it is occupied by a large stove or peech, flat at the top; on which many of them take their nocturnal rest; and during the day loll over its baking warmth, for hours. ... The apartment I am describing, rendered insufferably stifling by the stove, the breaths, and other fumigations, contained the postmaster, his wife, his mother, his wife's mother, an infant, and two men, apparently attached to the post department, as they wore green uniforms. There were others besides, who being rather withdrawn in a dark corner, we could not distinctly observe.

When we entered, the top of the oven was occupied by the three women and child, almost all in a state of nature. ... A bed with dirty curtains filled one corner of the room; a few benches and a table, completed the furniture. The walls were not quite so barren, being covered with uncouth prints and innumerable daubings. In one spot was placed a picture or effigy of our Saviour and the Virgin, decorated with silver plates. [150]

VII · A STUDY IN CONTRASTS: THE RUSSIAN HOUSEHOLD

I. THE COURTESY OF THE NOBILITY

ON DELIVERING our letters of introduction, we were welcomed with all the courtesies of friendship; and at the first salutation, were made to forget, by the true politeness of this generous people, that we were strangers. I have heard it said that hospitality is a mark of barbarism ... but certainly it had not its foundations at Mosco; for I never saw, in any part of the world, such general polish of manners as in this city. Their hospitality appears to me to arise from a confidence in the friend who gives the introduction that he will not recommend any person unworthy of their notice; not doubting this, their benevolence hesitates not to receive the introduced with kindness; and from their love of society, if he prove agreeable he soon finds himself on the most easy and pleasant terms with a large and elegant acquaintance. [153]

2. THE HONORING OF A HERO

Fortunately for us, our arrival and the Prince Bagration's[23] was nearly at the same time. We received cards from the English club (an association only so in name, not three of our nation belonging to it) inviting us to a dinner which they gave to the Prince in honour of his late gallant conduct with the armies. . . .

Its suite of splendid saloons, and the great marble hall in which dinner was served, were fitted up with the most unsparing magnificence. . . . The dinner was conducted with the nicest decorum; and the healths of the emperor and the Prince Bagration were drunk with the greatest enthusiasm . . . , and more than once it reminded me of similar meetings in honour of our glorious friend and hero, Sir Sidney Smith. Indeed, . . . several of the Russian nobility present asked me if it were not like the *fêtes* we dedicate to our heroes. I acknowledged the resemblance; but inwardly gave them the palm of general politeness; a grace in which this assembly far exceeded ours: I never in my life experienced so much attention as was there paid to us as strangers and Englishmen. [153-154]

[23] Prince Pëtr Ivanovich Bagration (1765-1812) the scion of a noble Georgian family and a disciple of the great Suvorov, under whom he served in his early years. His military daring and great personal courage had a strong appeal, both for Ker Porter and his contemporary, Sir Robert Wilson, who served with him in 1807, at Eylau and Friedland, and in 1812, at Smolensk. He was still adding to an international military reputation when his career was cut short in the same year at Borodino.

3. HARMONY AND DISCORD

Three-quarters of an hour finished the repast. . . . Part of the company withdrew to cards; and part (in which latter choice I united) preferred a saloon, where several vocal and instrumental military bands were stationed. . . . We had also the horn-music; which, as it is strange and curious, I will describe. It was invented by a Prince Gallitzin[24] in the year 1762. This instrument consists of forty persons, whose life is spent blowing one note. The sounds produced are precisely similar to those of an immense organ; . . . the effect possesses much sublimity, when the *performers are unseen*: but when they are visible, it is impossible to silence reflections which jar with their harmony. To see human nature *reduced to such a use*, calls up thoughts very inimical to admiration of strains so awakened. . . . Some of these individuals, thus destined to drag through a melancholy existence, play at different times on several pipes of various sizes which breathe the higher notes. But the bass pipes have each their unchanging blower: they are extremely long, and are laid upon a machine or trussel, close to which the performer stands. . . . The shape is exactly that of a hearing trumpet. . . . The performers are in general thin and pale: and I have little doubt but that the quantity of air the instrument takes, and the practice necessary for perfection in execution, must subtract many years from the otherwise natural term of their lives.

My introduction to Prince Bagration, who is not only one of the first of military heroes, but in his character as a man, is an honour to human nature, brought me to a sight the most degrading to our species. What a difference at once before my eyes! a great warrior, on whom all eyes were fixed with admiration; and a set of poor mechanized wretches, reduced to the level of a child's whistle! [154-156]

4. DWARFS, FOOLS, AND GIANTS

But this was not enough! I was to see the varieties of destiny yet more manifested, in the formation and fortunes of a race of rational beings called dwarfs. They are here the pages and the playthings of the great; and at almost all entertainments stand for hours by their lord's chair, holding his snuff-box, or awaiting his commands. There is scarcely a nobleman in this country who is not possessed of one or more of these frisks [freaks] of nature. . . .

[24] Probably Prince Dmitri Alekseevich Golitsyn (1738-1803), an ambassador to France and the Hague, as well as the author of several scientific treatises.

Besides these lilliputians, many of the nobility keep a fool or two, like the *motleys* of our court in the days of Elizabeth; but like in name only: for their wit, if they ever had any, is swallowed up by indolence. Savoury sauce and rich repasts swell their bodies to the most disgusting size; and lying about in the corners of some splendid saloon, they sleep profoundly, till awakened by the command of their lord to amuse the company. Shaking their enormous bulk they rise from their trance, and supporting their unwieldy trunks against the wall, drawl out their heavy nonsense, with as much grace as the motions of a sloth in the hands of a reptile fancier. One glance was sufficient for me of these imbruted creatures; and, with something like pleasure, I turned from them to the less humiliating view of human nature in the dwarf. . . .

Giants are also in request here: but they are not very numerous; and in stature fall far short of those which occasionally visit England from her sister island. . . . I assure you, the sight of a couple of these giants standing within the superb hall of a Russian nobleman, and the oddly caparisoned dwarfs, ushering you to the presence of their lord, would not a little strike you with its resemblance to a scene in romance. . . . [156-159]

5. THE RUSSIAN HOUSEHOLD: A BRITISH VIEW

Indeed, there are many sights exhibited in this country very strange to a British eye; and none more so to me than when I look from the great Russian noble in all the power of wealth, to the poor vassal in his train; who has not even an hour's liberty at his own command. Although I have been in this part of the world upwards of six months, I cannot yet prevail on myself to consider the Russian servant like the helots of the Spartans, as of a species so different from their masters, that to treat them like a horse or any other useful animal, is to pay them respect enough. There is something in the air of Britain which infuses into the generality of her sons as great a repugnance to make a slave, as to be one. Blessed, then, be the land of liberty! for it dispenses the good it enjoys, and by leaving every man free, allows him the rank in creation nature intended. Genius, industry, virtue, all find their proper spheres: and easily pass from the lower stations, into which accident might have placed them, to regions better calculated for the exercise of their powers. [175]

6. THE RUSSIAN HOUSEHOLD: A ROMANTIC VIEW

The houses of the nobility are filled with these vassals, or servants, both male and female, who line the halls, passages, and entrances of the rooms in splendid liveries. In almost every antichamber some of these domestics are placed, ready to obey the commands of their lord or his guests; and continually your ears are saluted with the theatrical call of "Who waits?" when two or three run in at the instant, as promptly as I ever saw the gentlemen-in-waiting answer the like summons from the boards of Drury-Lane or Covent-Garden. What with the dwarf pages, fools, numerous attendants, and customs of hospitality practised here, I cannot but be struck with its resemblance to the establishments of our old English barons; and sometimes almost fancy myself transported back to the feudal days of Britain. You, who are as romantic as myself in these particulars, can easily understand how these antiquated usages affect my imagination and set it to work: and indeed I find it no unamusing train of thought to pursue the progress of different nations through various stages of civilization, till I can with ease point out the periods in each when their customs and manners have exactly paralleled. Thus the present manners of some countries are only correspondent with what were the manners of a neighbouring nation a century ago. And so I go on, when I have nothing else to do, making the world pass before me, as we whirl about its effigy on a globe, with our finger. [175-176]

VIII · THE LIFE OF THE PEASANTS

I. FATHERS AND SONS

THESE people are particularly fond of children; a proof, I think, of the natural goodness of their hearts. You will more frequently see the men, when returning from toil, taking their infants in their arms and caressing them, than seeking the company of their wives. . . .

But while I am on the subject, I cannot omit mentioning a strange custom which they have amongst them; one very repugnant to nature, and to British feelings even shocking to think on. Fathers marry their sons to some blooming girl in the village at a very early age, and then send the young men either to Mosco or St. Petersburgh to seek employment, leaving their brides a few days after their marriage to the care of their parents. At the expiration of some years, when the son returns to his cottage, he finds himself the nominal father of several children, the offspring of his own parent! who had deemed it his duty thus to supply the place of a husband to the young wife. This is done all over Russia, and is never considered a hardship by the parties. . . . When the son becomes a resident in his native village, if he have a numerous stock thus raised to him, he marries them off, sends them a packing; and then enjoys himself, like a Turk in his seraglio. . . .

As it is the interest of the owner of slaves to increase their population, it is also to his advantage to allow of the emigration of the young men to the cities as much as possible; for, as he receives an annual pecuniary acknowledgement from all who leave his village to pursue their own plans, in proportion as they amass money, he may raise the rent they pay him for themselves; and so improve his revenue by their fortune. On these grounds, I suppose the horrid practice I have just mentioned, is permitted to pass uncensured. The nobleman finds his lands stocked with a growing generation of slaves, and he cares not by what means they were planted. This absorbing passion of self-interest, how does it possess the whole world; how does it even alloy natures which otherwise might not be far from heaven! [234-235]

2. MASTERS AND PEASANTS

That the Russian peasantry and servants are slaves, does not imply that their owners are tyrants. In most cases their comforts are very properly attended to; and cruelty or oppression is very seldom suffered to embitter their existence. You never hear them complain; and in fact they rarely have any cause of complaint; for, perfectly ignorant of the advantages of liberty, they desire it not; are quite content to be considered as much their master's property as his ox or his ass, provided they be foddered or fed as well. . . .[25]

Frequent instances have been mentioned to me of the cruelty with which some owners treat this unfortunate race. But I always found the anecdotes thus related were of very old date; and if not exaggerated,

[25] Lady Craven had assumed a similarly haughty and aristocratic tone on the peasant question, even prior to the French Revolution. In 1786, she had written: "It might appear to English minds, that a people who are in a manner the property of their lord suffer many of the afflictions that attend slavery; but the very circumstance of their persons being the property insures them the indulgence of their master for the preservation of their lives; and that master stands between them and the power of a despotic government and a brutal soldiery. Besides, my dear sir, the invaluable advantage which these peasants have, as in paying annually a very small sum each and cultivating as many acres of land as he thinks fit, his fortune depends entirely on his own industry. . . . If his lord would raise this tax too high, or make their vassals suffer, misery and desertion would ruin his fortune, not theirs. . . . It is very amusing to me to reflect, without prejudices of any kind, upon the ridiculous ideas of liberty and property that our English common people have. . . ." Such remarks as these illustrate the extent of the misconceptions to which tourists of the noble salons exposed themselves. Elizabeth Craven, *A Journey through the Crimea to Constantinople*, London, 1789, pp. 141-142.

time has so altered the minds of the Russians, that such barbarities very seldom, if ever, now occur.

The boors are all slaves. Each estate has its native boors by hundreds, who perform all its agricultural duties. They are extremely industrious; and when under a good owner, daily improve and become more valuable. Their attachment to their lord, when well treated, is generally as warm, as their enmity on the reverse. Indeed, I was told the other day of a gentleman, who, possessed of a large village with its inhabitants, and wanting money, was going to sell it and them. His slaves, who loved him, hearing of this intended transfer of them to some new, and perhaps less amiable proprietor, went in a body to him, and offered to collect amongst themselves all the little savings their labours had amassed; and if the sum were inadequate to supply the deficiency, several volunteered to be sold, if he would but consent still to remain master of the village. Happy was this man's temporary poverty, since it showed him his own worth, and proved to him the virtue of his slaves. From that day he must have considered them rather as his sons. . . .
[175-177] There exists an old law, happily now absolute, which empowered the proprietor of a slave, not only to receive his yearly rent, but on any pretence, to seize the harvest of his industry. Such is not tolerated now: on the reverse, a part of the hard earned riches of the serf is appropriated to purchase his freedom. Many of these industrious vassals are possessed of wealth to the amount of £30,000, and sometimes more.[26] [235]

3. THE FRUITS OF IGNORANCE: INJUSTICE

Uncultivated minds having nothing to restrain their passions, these ill starred men are very vehement in their hatred;[27] and sometimes,

[26] Ker Porter may have gained this impression either from the same source as John Carr, or directly from the latter's book, which he had read. In any case, Carr reported that "I one day saw a Russian, distinguished only from the commonest sort by the superiority of the cloth of his long coat, who had paid fifteen thousand pounds for his freedom, and had amassed by indefatigable industry, a fortune of one hundred thousand pounds; and not far from my hotel resided a Russian who, in the short space of twelve years, with a fair character, had amassed nearly a million sterling." John Carr, *Northern Summer*, Philadelphia, 1805, p. 164.

[27] Carr's far more sympathetic picture of the Russian peasant errs, perhaps, on the other side. "Amidst all the oppression that weighs him down to the earth, that half associates him with the rugged bear of his forest; and taught, as he is, that this condition can never know amelioration, this poor slave of the north has displayed the most heroic valour in the field, and the most gentle moderation in success, and the mildest unrepining philosophy in suffering. . . . No one who has remarked the Russian with candour, who judges from what he sees, and not from what he has heard or read, will hesitate to pronounce him one of the best tempered creatures in the creation. He will bear the curse and scorn and, frequently the blows of his superior, with mildness. Revenge, almost sanctioned by insults, never maddens his blood. . . ." *ibid.*, p. 166.

though seldom, they have no little provocation. When their owner exacts from them the produce of their earnings, after having perhaps received from them an exorbitant sum for allowing them to work at their respective trades, then, very frequently, they are wrought up to such resentment as to form formidable conspiracies against the life of their oppressor. One instance I can give you, which happened a few months ago. A gentleman having by some severities disobliged his slaves, they laid hold of him, and threw him into a large boiler of hot spirits in one of his own distilling houses. He was not discovered for some days. . . . [177]

These clowns are very summary in their resentments, clubbing all of a family together; if a father offends, so does the son; if a servant, so does his master, and so on: no individual bears the weight of his own follies, but all who happen to be in his company share the burthen. Another effect of complete ignorance, is this indiscrimination and injustice. [261]

4. THE FRUITS OF IGNORANCE: GREED

The eagerness with which gold was received as an equivalent for a whole skin, will show you the passion of the lower order of Russians for money. Indeed, when we consider the hardness of their fare, the ruggedness of their apparel, and the baseness of their abodes; and that these are the utmost of their ideas of actual enjoyment, is not their insatiable avidity inexplicable? Here and there we see a monster in nature who loves gold for its own sake: but in general the most avaricious have a further end in view, some particular pleasure to which they intend to devote their wealth. Contrary to this, with the Russian boor, it is a passion for which I cannot account; and rather seems a sort of wish imbibed originally, by imitation, in the cities; thence brought to the country, and so spread like an infection amongst the people, filling them with an aimless desire. For surely, to wish for gold for no other end but to possess it, is the most aimless, useless, joyless longing that ever occupied the breast of man. A Russian peasant will do any-thing, suffer any thing for money. [262]

IX · A STUDY IN CONTRASTS: THE SEASONS

I. THE ETHEREAL ELIXIR

THE CLIMATE of the old capital is even more salubrious than the new. Being situated on high grounds, it has a great advantage. Two fine rivers run through its centre. The streets are all so spacious that no foul air can stagnate in any one of them. The atmosphere is generally clear, and the weather settled. In summer, though it is hot, there are no noxious vapours to render it dangerous; and in winter the air is so pure, so bright and exhilarating, that you seem to inhale the very elixir of life into your lungs. It is impossible to describe the animating feelings which these ethereal breathings excite in the breast: and, as the bath of ether, through which we move, embraces every part, it seems to brace each nerve, and fill us with a spring of life enchanting and exhaustless. [200]

2. THE SUBTERRANEAN CLIMATES

I dined yesterday . . . and partook of a repast, which, at this sterile season of the year, teemed with all the luxuries of spring and autumn: fruits of every climate, ripened in hothouses; and vegetables of all descriptions raised in cellars.[28] A strange place, you will think, for the exercise of horticulture! But so it is; and by the exclusion of the cold air, and the admission of heat from the stoves, these subterraneous gardens produce summer vegetables all the year round. Green peas and asparagus are here as common at christmas, as potatoes and winter cabbages may be with you.

[28] Martha Wilmot, who, with her sister, enjoyed the same luxuries and even attended many of the same parties as Ker Porter, was equally struck by Russian ingenuity, but, unlike him, probed into its social origins: "We have been leading a very dissipated life. Balls without end; dinners that end after four hours' uninterrupted cramming of every delicacy that nature and art can produce—grapes freshly gathered, pine apples ditto, asparagus ditto, besides fruit, preserved with such care that there is a stout battle between nature and the cook for which is genuine. . . . I forgot to mention oranges which are at this moment clustering on thousands of orange trees in different parts of Moscow. Roses too are blooming in the midst of the sharpest degrees of cold; and even I have in my room this moment hyacinths of such beauty and fragrance as is really astonishing. 'Tis only a proof however that things are valued according to the difficulty of procuring them and not their intrinsic merit, for . . . they toil and moil here and at length laugh at all difficultys which oppose them. As a national trait I am told there is a proverb, to express the folly of supposing anything impossible; and it is very true that as the whym of the master is the law of the slave . . . the latter does not know (to all appearance at least) what inclination means, but does everything he is desired. . . . Nature has given them uncommon quickness, but perhaps 'tis to the caprice of their masters they owe their versatility of genius." Londonderry and Hyde, *op. cit.*, p. 75.

Indeed the Russians are very much indebted to the fostering care of our mother earth; for in her bosom do they also treasure the ice which, during the hot months, is used to cool their feverish bloods. In no country, not even Italy, can this attemperating substance be consumed in greater quantities. It is put down into the vaults appointed for its reception every year in such vast shoals, that, I am told, from the continual replenishing, (and using that first which lies a top, and consequently, the latest deposited,) there is ice in some of the cellars in Mosco, which has lain at their bottoms for nearly a century. . . .

Hence you see, between vegetables and ice, the two seasons (thus imprisoned during their own proper reigns, to break forth and invade each other's rights) occupy almost as great an extent of building underground as the city possesses above. [268]

3. THE BEAUTIES OF WINTER

I ascended the tower of the church of Ivan the Great, which commands a view of the whole surrounding plain. Although the monotonous paleness of winter then shrouded its bosom, yet the *coup-d'oeil* was transcendently magnificent. The sun shone with unattempered splendor through an atmosphere, whose clearness cannot be conceived in England; the variegated colours on the tops of innumerable buildings; the sparkling particles of snow on the earth and palaces; the fanes and crescents of the churches flashing their blazing gold; and, added to all, the busy world beneath, passing and repassing in their superb dresses and decorated sledges, presented such a scene of beauty and grandeur, that I should have thought myself repaid for my disagreeable journey, had I even been obliged to return to St. Petersburgh immediately, in beholding so glorious a view. [161-162]

4. THE TERRORS OF SPRING

It is now upwards of six weeks since I arrived in this city; a month of which was passed under all the rigours of winter, when the snow lay four feet deep in many of the streets, and the long lines of the frozen rivers, and the surrounding country, were covered with the same deathly garb. But in a moment, as if by an act of an enchanter's wand, a universal thaw dissolved the whole. Thousands of boors were seen breaking up with their hatchets the large masses of dissolving ice, and carrying it in their single horse sledges to the river, the sooner to make the ways passable, and rid them of their winter *shoub*.

During this operation, the road became extremely bad, having unavoidably, till all was cleared off, at different intervals, holes of a great depth, to the imminent peril of the passenger, whether in carriage or *en traineau*. Walking, at this season, is deemed a disgrace: and it is very well that prejudice sets so firmly against any attempt to change the mode, as it would be dangerous in the extreme: its inconveniencies could hardly be balanced. In the first place, to prevent the inveterate penetration of the snow water you must swathe your feet and legs in bandages of a hundred folds; and then thrust them into huge machines of most uncouth Russian materials, before you durst venture to set one foot to the ground in such a toe-destroying element. Common leather boots would be as mere blotting paper, and soak through in an instant. Then imagine all the muddy embroidery, which would skirt your pelisse even to the middle of your back, where the melting snows from the neighbouring houses, would greet it, like the meeting waters in Noah's flood. If you walk near the sides of the houses (the most eligible place in England), your death is threatened every moment. Here, during the long winter, the icicles accumulate to such a number and size, and hang in such a tremendous fringe from the eaves, that their appearance alone is sufficient to intimidate the boldest pedestrian. And yet some have been so rash that I have heard of frequent instances of persons passing under them at the commencement of the thaw, who, by the falling of these immense masses were crushed to pieces. . . . The snow is not only annoying, but equally perilous with the ice; and, as it slides by degrees to the bend of the roof, in some unexpected moment is precipitated in a sort of *avalanche* into the street below. I saw three natives, who were trudging by at the instant of a *chute de neige*, all embowelled at once. A considerable time was spent in digging them out, when they were brought forth, to a miracle alive, but much hurt.

It is a very amazing spectacle to observe how rapidly this frigid covering vanishes, and how soon the smiling face of spring appears. In one day the Moskva became liquid, and no trace of winter remained on its waters, except where floating masses of ice, and the fragments of dismantled cottages rolling down its current, reminding you of the yet recent devastations of its departing wrath. The disunited snows from the higher lands usually come down into the lower in such quantity and with such violence, that cattle, men, and often whole villages are swept away. The rivers receive the dreadful deposit: and thus, on the banks of the Moskva, at the moment when spring promises every vernal joy, you behold the wrecks of devastation, the memorials of a mischief and misery incalculable.

A great part of the city lying very low was for several days under water; but now all is cleared, and the trees are ready to bloom. It is hardly eight days since the thaw began, and there is scarcely a particle of snow to be found. What a fortnight ago was a dreary plain of ice, is now robed in verdure, and animated with budding trees and shrubs. The whole aspect of the city is so changed, that no one who did not witness the moment of alteration could believe it to be the same place. Mosco in summer and Mosco in winter has as much resemblance, as a butterfly to its chrysalis. [164-166]

X · MOSCOW: THE CARNIVAL CITY

1. A CITY OF MANY MANSIONS

AT PRESENT, it is like a world of palaces collected together: and really the idea given of it by Joseph the Second of Austria, who paid it a visit, is a better picture than I can draw. "Here, (said he) have all the chief lords of the empire set themselves down, surrounded each by his village, his church, and his vassals." The description is just; for it is not a city of houses in mere rank and file of streets, but rather a collection of mansions, each embosomed amidst its own lawns, gardens, pleasure grounds, and the dwellings of its necessary slaves. Some of the most ancient princes of the empire have very splendid palaces in Mosco, ornamented with basso relievo, gilding, and every Asiatic decoration. Indeed, this is a favourite residence with almost all the Russian nobility who have not employments at court or in the government.[29] [166]

[29] Catherine Wilmot contrasted the idyllic atmosphere of Moscow with the power and brilliance of St. Petersburg in a beautiful description with a somewhat different emphasis: "Moscow is the imperial terrestrial political Elysium of Russia. All those whose power existed in the reign of Catherine and of Paul and all those who are discarded or conceiv'd to be superannuated by Alexander hold an ideal consequence awarded by courtesy alone in this lazy, idle, magnificent, and Asiatic town, for all the effective power has long since pass'd as an inheritance to their successors who rule the imperial realm at Petersburg and flutter away their hours about the Court. Nevertheless, the ruffled decorated phantom of Prince Gallitzen [Galitsyn], Grand Chamberlain in the time of Catherine retains its orders, its stars, and its ribbons, which, added to the weight of four score years and ten, bends it double to the ground. It wears its key of diamonds, its bay and embroidery, and all its glittering baubles on its bones, and receives the homage of its brother ghosts who in former days shared with it the honors of state! . . . In short, the grandees—and in this circle, alas, we only move,—are, as I said before, of another world, and yet the same important gossip of court folly, the same vanity, the same puff'd up pride, the same ostentation sways them and creates their happiness and unhappiness, as if the grave did not yawn beneath their tottering feet to menace them, as it hourly does, with an earthly oblivion of their brocaded existence." *ibid.*, pp. 213-214.

INSIDE A RUSSIAN POSTHOUSE: SKETCH BY KER PORTER

MOSCOW: SKETCH BY KER PORTER

2. A ROUND OF PLEASURE

Owing to the peculiar circumstances of the inhabitants of this town, pleasure is ever the order of the day: it holds a continual carnival, where balls, private theatres, masquerades, and assemblies of all sorts, for ever vary the scene. . . .

Before I came into this country, I was led to believe that I should find the morals on a par with France. To me it seems totally the reverse. I never saw married people more happy, or apparently more affectionate towards each other: I never, in any country, met with young women more amiable and virtuous. Every country has its *mauvais sujets*! And anciently, as an unlimited license to pleasure was given here, and exampled by those high in influence, it might be supposed that the seeds of libertinism, once sown in a nation, could never be eradicated; but it grew so rank during its short season, that I believe all is exhausted, and that the last generation carried with them into the other world not only the fruits but the roots of their cultivation. In short, it appears from what I have hitherto been able to judge, that for a city, whose sole object is pleasure, Mosco possesses less of what is called fashionable vice, than may be found in countries where more seeming austerity is practised. [167-168]

3. THE PROMENADE À LA NOBLESSE

The Russians also are particularly fond of pleasures out of doors. Their cavalcades, promenades, and *fêtes champêtres* in the summer; and sledging parties in the winter, are not a little friendly to hilarity and health. A thousand gay excuses are formed to take them into the air; and so, for once, fashion is favourable to the wholesome. . . . [205]

The grounds around the mansions of the nobility afford romantic and charming morning walks. But their favourite amusement, is what they call the *promenade*. It consists of all the carriages in the city, perhaps to the number of seven thousand, trailing after each other in regal procession, through fixed parts of the town and its environs. The insides of these vehicles are filled with all the beauty and splendor of Mosco: and in my life I never beheld so many lovely women at one time.

The superiority of this metropolis over that of St. Petersburgh, in the general beauty of the females, is beyond comparison. Perhaps this may be accounted for, from the intermarriages of the noble families with those of countries celebrated for symmetry of features and graceful forms: namely, Circassia, Georgia, and Poland. The young ladies dress in rather the Parisian mode, but much improved by their own native taste. . . .

Were such a concourse of carriages to assemble in our island, as here meet on the banks of the Moskva, fractured poles, broken sides, and maimed coachmen, footmen, etc. would be the certain consequences; but a most admirable police is instituted . . . to prevent all confusion and disaster. This authority is invested in a detachment of soldiers, who having an imperious command over the procession, not only add to its magnificence but insure its safety. [167-168]

4. THE PROMENADE À LA BOURGEOISIE

On my return through the walks of these beautiful gardens, I found them filled with crowds of pedestrians of every description, (twice a week it being a fixed *promenade*); those which most forcibly attract the notice of a stranger are the wives of the native merchants. They are dressed in all the riches their husbands can afford, in a fashion, hot, stiff, and most discordant with their figures. . . . Every point about these dames is the opposite of beauty. Their eyes are tolerable, but totally divested of expression. Their complexions are besmeared with white and red paint, and their teeth most perversely stained with black; not a muscle of their face ever moves; and in general their usual attitude being stationary (hardly ever walking) with their hands knit together across their persons, they stand like a string of waxen figures, gazing on the passing groups of the higher orders. [183]

5. AN UNINSPIRED SPORT

One amusement I must not omit noticing, which they call coursing. In my mind, when managed with even the most plausible address, it can never be a humane pastime; and as it is ordered here it is a cruel one. With us it has an apology in the health produced by its attendant exercise, and the delights of a pleasurable suspense. But here the recreation is so simplified, that it hardly seems to contain any thing, but the murder of the animal. In England we have the social anxiety of beating an interesting and extensive country, and of following the game, when sprung, for several hours, in swift and jocund pursuit. The attention kept awake, the spirits exhilarated, and life imbibed in every coming gale, give an intoxication to the senses which may very readily make the huntsman forget the sufferings of the chase. But here all is the reverse. . . .

A concourse of people of all ranks was assembled, with about a hundred and twenty greyhounds. . . . On the same spot where the group had met, were boxes placed at certain distances, each containing a hare. . . . At an appointed moment the *amateur*, to whom the dogs belonged, and for whose entertainment this lively and humane pastime was prepared, gave the word! when suddenly one of the little creatures was let loose from its prison. . . . Of course the chase was very brief. The terrified animal was soon overtaken, and after a few doubles the canine pair buried their teeth in the heart of the panting fugitive. . . .

The promoter of the diversion did not seem to enjoy it greatly, and as small a degree of animation appeared in the faces of the spectators. Indeed, from what I have seen of this amusement, as well as of Russian horse-racing, I must suppose that the habits of this country are inimical to the activity of blood which rushes through the veins of an English hunter, shooter, or racer. Our early education to exercise of all sorts gives a stimulus to mind and body that impels Englishmen to undertake every enterprise with intrepidity, and confirms them to pursue it with an undaunted resolution to overcome. The severity of the Russian winter is sufficient excuse for the want I observed: an iron frost, with the threatened loss of toes or fingers, being no very attractive season for the sportsman to take the field. The extreme heat of summer is equally a foe to vigorous exercise which such amusements demand; and as for the temperate days of spring and autumn, they know them not. [205-207]

XI · TRAVELING SKETCHES: MOSCOW TO ST. PETERSBURG

I. A SCORCHING PLAIN

I TRAVELED this very road but a few months ago. In vain I now look round to recognise any object of my former observations: it seems totally a new scene. When I last beheld it, it was covered with snow; now, all is one wide stretch of green landscape. The one showed Winter in his direst reign; the other Summer, though I am sorry to say, not in her sweetest charms. All is flat and uninteresting. The villages boast no little spots cultivated with Swiss beauty and comfort. No tree, or creeping tendril grows near the doors and windows of these habitations. The russet cottages of England, overgrown with the blushing rose and fragrant honey-suckle; their pretty gardens, and domesticated animals, all are wanting here. The absence of the snow, and the unveiling of the grass, seem the only marks that winter has disappeared: at least the only pleasing assurance, for as to disagreeable proofs, in the forms of heat and dust, we have enough of them. A burning sun continually over our heads, scorching our very souls; and the dust, by way of soothing our pride, while it torments our skin, eyes, and lungs, makes us, like so many Eneases, always move in a cloud! [233]

2. A WATERY INTERLUDE

Amongst our scanty complement of entertainment . . . , the canal and falls of Borovitsky [Borovichi] struck across our recollection. . . . At Vislina Valochock [Vyshniy-Volochok] the canal is first descried, laden with vessels full of productions from the interior; human industry having here united the river Twertza [Tvertsa] with the Meutza [now called Tsna]; connecting . . . the Caspian with the Baltic Sea. We inquired whether there were any barks collected at the falls, in one of which we might descend; and being answered in the affirmative, we hired horses to take us to these torrents. . . .

We found numbers of craft on the eve of going down, and placing ourselves in one of them, soon entered on the descent, which was by no means tremendous, although the rapidity of the motion was surprising. This torrent is a long inclining surface of water of about thirty versts; and to give you an idea of the velocity with which the barks moved, we went twenty-five versts in three quarters of an hour. The most alarming circumstances in the exploit, is to see the constant changes the vessels make in their shapes from the violence of the waters. They bend like paper, and are so admirably constructed, as to take the undulating form of the rising wave. Were they of firmer texture they must inevitably be dashed to pieces. As it is, they bound like a feather on the water, and are carried by its impetuosity safely to the bottom of the fall. [236]

3. AN ENCHANTED EVENING

I found the city, on this my second entrance, rather to lose in comparison with the brilliant and festive Mosco. The summer had robbed it also of its principal inhabitants . . . , but as a kind of fairy favour, the *name-day* of the empress dowager came its annual round, and promised us some gay hours in those dedicated to its celebration. . . . The palace of Peterhoff and its gardens were to be the scene of the empress's *fête*. Vast crowds flocked towards the capital to witness the ceremony; and many thousands of all descriptions assembled in the gardens. The common people, by a gracious condescension of the imperial family, are admitted to a certain length, to share in all the grand festivities. And while the multitude thus roamed about, enjoying, in their minds, a paradise on earth, the court remained within the palace, amusing themselves from the windows with the passing groups. Everything around spoke the magnificence of the hand that designed the whole. Nothing could surpass the illuminations. Walks of not less than five or six miles, in various directions, bordered by fine trees, and carpeted with flowers of every hue and fragrance, were fantastically and brilliantly hung with millions of lamps. Temples blazing in light, as if constructed of myriads of precious stones, rubies, sapphires, topazes, and emeralds, darted their prismatic beams from a hundred openings in the shade.

Fountains, not to be equaled but at Versailles, played in every part of the gardens; throwing up their waters to an amazing height, and receiving them again, in basons of white marble decorated with gilded statues of the gods and water nymphs, whose bodies glittered through this shower of falling diamonds, like the lustrous forms of Amphitrite and her train. . . . In front of the palace a rapid torrent rolled down a flight of high granite steps. Having rows of lamps placed at the base of each, the rushing stream sparkled as it fled over the radiant platform; producing an admirable and marvellous effect, from the tremulous velocity of the water. In short, it appeared a work of enchantment; being more like a cataract of the brightest flame, than a fall of the colder element.

Light was here lavished; above, around, below, all was one continued blaze: for the numerous lakes in the grounds, reflecting the constellation of lamps, so bewildered the sight, that every step towards their margin seemed to announce a burning abyss. . . .

From the day having been previously rainy, and continuing cloudy, the night was extremely dark, which gloom, instead of being an inconvenience, gave more effect to the splendor of the scene; producing, to people who viewed it from a distance, the appearance of the conflagration of a great city. [241-243]

XII · DEPARTURE

I. THE COMMERCIAL SEPARATION

I FOUND our new ambassador the marquis of Douglas; and a political scene, somewhat different from that of Mosco. . . . The treaty of commerce with England had expired; and no hopes were entertained of its being renewed. . . . Nothing satisfactory on this head could be obtained. And indeed it is hardly to be expected that the leaders of the Russian commercial department, having learned the value of their own commerce, and the manner of carrying it on; will again put such advantages out of their own hands. The native merchants have been our apprentices for near three hundred years; so we must not be surprised they should now wish to set up for themselves, and reap the fruits of their own vineyard. To encourage them, is the interest of the nobles, whose vassals they in general are; and to see them prosperous is the delight of the monarch: for, considering himself the father of all his people, the happiness of the lower ranks is not less his object than that of the higher. And to show the trading part of his subjects the respect in which they should in future be held, a little while ago he gave them a magnificent dinner, at which he presided in person. . . . At present, the two great civic aims of this august monarch, are, to give gradual freedom to the vassals of the empire; and to establish its commerce on a wide and firm foundation. None can contemplate these projects without admiring the patriotic Alexander; and congratulating the people who are so happy as to be under his sway. [290-291]

2. THE POLITICAL RUPTURE

October: The battle of Friedland has been lost, the Treaty of Tilsit signed, and the whole face of affairs entirely changed. I could hardly believe that I am awake, did I not feel in every nerve the alteration which stabs my happiness. I see two countries that I love, on the point of variance: I see more in prospect than my heart at present can bear to dwell on. . . .

My lord Gower (having succeeded the marquis of Douglas) . . . received a note from the government, intimating, that as a British ambassador he was no longer necessary at the court of St. Petersburgh. Every thing is now preparing for his departure; and consequently, as the French interest is gaining ground, the British declines. All of our nation are eager to leave the country. Changed indeed is the face of things! But as it is the general idea that the new amity cannot last, and as abiding in the empire, under my peculiar circumstances, would militate against my feelings as an Englishman, who considers the duties he owes his king, and his own character as a loyal Briton, as paramount to all other interests; I shall make the earliest application for my passports. [293-294]

3. THE LEAVE-TAKING

My pictures I had finished. They were deposited in the hermitage with that of Peter the Great; and I now only waited for my passport to carry me across the frontiers into Sweden. . . .

The passport was sent to me. All was now closed with me in Russia, except to take my leave of the imperial head of the court in which I had experienced so much kindness. I was received with a condescension that redoubled my every hope; and as I received the most gratifying marks of the amiable Alexander's approbation, and interest in my fate; I withdrew from his presence with sentiments of never dying respect and gratitude, and with the dear conviction that "it would not be long before peace would reunite the two countries, and bring me back to Russia and to happiness!"

That night I slept not. I passed it in the saloons of some of my best friends; and freighted with many a gentle sigh to distant England, I parted from some. But from others, than *friendship dearer*! their tears are yet upon my cheek: and the blessings of those whom heaven, by age, seems particularly to have consecrated to itself, still dwell on my head; and, I trust were not breathed in vain.

The tenth of December, five in the morning! Remember that this day is the most fearful of his life to thy fortune-persecuted friend. [296]

CHAPTER SEVEN

Sir Robert Thomas Wilson

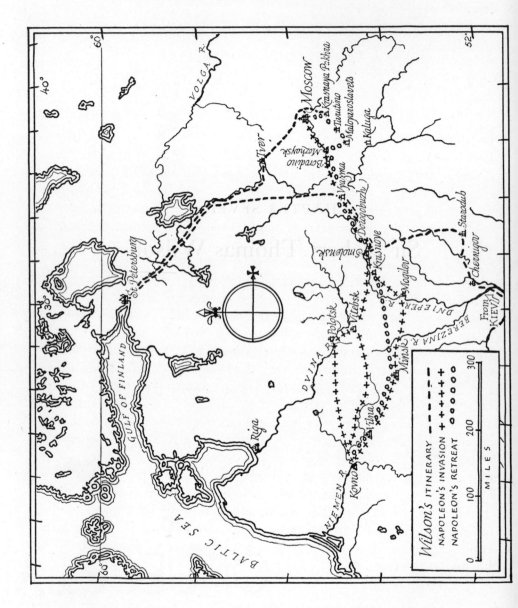

Wilson's Itinerary – – – –

Napoleon's Invasion + + + +

Napoleon's Retreat o o o o

MILES

0   100   200   300

Sir Robert Thomas Wilson:

CAVALIER OF CATACLYSM

(1812)

Of all the travelers dealt with in these pages, it is Brigadier General Sir Robert Thomas Wilson whose life story most easily lends itself to the language of romance. The grandson of a Leeds wool merchant, he was created a baron of the Holy Roman Empire and honored with the decorations of no less than six European monarchs. Orphaned by both parents when only twelve years of age, he lived to win an international reputation and the friendship of kings and emperors. During twenty years' service against the armies of the French Revolution, he campaigned from the Cape of Good Hope to the plains of Castile and from the burning sands of Egypt to the frozen snows of Russia. Having played to the hilt a role as the inveterate enemy of the Corsican tyrant, he quixotically assisted a leading Bonapartist, the Count de La Valette, to escape from Bourbon justice and was himself plunged into a dungeon of La Force by the authority of that very monarch for whose restoration he had so long been crusading. Having attained the height of his fame and popularity, he was disgraced and dismissed from the army by an order of George IV in 1821, yet managed to ride out the storm and vindicate his liberal principles as a member of the Reform Parliament of 1832. The child of a revolutionary era, he was nursed on the violence of a quarter of a century, whilst clinging to the chivalric ideals of a bygone age. As a contemporary said of him: "It is a pity Walter Scott does not know him, for with a tartan and a claymore he would make an admirable character for one of the novels, though his wild, romantic, enthusiastic, and chivalrous notions would be considered as out of real life and exaggerated."[1]

This romantic adventurer was born in London on August 17, 1777,[2]

[1] Henry Edward Fox, *Journal of the Hon. Henry Edward Fox, 1818-1830*, edited by the Earl of Ilchester, London, 1923, pp. 50-51.

[2] The great bulk of the biographical data has been derived from two biographies: Giovanni Costigan, *Sir Robert Wilson: A Soldier of Fortune in the Napoleonic Wars*, Madison, Wisconsin, 1932, and Herbert Randolph, ed., *Life of General Sir Robert Wilson*, 2 vols., London, 1862, which includes extensive quotation from Wilson's journals, memoirs, and correspondence.

as the fourth and favorite child of Benjamin Wilson, who, in addition to his success as a painter and the portraitist of such notables as the Duke of York, Lord Chesterfield, and David Garrick, enjoyed a considerable reputation as an amateur scientist. Had he lived, the old man might, perhaps, have instilled in his son the same cold calculating temper with which he had fashioned a successful career from the humblest origins. His death in 1788, followed, less than two years later, by that of his widow, placed young Robert in the care of quite a different sort of man. His uncle and guardian, William Bosville, distrusted the educational properties of the contemporary public schools and insisted on withdrawing the lad from Winchester and placing him under the care of a private tutor. At his uncle's house, he was exposed to influences which did much to shape his later career, for Bosville was a confirmed member of the opposition party, and he frequently entertained such prominent Whigs as Fox, Grey, Sheridan, Burdett, and the notorious pamphleteer of the American Revolution, Thomas Paine. As Wilson later remarked, his uncle's table at the Piazza Coffee House was a "hotbed for a young mind, and the passing events of the day were impressed on my attention, as I was appointed by the social meeting reader of the evening paper, the *Courier*, which, during the first part of the revolution, teemed daily with important news of what was passing in Paris, bulletins from the armies, etc."[3] It was this period which engraved on Wilson's mind those Whig principles which later impeded his professional advancement under a Tory ministry, and it is a strange paradox that it was ended by his decision to embark upon a career which was ultimately to devote more than twenty years to fighting that very revolution which at bottom it taught him to admire.

In 1794, fretted by the confinement of Bosville's wardship and fired by the call of adventure across the channel, the youth, not yet turned seventeen, saw an opportunity for escape in the military expedition of the Duke of York to Flanders. Relying on the court connections of his dead father, and abetted by the extraordinary personal magnetism he himself possessed, young Robert requested and received a commission as a cornet in the 15th Light Dragoons and joined his regiment in the spring of the year. His conduct and experience during this first terrible campaign were prophetic of his later career in several ways. Within less than a month of his arrival on the continent, he had displayed that impetuous courage, which was to be the admiration of an international

[3] Randolph, *op. cit.*, 1, 58.

acquaintance, by taking part in a daring cavalry charge later credited with saving the Emperor Francis II of Austria from imminent danger of capture. For his part in this action, he was ultimately rewarded by the Austrian government with the Cross of the Order of Maria Theresa and the rank of Baron of the Holy Roman Empire. From his own government he received, along with the "gracious" permission to accept such foreign distinctions, only the knighthood, which was to be his sole decoration for over twenty years' campaigning under an unsympathetic ministry. In the horrors of the frightful winter retreat which followed, he revealed that physical stamina which was the pride of many another campaign. Throughout, his humanitarian principles and youthful idealism recoiled from the cruel discipline, drunken licentiousness, and criminal incompetence which he observed in the British army; and the impatience with his superiors which this experience bred in him was to constitute a permanent handicap to his subsequent advancement. When he returned to England in February of 1796, he was a seasoned if somewhat disillusioned veteran of but eighteen summers.

For the next decade, Wilson's activities were carried on at a whirlwind pace. As a lieutenant in the encampment outside Weymouth, he met and eloped with a young heiress, Jemima, the daughter of Colonel William Belford, and in the following year, while he was serving against the rebellion in Ireland, their union was blessed by the first of the thirteen children she was to bear him in the succeeding fifteen years. In 1799, he took part in the disastrous Anglo-Russian expedition in Flanders, and in the following year as a major, he enjoyed his first taste of victory with the forces of Sir Ralph Abercrombie in Egypt. Having won military recognition in the award of the Order of the Crescent of the Ottoman Empire, he sought literary laurels in his *History of the British Expedition to Egypt.* Its calumnious account of Napoleonic atrocities was acclaimed, not only in England, but among anti-Bonapartists throughout the continent, and Wilson was honored by complimentary personal letters from both the Tsar Alexander and the Emperor Francis.

Flushed with this success, but restless under the inactivity following the Peace of Amiens in 1802, the chevalier made a nearly fatal attempt to keep his name in the public eye through a second publication in 1804, *The Enquiry into the Present State of the Military Forces of the British Empire.* Its criticism of such abuses as the system of life enlistment and corporal punishment impressed sincere reformers like the

Duke of Gloucester and William Windham but did nothing to ingratiate him with the royal favorites who still controlled the British army. Moreover, although it rejoiced the Whigs, his characterization of the general strategy as a series of poorly organized expeditions upon the periphery of the globe against an enemy invulnerable except in the heart of Europe so irritated Pitt that he is said to have sought Sir Robert's removal to India. Spared the humiliation of this exile, Sir Robert's insatiable thirst for action soon plunged him into another equally mortifying. In March of 1805, accepting a post as a lieutenant colonel, in one of those very peripheral expeditions which his book had attacked, he sailed for the Cape of Good Hope. A year's arduous and disappointing service convinced him that the policy of his commander, Sir David Baird, would soon transform it into "the Cape of Despair."[4] But in April 1806, the volatile chevalier's hopes took a sudden turn with the arrival of glorious news. His enemy Pitt was dead, and a coalition ministry which had been forced upon the Tory party included his old friend, Fox. Within less than six months, he had not only been released from his African exile, but was again embarking from England for the continent in another attempt to overthrow the Corsican tyrant.

Sir Robert's mission in November of 1806 was ideally suited to his temperament. He was attached to the special embassy of a personal friend, Lord Hutchinson, to the Court of Prussia. Armed with the prestige of a British officer, but freed from the restrictions of regular service, he was permitted to rove at will among the forces of England's Prussian and Russian allies. His diplomatic status gave him access to the Emperor Alexander as well as to the Prussian King and Queen, and his delight in their company was apparently reciprocated by signs of their royal favor. Only two years before, his conviction of the necessity of striking at Napoleon in Europe had almost persuaded him to desert the British army for the Russian service. Now, he not only won the friendship and respect of many of its highest officers, including General Bagration, Prince Benningsen,[5] Count Vorontsov,[6] and the Het-

[4] *ibid.*, 1, 308.

[5] Levin August Theophile Benningsen (1745-1826), a German-born general who entered the Russian army in 1773, serving in campaigns against Turkey, Poland, and Persia. He was prominent in the conspiracy to assassinate the Tsar Paul and commanded the Russian army at Eylau. For his services against the French, Alexander created him a count in 1813.

[6] Mikhail Sëmenovich Vorontsov (1782-1856), the son of Sëmen Romanovich Vorontsov, already well-known to Wilson in the capacity of ambassador to England, 1785-1806. The son, just launching upon a brilliant career, was wounded at Borodino in 1812 but later returned to the army. His administrative and military efforts in the regions of the Black Sea and the Caucasus utimately won him the title of prince and field marshal.

man Platov,[7] but was distinguished by the Emperor himself with the award of the coveted Order of St. George for his daring at Eylau. In the full tide of optimism which these circumstances generated, even the disaster at Friedland and the subsequent negotiations at Tilsit could not utterly dash his sanguine spirits. Long conversations with his Russian friends and two secret reconnaissances of Tilsit in a Cossack disguise, which did more to fortify his vanity than to enlighten his understanding, soon brought him to Prince Czartoryski's[8] persuasion that Alexander's "heart had not been changed, although he might have lost his head."[9] As a consequence, he conceived the idea of a journey to St. Petersburg, there to await the return of the Emperor, in order to sound his true feelings. On July 20, 1807, he set off with Lord Hutchinson from Memel on his first visit to the Russian capital.

Posting along the shores of the Baltic, and pausing only long enough to extend the list of his royal acquaintance by the addition of Louis XVIII in his shabby little exiled court at Mittau, he arrived some two weeks later in the city of St. Petersburg. "And what a city! Magnificent beyond description or imagination. It is, I am certain, unrivaled on the continent and in the modern world for the grandeur of its buildings."[10] Every line of his journal reflects his growing excitement. He made the round of the noble salons, visited the houses of the British merchants, and sounded the opinions of his Russian friends and fellow Britons. One of the latter was Robert Ker Porter, then petitioning the consent of his imperial idol for his marriage to the Princess Shcherbatov, and it is certain that the chevalier's confidence suffered no loss from this quarter. Everything confirmed him in the belief that the treaty was universally detested, and he was flattered to find that, whereas he was lionized on all occasions, the French envoy, General Savary, was refused admittance to all but a few houses. The Emperor's cordial welcome, the seat of honor at a royal banquet, and an "invitation to revisit Russia under imperial auspices"[11] served to convince him that Alexander se-

---

[7] Matvei Ivanovich Platov (1751-1818), appointed hetman of the Cossacks in 1801. Wilson became greatly attached to him, and, in 1812, interceded with Alexander to preserve his command. His bold harassing tactics in that year were rewarded with the title of count.

[8] Prince Adam Jersy Czartoryski (1770-1861), a scion of the great Polish family and later a revolutionary leader in the fight for Polish independence. As a hostage in St. Petersburg following the Polish insurrection of 1794, he had become the intimate of the young Alexander and had risen to the rank of assistant minister of foreign affairs when, in June 1806, his hostility to the Prussian alliance caused him to resign. He and Wilson carried on an intermittent, but life-long correspondence upon the subject of Polish aspirations. Adam Gielgud, *Memoirs of Prince Adam Czartoryski*, London, 1888, II, 240ff.

[9] Costigan, *op. cit.*, p. 40.   [10] Randolph, *op. cit.*, II, 344.

[11] *ibid.*, II, 354.

cretly repented the Tilsit betrayal. Impatient to be the bearer of such glad tidings, Sir Robert bade farewell to the Emperor on September 2. Their tête-à-tête was so familiar that Sir Robert, following "a conversation very interesting to England," was induced to favor the Russian autocrat with a reading of a private letter from his wife and was dismissed only after "many flattering assurances of his esteem."[12]

Colonel Wilson's arrival in London was the signal for a flurry of excitement. His friend Canning, knowing the flamboyant character of the chevalier, was at first reluctant to credit his glowing reports, but when these were at least partially confirmed by the official dispatches of the pessimistic Lord Gower in St. Petersburg, he determined to entrust the dashing colonel with a further errand. Even before he started, however, Wilson's negotiation had been foredoomed to failure. In addition to replying with stiff counterproposals to Alexander's offer of mediation with France, the British government had already committed an act of open aggression.[13] Ignorant of the exact nature of the secret terms of the Treaty of Tilsit, but mindful of French-inspired and Russian-led Baltic alliances of 1780 and 1800, the ministry determined to neutralize the maritime armament of Denmark before it could be enlisted on the side of Napoleon. Accordingly, a strong naval squadron had appeared off Copenhagen on September 1, and, when the pretense of an offer of "protection" for the Danish fleet had been indignantly declined, it had bombarded the capital and taken its navy in custody by force. This unprovoked assault upon a neutral power had excited anti-British hostility throughout the continent, and Russia was hardly disposed to accept England's offer of a partnership in the crime as a nominal guarantor of Danish independence.

More important than these diplomatic exchanges was the underlying shift in Russian policy signified by the appointment of Count Rumiantsev[14] to the ministry of foreign affairs. Rumiantsev was a strong advocate of Russian expansion in the Near East; and whereas Napoleon had recommended a wholesale partition of Ottoman territories, Wilson was empowered to offer only British recognition of the Russian annexation of Moldavia and Wallachia, and even this was to be

---

[12] *ibid.*, II, 365.

[13] A. A. Lobanov-Rostovsky, *Russia and Europe, 1789-1825*, Durham, North Carolina, 1947, pp. 160ff.

[14] Nikolai Petrovich Rumiantsev (1754-1826). A son of the famous general of Catherine's reign, he cherished her policy of expansion into the Black Sea and Mediterranean. Believing European diplomacy to be outside the orbit of Russia's true interests, he became in 1812 a leader of that school which thought the pursuit of Napoleon should end at the Russian frontier. Albert Vandal, *Napoleon et Alexandre Ier*, Paris, 1893, I, 157-159.

BRIGADIER GENERAL SIR ROBERT THOMAS WILSON

FIELD MARSHAL PRINCE MIKHAIL ILARIONOVICH KUTUSOV

made conditional upon the consent of Russia's arch-rival, Austria. It now seems clear that Alexander, eager for further Turkish acquisitions, had intended a rupture from the very beginning, and that his show of secret friendliness towards Wilson and Gower had been only a ruse to gain time until the Russian Mediterranean fleet could win to a safe haven and the approaching winter could secure his unprotected Baltic ports from just such a British attack as that which had ravaged Copenhagen. The "eastern chimera" which Napoleon had revived at Tilsit was as alluring to Alexander as it had been to his grandmother some forty years before, and the failure to recognize this fact was as disastrous to the mission of Sir Robert Wilson in 1807, as it had been to that of Sir James Harris in 1780.[15]

Quitting London on October 4, the unsuspecting chevalier undertook his ill-starred mission with customary gusto. Although the ice which had now closed the navigation of the Baltic, forced him to land in Sweden, at Gothenburg, where his vanity further delayed him at dinner with the newly exiled Louis XVIII, a furious gallop around the frozen coastline brought him to St. Petersburg only thirteen days later. His social versatility placed him in the limelight of every gathering. After dinner at the British Embassy, he gaily accepted Count Orlov's challenge to an impromptu wrestling match. "We broke two of Gower's chairs, and he was thrown thrice. Finding that though vanquished he persevered from mortification, I suffered him to press me down upon a sofa; choosing rather to retain a friend, than to acquire gymnastic glory."[16] At the theater, he could be seen, "going from one loge to another with the air of a general who inspects his troops and spurs them on to combat."[17] At one of the capital's splendid entertainments, he "had the honour of opening the Grand Ball with the Countess Lievin, which pleased me, as the French were mortified."[18]

For all his social triumphs, his official negotiation gained no headway. He could not obtain a private audience with the Emperor, and Count Rumiantsev was markedly chilly. In his overzealousness in the cause, Wilson, with the concurrence of Gower, then committed a fatal indiscretion. He circulated among his Russian friends copies of a British pamphlet entitled *Reflections on the Peace of Tilsit*, which contained several uncomplimentary allusions to Alexander. His explanations only partially satisfied Rumiantsev, and a letter of apology to the Emperor was returned unopened. Nevertheless, Wilson lingered on in St. Peters-

---

[15] *ibid.*, I, 152-170.
[17] Costigan, *op. cit.*, p. 46.
[16] Randolph, *op. cit.*, II, 381.
[18] Randolph, *op. cit.*, II, 380.

burg until the signs of Anglo-Russian hostility became unmistakable. On November 8, Lord Gower was given an angry note of dismissal, and with the dire prediction that this act might well cost Alexander "as dear as it did his father,"[19] Sir Robert, too, prepared for his departure. His passports were deliberately withheld for thirty-six hours so that a Russian courier might precede him with the news, but the indefatigible chevalier, after a mad dash across the frozen Gulf of Bothnia and a most hazardous sea voyage, arrived first in London, rousing Canning from his slumbers at four in the morning of December 2. His perilous speed permitted the capture of a Russian frigate, caught unawares by the outbreak of hostilities, and the closing episode of the first gloomy chapter of Sir Robert's Russian adventures was thereby furnished with a sorely needed balm for his wounded vanity.

Disappointed in his diplomatic adventures, the chevalier's thoughts turned again in search of military prospects. They had not far to seek, for in 1808 the French launched a full-scale offensive in the Iberian Peninsula to subdue native resistance and to drive the inferior British forces into the sea. Repeatedly frustrated in his attempts to obtain a regular command, his imaginative mind seized upon an even more promising alternative. Allying himself to the Chevalier de Souza, the ambassador from Portugal, and with the backing of the friendly Canning in the ministry, he petitioned for permission to organize and command a volunteer force of 3,000 troops, which was nominally to be assigned to the defense of the city of Oporto. When the harassed War Office finally accorded its consent, the delighted chevalier, who now held the rank of brigadier general in the Portuguese Army, immediately set about preparations for his departure. Collecting a handful of British officers and Portuguese exiles to serve as a nucleus, he set sail for Oporto with all possible speed and, upon his arrival on August 8, threw his full energies into organizing the native militia into the "Loyal Lustianian Legion.'" The diplomatic debacle of eight months before was quite forgotten in glorious daydreams of the campaign which was to hold his brightest hour.

General Wilson's position between the conflicting authorities of the disorganized little state and the British military command at Lisbon afforded him a latitude for independent action which he was not slow to grasp. In December, taking with him only 700 members of the Legion, he abandoned Oporto to the dismay of its inhabitants and set out inland across the mountains toward Spain. At a time when the

[19] *ibid.*, p. 382.

other British and Iberian forces were reeling before a fierce French offensive, he actually invaded Spanish territory, and on January 7, captured the town of Ciudad Rodrigo. Maintaining his headquarters there throughout the winter, he succeeded, by brilliant guerilla tactics, in immobilizing a corps of 9,000 French under Lapisse at Salamanca and thereby seriously disconcerted the plan which Napoleon had outlined for a three-pronged invasion of Portugal.[20] Moreover, Sir Robert's "unparalleled audacity" was as uplifting to the British morale, as it was disturbing to the French strategy. "The value of this service can only be estimated by those who were in the country at the time. Such was the consternation at Lisbon that his retreat would have been the signal for embarking every British soldier in the capital or its neighborhood."[21] Since Wilson's strategy had been devised entirely on his own initiative and, indeed, in actual opposition to the injunctions of his commander at Lisbon, he must be credited with an important share in sustaining the momentum and demonstrating the value of the operations in the Peninsula which were ultimately to do so much to drain the energies and sap the strength of French military might. If this be true, the full value of his services in a critical moment in 1809 could be appreciated only years afterwards, when the chevalier himself was confronting a Napoleonic host at the other end of Europe in the terrible campaign of 1812.

In grateful recognition of this service, Sir Robert was rewarded by the government of Portugal with the Order of the Tower and the Sword, but from the British military headquarters, he received only a peremptory order to retire to Oporto. Outraged, he resigned his commission in a fit of temper and was only persuaded to resume it at the instance of the newly arrived General Wellesley, who further showed his confidence by reinforcing the Legion. However, no commander could long tolerate a subordinate whose independent action habitually disregarded his instructions and Wellesley was no exception. On July 26, the chevalier far exceeded his orders to occupy Escalona and proceeded with 8,000 men to a point within three leagues of Madrid, from which he threatened the capture of the Spanish capital. This was too much for the future "Iron Duke," and on August 5, he reprimanded his unpredictable subordinate. "It is difficult for me to instruct you,

[20] Charles Oman, *A History of the Peninsular War*, Oxford, 1903, II, 257-258; J. W. Fortescue, *History of the British Army*, London, 1912, VII, 135-136.

[21] Holland, Henry Richard, 3rd Lord of *Further Memoirs of the Whig Party, 1807-1821*, New York, 1905, p. 25.

when every letter that I receive from you informs me that you have gone further off and are executing some plan of your own."[22] Retreating rapidly from the danger of French encirclement, Wilson had nearly made good his escape, when he unexpectedly encountered Ney with a force three times his own in the mountain pass of Baños. He extricated himself only with difficulty, and it was a thoroughly disheartened soldier who appeared in Oporto for the third and last time in early September. Deprived of his former independence and without prospects for further action in that year, the General applied for and was willingly granted his release from the Portuguese service.

For the next two and a half years, Sir Robert Thomas Wilson, the veteran of fifteen years' service and half a dozen campaigns in which he had won the decorations of four continental monarchs, fumed in impotence in London, while Wellesley won military glory and immortality as a relative newcomer to the field which he had voluntarily quitted. In the interim, his eulogistic history of the campaigns of Eylau and Friedland won him the gratitude of his former Russian comrades, and his diatribes against the conduct of the Peninsular War delighted his Whig friends, but his ceaseless petitions to the Tory ministry were treated with unceremonious indifference. When relief from inactivity came at last, it did so in a guise which promised exile rather than escape. On January 1, 1812, Sir Robert was informed that he had been attached to the staff of the aged Robert Liston, bound for Constantinople to mediate the negotiation of the Russo-Turkish peace then pending. The embassy at the Ottoman capital was held in general disregard by the majority of those in the foreign service. Both Lord Aberdeen and George Rose had previously refused it, and even the veteran Sir George Jackson expressed surprise upon Liston's acceptance "that he should wish for the thing."[23] Moreover, Sir Robert's role in this despised mission was to be strictly limited. Although he was accorded the rank of brigadier general in the army, he was to act in an advisory capacity only. His instructions explicitly denied him any initiative. "You are to consider yourself entirely attached to Mr. Liston's mission and are to regulate your conduct by his orders, and with him alone to correspond."[24] Lord Castlereagh, Canning's successor in the Foreign Office, must have felt quite satisfied that these restrictions would permit no repetition of the romantic diplomacy which had been the aftermath of Tilsit, but he had badly miscalculated both the character of his subordinate and the dynamics of the diplomatic situation.

[22] Oman, *op. cit.*, II, 254.   [23] Costigan, *op. cit.*, p. 106.   [24] *ibid.*, p. 107.

Constantinople was only one front of a European-wide conflict between the rapidly diverging French and Russian interests. Tension had been mounting ever since Alexander's refusal to permit the marriage of his sister with the Corsican upstart. Since that time, the Russian Secession from the Continental Blockade, disagreement over the status of Poland, the continuing occupation of Prussia by French troops, and Napoleon's seizure of Oldenburg, the domain of the Tsar's brother-in-law, had signalized a gradual disintegration of the Tilsit alliance, and the evidence suggests that Bonaparte had definitely decided for war as early as August 15, 1811.[25] Military mobilization was begun on both sides, and there ensued a period of feverish diplomatic activity in Prussia, Austria, Poland, Sweden, and Turkey. Napoleonic successes in central Europe were largely vitiated by a strong undercurrent of discontent, and Alexander had received secret assurances from Austria that she would provide only a minimum of assistance to her French ally. Moreover, he secured himself on the flanks by understandings with both Sweden and Turkey in the spring of 1812. In view of the fact that the preliminaries of the Russo-Turkish pacification had been signed in Bucharest in May, and that Napoleon had already begun the invasion of Russia by crossing the Niemen on June 24, Sir Robert's arrival in Constantinople on July 1 might seem to have placed him in the lamentable predicament of an actor who has arrived upon the stage only to find that the final curtain has fallen. In reality, however, there was a short afterpiece yet to be played, and in less than six weeks, Sir Robert's role in it had placed him a thousand miles away in the foreground of a far greater drama.

Anti-Russian feeling had been growing at Constantinople ever since the realization that the still unratified Treaty of Bucharest had failed to capitalize upon the danger of imminent French invasion of the Russian enemy. It grew still more hostile, shortly after Wilson's arrival, with the report of a Russian plan to march Admiral Chichagov's[26] Moldavian army across the Balkans, raising the standard of rebellion among the Slavs, in order to attack the French on the Austrian flank.

---

[25] Lobanov-Rostovsky, *op. cit.*, p. 201.

[26] In 1811, Admiral Pavel Vasilievich Chichagov had been appointed by the Tsar to the post of "Commander-in-Chief of Moldavia, Wallachia, and the Black Sea Fleet," and, when Kutusov following the preliminaries of the Treaty of Bucharest, returned to Russia, he was entrusted with the conclusion of the negotiation and assigned the unaccustomed role of the commander of a large army. His military capacity has been questioned, but the attempts to fix upon him the sole responsibility for failure to cut off Napoleon's retreat across the Berezina in November of 1812 seem entirely unjustified. Eugene Tarle, *Napoleon's Invasion of Russia, 1812*, New York, 1942, pp. 379-380.

Indeed, Liston began to fear that the Sultan would "advance pretensions even beyond the status quo ante bellum,"[27] and his apprehensions for the ratification were increased by his uncertainty as to what was passing at the scene of the negotiation in Bucharest, five hundred miles away over terrain virtually impassable for a man of his years. In his uncertainty, he fell easy prey to one of those schemes for which the active mind of the ardent chevalier was never at a loss, and, disregarding Castlereagh's wishes to confine him to the role of a mere military adviser, he determined to dispatch Wilson to Bucharest as a mediator of the pacification. Far more important from Sir Robert's viewpoint, he authorized him, should the success of the negotiation still remain in doubt, to proceed to Russia for a conference with Alexander. His determination to pursue this course in any event was made eminently clear even prior to his departure from Constantinople. In a letter to Lord Castlereagh, he joyfully outlined his future itinerary and concluded by requesting his Tory nemesis to be allowed "to continue in an official capacity with the Russian Army. Attachments already formed, the hope of being useful, and the assurance of this appointment being agreeable to his majesty, the Emperor, prompt me to the request, and will, I hope, obtain for me your Lordship's sanction."[28] On July 25, accompanied by a tartar interpreter and an escort of British Dragoons, but quite unencumbered by so empty a formality as the consent of the Foreign Office, he took the road for Bucharest, secure in the conviction that it would open for him the freedom to roam at will throughout eastern Europe.

Proceeding at breakneck speed, he arrived in Shumla on July 31, where a flying conference with the Grand Vizier convinced him of the pacific intentions of that potentate. He was off again on the same day and reported in Bucharest on the next, where he proudly noted that he had "ridden four hundred and twenty-five miles, rowed six miles on the Danube, and travelled eighty by carriage, in five hours less than five days, including the nine hours passed at Shumla."[29] He assumed as much credit for his diplomatic progress as for his equestrian pace, for "on the day after my arrival, Kalib Effendi, the Turkish plenipotentiary, told me that if I had come out ten months before, peace would then have been made. Admiral Tchichagow expressed as much. . . ."[30] In reality, the peace had been nearly inevitable, for the

[27] Costigan, *op. cit.*, p. 112.   [28] *ibid.*, p. 113.
[29] Robert Thomas Wilson, *Private Diary*, London, 1861, 1, 138.
[30] *ibid.*, p. 139.

Turkish army was well nigh exhausted and that of Chichagov was so sorely needed against Napoleon in Russia that an Adriatic expedition was unthinkable.[31] Nevertheless, Liston in Constantinople apparently credited Sir Robert's naïve boasts for he wrote his mercurial emissary expressing "a very high satisfaction in the able manner in which you have executed the commission I ventured to entrust to your charge."[32] The British General, for his part, was already speeding on toward Smolensk, where he arrived on August 12 in the direct path of the retreating Russian army.

The experiences of the next few months were the most dramatic of the chevalier's long and theatrical career. The emotional impact of this campaign cannot be explained in terms of its magnitude alone. In fact, its statistical dimensions, unprecedented in the history of Europe, were not to be equaled for more than a century, but it is more than mere size that men have seen in it. Romantics have been disposed to view it as the personal drama of two gigantic principals on an enormous stage; the tall, handsome, enigmatic Tsar, marshaling the forces of his vast semi-oriental empire against the little French Emperor, brooding amid the flaming ruins of Moscow. Tolstoi, intent upon the destruction of the Napoleonic legend, has reduced the leading actors to mere puppets caught up in the grip of forces which they did not understand: "Providence compelled all these men, striving to attain personal aims, to further the accomplishment of a stupendous result no one of them at all expected. . . ."[33] The truth, perhaps, synthesizes these two opposing views. It is the peculiar quality of military history that, from among the countless altogether mediocre figures who crowd its pages, it occasionally produces personalities of extraordinary stature whom fate or providence has chosen to manipulate immense power in such a way as to effect cataclysmic alterations quite foreign to the relatively gradual evolution of political, economic, or cultural development. Such profoundly influential phenomena as the Islamic conquests in the Mediterranean, the Norman conquest of England and the Mongolian conquest

---

[31] Driault attributes the abandonment of the Adriatic expedition to this latter exigency, in combination with the fear that such an expedition might yet goad the Turks into a French alliance, and Sorel adds to this that the Austrian promise to Alexander of a tacit "neutrality" made it inexpedient to provide an occasion for active hostility in that quarter. Moreover, Alexander's advisers suggested that the agitation of Balkan aspirations for an independent Slavic state might create a dangerous contagion of revolt, which, were it to spread to Poland, would hamper Russian designs in that country. Edouard Driault, *La Question d'Orient*, Paris, 1898, p. 98; Albert Sorel, *L'Europe et la Révolution Française*, Paris, 1911, VII, 570.

[32] Costigan, *op. cit.*, p. 115.

[33] Leo Tolstoi, *War and Peace*, New York, 1942, p. 761.

of Russia are unthinkable apart from the altogether exceptional personalities of Mohammed, William the Conqueror, and Genghiz Khan.[34] Napoleon and, perhaps to a lesser extent, Alexander were such cataclysmic personalities nominated by history to direct cataclysmic forces, and the aura of myth which has grown up about their collision, like every other legend, has originated in the attempt to dramatize a profound historical experience.

Perhaps the most unexpected of the "stupendous results" of Napoleon's domination of Europe was its awakening of the spirit of nationalism among the subject peoples. The new cult of "la patrie" had appeared first in France, where the ideology of the Revolution, transforming French society, had firmly united the interest of the liberated individual to the welfare of the Republic which set him free. In the crisis of the attack of the coalesced monarchs of the continent, the Republic had been saved by a patriotic enthusiasm which, translated into military terms, had organized a democratic citizen army, devised a strategy of mobility and decisive conflict, and crushed the cautious and slow-moving professional mercenaries of the enemy. Dazzled by its own success, the French Revolution militant became the French Imperium, whose doctrine was spread, not by the word, but by the sword. In the end, however, the lesson which it taught destroyed its own power, and the various subject states, adapting their own forms of nationalism, were endowed with the energy to resist the explosive combination of French patriotic fervor and Napoleonic military genius. Wilson had witnessed the stirring of the nationalistic reaction in Spain, but at a time when the poverty of military means at its disposal had rendered its operations less than decisive. In Russia, in 1812, he saw how a fanatical nationalistic spirit could inspire an effective military force, operating under favorable conditions of geography and climate to create an insuperable barrier against which the very weight and momentum of the invading host were not only ineffectual but positively self-destructive.

The French invasion of Russia pitted a mere army against an entire nation, but the Grand Army of Napoleon was less than French, and the champions of Russia were more than national. The composition of the military combatants demonstrated this significant paradox, for while the French generals commanded a heterogeneous mixture of Portuguese, Spanish, Italian, Swiss, Belgian, Polish, and German troops,

[34] Charles Oman, *Studies in the Napoleonic Wars*, New York, 1930, pp. 24-31.

with only a small proportion of Frenchmen,[35] the homogeneous Russian soldiery was officered by a nobility which the past century had largely Europeanized. Moreover, the identification of the Russian cause with a European-wide resistance to the oppression of the French Imperium was symbolized by the presence of a number of distinguished anti-Bonapartists. In St. Petersburg, were Madame de Staël, the famous French woman of letters, Joseph de Maistre, the Sardinian Ambassador and religious philosopher of the reaction, Baron Stein, the regenerator of Prussia, and Prince Adam Czartoryski, the Polish patriot. With the army were the Prussian General Pfuhl, councilor of the strategy of evasion, and Colonel Clausewicz, the disciple of the "war of perfection," the French General Langeron, émigré and careerist, the Swedish General Armfeldt, chief architect of the Russo-Swedish alliance, the Dukes of Oldenburg and Württemberg, the Tsar's kinsmen, and, of course, the British General Wilson himself. Hence, the campaign which marked an epoch in the development of nationalism in a semi-Asiatic state, was also an international crusade deciding the fate of Europe. The French Revolution made strange bedfellows. The peasants of Siberia and the merchants of Liverpool were linked for a moment in history. Brigadier General Sir Robert Thomas Wilson stood at the point of their juncture during the critical days of that epoch.

Wilson's character, past experience, and the peculiar nature of his position in the Russian army, all influenced his perspective of these eventful days. His movements enabled him to observe the important battle of Smolensk, and although diplomatic errands in the capital absented him during the battle of Borodino and the evacuation of Moscow, he rejoined the main army shortly thereafter and remained with it until the end of the year. His freedom from the duties of regular service, coupled with his iron constitution and physical energy, permitted him to range widely over the field of action. In addition, his popularity, his many friendships, and his prestige as a British officer gained him access to important sources of intelligence. Only thirty-five years of age on August 17, 1812, he was, nevertheless, upon arrival in Russia, the oldest of all the British travelers with whom these pages have dealt, and eighteen years of active campaigning had furnished him with a reservoir of professional experience which the others had lacked. On the

[35] Besides 200,000 French soldiers, the Grand Army of nearly 600,000 troops who invaded Russia included 147,000 Germans, 80,000 Italians, 60,000 Poles, and a miscellany of smaller units from other nations under Napoleonic domination. In addition, 50,000 troops of the Prussian and Austrian allies guarded the northern and southern flanks, respectively. J. Holland Rose, *The Life of Napoleon I*, New York, 1902, II, 221.

other hand, Wilson's vanity and love of the theatrical caused him to exaggerate the significance of specific events, particularly those in which he was himself an actor, and his emotional involvement in his own narrative is one of the most striking points of differentiation from his fellow travelers. Unlike Ker Porter, his participation in the history of his time was real, as well as vicarious. Between the pressure of events and his insatiable thirst for action, he had neither time nor taste for objective meditation. He sought not the speculative pleasures of the humanist, the scholar, or the aesthete, but the violent overthrow of Napoleon and, inevitably for him, his own glory and advancement. For this reason, his interpretation of the elements underlying the Napoleonic disaster must be sought in his incidental reactions to the daily occurrences of the campaign. Nevertheless, the scope and vitality of a romantic imagination, fed by the contemplation of twenty years of international warfare, frequently enabled him to generalize from his immediate impressions with real insight, and the reader of his memoirs is inclined to agree with Sir George Jackson that, "though it cannot be denied that he is one of the most harum-scarum fellows that ever existed, yet there is an immense deal of good in him, and much sound judgement at bottom."[36]

It is notable that, from the very outset, Sir Robert was convinced that Russia possessed the military means of victory. On August 14, he wrote: "I have . . . no doubt of Russia having at this moment, by an extraordinary national energy, arrayed a force far more than sufficient for the contest, if its direction be but worthy the character of the soldiers."[37] Taking for granted her vast natural resources, physical extent, and abundance of military supplies and manpower, he turned his immediate attention to the condition of the army itself. Although dissatisfied with certain aspects of the internal organization, he confirmed many happy recollections from the campaigns of five years before in which he had praised the fanatical courage of the soldiers, the justice of the discipline, the absence of intemperance, the superb condition of the horses, and the excellence of the artillery.[38] The temporary numerical superiority of the

[36] George Jackson, *The Bath Archives*, edited by Lady Jackson, London, 1873, ii, 109.

[37] Wilson to Cathcart, August 14, 1812, Robert Thomas Wilson, *Narrative of Events during the Invasion of Russia*, edited by Herbert Randolph, London, 1861, p. 383.

[38] Robert Thomas Wilson, *Brief Remarks on the Character and Composition of the Russian Army*, London, 1810, pp. 8-11, 21-22. Wilson's estimate of the Russian ordinance, characteristically optimistic, but, on the whole, just, is interesting in the light of Dr. Clarke's gibes at the expense of the Tula arms factory: "The machinery is ill constructed, and worse preserved. Every thing seemed out of order. Workmen, with long beards, stood staring at each other, wondering what was to be done next; while their intendants or directors were drunk or asleep.

Grand Army, composed of unwilling conscripts of subject peoples, was more than offset by the superior morale and determination of the unified Russian soldiery defending its native soil. Reassured on all these grounds, Sir Robert's only fears centered upon the character of the direction of the Russian forces.

A comparison with Perry's view of Russia is here illuminating. Both Perry and Wilson believed Russia to be naturally endowed with adequate means for the accomplishment of purposes in which their sympathies were wholeheartedly enlisted. Both men identified their interests with those of the absolute sovereign, and both saw the main obstacle to their grand designs in administrative defects which aroused their unbounded personal indignation. In strong contrast, however, Perry's ultimate object was the improvement of Russian commerce and industry, which, however much they might be benefited by limited mercantilist wars, were peaceful pursuits, while the furthest horizon of Wilson's ambition extended only to the overthrow of Napoleon in a war of a magnitude and intensity undreamed of in Perry's day. The engineer lamented the peasant's lack of initiative and incentive to economic exertion, while the soldier rejoiced in the hatred of the foreigner which animated all ranks of society. To Wilson, the primitive state of the Russian economy was not only no handicap, but a positive military advantage, for whereas it greatly increased the difficulties of supplying the needs of the Grand Army, it minimized the value of every conquest on the road to Moscow. Napoleon succeeded only in capturing an economic desert, and even the occupation of Moscow did not bring those material advantages which might have been expected from the conquest of any other European metropolis. The primitive Russians had "preserved so much of their nomad habits that they were much more quickly packed and equipped for their emigration than the inhabitants of any other European city would have been,"[39] and the Grand Army entered, not a teeming capital, but a ghost town. Perry saw the great check to the economic progress he desired in the tyranny and obscurantism of the boyars and he expanded his hatred of a few personal enemies into a sweeping condemnation of an entire class, whereas Wilson, admiring the courage and energy of the great bulk

---

Notwithstanding all this, they pretended to issue from the manufactory . . . thirteen hundred muskets in a week. But the name of musket is almost all that connects the appearance with the reality. It is wonderful any troops can use them; besides being clumsy and heavy, they miss fire five times out of six, and are liable to burst whenever dicharged." Edward Daniel Clarke, *Travels*, London, 1811, I, 148.

[39] Wilson, *Narrative*, p. 155.

of his allies in the international crusade, concentrated his perennial irritation with all military superiors into a personal animosity which ultimately focused upon a single Russian commander.

The resulting combination of hope and despair, which permeated all his observations, joyous enthusiasm at the strength of the Russian army and black indignation at the evasive strategy of the Russian command, was manifest from the moment of his joining the army, and within less than a week, he had plunged deep into a military conspiracy. General Barclay's eminently reasonable decision to abandon Smolensk had aroused a storm of protest among the other Russian generals. Barclay's patriotic integrity was seriously questioned, and the impetuous Wilson, who was obliged by his diplomatic mission to proceed to St. Petersburg, was readily persuaded by his former comrades to be the bearer of an extraordinary message to the Tsar. Demanding the dismissal of both General Barclay, the commander-in-chief, and Count Rumiantsev, the reputably Francophile foreign minister, the officers highhandedly declared their defiant intention of fighting the war to the death, in which determination they would regard any instructions from the capital to cease hostilities as the product of treasonable counsel, contrary to the Emperor's true desires. Whatever the diplomatic verbiage, this was strong medicine for the theoretically supreme autocrat, but Sir Robert was equal to the occasion, and, in an historic interview with Alexander on September 4, he administered the dose as painlessly as the situation would admit. His efforts did not go unrewarded. Even before Wilson's arrival, the Tsar had appointed General Kutusov as Barclay's successor, and he refused to dismiss Count Rumiantsev, but he swore to the British General in the most solemn manner that he would not negotiate for peace as long as a single French soldier remained in arms on Russian soil. Even more personally gratifying, he was authorized by the Emperor to return to the army with specific instructions to interfere in any negotiations prejudicial to that pledge. From a minor official of a discredited embassy whose appointed post was fifteen hundred miles away, Sir Robert had maneuvered himself, within six weeks, into a position as the confidant of one of the most powerful sovereigns in the world and the official guardian of Russian honor in the extremity of her fatal encounter with the enemy of all mankind.

On his return to the main army outside Moscow, Wilson's spirits rose even higher. The defeat at Borodino and the loss of Moscow were as nothing provided the will to resist remained, and here, in addition to the fervent assurances of the Emperor, Sir Robert saw ample testimony of this resolution among civilians and soldiers, nobles and peasants alike. He became ecstatic over acts of *"not Roman, but more than Roman—Russian dignity."*[40] Moreover, this nobility of spirit was expressed, not only in the voluntary destruction of the enemy's destined booty, but in an extraordinary national zeal to supply reinforcements of men and material to the military encampment. Wilson displayed an acute awareness of the psychological disadvantages of the enemy. Throughout the campaign, he attempted to spread disaffection and encourage desertion among the non-French elements of the "confederate army." He rejoiced in the predatory raids of both Cossacks and peasant bands, not only as a means of disrupting communications, but as the poisons to morale and discipline. Finally, he was quick to realize the strategic superiority of the Russian position as its rapidly augmenting army stood sentinel south of Moscow barring the inevitable retreat of the weakening French forces from the desolated city and his confidence of ultimate victory hourly increased.

This confidence gave way to outraged consternation on the morning of October 4 with the surprising information that Kutusov had agreed to a secret midnight rendezvous beyond the advanced posts with General Lauriston, Napoleon's aide-de-camp. For some days, both before and after this time, Russian and French officers had been engaging in informal conversations on the picket lines, and although Wilson theoretically disapproved this breach in the façade of hostility, he had rejoiced in the witty thrusts of the Russian generals. Now, however, he was thoroughly alarmed and availed himself of the equal indignation of his Russian comrades to foil the Marshal's scheme. Mustering the support of the Dukes of Oldenburg and Württemberg, and citing his own prerogative to interfere in such matters, he forced the angry Kutusov to revoke his original intention and succeeded, since he still persisted in meeting Lauriston, in removing the interview to the Russian headquarters at Tarutino where it might be conducted under his personal surveillance. Under these circumstances, no Franco-Russian armistice was possible, and Sir Robert, in recounting this episode, obviously felt himself to have been an important instrument in the preservation of Europe.

It has been suggested that the cunning old Marshal wished only to feign a negotiation in order to delay Napoleon's departure from Moscow until the arrival of cold weather,[41] yet even his most competent

[40] *ibid.*, p. 179.
[41] H. B. George, *Napoleon's Invasion of Russia*, London, 1899, p. 232.

apologist admits that Kutusov's single purpose in this campaign was not the overthrow of Napoleonic power but the liberation of Russia from the invader with the smallest possible loss to his army.[42] Certainly, the negotiation of such a military armistice as Lauriston had desired would have accorded well with this aim, and Wilson's suspicions of the Marshal were probably justified. In any event, to Sir Robert, to whom the destruction of Napoleon meant the salvation of all Europe, Kutusov's parochial concern for the preservation of Russian life was little short of heresy, and he began to regard the Marshal as second only to the Corsican in the record of iniquity.

The most important aspect of the conversations between French and Russian officers is neither their revelation of a cleavage in Russian military policy, nor even their termination in the refusal of an armistice, but the consciousness which they show of the elemental force of the resistance of the Russian people to any idea of peace with Napoleon. When Kutusov likened the anger of the civilian population to that which they would have felt toward "a marauding force of Tartars under a Ginghis Khan," he suggested the existence of one of those phenomena which Barzun has termed "national neuroses." "They are neuroses, and they are national, because the common forms of national behavior derive from the arbitrary memories of the nation's past. What a people remembers are the bad times, or the glorious times, or the eleventh hour measures of salvation, which then inspire repetition in the mechanical manner of a neurotic trait. The Russian phobia against foreigners is that of a much conquered people. . . ."[43] As here applied, this suggests that the advance of the Grand Army in 1812 revived ancient memories of invading Mongols, Tartars, Poles, Swedes, and, in short, the cumulative historical experience of foreign aggression which had provided the original justification for Russia's military autocracy and servile institutions, and that these memories, awakening the dormant devotion to that autocracy and uniting noble and peasant

[42] Eugene Tarle, the eminent Russian historian, whose recent account of the campaign of 1812 is a classic, is wantonly partisan in his support of Kutusov in the latter's quarrels with Wilson. He calls Sir Robert "the British commissioner and spy" and interprets his actions as part of an English bourgeois conspiracy to employ the blood of Russian patriots to obtain new markets for the London merchants and Birmingham manufacturers. In this, he ignores the fact that the chevalier, discredited by the British government in general and by the Foreign Office in particular, had been repeatedly instructed to play no part in questions of policy and was prompted rather by romantic dreams of glory in the overthrow of "the World's enemy," than by banal considerations of mercantile profits. Tarle, *op. cit.*, pp. 307ff., 334-335; compare Costigan, *op. cit.*, pp. 125ff.

[43] Jacques Barzun, "Whence the Russians and Why the French?" *Harper's Magazine*, May 1948.

in a common cause, fanned the hatred of the foreigner and steeled the determination to avenge his desecration of Russian soil. It might further imply that this confirmation of a remembered heritage had inspired the Russian people with a new sense of their national identity and unique patriotic mission, but whatever the reactions of the people as a whole, Kutusov, in his remarks to Lauriston, betrayed a distinct awareness of the Russian past, and the other Russian officers, as well as the British General himself, revealed a kind of awed reverence for the inscrutable force of the popular will.

If the resistance of the Russian peasants was occasionally viewed in the light of a distinctive national history, their behavior is intelligible on the grounds that they belonged to the genus "peasant," as well as to the species "Russian." Peasants in all lands lean toward an instinctive dislike of foreigners, and the Grand Army had done nothing to allay the hostility of the Russian serf. Its coming brought him, not the enlightenment, liberation, and humanitarian reforms of the Revolution, but the confiscations of foraging parties and the humiliating affronts of military occupation. The peasant whose livestock and provisions had been appropriated by force needed no atavistic memories of warrior nomads to excite his hatred of the invader, and in his rage at the predatory newcomer he tended to forget his grievances against the native landlord whose exactions, at least, had been sanctified by ancient usage. In this light, both the causes and the forms of peasant resistance in Russia recalled those of Spanish guerillas and Tirolese partisans at an earlier date. Wilson was not oblivious to certain of these extranational precedents and parallels; yet he seems to have felt something distinctive in the fanatic fury of the Russian spirit, and he was profoundly moved by the scope and violence of peasant and partisan operations which attended the military abnormalities of the campaign.

The fiery Sir Robert was repeatedly frustrated in his desire for one of those momentous and decisive pitched battles so long associated with the name of Napoleon. At the outset, "scorched earth," and toward the close, the winter snows made inaccessible to the French the material resources of a countryside which, in any case, was too poor to supply the needs of such vast numbers, and the resulting logistical difficulties at that distance from home impeded the progress of the unwieldy force. As Russian strategy continued to elude Napoleon's maneuvers to force a battle, the posting of garrisons, the detachment of flanking forces, the friction of long marches, disease, desertion, and the casualties of minor engagements so reduced the numerical superiority of the main army of Napoleon, that, when he finally brought the enemy to bay at Borodino, his assault lacked its wonted impetuosity, and he refused even to commit his elite reserve, the Young Guard.[44] The battle was extremely bloody, but its results were inconclusive. For five weeks, thereafter, the steadily weakening Grand Army lingered in the ruins of Moscow, while its commander deluded himself with hopes of another Tilsit to be followed by a joint Franco-Russian expedition against British India. In the inevitable retreat, he lacked the strength, and Kutusov, the inclination to seek a major battle. Therefore, although the pursuit by the Russian main army posed an important strategic threat, and although it inflicted heavy casualties in several minor engagements, the great decisive conflict for which the chevalier yearned was never fought. Hence, a major role in the annihilation of the Grand Army was assigned to Cossack detachments, militia bands, and peasant partisans who vented the national fury by killing, capturing, or exposing to starvation and biting cold tens of thousands of the demoralized enemy.[45]

Wilson's attitude toward this fanatic hatred of the foreign invader is significant of his character and military principles. He rejoiced in it as a manifestation of national spirit, and he welcomed it as the instrument of the policy of uncompromising aggression which he himself advocated. It was the preservation of Russian morale and the determination to resist which had most vitally concerned him at both St. Petersburg and Tarutino, and he more than once implied that the widespread Russian Xenophobia had put the power of pacification beyond the reach of even the Emperor. Such patriotic fervor was productive of the highest good, and he prophesied that the stimulus to national energy and the consciousness of national greatness which this campaign had engendered would advance the progress of Russia more than a century. According to his code, however, national energy ought not to be expressed in national brutality, and the consciousness of national greatness ought not to be founded upon indiscriminate contempt for all things foreign. He could not have supported the aggressive Slavophilism of

[44] Even prior to the taking of Smolensk, before any real fighting had begun, the main French army had lost an estimated 100,000 men through the effects of fatigue, desertion, and disease. The French troops at Borodino, calculated at between 125,000 and 135,000, enjoyed a relatively small numerical superiority over Kutusov's 120,000 Russians, and Napoleon, a great artilleryman, suffered an unaccustomed disadvantage in the number of his cannon. Lobanov-Rostovsky, *op. cit.*, pp. 220, 222, 226.

[45] Recent communist historians have tended to emphasize the importance of the peasant proletariat, glorifying the exalted national spirit, and Tarle, a leader of this school, has devoted very considerable space to the role of the peasant, an aspect virtually neglected by earlier military historians of the Nineteenth Century. Tarle, *op. cit.*, pp. 257-288.

Karamzin,[46] who had written, in 1810: "After more than a century of foreign education, . . . we call all the Europeans brothers whom we formerly called infidels; I ask, For whom will it be easier to subdue Russia, for infidels or brothers?"[47] For all his hatred of the Corsican, Sir Robert yet regarded the French people as his European brothers, and his international chivalry respected heroism on either side. For this gallant crusader, it was rather the cruel Russian peasants, whom he had formerly hailed as brothers, than the courageous French captives they brutally martyred who appeared in the guise of infidels.

This horror of useless suffering reinforced his anger at the strategy of Kutusov, which permitted the campaign such scope while neglecting the one course which could bring it to a speedy and successful conclusion. To Wilson, no war against the French Imperium could be successful apart from the actual capture or death of the Corsican, and he was convinced that this could be achieved only by that decisive conflict of the main armies for which he had so long been agitating. Yet Kutusov deliberately refused a second Borodino at Maloyaroslavets, at Vyazma, and on the Berezina, preferring to offer the enemy "a bridge of gold" on his departure from Russia. The main prize was being allowed to escape while marauding bands, weary marches, the pangs of starvation, and the torments of winter were inflicting unprecedented suffering upon the participants of both sides. Kutusov's concern for the single object of ridding Russia of her invaders as quickly as possible, without reference to the international aspects of the war, were unintelligible to Sir Robert except as cowardice, senility, or downright treachery. In black despair at the close of 1812, he concluded that the campaign had been a failure and that it was Kutusov, and Kutusov alone, who had betrayed the great crusade in the very moment of victory.

Sir Robert's emotional predicament in the invasion of Russia was that of a chivalrous and romantic schoolboy, plunged into the midst of a cataclysmic upheaval which indiscriminately laid bare not only the noble heroism and unselfish devotion, but also the savage brutality and sadistic cruelty of his fellow human beings. He was the advocate of total war in a conflict of unprecedented dimen-

---

[46] Nikolai Mikhailovich Karamzin (1766-1826), the historian and novelist, exemplified a change from liberal cosmopolitanism to a narrow nationalism about the turn of the century. His eight-volume history of Russia, written in a style which did much to demonstrate the great potential beauty of the Russian language to later writers, extolled the institutions of the ancient Muscovite past prior to the pernicious westernizing influence of Peter, and his ideas received wide currency through the popular acclaim with which it met. Hans Kohn, *The Idea of Nationalism*, New York, 1945, pp. 569ff.

[47] Hans Kohn, *op. cit.*, p. 571.

sions, but total warfare, as he understood it, like a schoolboy's athletic contests, was waged under an unwritten ethical code. He was a keen competitor and showed no mercy within the rules, rejoicing in the physical and psychological attrition wrought on the Grand Army by its diet of "horseflesh and Cossack iron." This was to be considered as no end in itself, however, but only as a means of forcing that final Armageddon which would hold out the prize of victory to the strong, the righteous, and the brave. He shrank from neither bloodshed, nor suffering, and his concept of the overall strategy, however flamboyant and egotistical, was never merely naïve, but, with many of his generation, he retained the childish innocence of his faith in the humanitarian purposes of the crusade to which he had dedicated himself. Hypocrisy was not in him, and there is no basis in fact for the communist historians' characterization of him as the cunning intriguer of a British capitalist conspiracy to secure the economic domination of Europe. It was just because his own patriotism was founded upon an international code of chivalry that he recoiled alike from Kutusov's narrower national aims and the peasantry's unrestrained Xenophobe ferocity. Under all these circumstances, his mind shrank from the emotional impact and the terrible dimensions of the events he had witnessed, and, even years later, when it became apparent that the campaign had redeemed its promise in breaking the power of Bonaparte, he betrayed an instinctive dissatisfaction with his explanation of its causes and character. As if in tacit recognition that rational analysis alone was inadequate, the closing lines of his *Narrative* made their final appeal "to that Almighty Being, who rode on the whirlwind and directed the storm."[48]

[48] Wilson, *Narrative*, p. 370.

EXTRACTS FROM: *Narrative of Events during the Invasion of Russia by Napoleon Bonaparte and the Retreat of the French Army, 1812.*

AND

Private Diary of Travels, Personal Services and Public Events during Mission and Employment with the European Armies in the Campaigns of 1812, 1813, 1814.

by General Sir Robert Thomas Wilson

CONTENTS

....

I · ARRIVAL IN RUSSIA

I. A WRETCHED NIGHT AND A SUPERB RECEPTION: JASSY

August 6: Towards the evening, a second Danube thunder storm
broke over our heads. If I had not been one of the dramatis personae,
I should have enjoyed the scene; but the harder it poured the faster my
postilion galloped, and my voiture soon became a mud-cart. I never
was more wretched except when we came to the next post-shed, and
found all flown, so that we were obliged to proceed with the same

horses: but who can say that he has attained the extreme of misery?
A third post-station was also abandoned, and our cattle could do no
more. By bribing, we prevailed on the postilions to . . . let them graze
for two hours—We, in the interval, lay in our waggon with a cloak
over us; but the dew from the heavens and the earth soon thoroughly
soaked it, and then we steamed throughout; for our hay, which formed
the bed, became like manure. I will not, however, dwell on these
troubles, but announce our arrival at Jassy this morning, where the
commandant assigned me a superb quarter in the house of the principal Boyard [Boyar] and where I have been entertained with hospitality
and costly magnificence. . . . The room in which I dined this day was
one hundred and twenty feet long, and the other apartments are in
proportion. . . . Almost every moment, from high and from low, some
incident occurs to show the world's estimation of the British character.
[*Diary*, 140-142]

2. THE PASSAGE OF THE FRONTIER: KIEV

August 10: At Jitomir [Zhitomir], I found my ancient friend, General Sacken, in command of a division. He gave me a most cordial
welcome, and I remained two hours. . . . We then resumed our course
. . . and, aided by better roads, we arrived here to dine.

Kiew is a very large city, has a considerable citadel and appears to be
an important place. The country round is beautiful, and richly cultivated. If Dr. Clarke[49] had been here, I think he would have made one
exception to his sweeping clause against the establishments of this
empire. [*Diary*, 144]

3. LA PETITE RUSSIA: SMOLENSK

August 14: From Kiew we rolled over a rich country to Tchernigow
[Chernigov]. . . . The next day we dined with a Russian merchant at
Starodoub [Starodub], where we experienced the kindest hospitality.
Here we found the Vice-governor of Wilna's [Vilna] wife, an emi-
grant, who told her woes and the loss of nine waggons laden with
property in a manner that would have entitled her to a niche in the
Stoic school, but it was *d'accord* with the general patriotism. An Eng-
lishman was a rare being in this part of the world, but a welcome per-

---

[49] Edward Daniel Clarke (1769-1822), the distinguished scientist and traveler, who had been
acting as a traveling tutor when Wilson had first met him during the Egyptian campaign. The
first volume of his travels, published in 1810, had depicted Russia and the Russians in an
extremely unfavorable light.

son and much esteemed, for in that quarter the great flax purchases are made. I enjoyed the curiosity and the honest feelings of these rural merchants greatly. . . . This morning we reached Smolensk, having performed a very severe journey, but much mitigated in its severity by the universal kindness we experienced, and latterly by the scenes of a most beautiful country. I was greatly surprised in "la petite Russie" to see as great a population and as richly cultivated land as almost any province in England can produce. I do not think we saw a barren acre for five hundred miles. [*Diary*, 144-145]

II · THE RETREAT FROM SMOLENSK

I. A JOYOUS REUNION

AT SMOLENSK, I found General Beningsen [Bennigsen], . . . Prince Galitzin [Golitsyn], and many others. No meeting could be more sincerely affectionate. . . . To-morrow, I go to the armies of Barclay and Bagrathion [Bagration]. God grant that the Emperor may move up from S. Petersburg, for I abhor the idea of retiring from service and, moreover, journeying five hundred miles. . . .

On the 15th . . . the enemy were supposed to be approaching. By the active exertions of Prince Galitzin, I was myself equipped for the field, and conveyance was secured for my dragoons. . . . After proceeding about twenty-five wersts [versts] . . . we met Barclay's advanced guard: we therefore halted, saw the army file before us to Smolensk, and then joined the General, who received me very graciously, invited me to remain with his army, and to live at his head-quarters. . . . On the march we dined. In the evening, joined Prince Bagrathion's army on the heights opposite Smolensk, and I flew to the Prince and Woronzow [Vorontsov]. Quelle moment de bon heure! . . .

I stayed in his tent until the march at midnight. . . . He then gave me a very fine horse to ride, equipped me with a great coat, (for the nights are bitterly cold) and a Russian cap, in case of a mêlée in battle, that I might be recognised.

As soon as day dawned I accompanied the General into Smolensk. The action on the right soon commenced. . . . [*Diary*, 145-148]

2. THE STRATEGIC DECISION TO WITHDRAW

A cannonade and musketry fire continued until sunset, when the enemy fell back into their original position, with a loss of not less than ten thousand men.

The Russians had been favoured by the shelter of ramparts and battlements, but their loss amounted to six thousand men, exclusive of many officers, amongst whom were two generals.

The retention or evacuation of Smolensk was a question of measures that excited the deepest interest in the Russian army; every commander, officer, and soldier was desirous of forming its garrison, and resisting the future attacks of the enemy, who, notwithstanding his severe check, would, it was hoped, from a characteristic irritation of temper, persevere in an attempt to storm the town, and thus fruitlessly expend his bravest men.

But General Barclay conceived that the enemy might make a movement towards its left, which would oblige him to evacuate Smolensk in the day time, an operation that he thought would be attended with great inconvenience; and, moreover, he did not choose to engage in a defence that would require a daily expenditure of his own men, and thus perhaps enfeeble his army too much for the execution of his other plans.

General Barclay therefore resolved to withdraw from Smolensk. . . . [*Narrative*, 104-105][50]

3. THE INDIGNANT DETERMINATION TO REMAIN

In order to counteract the intention of General Barclay to quit Smolensk, I was, about ten o'clock at night, obliged to mount again and reenter the town to take the opinions of General Doctorow [Dokhturov] and Prince Eugène of Wurtemberg,[51] as to the capability of longer defence. . . . The latter engaged, with eight thousand men, to defend the city ten days, and begged of me to assure the General of the necessity of further defence. I had at least a dozen letters from officers of rank on the subject, as they thought I had access to and influence with the Commander-in-chief that no one else had. . . . [*Diary*, 148]

After I had . . . urged the detrimental moral effects which . . . would

[50] Wilson's *Narrative of Events during the Invasion of Russia*, published posthumously, was written some time after 1812, probably in the comparative leisure of the decade following the Vienna settlement. For this reason, except in those cases when it includes extracts of his original correspondence, it tends to lack the immediacy of the journals of the campaign, for the General affected the third person in describing his own actions. However, comparison with the *Private Diary* reveals very little alteration in his original observations, and in these extracts, considerations of succinctness have occasionally given the preference to the *Narrative*. The distinction between the two sources is observed within the brackets containing the page references at the close of each passage.

[51] Eugen, Duke of Württemberg (1788-1857), Russian general, nephew of Alexander's mother, hence the Tsar's first cousin.

be made on the country by the evacuation of "the venerated city of Smolensk," he observed—"There is nothing to fear on that account; I have provided against it: the Holy Virgin" (a picture) "is safe, and we have her in our camp; she is the only object that gives importance to the city in the eyes of the Russians; she shall be carried in a car of triumph with the army, and a battalion constantly appointed to escort and mount guard over her." . . . [*Narrative*, 105]

I cannot express the indignation that prevailed. The sacrifice of so many brave men; the destruction of an important town unnecessarily; the suspicion that Buonaparte directed Russian counsels, the sight of the holy city in flames, etc., etc., worked strongly on the feelings of the Russians. I even, in this moment of disappointment and wrath, regretted the exertions I had made and the hazards I had run (for I had my "hair-breadth scrapes") for objects which the General seemed to determine should be unattainable. . . . [*Diary*, 149]

4. A HAZARDOUS MARCH

The direct route on Dorogobouche [Dorogobuzh] from General Barclay's position ran parallel with the Dnieper for five wersts, but was commanded by the enemy's guns and musketry; the general therefore judged it necessary to march by a cross road.

The march of so considerable an army with more than five hundred pieces of cannon, even in two columns, must in any case have been attended under existing circumstances with great embarrassment; but unfortunately in this instance there were two very steep hills on the route of General Barclay's column, and the Russian ammunition waggons on two wheels had not proper aid in carriage-tackle or harness, there being no breechings or other apparatus for their safe descent.

I had been sent forward by General Barclay to ascertain why the column was halted, and I found that the first four ammunition waggons, with two pieces of cannon, twelve-pounders, had overpowered the horses in the descent of the nearest hill, and that they lay at the bottom, with wheels or limbers[52] broken, and all the horses killed or maimed; every succeeding gun and ammunition waggon had therefore to be held back by the soldiers fixing ropes on them, and that could not be done till daylight; and moreover, as too frequently occurs in night marches, most of the drivers fell asleep. [*Narrative*, 106-107]

---

[52] The detachable fore-part of a guncarriage or caisson, consisting of two wheels, an axle, and a pole.

Baron Brinken, a Courland nobleman, who afterwards became my aide-de-camp, was with me. He will bear witness to my toil for three hours, on account of the difficulty of descent. . . . I verily believe that my vigilance saved a great misfortune to the world. A longer delay would have infallibly enabled the enemy afterwards to execute what he proposed; but, in consequence of our onward movement he could not effect it in time. . . .

I was "here, there, and everywhere," until sunset, when I must particularize my being with General Barclay, going forward with him, and at last charging with the column that saved the day, and with it, the independence of Europe.[53] [*Diary*, 150-151]

5. THE PRESERVATION OF POWER

Having been a participator in the events which I have partially traced . . . I can with authority assure . . . that, notwithstanding the painful marches which the Russian army has incessantly made, notwithstanding its harassing retreats and severe services, its original high condition is but little impared, and that its confidence has augmented by the incidents in every field of combat. An impatience for a decisive battle is perhaps expressed in a tone that infringes on strict discipline; but the sight of a much loved country in desolation adds to the feeling of mortification which each individual experiences, under the buoyant belief "that it has been an unnecessary sacrifice of reputation and property."

Against the undeniable numerical superiority of the enemy, it is urged . . . "that the enemy does not present a national force, nor one of that same experienced description against which they had to contend before the Spanish War. They insist upon the reduced condition of the enemy's cavalry, and the comparatively increased vigour of their own; the indisputably greater efficiency of their artillery, although weaker in point of numerical amount; and finally, the devotion of every man in the army, as if the fate of the country depended on his single efforts." [*Narrative*, 110-111]

[53] Five versts east of Smolensk, the parallel route of Barclay's army made a juncture with the main road along the Dnieper at Valutino. Here, the corps of Ney made a strong effort to cut off the Russian retreat, and had Marshal Junot, who was in the vicinity, seconded Ney with vigor, Valutino might well have been a second Austerlitz. As it was, however, the stout defense of the Russian rear guard, of which the charge Wilson here described was a part, beat off the determined assault of Ney and the main army was preserved from what was probably the most dangerous threat of the entire campaign.

6. THE BREAKDOWN OF AUTHORITY

It is my duty to state that I consider General Barclay as terrorised (if I may use the expression) by the reputation of his enemy. That I am certain he is not making a war of manoeuvre upon any fixed and pre-arranged military system, but a war of marches without sufficient arrangement and method to avoid serious misfortune, if the enemy should press with more energy than they have hitherto done. . . .

The state of affairs is too desperate to admit of any attempt to enforce the maintenance of his authority.

I cannot give . . . a stronger specimen of the degree of opposition to the proceedings that have occurred than by citing the words of General Platow [Platov], in my presence, to General Barclay, after the evacuation of Smolensk: "You see, Sir, I wear only a cloak. I will no longer put on a Russian uniform; I consider it as a dishonour!" [*Narrative*, 384-385]

III · THE MISSION TO ST. PETERSBURG

1. THE MESSENGER OF THE ARMY

WHEN Sir Robert Wilson reached the Russian army he found the Generals in open discussion with the Commander-in-chief, General Barclay, for having already suffered the enemy to overrun so many provinces, and for not making any serious disposition to defend the line of the Dnieper. . . . Before his departure for S. Petersburg, however, it had been resolved to send to the Emperor not only the request of the army "for a new chief," but a declaration in the name of the army, "that if any order came from S. Petersburg to suspend hostilities, and treat the invaders as friends (which was apprehended to be the true motive of the retrograde movements, in deference to the policy of Count Romanzow) [Rumiantsev], such an order would be regarded as one which did not express His Imperial Majesty's real sentiments and wishes, but had been extracted from His Majesty under false representations or external control; and that the army would continue to maintain his pledge and pursue the contest till the invader was driven beyond the frontier." Since the execution of such a commission might expose a Russian officer to future punishment, and the conveyance of such a communication by a subject to the Sovereign was calculated to pain and give offence, when no offence was proposed, it was communicated by a body of generals to Sir Robert Wilson, "that under the circumstances of his known attachment to the Emperor, and His Imperial Majesty's equally well known feelings towards him,[54] no person was considered so properly qualified as himself to put the Emperor in possession of the sentiments of the army. . . ."

Sir Robert Wilson, after that deliberation which such a grave proposition required, agreed to be the bearer of the message, as far as the question of war and peace was concerned; but agreed solely that he might mitigate the unavoidable distress which the Emperor must experience during the execution of such a commission. [*Narrative*, 111-112]

2. THE PROPAGANDIST OF THE ALLIES

Before I left the army . . . I distributed several hundred proclamations of the Duque del Infantado,[55] which gave me full powers to treat with Spanish officers and soldiers; and by which, as Regent, His Highness pledged himself to ratify my engagements; and General Barclay agreed to leave several wounded Spaniards on the march with the proclamations sewed in their clothes, and with such verbal encouragements as, I hope, will produce a considerable defection from the enemy, if any Spaniards and Portuguese survive his prodigal expenditure of them. . . .

The English name stands so high in the enemy's army, that numbers of the confederates would flock to a British standard if His Majesty's Government thought it expedient; but I have confined myself, until I receive further orders, to negotiation with the countrymen of our allies. [*Narrative*, 386-387]

3. THE DEPARTURE FOR ST. PETERSBURG

A little before daybreak we moved. Head-quarters were in a miserable village; but I found good fare with the Duke of Oldenburg, and enjoyed the luxury of a toilette under the shelter of a pig-stye.

As I did not think there would be a general battle, . . . and as I had urgent motives to communicate with the Emperor . . . I took my corporal with me, my dragoon being very ill with fatigue, and, accompanied by Baron Brinken, set out for S. Petersburg. . . .

[54] Sir Robert's elastic disposition had apparently suppressed the memory of his last visit to St. Petersburg when the Emperor had not only refused him an audience, but had actually returned a letter addressed to him unopened.

[55] Infantado, an intriguing intimate of the future Ferdinand VII, who had been forced to renounce his right to the Spanish throne in 1808 and was even then being held hostage in France.

At Wiazma [Vyazma], we were entertained at breakfast by Mr. Birt, an English doctor, who is greatly esteemed by the Russians, and who has, on the present occasion, assisted the wounded with a liberality that will long be recorded in Russia. [*Diary*, 151-152]

4. ROADSIDE INTERVIEWS

Count Panin[56]

Stopped about fifty wersts from Wiazma, to call on Count Panin. It was night when we entered the court-yard, and it appeared an enchanted residence; but on a sudden we found ourselves surrounded by a square of palaces with a hugh church in the centre. I never saw a more magnificent establishment, nor one which accorded more with my sense of adaptation, especially in the nursery arrangements. Count Panin received me with great cordiality, and for four hours, we maintained a tête-à-tête, equally interesting to both, and which put me in possession of more knowledge with regard to the state of the Russian empire than as many years would have done "en particulier." [*Diary*, 152]

The Grand Duke Konstantin[57]

From Wiazma, we had proceeded across the country, which was everywhere very richly cultivated. Indeed, I may say again, that for five hundred wersts I did not see a barren acre. When we gained the high Moscow road, about three hundred wersts from S. Petersburg, the Grand Duke Constantine overtook me from the army, entered my room just as I had washed and changed, and made me sit down by him to talk for an hour. . . . In the midst of our discourse, he spoke of *Napoleon*. I called him *Buonaparte*[58] in my answer.

"Whom do you speak of?" he asked.

"Why, Sir," I answered, "Buonaparte, Buonaparte!"

[56] Count Nikita Pëtrovich Panin (1770-1837), the nephew of Catherine's famous foreign minister and the son of General Pëtr Ivanovich Panin. His early career had shown great promise, and as one of the conspirators against Paul, he had prepared Alexander's mind for the ultimate deposition of his father. Later, overcome with remorse and chagrin at his father's murder, Alexander had dismissed him, with several other leading conspirators, and he was now living in retirement.

[57] Grand Duke Konstantin Pavlovich (1779-1813), Alexander's younger brother. He was an ardent militarist, but feared and disliked war "because it spoiled the army." His personal cowardice kept him far removed from action throughout the campaign.

[58] Although the flamboyant chevalier continued this affectation throughout Napoleon's halcyon days, the ponderous dullness of the Bourbon Restoration gradually created in him a secret nostalgia for his ancient enemy, and, in his later recollections, he was far from begrudging "the hideous Corse" his imperial title.

"I thought," he said, "you meant *Lucien,* not *Napoleon Emperor of France, King of Italy,*" etc.

"I know, Sir," I replied again, "that you have made his acquaintance under these titles, and I am sure, Sir, you repent it: Thank God! I am not in that situation, and I cannot, even *en etiquette,* address him with any term of respect." [*Diary,* 152-153]

Prince Kutusov[59]

About a hundred wersts further, I met Prince Kutusow [Kutusov], on his way to command the armies. . . . The Prince alighted from his carriage, and we talked under a shed for about an hour. . . . I was much flattered by his cordial invitation to rejoin the army. Taking me by the hand, he said, "Lose no time to return; I have great need of such a comrade as yourself in the cabinet and in the field."

Brinken, who was with me, accustomed to see these high personages treat all others with dignified reserve, if not with offensive hauteur, could scarcely believe all that he saw on my travels, and is still in a trance of surprise from what has occurred here. [*Diary,* 153]

5. DIPLOMATIC PRETENSIONS

On the 27th, in the evening, I reached S. Petersburg very much fagged when in my telaga, but not in the least when I got out. I drove to the Hôtel de l'Europe. . . . The same evening I wrote despatches, and called on one or two friendly ministers.

The next morning, I had a great deal of official business to transact, which, with the despatches for Lord Castlereagh and Lord Cathcart,[60] occupied the whole day and night. . . . I should presume their contents will not be a dead letter in the Russian, British, or French archives. I have, if successful, gained a greater victory over Buonaparte than if I had preserved fifty Smolensks, nay, driven him beyond the Vistula. [*Diary,* 153-154]

[59] Prince Mikhail Ilarionovich Kutusov (1745-1813), a highly respected military commander with a long record. His popularity with the nobility had compelled his appointment to the post of commander in chief, although Alexander had personally disliked him ever since his own strategy, forced upon the latter over his stubborn objections, at Austerlitz in 1805 had resulted in a defeat which made of it a synonym for military disaster.

[60] Sir William Schaw, 1st Earl Cathcart, a proud and stubborn man, the former pupil of William Richardson in St. Petersburg and the current British ambassador to Russia. He was entirely ungifted as either a soldier or a diplomat. In this dual capacity, however, he served his country for nearly fifty years. He took a strong dislike to the dashing Sir Robert, whose freedom of action he sought to limit from the very outset and whom, in 1813, he spent the better part of six months to have recalled. Costigan, *op. cit.,* pp. 117-153.

IV · IN THE CAPITAL: A CHANGE OF ROLES

I. A BOLD AND HIGH PART

MOST of the families are in the country; but I have seen the Strogonows [Straganovs], the Orloffs, the Galitzins, and the Nariskins, etc. I have been an hour with the Empress Elizabeth, and two hours with the Empress-mother, who, on my going away, after many gracious speeches, notwithstanding the *language of truth* which I had thought it my duty to use, and which is so seldom respected by Princes, observed, "General, your coming here has rendered my son and the empire the greatest service. It is an obligation that we owe you, in addition to many former ones. I hope to see a great deal of you while you stay here." And the Orloffs told me that during the dinner yesterday, her expressions of favour were incessant. . . . The social hours here are very late; and the necessity of devoting some of the night or early dawn to business renders it impossible for me to be in bed more than four hours. . . .

I have found day and night too short. . . . However, I trust that my occupation here will long be remembered, as essentially contributing to the welfare of Russia and the triumph of the common cause.

I have been playing a bold and high part on this stage. I have been the organ of the Russian army and nation, and I hope one of the best friends that a sovereign ever had in a foreigner. . . . [*Diary*, 154-156]

2. A DIFFICULT SCENE

The Emperor arrived on the 3rd of September at S. Petersburg, and Sir Robert Wilson was immediately honoured by a command to dine with him. . . .

When the dinner was over, the Emperor withdrew with Sir Robert Wilson to his cabinet, where the conference commenced. . . . The Emperor . . . directed the conversation to the dissensions existing among the Generals. . . .

Sir Robert Wilson observed ". . . that he had undertaken a charge which his affection and gratitude towards His Majesty had made a duty under all circumstances; that in incurring the chance of displeasure, he was devoting himself to the Emperor's service, and for the protection of his dignity;" and then, entering at once into the matter . . . he concluded "by earnestly imploring His Majesty to bear in mind the perilous state of the empire, which might justify patriotic alarm, and which alarm, from the gravity of its cause, extenuated a trespass on authority instigated by the purest motives, and intended for the permanent preservation of that authority itself; that the chiefs were animated by the most affectionate attachment to the Emperor and his family; and if they were but assured that His Majesty would no longer give his confidence to advisers whose policy they mistrusted, they would testify their allegiance by exertions and sacrifices, which would add splendour to the crown, and security to the throne under every adversity."

During this exposition the Emperor's colour, occasionally visited and left his cheek. When Sir Robert Wilson had terminated his appeal, there was a minute or two of pause, and His Majesty drew towards the window, as if desirous of recovering an unembarrassed air before he replied. After a few struggles, however, he came up to Sir Robert Wilson, took him by the hand, and kissed him on the forehead and cheek, according to the Russian custom. "You are the only person," then said His Majesty, "from whom I could or would have heard such a communication. In the former war you proved your attachment towards me by your services, and you entitled yourself to my most intimate confidence; but you must be aware that you have placed me in a very distressing position. Moi! Souverain de la Russie!—to hear such things from any one! But the army is mistaken in Romanzow: he really has not advised submission to the Emperor Napoleon; and I have a great respect for him, since he is almost the only one who never asked me in his life for anything on his own account. . . . I am to be pitied, for I have few about me who have any sound education or fixed principles: my grandmother's court vitiated the whole education of the empire, confining it to the acquisition of the French language, French frivolities and vices, particularly gaming. I have little, therefore, on which I can rely firmly . . . but I will think on all you have said." His Majesty then embraced Sir Robert Wilson again, and appointed the next day for his further attendance. [*Narrative*, 114-117]

3. THE AMBASSADOR OF THE REBELS

Sir Robert Wilson obeyed His Majesty's commands, who renewed the subject almost immediately by saying "Well! *Monsieur l'Ambassadeur des rebelles*—I have reflected seriously during the whole night upon the conversation of yesterday, and I have not done you injustice. You shall carry back to the army pledges of my determination to continue the war against Napoleon whilst a Frenchman is in arms on this side the frontier. I will not desert my engagements, come what may. I will abide the worst. I am ready to remove my family into the interior, and undergo every sacrifice; but I must not give way on the point of choosing my own ministers; *that* concession might induce other demands, still more inconvenient and indecorous for me to grant. Count Romanzow shall not be the means of any disunion or difference. . . . Give me a little time—All will be satisfactorily arranged." [*Narrative*, 117]

4. THE REWARDS OF DARING

The next morning I received a note to dine with the Emperor. . . . The dinner was magnificent. The Empress-mother, the Empress, the Grand Duchess, the Duchess of Wurtemberg, the Princess Amelia, etc. were present. The party seemed to be made for particular distinction, as such a meeting is very rare. Before dinner the Emperor and Empress especially addressed themselves to me; and after dinner, in the adjoining room, the Empress first spoke with me for a quarter of an hour, and then the Emperor for a full half-hour. The compliment was so marked—since neither conversed with any other person above a few moments, and even so much only with two or three grandees—that every one of my friends noticed it to me afterwards. . . .

At night, I went to several parties. With Countess Potoski, I passed a most agreeable hour, as she is one of the most accomplished women I ever met with: and as Madame de Stael is going away, I joined her party for another hour, and adventured in the presence of such a bel esprit to discuss several topics very vehemently. "Fortune favours the bold"; and I retired in full possession of her favour, and loaded with her encomiums, which I appreciate highly, as she is certainly a very clever woman, and I strongly recommend her to the attentions of my friends, in England when she goes there. [*Diary*, 157-159]

5. THE PENALTIES OF SINCERITY

Yesterday was incessantly occupied with business until dinner time, when I made myself chaperon to Captain Bowles of the Navy, Macdonald, and several of Lord Cathcart's staff. We nearly mustered a regiment in the several houses to which we went, but all were delighted at the sight of the "*masse en rouge*.". . . The group is very respectable, and I make no doubt will continue popular. . . .

Every hour endears Russia more and more to me. I do not know, however, that my popularity may not receive a shock. My Russian work[61] is being translated into Russian, French, and German, so it will be universally read, and no man could ever yet please all the world with

[61] *Brief Remarks on the Character and Composition of the Russian Army*, London, 1810, mentioned in the biographical sketch above.

a picture. Still, if any are offended, I shall say: "Amicus Plato, amicus Socrates, sed magis amica veritas": what is an Englishman without sincerity? the most despicable abortion in nature! [*Diary*, 160-161]

6. THE TIDINGS OF VICTORY

I have just returned from one of the most interesting and magnificent scenes in the world—the ceremony in the Church of Alexander Neufsky [Nevskii] on the baptism day of the Emperor. So splendid a sight I never beheld. . . . After the service, Prince Gortschakow read a despatch from Marshal Kutusow, announcing the defeat of Buonaparte in a great battle. The effect was glorious. . . . Two hundred thousand roubles (two shillings each) to Prince Kutusow, with the rank of Marshal: twenty-five roubles to each private soldier. . . . I am more than ever impatient to return, that I may be of use . . . as well as to pursue the career of true glory. [*Diary*, 162]

7. THE AMBASSADOR OF THE EMPEROR

During the stay of Sir Robert Wilson at S. Petersburg, His Imperial Majesty continued to heap distinctions on him, as if anxious to make more manifest through him his sentiments and feelings towards the parties whom he had represented; and when the Emperor sanctioned his return, His Majesty, with the greatest solemnity, "declared upon his honour, and directed him to repeat in the most formal manner the declaration, that His Majesty would not enter into or permit any negotiation with Napoleon as long as an armed Frenchman remained in the territories of Russia." His Imperial Majesty said, "he would sooner let his beard grow to his waist, and eat potatoes in Siberia." At the same time he *especially authorized Sir Robert Wilson* (who was to reside with the Russian army as British Commissioner) *to interpose, and intervene with all the power and influence he could exert, to protect the interests of the Imperial Crown in conformity with that pledge, whenever he saw any disposition or design to contravene or prejudice them.*" [*Narrative*, 119]

V · OUTSIDE MOSCOW: THE RISING SPIRIT

1. A BURNING LOSS

ON THE 15th of September . . . Lord Tyrconnel,[62] and I, my corporal, Lord T's servant, and a field-jager left S. Petersburg. . . . My mode of

---

[62] Earl of Tyrconnel, a young nobleman and personal friend of Castlereagh's, who had been attached to Sir Robert from Lord Cathcart's embassy by the dour old Scot in order to keep him under observation and prevent unauthorized diplomatic maneuvers. Wilson subsequently

conveyance was improved, for I now had a carriage with hind springs, which broke in some degree the violence of the action upon the wooden roads; but still I was far from personal ease. My mind was, however, quite comfortable, for I felt that my residence had been *eminently* useful at S. Petersburg, and that every succeeding day would more and more exemplify that fact. We travelled unremittingly day and night, without any remarkable incident, until we reached Tver [Tver], a hundred and twenty wersts from Moscow, where we heard the fall and the firing of that city. . . .

We then proceeded within fifty wersts from Moscow, rounded the burning city, whose flames fired the whole sky, keeping about that distance until we reached . . . on the seventh day, the head-quarters at Krasnoi Pakra [Krasnaya Pakhra] thirty-two wersts distant from Moscow, on the Kaluga road. . . .

The bearing of the fugitive nobility and commonalty from Moscow, who covered the country, was a noble specimen of patriotism, that made us forget our own disappointments and vexations. There was not one who did not disdain to mourn over his own particular afflictions, and when I told them of the Emperor's resolution to continue the war without remission whilst a Frenchman remained in arms on Russian territory, many wept for joy, many kissed me (*young and fair, as well as old*) and they cheered as others might have done when their losses were repaired and their wanderings had ceased. The same sentiment animates all classes in this illustrious army. It was their first question, and I was almost suffocated with caresses when I pledged the Emperor's perseverance. [*Diary*, 164-165]

2. A FLAMING PRIZE

On the 14th of September, the Russian rear-guard commenced its movement through the city. . . . When Murat entered, the Crown magazines of forage, of wine (not less than thirteen millions of quarts), of brandy, of military stores, and of powder were blazing. As he approached the arsenal, the populace, frantic, rushed upon him and his troops.

The enemy, victorious, hoped and expected to repose in an emporium of riches and luxuriant abundance until that peace was made which Buonaparte promised to his army at Smolensk. But the Russians resolved on inflicting a species of vengeance more disastrous in its con-

---

dispatched him as an observer to the Moldavian army, and he died prematurely of an epidemic illness at Vilna in December, 1812. Costigan, *op. cit.*, p. 127.

sequences than the slaughter of the sword. All the houses of the nobility, all the ware-houses of the merchants, all the shops, etc. were fired; and, notwithstanding every effort of the enemy, the conflagration raged and rendered Moscow one flaming pile; so that, as the enemy stated themselves, they occupied only the site where the city stood, and their embarrassments were increased by an erroneous calculation that their needs would be supplied by the resources of Moscow. [*Diary*, 172]

3. AN HONORABLE EPHESUS

Last night [September 26], as it was found that the provisions for the army came in slowly on account of the roads being spoilt by the incessant rain, Prince Kutusow resolved to march his army on the Kaluga road, whence his supplies come, nine wersts in the course of the day. I therefore resolved to come on with General Beningsen, Count Rostopchin,[63] the Governor of Moscow, and Platow, who is a little unwell. Last night . . . we proceeded to the Count's house, which is one of the most superb edifices I ever saw.

There are two groups of figures from the antique—grooms holding rampant horses—placed upon Saracen towers at the extremity of his stables, which, for gigantic mould and skilful execution, are worthy of the original Roman design. They are modelled from the Monte Cavallo horses.

The whole suite is in the best style of building, and the grounds equal in scenery, from eminence and distribution of wood and water, any residence in the British dominions. [*Diary*, 167]

This morning [October 1], the army marched ten wersts. I waited, with Count Rostopchin, to see him fire his palace and all surrounding premises. It was a magnificent act, executed with feeling, dignity, and philosophy. The motive was pure patriotism.

On the preceding day, seventeen hundred and twenty of his peasants (all on this property) came in a body to request permission to leave their houses, effects, and the bones of their fathers, and retire to the Count's estates in the interior of Russia, which leave was granted. Never was a more affecting procession. But what a country is this Russia! What patriotic virtue! What nobility of spirit! Shame! For shame on Dr. Clark who has calumniated such a nation. The flames

[63] Count Fëdor Vasilievich Rostopchin (1763-1826), a soldier, politician, and writer, who had been favored by Paul and was currently the Governor of Moscow. Prior to its evacuation, he had issued bombastic proclamations assuring the population of a vigorous defense and was loud in his recriminations against Kutusov both for his decision to abandon the city and for his failure to notify him in time to organize a systematic conflagration.

had raged about two hours, when we received advice that the enemy had retreated, but the Count expressed no regret; on the contrary, he conversed quite calmly with me, and waited until we saw some colossal statues of men and horses fall. Certainly the property destroyed could not be replaced for a hundred thousand pounds. The house and premises rival any that we have in England. The firing of Ephesus won a dishonourable immortality; the firing of Woronowo ought to insure, and will insure, a lasting record of Russian patriotism! [*Diary*, 177-178]

4. SPANISH TACTICS AND RUSSIAN COURAGE

Every day since we have been here, prisoners in parties of fifty, and even of a hundred, have been brought in, chiefly wounded. During the five days that we remained at Krasnoi Pakra, thirteen hundred and forty-two were delivered to the commandant at head-quarters. Of course many more are killed; for such is the inveteracy of the peasants that they buy prisoners of the Cossacks for several roubles to *put them to death*. Two guns have been taken by the peasants; vast quantities of baggage, etc., both going to and from Moscow; much melted silver, which I myself have seen: and some of the guards—of whom two squadrons were taken—told me that they had been obliged to blow up a convoy of sixty powder-waggons, rather than suffer them to be made a prize. In brief, the Spanish guerrilla warfare never was more successful, and certainly was not so formidable to the enemy. . . . When fate presides, and Russian courage is its instrument, chiefs may wrangle or may err, due precautions may be neglected, but he *must fall*! [*Diary*, 174-175]

5. FINE FELLOWS AND COMRADES

September 27: The Cossacks continue to obtain great success. Five hundred Frenchmen have been taken by them as the enemy's column retrograded from the Kolomna road; and yesterday fourteen carts, two of which contained gold and silver to the amount of fifteen thousand ducats, were taken on the Podolsk road. All the prisoners concur in stating that the French army is in the state we desire; and it appears that Buonaparte is in some danger in Moscow. . . . [*Diary*, 176]

October 1: The day before yesterday, General Milaradowitch[64]

[64] Mikhail Andreevich Miloradovich (1771-1825), who had been a general at Austerlitz, revealed excellent qualities as a commander in large scale harassing operations in 1812. His death in 1825 as the Governor of St. Petersburg was remarkable as being one of the few loyalist casualties in the Decembrist uprising in the capital.

attacked and drove back the enemy with some loss . . . and, in the night, General Fevrier, with two aides-de-camp, was taken by the Cossacks. . . . He seems to be a person of some consideration for Murat sent immediately to have him exchanged, which was refused. . . . At night the Cossacks attacked and killed two hundred Cuirassiers on a foraging party, and made eighty-five prisoners. [*Diary*, 177]

October 3: At night the Cossacks attacked a convoy, made eighty-four prisoners, and possessed themselves of many waggons laden with bread. . . . [*Diary*, 179]

October 4: The cannonade recommenced about noon, and the French cavalry fell into a Cossack ambuscade—five hundred were killed and a hundred and eighty made prisoners. It was a very gallant affair, most ably conducted. . . . Platow is about to vault again into the saddle. . . . The cannonade recommences, and I must go and see my fine fellows and comrades, the Cossacks, work. I am happy to say that from services rendered to their Hetman, I am more popular than ever with them. With regard to the army at large, I remain, as heretofore, the object of every attention. [*Diary*, 179-181]

VI · IN THE CAMP: THE SINEWS OF WAR

I. THE STREAM OF TROOPS

THE CALCULATION of reinforcement to the Russian army by the Council of War has been fully answered. I myself have seen a hundred and forty-four pieces of cannon refused, and eight thousand as fine troops as any in the regular army arrive, with several thousand militia. Tomorrow and on the ensuing days of next week, fifteen thousand regular infantry, under Prince Labonow [Lobanov] are expected; four thousand Cossacks will be here in eight days . . . two thousand horses given by the province of Toula [Tula], and two thousand horses for the remnant [remount] of the cavalry and artillery of this army, also given by that province exclusive of its militia contingent, are in our camp; while eighty-four thousand militia are on their march from the neighbouring provinces to be fused into the ranks of the regular army, and will successively arrive in the month of October. Exclusively of these supplies, an immense army is forming in the province of Kasan [Kazan]. . . .

With the means of such an empire, with the spirit of such a people, with the base of such an army, can I doubt of Russia's triumph and the establishment of at least one independent State in the North of Europe? [*Diary*, 173-174]

2. A COMPARATIVE BANQUET

White bread is six shillings a loaf; sugar, ten shillings a lb.; butter, not to be had; and very little of anything in camp but meat and black biscuit; yet all are well and gay, and, by some means or another, we have daily a comparative banquet. For want of . . . my canteens from Constantinople, I cannot yet boast of a good breakfast or tea establishment; but I mean to be *fort* in both, and Prince Galitzin yesterday gave me a cow to assist my good intentions. [*Diary*, 182]

3. A SURGICAL SUCCESS

I wish Keate[65] to be told, that the day before yesterday I saw a Cossack have his arm extracted from the shoulder joint, who had ridden twenty miles after having been struck by a cannon shot. He never spoke during the operation, which was performed by Dr. Wiley[66] in less than four minutes; but he talked afterwards quite composedly. The next morning, he drank tea, walked about his room, and then got into a cart, which carried him fourteen miles. He is now proceeding several hundred miles to the Don, and is, according to the last report, doing very well. This operation of extracting the arm is a frequent operation here, and seldom fails of cure. [*Diary*, 182]

4. WELCOME GUESTS

The bearded warriors of the Don . . . continue to arrive, and *General Winter*, who is our most powerful ally, has already presented the torrents of his advanced guard. . . . Platow loaded me with pears, Don wine, better in my opinion than Champagne, and a fine dried sturgeon to eat like smoked salmon. I value this present the more as it enables me to distribute "the goods the Gods provide.". . .

While I was dining with Platow and a great party of general officers the day before yesterday, Platow received a letter from one of the Tartar regiments, informing him that they had made prize of a consider-

[65] Dr. Robert Keate (1777-1857), an eminent surgeon and the personal physician of four British sovereigns, who was an intimate friend of Sir Robert's.

[66] Dr. James Wylie, a Scottish physician, who spent many years in the Russian capital, having made himself grateful to the court by mixing medicine with politics and diplomatically assigning apoplexy as the cause of death in Paul's assassination in 1801. Archibald Steuart, *Scottish Influences in Russian History*, Glasgow, 1913, p. 121.

able sum of gold and silver, which had been melted by the enemy from church ornaments; but that they placed their prize at his disposal, as they thought it a sacrilege to take it from their country. "Le beau sentiment" is not extinguished here, however rare in these times, and I could write a many-paged book of verified anecdotes that would shame the niggardliness of other more civilized countries.

It is true the light troops have no want of unrighteous gold; they have taken so many horses, watches, Louis d'ors, etc., that one Cossack regiment has divided booty that gives every man eighty-four pounds sterling. . . . The Don regiments continue to pour in. Such a reinforcement of cavalry was perhaps never equaled. . . . They bring us the most agreeable wines, sturgeon, caviare, and large barrels of red and white grapes, of which Platow has given me a superabundant share. [*Diary*, 193-196]

5. A GRATEFUL LARGESSE

The reinforcement and provisioning of the assembling army was one of the most extraordinary efforts of national zeal ever made. No Russian who possessed any article which could be rendered serviceable to the state withheld it: horses, arms, equipment, provisions, and, in brief, every thing that can be imagined was poured into the camps.

Militia performed the most remarkable marches, even for Russians, to reach the head-quarters.

Old and young, over and under the regulated ages, flocked to the standards, and would not be refused service. Fathers of families, many seventy years of age and upwards, placed themselves in the ranks, and encountered every fatigue as well as peril with all the ardour of youth. Governors of distant provinces, without waiting for orders or requisitions, urged forward every supply they could collect; and so many cannon were despatched by relays, that a hundred and sixty beautiful new guns were in one day sent away as superfluous.

When the army amounted to a hundred and ten thousand men, not only were they regularly fed, but fifty thousand horses received full rations of hay and corn without the extension of the foraging range above twenty miles.

The camp resembled a bee-hive in the activity of its swarming hosts. The whole nation was solicitous to fill it with stores and useful largesses. [*Narrative*, 194-195]

6. AN AWFUL EPOCH

We are now in a commanding position, strongly reinforced, and all wears the face of successful promise. Our main army is as numerous as that of the enemy—I believe, indeed, stronger. He is environed by numerous difficulties, and very superior forces pressing upon his flanks and rear. We have our supplies; he wants them. We are habituated to climate; he has everything to fear from it.

It is a great moment—an awful epoch! The operations of the last seventeen years, the victories of France, the errors of the continental Powers are all now gathered together, and await the decision of the fate of ninety thousand men plunged above five hundred miles into the heart of a warlike and powerful nation, whose army has never yet, during this war, suffered actual defeat. [*Diary*, 179-180]

VII · AT THE ADVANCED POSTS:
AN IRON DOOR

1. "A TERRIBLE PEOPLE"

SINCE the Russian main army had taken up its position at Taroutino [Tarutino], and Murat at Winkowo, conversations had daily been held at the advanced posts by the principal Russian officers with Murat and his generals. They had commenced with the cessation of daily morning skirmishing, mutual courtesies followed as the lines of videttes were visited; and finally such civilities were interchanged that the intervening ground was respected as neutral, where both parties might meet and confer in security at pleasure.

Murat, on one of these occasions, expressed a wish to meet Beningsen next day, who inconsiderately (for it was contrary to the Emperor's orders) kept the appointment.

After some personal compliments, Murat said, "Peace is necessary—I wish it as King of Naples, who have a country to govern."

Beningsen answered, "As much as you wish it, in so much do we prefer war: besides, if the *Emperor would*, the Russians *would not*; and, to speak frankly, I belong to that party."

Murat observed, "National prejudices might be overcome."

"Oh no," replied Beningsen, "not in Russia; the Russians are a terrible people, and would kill any man instantly who even talked of negotiation." [*Narrative*, 200]

2. "A MARAUDING FORCE OF TARTARS"

The next morning Buonaparte sent a letter to request permission for an aide-de-camp-general to come to head-quarters, and speak on important matters with Marshal Kutusow. The Marshal had answered that he himself would meet him beyond the advanced posts, before I knew of his flag of truce.

However, on my *strong representations* against the intercourse, and my statement of the mischievous consequences of such a proceeding—such an impressement to enter into negotiations with the enemy—in which representations I was supported by the Duke of Wurtemberg and Prince Oldenburg whom I brought to the Marshal for that purpose, the Marshal consented to send Prince Wolkonsky to the advanced posts.

The Prince went as aide-de-camp-general of the Emperor, and met General Lauriston, who told him that he had important matters to communicate to the Marshal in person: it was then settled that General Lauriston should at night see the Marshal in his own head-quarters. . . .

At night, Marshal Kutusow wished the Duke of Wurtemberg and myself to be present when Lauriston entered, that we might let him see how he was *entouré en conseil*. After mutual salutations from the Marshal, that Lauriston might not be ignorant who we were, we retired, but waited very near, and saw that the conversation was very animated on the part of the Marshal by his gestures.

In half an hour, Prince Wolkonsky was called in, and a quarter of an hour afterwards, General Lauriston came out with a very discontented air, and spoke in such a manner that every person was satisfied he had been disappointed. The Marshal, on our entering, told us what had passed.

General Lauriston had complained, first, of the barbarity of the Russians towards the French. The Marshal answered, that he could not civilize a nation in three months who regarded the enemy as a marauding force of Tartars under a Ginghis Khan.

Lauriston said, "But at least there is some difference."

"In fact," said the Marshal, "there may be, but none in the eyes of the people: I can only answer for my own troops."

General Lauriston had no complaint to make against them. He then adverted to an armistice, saying that "Nature herself would, in short time, oblige it." The Marshal said he had no authority on that head. . . .

The burden of his tale was an armistice; and I presume that this, and a convention for the retreat of the army, were the subjects to which Buonaparte alluded in his letter to the Marshal. . . . [*Diary*, 183-186]

3. "FRENCH LEAVE"

General Korf, who is a most excellent man, with a fund of dry humour, on the same day met General Amande at the advanced posts. Their conversation soon turned on peace. General Amande observed, "We are really quite tired of this war: give us passports and we will depart." "Oh! no, General," said Korf. "You came without being invited; when you go away, you must take French leave." "Ah!" said General Amande, "but it is really a pity that two nations who esteem each other should be carrying on a war of extermination: we will make our excuses for having intruded, and shake hands upon our respective frontiers." "Yes," replied the Russian, "We believe that you have lately learned to esteem us, but would you continue to do so if we suffered you to escape with arms in your hands?" "Parbleu!" sighed Monsieur Amande, "I see that there is no talking to you about peace now, and that we shall not be able to make it." [*Diary*, 188]

4. DOMESTICATED MYRMIDONS

The language of Murat and General Amande is the universal language of all who communicate with us, or who are taken. It is the content of every letter found in the pockets of the enemy. . . . Discontent, and need, and apprehension are hourly augmenting the difficulties of Buonaparte. These, added to the daily multiplying forces of the Russians, and the approaching rudeness of the climate, will, I think, very soon render his case desperate. . . .

Sixty thousand militia, with some regulars and corps of Cossacks, occupy all the roads leading to Moscow, and daily destroy escorts, convoys, etc. . . .

Yesterday, two hundred French cuirassier foragers were made prisoners. A general came with a flag of truce to remonstrate against the cruelty of the Cossacks in falling upon "poor men, only going in search of a little hay!" Sweet innocents! How tender! how humane! how considerate these Myrmidons have become! [*Diary*, 188-190]

5. CAVALIERS "CUM DES POULES"

My leg improved a little,[67] and therefore I thought I might venture to get as far as General Milaradowitch. The General had, the day be-

[67] Driving home to his quarters on the night of Lauriston's interview with Kutusov, Sir

fore, seen Murat, who asked him personally to let his cavalry forage to the right and left.

Milaradowitch answered, "Why, would you wish to deprive us of the pleasure of taking your finest cavaliers of France 'cum des poules'?"

"Oh! Then I shall take my measures: I shall march my foraging columns with infantry and artillery on the flanks." "It is exactly what I wish, that I may order my regiments to give them the rencontre."

Murat galloped off, and instead of his marching the columns to protect the foragers, the Cossacks took last night forty-three cuirassiers and carabineers, and fifty-three this morning. [*Diary*, 191-192]

6. DISMISSAL TO COVENTRY

The day before yesterday, I rode to the French posts, passed within half pistol shot, accompanied by my dragoon and Colonel Potemkin, that I might introduce myself and dragoon ... to the knowledge of our friends in the enemy's army. As I was resolved that they should be under no mistake, I persuaded Potemkin to make some excuse and speak to a French officer whom we saw by one of the videttes, under some pretext. He did so, and in the course of conversation let him know who I was. A party of cavalry turned out from a neighbouring wood, and then we leisurely fell back. Soon afterwards, Murat came and wished to speak to General Korf, but Korf sent him to Coventry and would have no more communication with him. [*Diary*, 192-193]

7. THE END OF MODERATION

I feel confident that in another fortnight Moscow will be evacuated, and the enemy in that desperate condition which leaves him no alternative but ... surrender at discretion. As his army is not national, the greater part will probably prefer the "crooking of the knees.". . .

More prisoners are momentarily brought in. Above fifteen hundred are now before our eyes, in wretched condition, with teeth chattering. The peasants have bought numbers from the Cossacks, at two silver roubles a head, to kill them. . . . This town is a complete heap of ruins. It is impossible to see such devastation and not find some excuse for the vengeance of the Russians.

Robert's carriage had overturned, pinning his ankle to the ground and causing him considerable pain and discomfort for the succeeding two weeks. It is remarkable that this accident, together with a frostbitten nose in the following December, and a wasp sting on the tongue in the Peninsular Campaign, were the only casualties of an apparently charmed life exposed to every danger of the battlefield for more than twenty years.

On the 21st, a colonel . . . brought a letter from General Berthier, who, in the name of the Emperor . . . expressed his surprise "that no answer had been received from S. Petersburg to his demand for a change in the character of the war, and the restoration of order in the country." Baron Arnsted wrote the answer, which was extremely well expressed; and he concluded by observing, "that no person dared to speak to the exasperated inhabitants on the subject of moderation." [*Diary*, 198-200]

VIII · THE ESCAPE FROM MOSCOW:
A BRIDGE OF GOLD

I. BUONAPARTE ON MARCH

On the 22nd, I marched with the corps of General Doctorow's comprised of twelve thousand infantry, three thousand cavalry, and eighty cannon, to effect a coup-de-main against a corps of ten thousand French, supposed to be at Fominskoi [Fominskoye], distant thirty wersts.

When we came within seven wersts, I saw that the attempt was madly rash: the enemy's corps was not posted in any town, consequently could resist and retreat; the grand army was known to be at Woronowo, distant only twenty wersts, the day before; and all reasonable conjecture induced the assurance that Buonaparte was on the alert, and moving to his right that he might gain our left. . . .

I prevailed so far as to obtain a delay for better information. At dusk, we received full assurance that Buonaparte, having evacuated Moscow, was with his guards and Davoust's corps only four wersts from Fominskoi. . . . [*Diary*, 201-202]

2. A CRITICAL MOMENT

Doctorow sent to the Marshal for further reinforcements, and immediately began his march on Malo-Jaroslavets [Maloyaroslavets], distant thirty wersts. We made every possible effort, but the enemy from Barowsk [Borovsk] had lodged themselves before our arrival. . . .

I had the honour to open the ball, and plant the first guns that saved the town, for the enemy were pouring in. Our corps was in the greatest confusion, ignorant of the Kalouga-road, and having to defile with all our incumbrances round the town to gain it. It was a most critical moment, and the hour so saved enabled the resistance which was afterwards so obstinately made. I pushed the guns into short grape distance.

After the first four rounds, the enemy's columns broke. . . . The slaughter must have been considerable. . . . The Russians and the enemy fought desperately. The town of Aspern was not more heroically contended for.[68] But whenever the enemy appeared out of the town, the Russians gained an easy victory, even over the Guards, who latterly were engaged, and whom Buonaparte was seen to be addressing as they descended the hill to pass the river. [*Diary*, 202-203]

3. THE RUSSIAN CANUTE

The shot, shell, and balls fell in showers from time to time in all parts of the field, but there was no time at that moment for consideration of peril. . . . The Russians only accuse *one person* of being *deficient in example*; in addition to the heavy charges which can be brought against him for ignorance in the conduct of the troops, for sloth, for indecision of counsels, for panic operations, and for "a desire to let the enemy pass unmolested."

Marshal Kutusow affords a memorable instance of incapacity in a chief, of the absence of any quality that ought to distinguish a commander. Although within five wersts of the action from day-break, he never had even the curiosity to appear in the field until five o'clock in the evening; and when he did come he never went forward, but, like Canute on the sea-shore, took his station and said to the balls, "Come no further than three hundred paces from me," and they, unlike the rebel waves, obeyed. . . . I have done my duty, and put those in possession of the facts who can prevent their pernicious repetition.[69] [*Diary*, 203-204]

[68] The battle of Aspern-Essling on the Danube in 1809 had been one of the bitterest of Napoleon's career. In it, the Archduke Charles had inflicted losses of more than 25,000 men on the French forces, and only the iron will of the French commander had saved him from a disaster.

[69] Here, as elsewhere, Sir Robert's literary style did not run to understatement. Nevertheless, attempts to defend Kutusov's conduct at Maloyaroslavets have been notably ineffectual. The Marshal's army spent 38 precious hours in marching only 28 versts, while Dokhturov's corps made a forced night march over pathless country, reached Maloyaroslavets only to find it occupied, circled the town to bar a further progress southward, and waged a fierce offensive action to gain possession. The town changed hands no less than eight times. Had Napoleon been able to force a passage through it to Kaluga, the immense supply of military stores and provisions awaiting him there and a route through an untouched country would have greatly facilitated his withdrawal to Smolensk. Yet Tarle, admitting all this, defends Kutusov on the ground that he wished to preserve his army by avoiding decisive conflict. To this, it must be objected that Kutusov's conduct actually invited attack by placing an inferior force between the enemy and a much needed prize. Yet despite his blunder, the heroic resistance of Maloyaroslavets resulted in a French withdrawal. For all that the casualties were relatively small, about 15,000 on both sides, this issue made it one of the decisive battles of a decisive campaign. Tarle, *op. cit.*, pp. 331-332.

4. THE "PONT D'OR"

About two in the morning, the generals were . . . summoned. . . .

Kutusow, sitting in the midst of the circle, shortly acquainted them that "he had received information which had induced him to relinquish the intention of defending the ground in front of Malo-Jaroslavets and determined him to retire . . . to secure the road to Kalouga. . . ."

This announcement was a thunderbolt that caused a momentary stupor. It was, however, represented to him, "that such a movement, in such a moment, and under the circumstances of darkness and the narrow causeway on the line of retreat, could not be executed without perilous confusion; and that the enemy, seeing this, would doubtless endeavour to increase it by an attack; that the whole army would be placed in jeopardy, and the rear guard inevitably lost. . . ."

The English General enforcing these considerations, was told by the Marshal, "I don't care for your objections. I prefer giving my enemy a 'pont d'or,' as you call it, to receiving a 'coup de collier': besides, I will say again, as I have told you before, that I am by no means sure that the total destruction of the Emperor Napoleon and his army would be such a benefit to the world; his succession would not fall to Russia or any other continental power, but to that which already commands the sea, and whose domination would then be intolerable." [*Narrative*, 233-234]

5. HYMNS OF LAMENTATION

The firing of the town was a terrible expedient. All the wounded who could not move were burnt, but I have seen this so often that I cease to feel the same horror that I felt at first. . . . The columns clashed, the horses could not draw through the mud, the bridges over the marsh were broken, the wounded crawling away were crying for aid; and such a scene of confusion ensued as determined me to take my part with the rear guard as the least evil.

The good countenance, however, of this rear guard checked the advance of the enemy. Gradually the difficulties diminished, the army collected three wersts from the town, order was re-established, and there was not a man but the Marshal who would not have thanked Providence for a general battle at that very moment. The transitions from confidence to fear, from joy to despair, are as frequent as the movements of this army and its occupation of positions; for courage is our only shield. . . .

This morning, the enemy was retreating, probably to gain the Smolensk road. The Marshal will sing *Te Deum*, but the rest of the army, "hymns of lamentation," if the French army is not wrecked before it reaches the frontier, the Marshal, old and infirm as he is, ought to be shot. [*Diary*, 204-205]

IX · THE FLIGHT TO VYAZMA: A LEADEN PURSUIT

I. THE ENERGY OF THE NATION

THIS nation has now solidly established its independence—by great sacrifices, assuredly, but they have produced an energy that advances the growth of Russia a century at least.

No person had previously to this war a just knowledge of the power and resources of the Russian empire. . . . There is one universal emulation of patriotism, one general spirit of vengeance.

In all the late affairs the rude peasants charge *en masse* with the veteran troops, and the pike in their hands is no less formidable to the enemy than the bayonet in those of the regular Russian soldier. [*Narrative*, 395]

2. THE MEANS OF REINFORCMENT

If the smallest corps of British could . . . be landed, such co-operation would have a most advantageous moral influence, and still more because of our notorious exertions in the Peninsula.

Upon such a corps we might form a German army to any extent we chose. I am sure that I could have enlisted ten thousand men from the enemy alone, without a shilling bounty. Russia can not recruit with any success amongst the foreigners. Language, prejudice, Siberian tales, form a rampart of separation which cannot be removed in one campaign, and the finances of Russia cannot support the expense. [*Narrative*, 395-396]

3. THE FEEBLENESS OF THE MARSHAL

Yesterday [October 29], we marched to Poloianameya, a great cloth-manufactury. There is not in England a more extensive establishment or a mercantile residence more magnificent. I was lodged in some of the best apartments, but I would gladly have exchanged for any ordinary hovel, as the day was bitterly cold, and the stoves smoked so much that they could not be used. . . .

This morning we marched to Medinsk, where the Cossacks defeated the advance guard of Prince Poniatowski[70] . . . destroying a great many men and capturing five pieces of cannon. The ground is still covered with dead horses and men. . . .

We are now in pursuit of the enemy, who is flying with all expedition: he has already destroyed above a thousand waggons. The army is highly indignant with the Marshal for his conduct of the operations: by a false movement, occasioned by his personal terror, rather than by an error of judgment, he has made a circuit of near eighty wersts and has lost sight of the enemy, whom he ought to have daily brought to action and never to have quitted with his main army while ten thousand men remained together.

I can scarcely behave with common decency in his presence. His feebleness outrages me to such a degree that I have declared, if he remains Commander-in-chief, that I must retire from this army.

November 1. Selino [Semlevo]: This day we marched here. . . . The whole road to Mojaisk [Mozhaisk] was enveloped in smoke; we saw various explosions of powder waggons and heard a cannonade in the line forward . . . but we have fifty wersts to reach Wiasma, and I fear much that we shall not arrive in time. . . . The army has been without food the whole of this day, and I fear we must march to-morrow without any, as the provision-waggons are left far behind, but the troops support every privation with wonderful spirit. How lamentable that they should have been so commanded! that they should have been deprived of the recompense their courage merited! that their toils should have been so unnecessarily continued! and that so much more blood must be shed to effect partial success, when the whole prize was in their hands! [*Diary*, 206-209]

4. THE RELENTLESSNESS OF THE PEASANTRY

The peasants of the village in which we now are have wreaked dreadful vengeance on many of the enemy. Fifty were seized here and buried alive. A dog, belonging to one of the unfortunate men, daily went to the French camp and returned to his master's grave. The peasants

---

[70] Prince Józef Antoni Poniatowski (1763-1813), the nephew of the former King of Poland, fought in the Polish revolt against Russia under Kosciusko in 1792-1794. He joined the French army in 1800 where, both in 1807 and in 1812, he continued to seek revenge against Russia. Shortly before his death in 1813, he became a Marshal of France.

were afraid of discovery, but they were a fortnight before they could kill the faithful animal. . . . All the peasants, and the few prisoners who escape death, declare that famine makes great havoc. Their only nourishment is horse-flesh, which many cannot eat as it produces dysentery.

When the poor fellows are taken, they place the fusees of the peasants at their own heads or hearts that they may be sooner destroyed; but this indulgence is not always allowed them. The peasant who grants this grace thinks himself almost guilty of a sin. [*Diary*, 209-210]

5. THE INDULGENCE OF THE CLIMATE

All the letters, and all the Frenchmen with whom I have conversed, state that four things have greatly surprised them in Russia:

1. The population and cultivation.
2. The goodness of the roads.
3. The sacrifices made by the nobility.
4. The obedience and attachment of the peasantry to their masters.

Had they waited a little longer, the French would have been astonished by the cold, but they chose a most auspicious moment to retire: a season unknown to Russia. However, it has favoured us also; for we could not in ordinary time have passed the cross-roads, as we have done, to remedy the Marshal's *ignorance*, to use the the lightest term. [*Diary*, 210]

6. THE LOSS OF THE QUARRY

November 5th, Wiasma: We marched on the 2nd again. Another forced march. Saw the enemy's line of retreat by the uninterrupted train of flames and smoke, that extended many wersts.

On the third . . . I determined to wait no longer with the main army, which had wearied itself with wanderings; I therefore took three Cossacks and my dragoons, with Brinken; the cannonade which we soon heard directed our course. . . .

General Milaradowitch had engaged the enemy soon after day-break, driving before him . . . Marshals Murat, Davoust, and Beauharnois [Beauharnais]. . . .

The French . . . obliged to give way incessantly for twelve wersts, blew up numbers of powder-waggons, and abandoned carriages, cars, and baggage of every description and all his wounded that could not walk. The route and the fields were covered with their ruins, and for many years the French have not seen such an unhappy day: they could not have lost less than six thousand men. . . . Had our army been well directed, we should have been at Wiasma two days before the enemy, and the whole fifty thousand men that engaged us yesterday must have surrendered. . . .

The misconduct of the Marshal quite makes me wild. However, much has been done and much more will be done, for the enemy has a long gauntlet yet to run. [*Diary*, 210-211]

X · A GAUNTLET OF HORROR: NOVEMBER

1. THE ONSLAUGHT OF WINTER

November. On the morning of the 4th, the snow . . . had first fallen in large flakes so as to cover the soil.

On the 5th the quantity increased considerably.

On the 6th rose that razor-cutting wind which hardened the snow and made it sparkle as it fell like small diamonds, whilst the air, under the effect of its contracting action, was filled with a continual ringing sound.

The atmosphere seemed to be rarified till it became quite crisp and brittle.

The enemy, already afflicted by hunger, fatigue, sickness, and wounds, were ill prepared for this new, though always certain calamity. . . .

On coming to the first enemy's bivouac on the morning of the 5th, some Cossacks, accompanying the English General, seeing a gun and several tumbrils at the bottom of a ravine, with the horses lying on the ground, dismounted, and taking up the feet of several, hallooed, ran, and kissed the English General's knees and horse, danced, and made fantastic gestures like crazy men. When the delirium had somewhat subsided, they pointed to the horses' shoes and said, "God has made Napoleon forget that there was a winter in our country. In spite of Kutusow the enemy's bones shall remain in Russia."

It was soon ascertained that all horses of the enemy's army were in the same improperly-shod state, except those of the Polish corps, and the Emperor's own . . . kept always roughshod, as is the usage of the Russians.

From that time the road was strewn with guns, tumbrils, equipages, men, and horses; for no foraging parties could quit the high-road in search of provisions, and consequently the debility hourly increased.

Thousands of horses soon lay groaning on the route, with great pieces of flesh cut off their necks and most fleshly parts by the passing soldiery for food; whilst thousands of naked wretches were wandering like spectres, who seemed to have no sight or sense, and who only kept reeling on till frost, famine, or the Cossack lance put an end to their power of motion. [*Narrative*, 253-255]

2. AN HONORABLE EXCEPTION TO A GENERAL FRENZY

From this time a state of feeling prevailed that denaturalized humanity—a general recklessness pervaded all—a callousness to every consideration but selfish momentary relief, with one *honourable exception* in favour of the French, who, *when captive, could not be induced by any temptation, by any threats, by any privations; to cast reproach on their Emperor as the cause of their misfortunes and sufferings*. . . . The famished, dying of hunger, refused food rather than utter an injurious word against their chief to indulge and humour vindictive inquirers.

With this excepted trait, rage appeared to madden all. Everything that could be fired was set in flames; and the same ruthless violence was directed against helpless comrades as against foes.

The maniacs tore away the clothing of their own companions when they were to be abandoned. If any food was found, they turned their arms against each other. They repulsed with force every one who endeavoured to share their bivouac fire when one could be lighted, and they mercilessly killed every prisoner.

Nor was the Russian peasant, victim of the enemy's fury in his advance as well as retreat, less ferociously savage.

A demoniacal frenzy infuriated Russians and French alike. [*Narrative*, 254-255]

3. A PANORAMA OF SUFFERING

November 13th, I returned to Wiasma. . . . The first day I proceeded forty wersts, the next, seventeen, the next, twenty-five, when we entered Dorogobouche by force. . . . The marches were very severe, as the weather was of the most desperate character; but the scene for the whole route presented such a spectacle that every personal consideration was absorbed by the feelings that the sight of so much woe excited. . . .

The naked masses of dead and dying men; the mangled carcases of ten thousand horses, which, had in some cases, been cut for food before life had ceased, the craving of famine at other points forming groups of *cannibals*; the air enveloped in flame and smoke; the prayers of hundreds of naked wretches, flying from the peasantry, whose shouts of vengeance echoed incessantly through the woods; the wrecks of cannon, powder-waggons; military stores of all descriptions, and every ordinary as well as extraordinary ill of war combined with the asperity of the climate formed such a scene as probably was never witnessed to such an extent in the history of the world. [*Diary*, 213-214]

4. A TERRIBLE TRIPTYCH

But these terrible acts of ferocity were minor features,—they ended in death with comparatively little protracted suffering. Here, death so much invited, so solicited as a friend, came with dilatory step. . . .

I will cite three or four of the most painful incidents that I witnessed:

1. A number of naked men, whose backs had been frozen while they warmed the front of their bodies, sat round the burning embers of a hut. Sensible at last to the chill of the air, they had succeeded in turning themselves, when the fire caught the congealed flesh, and a hard burnt crust covered the whole of their backs. The wretches were still living as I passed.

2. Sixty dying naked men, whose necks were laid upon a felled tree, while Russian men and women with large faggot-sticks, singing in chorus and hopping round, with repeated blows, struck out their brains in succession.

3. A group of wounded men, at the ashes of another cottage, sitting and lying over the body of a comrade which they had roasted and the flesh of which they had begun to eat. . . .

I could cite a variety of other sad and sorry calamities, but the very recollection is loathsome. [*Diary*, 214-215]

5. THE SPORT OF THE PEASANTRY

The Emperor has granted me permission for all Piedmontese to be sent to Odessa at the Russian charge, but thence to be transported at our charge or the King of Sardinia's; and . . . if twenty thousand Germans are wanted as soldiers, I venture to affirm that England may have them in six weeks.

From want of a protection for them, I calculate that six thousand have been murdered by the peasants and as many by the Cossacks. [*Diary*, 221]

All prisoners . . . were immediately and invariably stripped stark naked and marched in columns in that state, or turned adrift to be the sport and victims of the peasantry. [*Narrative*, 256]

6. THE HUMANITY OF THE GRAND DUKE

When General Beningsen and the English General, with their staffs, were one afternoon on the march, they fell in with a column of seven hundred naked prisoners under a Cossack escort. . . . Amongst this wretched convoy was a young man who attracted notice by his appearance. . . . One of General Beningsen's staff, of high titular rank [the Grand Duke Konstantin],[71] . . . asked him "if he did not under present circumstances wish for death?" "Yes," said the unhappy man, "I do . . . for I know I must in a few hours perish by inanition, or by the Cossack lance, as I have seen so many hundred comrades do. . . ." The questioner then said that "from the bottom of his heart he pitied his fate, but . . . if, however, he really wished to die at once, and would lie down on his back, to give proof of the interest he took in him, he himself would inflict the death blow on his throat." . . . The English General spurred forward to overtake and bring back General Beningsen; but happening to turn round before he could reach him, he saw the Russian officer, who had dismounted, strike with his sabre the fatal blow that severed the head nearly from the body! Nor could this officer afterwards be made to think that he had done a reprehensible act. [*Narrative*, 257-258]

XI · IN THE WAKE OF THE ARMIES: DECEMBER

I. BALANCE OF THE SCALES

A Gigantic Ruin

THE baggage taken is enormous, and its value immense. One waggon was full of gold and silver ingots. Another military chest had two hundred thousand pounds in specie.[72] Davoust's carriage had his Marshal's

---

[71] From considerations of tact, Wilson had at first suppressed the identity of the Grand Duke, but it has been supplied in a footnote by the editor of his *Narrative* from other evidence at his disposal.

[72] Another of the prizes taken at this time was a fourgon (or baggage wagon) "in which were the maps and plans, not only of Russia and Turkey, but of central Asia and India; for Napoleon

staff, all his insignia, private correspondence, the French ciphers, manuscript maps, etc. Others had all Beauharnois' property and effects.

Buonaparte has now lost, since the commencement of the campaign, two hundred thousand men, of whom eighty-two thousand are actually prisoners; seventeen generals are captives; above four hundred cannon are in the Russian parks; more than forty standards are in, or on their way to, the Palace of S. Petersburg; and a vast variety of trophies will deck the hall of victory.[73]

The ruin is gigantic in the aggregate. It might have been complete, and the column of Russian glory might now have been fixed on the tomb of the world's enemy. [*Diary*, 226-227]

An Heraldic Stain

It is now that all will regret opportunities lost. . . . When will fortune again woo us to achieve without peril or loss in one day what so many years, so much treasure, so many brave armies had in vain attempted heretofore? How many toilsome marches, how many doubtful conflicts, how many anxious days and nights, how much life, how much property would have been saved merely by an attitude of resistance! I give to the Russians all *due*, and that is *high* honour, for their patriotism and courage; but the escape of Buonaparte with a train carrying arms is a stain upon their escutcheon. [*Diary*, 238]

The Modern Xenophon

The loss of property to Russia in this war is immense; Moscow alone

---

had projected the invasion of Hindustan as one of the articles of peace with Alexander. . . ." Speaking on the subject of this prize, a concrete evidence of the oriental dreams which may have clouded Napoleon's vision of the stark realities of the Russian campaign, Alexander later had a remarkable conversation with Sir Robert, clearly foreshadowing a source of uneasiness between England and Russia in the century to come. The Emperor remarked: " 'England owes me a greater service than she imagines; for by my rejection of peace her eastern empire has perhaps been preserved.' On which the English General observed, 'To complete the act of grace and remove all temptation, Your Majesty had better send her the whole fourgon. . . .' 'No, No,' answered Alexander jocularly, 'the contents are in very good keeping in my chancellory; but I confess I wonder that you did not contrive to blow up the fourgon when you had it in your possession, on finding that you could not carry it off. Tell me, have you and Cathcart not orders to burn all manufacturing establishments when you get into Prussia and Germany?' " Wilson, *Narrative*, p. 274.

[73] Wilson's estimate of casualties was made on November 19 well before the end of the disastrous retreat and without the benefit of figures from the further reaches of the action. Even the final computation could not be accurate in the face of the terrible confusion, but the figures of the official *Russian Gazette de St. Petersbourg* calculated Napoleon's losses at 6,000 officers and 130,000 soldiers made prisoner and 308,000 corpses cremated. Lobanov-Rostovsky, *op. cit.*, p. 240.

twenty-five millions sterling; but she has gained solid power in the knowledge of her own strength, and prosperity will be the consequence. For the moment, she may want aid, particularly in cloth for her armies; but that is an aid for which, I hope, we shall not have to solicit. It should come spontaneously from England, and she will soon repay herself.

To give an idea of the forces of this empire, I will state that the Marshal ordered the militia of Little Russia to advance upon Moghilev [Mohilev], thinking that fifteen thousand would arrive: but twenty thousand horse and twenty-six thousand foot made their appearance! And yet Buonaparte, without any talent, did escape from such a multitude of real warriors! Xenophon's retreat was more glorious, but it was not so marvelous. [*Diary*, 240-242]

2. THE PLAINS OF MISERY

The next morning, the Duke of Wurtemberg and myself resolved to go to Wilna. . . . I rode on horseback in twenty-eight degrees of cold. . . . The fear of the wolves even, now in their raging season, had not warmed my blood. I . . . missed my road; so, instead of being with the Duke, I found myself with General Milaradowitch. As soon as I entered the room, I found various hands pointing to my face, which was generally frozen, but, by the application of snow immediately, after some time, the blood returned. General Milaradowitch was himself laid up with a frozen eye, and almost every one present was a sufferer from the inclement weather. I passed a very agreeable day, and this morning came into Wilna along a road covered with human carcases, frozen in the contortions of expiring agonies. The entrance of the town was literally choked with dead bodies of men and horses, tumbrils, guns, carts, etc. and the streets were filled with traineaus carrying off the dead that still crowded the way. Painters and sculptors would be benefited by the specimens. Accustomed as I am to scenes of carnage and distress, it is a repeated picture that I loathe the more that I see of it. For the last two months, I have seen very nearly as many dead and dying as living beings. The enemy have a disease internally, occasioned by eating horse-flesh without bread and salt, that carries off nine-tenths even of those who survive the field and epidemic sickness. Change of diet causes almost instant death, unless very carefully regulated. I have seen comparatively hale men, after a little food, lie down, doze, and die in half an hour. The dead, however, are to be envied. With frost to twenty-eight and thirty degrees, naked bodies and infirm health offer but subjects for terrible torments: imagination cannot conceive the reality. . . . *Yesterday, I saw four men grouped together, hands and legs frozen, minds yet vigorous, and two dogs tearing their feet.*

I arrived at Wilna just as the Marshal was going to dine. From the plains of misery, I passed to the banquet. [*Diary*, 251-252]

3. MAGNIFICENT DISCOMFORT

After dinner, I found my quarters—a magnificent summer palace, but a winter ice-house;—no fire-place, and only one stove; so that there are eighteen degrees of frost in the room in which I was obliged to sit and to rest at night. . . . This evening I went to the play, and was almost frozen. As it was a state occasion, I was obliged to remain till the conclusion; but my teeth chattered again, and when I rose to go I could scarcely use my limbs. There was not one lady in the house, which added to the wretchedness. I now come to my quarters, and although sitting close to the stove, my feet are as ice, and my hand can scarcely hold the pen. [*Diary*, 252-253]

4. A CHARNEL CITY

Sickness has made very serious progress in this city. In fifteen days, nine thousand prisoners have died, and in *one eighteen hours, seven hundred.* The mortality has extended of course to the inhabitants. The physicians have ordered straw to be burnt before every house, but the pestilential atmosphere is not to be corrected by such lenitives; and, as if fate resolved to spread the contagion to the utmost, there has been a thaw for the last twenty-four hours.

In the spring, Wilna must be a complete charnel-house. All the carcasses which are removed from the streets and hospitals are laid at a short distance from the town in great masses; and then, such parts as the wolves have not devoured during the winter will throw pestiferous miasmata back upon the city which, from its position, is always shrouded in vapour. [*Diary*, 256-257]

5. THE MONUMENTS OF MORTALITY

I rode yesterday round the town. . . . In all directions I saw mountains of human bodies and carcasses of beasts. Disgusting as the sight was, I could not help occasionally stopping to contemplate the attitudes in which those who had been frozen had died. The greater part happened to have been writhing with some agony at the instant their hearts blood congealed; some were raised upon their hands with their heads bent back and their eyes uplifted, as if still imploring aid from the passers-by. [*Diary*, 257]

6. "A PEST LAZARETTO"

The present state of the Russian force will afford a severe comment on the policy of those who considered that the evasion of resistance would economise the Russian strength. The march has certainly not cost less to the Russian armies than eighty thousand, and every day the effects extend with alarming violence. Few of our battalions muster more than two hundred men under arms; and all the armies now moving on the Vistula cannot bring into the field more than seventy thousand effectives.

We are taught to expect great reinforcements in the spring . . . but the whole line of march is a pest lazaretto, so bad, that of ten thousand men who marched from Rayan, only two thousand five hundred entered Wilna a fortnight since, and the greater portion of that number has remained there in the hospitals where eight thousand bodies still remain unburied. [*Narrative*, 398-399]

7. "THE WORLD'S PUPPETS"

In the evening, the Emperor glided into the town. The next morning, there was a great levee. . . . Yesterday was the Emperor's birthday. Parade, a confidential conference with the Emperor, mess, and twenty-five degrees of frost, were the incidents of the morning. The Marshal gave a great state dinner to the Emperor afterwards, on the occasion of his receiving the *Order of St. George of the First Class.* "It is a strange world," quoth Adam . . . and so will his posterity again say. Glory for me has lost all her charms. I shall become a Timon from contempt of the world's puppets. Happy are they who know not the Arcana of the mechanism that conducts the world's affairs. Happy are they who never reason on causes or effects. [*Diary*, 254-255]

CONCLUSION

IN THE PRECEDING CRITICAL ANALYSIS, every effort has been made to distinguish the viewpoint of one traveler from another by emphasizing the differences in their personalities, their early training, and the circumstances of their visits. In particular, it has been pointed out how the distinctive professional character of each of these men influenced his perspective of the Russian nation. Perry's engineering ambitions were excited by the potentialities of the natural wealth of the country, but frustrated by the poverty of the human means available for their exploitation. Hanway, a merchant, viewed Russia as a vast commercial emporium, God-given, as it were, to provide a theater for British mercantile activity, but he displayed little interest in the other facets of the national life. Richardson, a humanist, was virtually blind to either the natural or commercial wealth of Russia, seeing only the degradation of that human dignity which he regarded as the true measure of social and political progress. As a diplomat, Harris confined his view of Russia to the court at St. Petersburg and a foreign policy which, thanks to his stubborn convictions as to the inevitability of Anglo-Russian cooperation in the face of Catherine's new interests in the Black Sea, he largely misunderstood and violently condemned. The traveling tutor, Coxe, a scholar and a cosmopolitan, made an objective effort to grasp all aspects of Russian society, which, with his faith in progress and his long historical perspective, he interpreted as moving by slow steps toward a higher level of civilization. Ker Porter, the painter, saw Russian life as a rather disconnected series of pictorial images, either delightful or disgusting on purely romantic and aesthetic grounds, and Wilson, the chivalrous soldier of an international crusade, who despised the "pusillanimous" strategy of Kutusov and recoiled from the barbarous cruelty of the enraged serfs, praised the heroic gallantry and patriotic devotion of his allies in the conflict with Britain's and the world's great enemy. Despite the specialization of their viewpoints as individual personalities with varying professional aspirations, both as travelers and as heirs of a common national culture, their reactions, impressions, and conclusions as to the nature of Russian society were subject to many important common influences.

With a keenness of observation, whetted by the novelty of his surroundings, each of these travelers described some phase of his foreign adventures with a sense of detail which helps to recreate the flavor of some aspect of Eighteenth Century Russia, and the reader finds himself sharing a vivid moment in the author's experience. With Perry, he wonders at the wild beauty and fertile abundance of the uninhabited steppe. With Hanway, he embarks at Tsaritsyn for the passage down the great Volga, winding for hundreds of miles across the vast Eurasian plain. He smiles with Richardson at the sight of the gorgeous nobles, starting forth from their winter furs, like butterflies shedding their hairy cocoons. Through the dry official language of Harris's despatches, he savors the conspiratorial atmosphere and intrigue of Catherine's court, and with Coxe's ears, he listens in the still night to the songs of the itinerant herdsmen echoing through the dark forests lining the great Moscow highway. He follows Ker Porter through festive throngs of nobles and peasants in the frozen enchantment of a market upon the ice-covered Neva or ranges with Wilson's hard-riding Cossacks through a panorama of death and destruction on the heels of the Grand Army of France. Such picturesque images are not the main preoccupation of the historian, but they are the inevitable reflection of the traveler's experience and may serve even the serious student to animate the narrative of a significant chapter in the history of Russia. As such, the record which these travelers compiled in the midst of social distractions, professional difficulties, and even physical hardship and personal danger, evokes both the gratitude and admiration of the reader.

If the stimulus of novelty tended to sharpen these travelers' eyes for the surface details of the Russian scene, both their status as strangers and their perspective as Britons obscured their understanding of the inner conflicts and psychological ramifications of Russia's unique position between east and west. Of all the similarities which linked them together, it was, perhaps, this mental astigmatism which provided the strongest common bond. In explanation, it is clear, that any foreigner must have found it difficult to fathom the impact of Russia's peculiar cultural dichotomy upon the intimate workings of the Russian mind. For the same reason, many British travelers in nineteenth century United States had noted and ridiculed the absurd American sensitivity to any sort of foreign criticism without any appreciation of the childish sense of inferiority which lay at its base, yet in point of language, religion, and political tradition, these men faced far fewer barriers than those which confronted their eighteenth century ancestors in Russia. Irrespective of their handicaps as travelers, however, it must be sug-

gested that the national culture in which they had been bred had provided them with few opportunities to develop an insight into the
nature of the nearly unique problems facing the upper class Russian
from the time of Peter.

For centuries, the British people, whatever their colonial and commercial adventures, had made their home on the same snug little island
securely bounded by an unchanging coastline, while the Russians
spilled out across a vast plain, spanning two continents. The elasticity
of British social organization had fostered a strong sense of solidarity
among all classes, whereas the transformation of ancient Muscovy into
the new Russia had driven a gaping chasm between nobles and peasants
which was never again bridged. British political institutions had absorbed the shock of the Protestant Reformation and the Puritan Revolt
with a continuity and ease in marked contrast to the violence of the
religious wars in Germany and the Revolution in France, while the
preservation of the Romanov dynasty had been marked by periodic
regicide, purges of the nobility, and bloody supression of countless
peasant revolts. Finally, although subject to periods of foreign influences, Britain had not, since the Norman conquest, witnessed the
collision of two mutually hostile traditions such as that of the Moslem
and Christian civilizations in Spain, or that of the classical and medieval
cultures in Italy, whereas Russia, throughout the eighteenth century
and for long thereafter, was the theater of a violent cultural conflict
between Europe and Asia.

The consciousness of his social solidarity, political continuity, and
cultural unity endowed the Briton with a sense of national superiority
denied to the Russian, under the pressure of reconciling the underlying
cultural dichotomy of his national life. Forced, from his earliest years,
to choose between the heritages of east and west, either to experience
the humiliation of conscious inferiority to his European neighbors, or
to suffer a total estrangement from the powerful, if primitive traditions
of his native land, the sensitive intellectual was ground between the
millstones of two hostile worlds. The ethical and spiritual consequences
of this choice were for long a central problem of the educated Russian.
In the nineteenth century, a host of literary figures, Onegin, "the superfluous man," Basarov, the nihilist, and Raskolnikov, the moral rebel,
would demonstrate the hazards inherent in the problem which underlay "the unbearable sadness of Russian life." In the eighteenth century,
many Britons saw and ridiculed members of the Russian aristocracy,
either because they chose to become slavish imitators of the west, or

because they preferred to cling to the traditions of ancient Muscovy. They were unsympathetic, because they were ignorant of the basic impact of the Russian dilemma. Like Robinson Crusoe, the literary symbol of the empire builder, self-confident and self-reliant, they tended to remain unaware of any but the external problems which nature imposed and which they knew how to combat with admirable resourcefulness and practical ability. They refused to admit of any reasoning in favor of deviation from western influence. Whether it was Perry denouncing Golitsyn for his conservative opposition to the Don-Volga canal, Harris lampooning Potemkin's absurd preoccupation with "the Eastern chimera," or Wilson raging at Kutusov's parochial insistence upon the exclusively Russian interests in the Napoleonic invasion, all shared a common conviction of their own essential rightness which blinded them to the Asiatic horn of the Russian dilemma and distorted their portraits of the Russian people.

Equally harsh in their judgments of the Russian national character as in their reactions to specific personalities, the British travelers, as a whole, showed a firmer grasp of their problem. To be sure, they arrived at their estimates by the simplified process of exalting the ethical standards of their native milieu to the rank of absolute criteria, and, in so doing, they occasionally permitted their preoccupation with good Puritan virtues to obscure the subtler nuances of the Russian spirit. The court of Catherine with its scheming factions, corrupt favorites, and conspiratorial secret agents, would have been far less of an enigma to the crafty Machiavelli than it was to the priggish Harris, and, as the product of an era of similar political instability and cultural conflict, the Florentine would, perhaps, have seen *virtu*, where Harris saw only evil. Trained to the Protestant bourgeois virtues of honesty, sincerity, industry, and thrift, the Briton was sometimes too quick to equate cunning with treachery, eloquence with flattery, patience with indolence, and display with waste. Such minor distortions are, however, more desirable, perhaps, than that historical relativism which, by explaining all moral behavior as merely the product of varying political, economic, and social conditions, destroys the possibility of ethical evaluation. Having exposed the unquestionable cruelty, sensuality, and corruption of Russian life, the British travelers collectively displayed considerable acumen in tracing to their underlying causes the moral defects which they so violently condemned.

As in nearly every other instance, their explanation of the causes of Russian immorality varied from one traveler to another. Perry emphasized the influence of Greek Orthodoxy as the sponsor of general depravity. Richardson saw political tyranny as the sole source of degradation. Harris attributed the vice of the court to the conduct and example of Catherine. And Ker Porter tended to dismiss the barbarous behavior of the peasants with the contemptuous reflection that they were after all, only *canaille*. Above and beyond their diversified special interests, a number of these travelers shared in common with their countrymen a propensity for amateur social and political philosophy. When engaged in any analysis of the character of Russian society, therefore, they almost invariably placed the responsibility upon the defective political administration. Typical eighteenth century Britons, their concern was not for political democracy, but for executive method, and they were less interested in a theoretical constitution than in practical civil liberties. Even a legally absolute monarchy might, under certain circumstances, provide security of person and property, but the political instability of Russia, where the succession to the throne was dependent upon the whim of the nobility, and the power of the noble upon the caprice of the ruler, transformed monarchs into despots, and nobles into tyrants. As Richardson had most effectively pointed out, the insecurity of Russian life invaded all ranks of society and basically affected every aspect of the behavior of its members. Initiative and industry were discouraged, for exertion toward the acquisition of neither technical knowledge nor material wealth could promise more than temporary benefits. As tsar or noble, merchant or peasant, artist or craftsman, the status of the Russian was forever precarious. Denied any faith in the future, he lived only in the present, and his behavior, political, economic, or ethical, conformed to the exigency of the moment as its highest law. Thus, the wheels of progress were forever spinning in the shifting sands of a capricious despotism.

In conclusion, a grateful tribute is owing to the formidable contribution of British travel literature as a whole in this period. Allowing for occasional exaggerations and undue preoccupation with the exotic or the unusual, the eye-witness accounts of these travelers add color and animation to the events of an historical epoch. The seven men most specifically discussed attained considerable distinction in their chosen professions, and, if they were too often prejudiced and inaccurate in their reports of other aspects of Russian life, they were always conscientious and usually keen observers in the field of their special interests. The severity of their pronouncements upon the Russian national character reveals a certain Puritanical conviction of their own self-righteousness, but they were, in the main, high-minded, and the standards by which they judged the behavior of the Russians have still sufficient currency to weigh in the modern scales. Finally, if they were overly complacent in their admiration of the social virtues of the British nation, they were members of the most liberal political and economic system of their day, and their reflections upon the nature of Russian society were rooted in a social philosophy which yet survives. The self-interest and freedom of enterprise which they respected are still basic concepts of modern capitalism and the ideal of liberty under law, which they found in their beloved Britain, still serves as the foundation of a great political tradition. In short, the ethical, economic, and political values of the eighteenth century Briton are part of the heritage of modern democratic and capitalistic society, and the heir to the tradition of Anglo-American culture may find new confirmation of their vigor in their application to the older Russia, whose features are still discernible under the hostile ideology of the Soviet Union.

BIBLIOGRAPHY

THE following is a list of the published works of British travelers in Russia between 1698 and 1812. The official diplomatic correspondence published by the Russian Historical Society, although it does not correctly belong to the category of travel literature, strictly defined, has been included because it has been used as a primary source for the reactions of diplomatic visitors of the period. The same might be said of the diaries and correspondence of Sir James Harris, which confine themselves almost entirely to official diplomatic business. They are here included, however, because they have been so often quoted, whereas the official diaries and correspondence of a number of other diplomats have not been mentioned because they were not cited in the text.

An Authentic Narrative of the Russian expedition against the Turks by sea and land. . . . Compiled from several authentic journals, by an officer on board the Russian Fleet. London: Printed for S. Hooper, 1772.

Bell, John, *Travels from St. Petersburg in Russia, to various parts of Asia.* 2nd ed. Edinburgh: Printed for W. Creech, 1806.

Bentham, Jeremy, *The Works of Jeremy Bentham.* Edited by John Bowring, vols. IV, x, Edinburgh: W. Tait; London: Simkins, Marshall, and Co., 1843.

Bruce, Peter Henry, *Memoirs of Peter Henry Bruce, esq. a military officer in the services of Prussia, Russia, and Great Britain. Containing an account of his travels in Germany, Russia, Tartary, Turkey, the West Indies etc., as also, several very interesting private anecdotes of the Czar, Peter I, of Russia.* London; T. Payne and Sons, 1782.

Carr, John, *Northern Summer; or Travels round the Baltic through Denmark, Sweden, Russia, Prussia and part of Germany, in the year 1804.* Philadelphia: Samuel F. Bradford, 1805.

Clarke, Edward Daniel, *Travels in Various Countries of Europe and Africa.* Vol. I, London: T. Cadell and W. Davies, 1811.

Cook, John, *Voyages and Travels through the Russian empire, Tartary and part of the kingdom of Persia.* 2 vols., Edinburgh: Printed for the author, 1770.

Coxe, William, *Travels in Poland, Russia, Sweden, and Denmark.* 6th ed., 3 vols., London: T. Cadell and W. Davies, 1803.

Craven, Elizabeth, *A Journey through the Crimea to Constantinople in a series of Letters.* London: G. G. J. and J. Robinson, 1789.

Gordon, Patrick, *Passages from the Diary of General Patrick Gordon of Auchleuchries.* Aberdeen: The Spalding Club, 1859.

Guthrie, Marie, *A Tour performed in the years 1795-1796, through the Taurida, or Crimea.* London: T. Cadell and W. Davies, 1802.

Hanway, Jonas, *An Historical Account of the British Trade over the Caspian Sea: with the author's Journal of Travels from England through Russia into Persia; and back through Russia, Germany and Holland.* 2nd ed., 2 vols., London: D. Brown, T. and T. Longman, C. Davies, C. Hitch, L. Haines, A. Millar, J. Whiston, B. White, R. Dodsley, J. and J. Rivington, 1754.

Harris, James, *Diaries and Correspondence of James Harris, First Earl of Malmesbury.* Edited by the Third Earl of Malmesbury, 2nd ed., vol. I, London: Richard Bentley, 1845.

History of the Russian Fleet during the reign of Peter the Great by a contemporary Englishman. Edited by C. A. P. Bridge, London: Navy Records Society, 1899.

Justice, Elizabeth, *A Voyage to Russia: describing the laws, manners, and customs of that great empire, as governed at this present by that excellent princess the czarina. Shewing the beauty of her palace, the grandeur of her courtiers, the forms of building at Petersburgh, and other places: with several entertaining adventures that happened in the passage by sea and land. To which is added four letters, wrote by the author when at Russia to a gentleman in London.* 2nd ed., London: Printed for the author, 1746.

Macartney, George, "An Account of Russia in the year 1767." *Some Account of the Public Life of the Earl of Macartney.* Edited by John Barrow, vol. II, London: T. Cadell and W. Davies, 1807.

Marshall, Joseph, *Travels through Holland, Flanders, Germany, Denmark, Sweden, Lapland, Russia, the Ukraine and Poland, in the years 1768, 1769, and 1770.* 2nd ed., vol. III, London: J. Almond, 1773.

Perry, John, *The State of Russia under the Present Czar. . . .* London: B. Tooke, 1716.

Porter, Robert Ker, *Travelling Sketches in Russia and Sweden, 1805, 1806, 1807, 1808.* Philadelphia: Hopkins and Earle, 1809.

Richards, John, *A Tour from London to Petersburgh and from thence to Moscow.* Dublin: William Wilson, 1781.

Richardson, William, *Anecdotes of the Russian Empire. In a series of Letters written a few years ago from St. Petersburg.* London: W. Strahan and T. Cadell, 1784.

Sbornik Russkogo Istoricheskogo Obshchestvo. (Journal of the Russian Historical Society.) Vols. XII, XIX, XXXIX, LXI, St. Petersburg: 1875-1898.

Swinton, Andrew, *Travels into Norway, Denmark and Russia in 1788, 1789, 1790, 1791.* London: G. G. J. and J. Robinson, 1792.

Tooke, William, *View of the Russian empire during the reign of Catherine the Second, and to the close of the eighteenth century.* 2nd ed., London: T. N. Longman, 1800.

Vigor, Mrs. William, *Letters from a lady who resided some years in Russia, to her friend in England, 1775.* 2nd ed., London: J. Dodsley, 1777.

Whitworth, Charles, *An Account of Russia as it was in the Year 1710.* Printed at Strawberry-hill, 1758.

Williams, John, *The Rise, Progress, and Present State of the Northern Governments; viz. The United Provinces, Denmark, Sweden, Russia, and Poland: or Observations on the Nature, Constitution, Religion, Laws, Policy, Customs, and Commerce of each Government; the Manners and Dispositions of the People; their Military Forces by Land and Sea; the Revenues and Resources of each Power.* . . . 2 vols., London: T. Becket, 1777.

Wilmot, Martha and Catherine, *The Russian Journals of Martha and Catherine Wilmot.* Edited by The Marchioness of Londonderry and H. M. Hyde, London: Macmillan and Co., 1934.

Wilson, Robert Thomas, *Private Diary of Travels, Personal Services and Public Events during Mission and Employment with the European armies in the Campaigns of 1812, 1813, 1814. From the Invasion of Russia to the Capture of Paris.* Edited by Rev. Herbert Randolph, London: John Murray, 1860.

——, *Narrative of Events during the Invasion of Russia by Napoleon Bonaparte and the Retreat of the French Army, 1812.* Edited by Rev. Herbert Randolph, London: John Murray, 1860.

Wraxall, Nathaniel, *A Tour through some of the Northern parts of Europe, particularly Copenhagen, Stockholm, and Petersburgh. In a series of letters.* 2nd ed., London: T. Cadell, 1775.

INDEX

abacus, 34n., 289n.

administration, corruption and confusion of powers of, under Peter I, 16-17, 44-45; connection of civil and military, 17; harmful commercial practices under Peter I, 18, 53-61; regulations of travel, 108-109, 116-117; indolence and confusion of, under Catherine II, 201-202, 203-204, 208; reformed by Catherine II, 279-280

agriculture, British and Russian compared, xiv-xv; and taxation, 162-163; Society for the Promotion of, 272; fertility of the Ukraine, xv, 149, 371-372; *see also* gardens

Alexander I (1777-1825), birth of, 198, 200; appearance of, 316; and Ker Porter, 297, 299-300; magnificence of the court of, 317-318, 338-339; liberalism of, xi, 315-316, 340; British prestige under, 324, 371-372, 378, 382; reaction to French Revolution under, 301-302, 359; and England, 300, 350-351; Eastern ambitions of, 350-351, 403-404n.; and Napoleon, 355, 358; and Wilson, 347, 348, 349-350, 351, 356, 362, 377, 380-383; and the rejection of compromise (1812), 362, 376, 380-383, 384, 390

amusements, as revealing national character, 170-171; aversion to bodily exercise, 170-171, 312, 337; Easter festival, 154-155; of the peasants: ice-hills, 171, dancing, 171, boxing, 261, games, 171, 269, feasts, 268-270; of the nobles: parties, 311-312, 325, music, 312, 325, the promenade, 335-336, coursing, 336-337, cards, 146, 200, 202, 206, 217, 218, 255, 311-312, fireworks, 153, 339; *see also* food, drink, and court

Apraxin, Fëdor Matveevich (1671-1728), 6; feud with Perry, 7; character of, 8

Archangel, discovery of (1553), xvi, xvii; character of inhabitants of, 176, 248, 286-287

Armed Neutrality (1780), xx, xxv, 189, 194, 214-217, 220, 227-228; (1800), xx, 82, 300

Armenia, merchants of, 73, 79, 83, 104, 108, 109, 110, 112, 113

Armfeldt, Gustaf Mauritz (1757-1814), 359

Armies, Napoleonic (1812), non-national elements of, 358-359, 377, 393, 397, 402; loyalty of French soldiers in, 401; losses of, 366n., 373, 386, 387, 392, 393, 400, 403-404; starvation and exposure of, 400-401, 401-402, 402-403, 405-406

Army, Russian, successes of, xiii-xiv, xix-xx;

reforms of Peter I, 17, 48-50; British and foreign officers in, xvii-xviii, xxii, 133n., 358-359; Cossacks in, 319, 363, 366, 386, 387, 388-389; peasants in, 309-310, 320-321, 389, 397; courage of, 321, 360, 386; discipline of, 320, 360; uniforms of, 319-320; artillery of, 360, 366n., 374, 387, 389; arms of, 53, 319-320, 360-361n.; horses of, 319, 387, 389

artel, 276

Arts, Academy of, 128, 271-272; obstacles to, 271-272, 315; of peasants, 321-322; *see also* literature

Astrakhan, description of, 111-112; locusts of, 112-113, commerce of, 113-114

Austerlitz, battle of (1805), xiv, 300

ax, Russian use of, 104-105, 169, 256-257, 262, 263-264, 265, 309

Azov, taken from Turks (1696), 28; by Turks (1711), 9-10

Bagration, Pëtr Ivanovich (1765-1812), 312, 324; and Wilson, 348, 372

Baird, Sir David (1757-1829), 296, 348

Baltic Provinces, conquered by Peter I, xiii, xviii; 86-88, 142

Barclay de Tolly, Mikhail (1761-1818), resentment against, 262, 373-374, 375, 376; and Wilson, 372, 373, 375, 377

batoags, 43, 61

beards, shaved by Peter I, 38-39; revered by Russians, 282

Bell, John (1691-1780), Russian *Travels*, xxii

Benningsen, Levin August Theophile (1745-1825), 348, 372, 385, 390-391

Bentham, Jeremy (1748-1832), xi, xxvi

Bentham, Samuel (1757-1831), xxvi

Black Sea, Russian ambitions in: under Peter I, 26-27, 28-29; under Catherine II, 224n., 276-277

Blackstone, Sir William (1723-1780), *Commentaries*, x; 130, 210

Borodino, battle of, 359, 362, 366, 383

Bruce, Count James, xviii

Bruce, Peter Henry, 9; Russian *Memoirs*, xxii

Bruce, Countess, 133, 207n.

Burke, Edmund (1729-1797), x, 140, 247

calendar, Russian, 197n., 259

canals, obstacles to construction of, 5-6; Don